TOWARDS AFRICA'S RENEWAL

Towards Africa's Renewal

Edited by

JEGGAN C. SENGHOR and NANA K. POKU

LONDON AND NEW YORK

First published 2007 by Ashgate Publishing

Reissued 2018 by Routledge
2 Park Square, Milton Park, Abingdon, Oxon, OX14 4RN
605 Third Avenue, New York, NY 10017

First issued in paperback 2021

Routledge is an imprint of the Taylor & Francis Group, an informa business

© Jeggan C. Senghor and Nana K. Poku 2007

Jeggan C. Senghor and Nana K. Poku have asserted their moral right under the Copyright, Designs and Patents Act, 1988, to be identified as the editors of this work.

All rights reserved. No part of this book may be reprinted or reproduced or utilised in any form or by any electronic, mechanical, or other means, now known or hereafter invented, including photocopying and recording, or in any information storage or retrieval system, without permission in writing from the publishers.

A Library of Congress record exists under LC control number: 2006103147

Notice:
Product or corporate names may be trademarks or registered trademarks, and are used only for identification and explanation without intent to infringe.

Publisher's Note
The publisher has gone to great lengths to ensure the quality of this reprint but points out that some imperfections in the original copies may be apparent.

Disclaimer
The publisher has made every effort to trace copyright holders and welcomes correspondence from those they have been unable to contact.

ISBN 13: 978-0-815-39851-6 (hbk)
ISBN 13: 978-1-351-14444-5 (ebk)
ISBN 13: 978-1-138-35775-4 (pbk)

DOI: 10.4324/9781351144445

Contents

List of Figures		*vii*
List of Tables		*viii*
Notes on Contributors		*ix*
Preface		*xii*

An Introduction: Africa: Amid Renewal, Deepening Crisis 1
Nana K. Poku

1   The African State
       I William Zartman   17

2   The Post-colonial African State: Issues of Citizenship and Subjectivity
       Lawrence Flint   35

3   Liberalization, Democratization and Political Leadership in Africa
       Edward Kannyo   63

4   Africa's Industrialization: An Alternative Approach
       Daniel B. Ndlela   85

5   Revisiting the African Development Trajectory: From LPA to NEPAD
       Mbaya J. Kankwenda   107

6   Institutional Architecture for Managing Integration in the ECOWAS Region: An Empirical Investigation
       Jeggan C. Senghor   143

7   Vassal States, Development Options and African Development
       Anthony V. Obeng   179

8   Instabilities and Development in Africa
       Augustin Kwasi Fosu   209

9   Trade Regimes, Liberalization and Macroeconomic Instability in Africa
       Chantal Dupasquier and Patrick N. Osakwe   225

10   Civil Society Organizations: The Search for Empowerment
       Amy S. Patterson   255

11	Gender and Development *Christine Obbo*	279
12	Migrants' Remittances and the Nigerian Economy: Theoretical and Impact Issues *Siyanbola Tomori and Michael A. Adebiyi*	295
13	The Nigerian Federation at the Crossroads: The Way Forward *Ladipo Adamolekun*	319
Index		*335*

List of Figures

1.1	Deaths from Conflict 1994-2006, World Regions	5
4.1	The Duality of the African Economy	89
9.1	Output Equation	247
9.2	Consumption Equation	248
9.3	Investment Equation	249
12.1	Net Capital Inflow and Direct Investment Income Remittances for Nigeria, 1970-2004	308
12.2	Direct Investment Income Remittances to and from Nigeria	309
12.3	Direct Investment Income Remittances from Nigeria as a Ratio of Export and Gross Domestic Product	310
12.4	Ratio of Direct Investment Income Remittances from Nigeria to Net Direct Foreign Investment Inflow, GDP, and External Reserves	311

List of Tables

1.1	Selected Macro-economic Indicators, Sub-Saharan Africa and South Asia: 1963-1980	8
1.2	Foreign Direction Investment (as Percentage of global FDI flows) 1997-2006	9
1.3	GDP Growth Under Adjustment – Agriculture-growth Rate (median) sub Saharan Africa, 1981-83, 1987-91 and 1992-97	9
1.4	Impact of Common Structural Adjustment Measures on Health Determinants	10
1.5	Circle of Decline and Vulnerability: The impacts of SAP on African Societies	11
1.6	Debt to Health and Education Profile: Selected African Countries	13
5.1	Economic Growth in Africa and in the World 1980-2004	112
5.2	Real Economic Growth Between Africa and Asia	114
5.3	Real Economic Growth Per Head Between Africa and Asia	114
6.1	Location and Reporting Arrangements	152
6.2	Structures	154
6.3	Functions	155
6.4	Resources	157
6.5	Relations with Sector Ministries	160
9.1	Selected Indicators on African Economies	227
9.2	Structure of African Economies (% of GDP)	228
9.3	Output Volatility	230
9.4	Consumption Volatility	231
9.5	Investment Volatility	232
9.6	Trade Liberalization Episodes in Selected Countries	234
9.7	Benchmark Estimation Using Trade Regime Measure 1	240
9.8	Benchmark Estimation Using Trade Regime Measure 2	241
9.9	Benchmark Estimation Using Trade Regime Measure 3	242
9.10	Excluding the Terms of Trade	243
9.11	Sub-Saharan Africa	244
9.12	System Estimation (SURE)	246
12.1	Flow of Workers' Remittances and its Share in Imports and Exports of Goods in Nigeria	305
12.2	Formal Remittances and Related Macroeconomic Indicators in Nigeria (1990-2005)	306
12.3	Determinants of Remittances in Nigeria, 1990-2005	307

Notes on Contributors

Michael Adebayo Adebiyi is a Senior Lecturer in economics at the University of Lagos, Nigeria, from where he also received his doctorate and other degrees. His research interests are in econometrics, monetary and development economics, in which subject areas he has published extensively.

Ladipo Adamolekun is a part-time Professor of Management at the Federal University of Technology, Akure, Nigeria. He is the author/co-author or editor/co-editor of over twenty books and monographs and numerous articles and contributions to books on politics and public administration in Africa. He is editor of *Public Administration: Main Issues and Selected Country Studies* (1999).

Chantal Dupasquier is the Leader of the Policy Coordination and Technical Cooperation Team in the Office of Policy and Programme Coordination at the UN Economic Commission for Africa (ECA) in Addis Ababa, Ethiopia. Prior to joining the United Nations, Chantal worked as a monetary operations advisor at the International Monetary Fund, Washington, and contributed to the design and development of a new and effective monetary policy framework for Burundi.

Lawrence Flint is Executive Director of the Africa Information Centre, a research and development consultancy based in Birmingham, UK. He is also Visiting Lecturer at the Centre of African Studies, University of Copenhagen and Guest Researcher at the Department of International Development, University of Roskilde, Denmark. His current research interests include identity construction, social and environmental history of Central and Southern Africa, contemporary representations of history and heritage in Africa, climate change and adaptation strategies in the developing world.

Augustin Kwasi Fosu, is a co-editor of the *Journal of African Economies* (Oxford). He has been the Director of Research of the African Economic Research Consortium (AERC), Nairobi, Kenya. He was also a Professor of Economics at Oakland University, Michigan, USA. Professor Fosu has served as a consultant for a number of both national and international entities. He has published numerous articles in major international academic journals on labour economics as well as on economic growth and development, focusing on the impacts of economic and political instabilities, the external sector and debt on the growth of developing economies. He has also edited several volumes/books, and contributed chapters to many others.

Mbaya J. Kankwenda is currently Director of the Congolese Institute for Development Research and Strategic Studies (CIDRESS). He is a former Professor of Economics at the Institute of Information Science and Technology at the University of Kinshasa,

Democratic Republic of The Congo. Prior to that he was successively General Manager, Institute of Scientific Research; Economic Adviser to the Minister of Planning; and Minister of State for National Economy and Industry.

Edward Kannyo has been an Associate Professor at SUNY, Geneseo, and is currently Associate Professor of Political Science in the College of Liberal Arts, Rochester Institute of Technology, New York (USA). His research interests include human rights, democratization and international environmental protection.

Daniel B. Ndlela is co-director of Zimconsult a private consultancy firm specializing in industrialization and trade policy (GTAP issues, WTO, EPAs), regional economic cooperation and integration, macro-economic policy/modeling, and economic planning models (World Bank/ADB's macro-modeling, CSPs), and project evaluation. He was previously Senior Lecturer in economics at the University of Zimbabwe.

Christine Obbo is a distinguished Professor of African Anthropology and has taught at a number of American Universities. She has written extensively on work, urbanisation and gender in Africa. Obbo is the author of *African Women* and has in the last two decades been working on HIV/AIDS and gender issues in Africa. She has also written many other articles and contributed chapters to many other books.

Anthony V. Obeng was Research and Editorial Assistant at the Encyclopedia Africana Secretariat in Accra, Ghana, followed by various professional positions at the African Training and Research Centre in Administration for Development (CAFRAD), in Tangier, Morocco. After a stint as Research Officer at the Institute of Development Studies, University of Sussex (Brighton, England) he moved to the United Nations African Institute for Economic Development and Planning (IDEP), in Dakar, Senegal, as lecturer. In his subsequent career in the UN Food and Agriculture Organization (FAO) positions held included Regional Cooperation and Liaison Officer (Regional Office, Accra) and head of its OAU/ECA Unit (Addis Ababa, Ethiopia), concurrently with the representation of FAO in Ethiopia and Djibouti.

Patrick N. Osakwe holds M.A. and Ph.D degrees in economics from Queen's University, Kingston, Canada. He is currently the Leader of the Trade Policy Analysis Team in the Trade and Regional Integration Division of the UN Economic Commission for Africa (ECA) in Addis Ababa, Ethiopia. Previously, he was Leader of the Macroeconomics and Finance Team in the Economic and Social Policy Division of the ECA.

Amy S. Patterson is Professor of Political Science at Calvin College in Grand Rapids, Michigan. She teaches African and Latin American politics, international relations, and international development. Some of her published works are: *The Politics of AIDS in Africa*. (Boulder, CO: Lynne Rienner Publishers), (editor) *The African State and the AIDS Crisis*. Aldershot, UK: Ashgate); 'Power Inequalities and the Institutions of Senegalese Development Organizations.' (African Studies Review

46, 3). Her research interests include the politics of HIV/AIDS in Africa, women in development, and democratization (apatters@calvin.edu).

Nana K. Poku is John Ferguson Chair and Professor of African Studies at the University of Bradford. Before joining Bradford, he was Director of the United Nations Commission on HIV/AIDS and Governance in Africa (CHGA) and Senior Advisor (Health) to the office of the United Nations Secretary General. His recent publications include: *Africa's AIDS Crisis: how the poor are dying* (2006); *Globalization and the developing World* (2007) with Tony McGrew; and *AIDS and Governance*, (2007) with Alan Whiteside and Bjorg Sandkjaer.

Jeggan C. Senghor is at present a Senior Research Fellow at the Institute of Commonwealth Studies, School of Advanced Study, University of London. Much of Dr. Senghor's career was in the United Nations Secretariat where he served in several duty stations including: Chief, Public Management Programme in the UN Economic Commission for Africa (UNECA), Director of the UN Institute for Economic Development and Planning (UN-IDEP) in Dakar, and Director, ECA Office for West Africa, Niamey, Niger. Dr. Senghor's areas of research interest are regional integration and public sector reform and management.

Siyanbola Tomori is a professor of economics at the University of Lagos (Lagos, Nigeria). He has been Visiting Senior Lecturer, University of Ife (Obafemi Awolowo University) and Visiting Professor of Economics, Federal University of Technology, Akure. Among his books are the co-edited *The Political Economy of Development: An African Perspective*, vols. 1 and 2 (ICIPE Science Press, Nairobi). He is a former President of the Nigerian Economics Society and former President of the African Economics Association.

William Zartman is Jacob Blaustein Professor of International Organizations and Conflict Resolution and Director of Conflict Management at the John Hopkins University. He was formerly on the faculty of the University of South Carolina and New York University; served as Olin Professor at the U.S. Naval Academy, was Halevy Professor at the Institute of Political Studies in Paris and was visiting professor at the American University in Paris.

Preface

This volume has had a rather longer gestation than we both care to admit but we hope that it has matured in the process. It has involved a truly global collaboration, as the list of contributors attest, whilst for the editors the process has involved a truly intercontinental collaboration – from Ethiopia to United Kingdom to Sierra Leone – where the book was finally completed with the assistance of the 2007 Africa field visit class from Bradford University's Peace Studies Department. We would like to thank particularly our extremely patient Publisher at Ashgate, Kirstin Howgate, who provided considerable support at various stages and never despaired – or at least did not communicate it to us! The contributors to the volume also deserve praise for working to tight deadlines and responding to our editorial queries. The Senior Desk Editor, Gemma Lowle, also deserves a particular mention because she has made many helpful refinements to the text. Grace Maina also worked tirelessly to assist me in getting the project into a publishable shape as well as dealing with all the editorial queries. Finally, many thanks and gratitude to the Peace Studies class of 2007 for their energy, drive and enthusiasm for the study of African Politics and Society. It is to them that this book is dedicated.

African Study Visit Members 2007

Alisa Buma	Canada
Atsuko Ishizuka	Japan
Christina Pell Fleming	United States
Denise Bentrovato	Italy
Donna Garton	United States
Hajime Usukura	Japan
John Jumbe Ackah Sarbah	Ghana
Kathrin Nutt	Germany
Kazuyo Mitsuhashi	Japan
Kolawole Olugboyega Olagbaiye	Nigeria
Laura Gilchrist	United Kingdom
Miguel D. Ramirez	United States
Mariko Oshio	Japan
Sunghye Jee	South Korea
Tanya C. Walmsley	United Kingdom
Tobias Schuldt	Germany
W. Marc Douglas	Canada
Yuki Sugihara	Japan

An Introduction
Africa: Amid Renewal, Deepening Crisis

Nana K. Poku

'To achieve the possible is not failure but success, however inadequate the success may prove in the end.'
Joseph Schumpeter

'[The] struggle of man against power is the struggle of memory against forgetting'
Milan Kundera

Ghana's independence in 1957 marked the beginning of the end of direct colonial rule in Africa. In the short period between 1957 and 1961, most of West and Equatorial Africa had won its independence. So had North Africa, except Algeria where a war of liberation was being fought. East and Central Africa were well on their way. Africans grew confident that southern Africa would soon follow this path; but in the event, it took over three decades for southern Africa to be fully liberated from minority rule. By 1967, no less than 46 countries had revolted against colonial rule and won their independence in Africa.

Writing at the time, Immanuel Wallerstein concludes that, 'Ghana's independence marked an optimistic and glorious period in contemporary African history.' A mere fifty years on, however, the aura of 'optimism' has largely faded, while the debilitating effects of decades of misguided policies assume new realities. The political norm has been near-absolute power in the hands of Africa's political elites (the Big Men) who tolerate no opposition, manipulate elections and regard state revenues as their personal income. Meanwhile, ordinary Africans lurch between an alien superstructure (the legacy of the colonial state) and decaying traditional African past. Their loyalties stretched between predatory elites and disintegration tribal systems as many of them head to the melting pots of ever expanding cities in pursuit of the elusive dividends of independence.

The ensuing struggle for power and wealth has seen the continent engulfed in an avalanche of conflicts and crisis. Progress on one front is so often accompanied by regression on another. As a faint glimmer of hope begins to emerge in the appalling conflicts in Sudan with the signing of the Comprehensive Peace Agreement and the Darfur Peace Agreement, the situation in Somalia deteriorate, threatening to draw in Ethiopia. And the Ethiopia/Eritrea border one again a tinder box. In 2006 alone, roughly 40 percent of Africa's 53 states were affected by conflict. The resulting social decay presents a dramatic picture of insecurity of ordinary people in circumstances where states – and the international system of states – are either unable to provide protection or are themselves the principal sources of violence.

The on-going conflicts over the remains of Somalia, for example, gives a poignant reminder of the plight of ordinary folks on the continent who are without protection from any state – some falling prey to the remnants of the very state that was once supposed to be their protector. Similarly, the periodic descent of countries like Sierra Leone, Ivory Coast, Liberia, Chad, Somalia, Rwanda to mention but a few, into anarchy or something close to it, demonstrate in the most dramatic way the exposure of vast numbers of people not only to the dangers of violence from marauding hordes of warriors and bandits, in a manner reminiscent of medieval times, but to hunger and disease on a cataclysmic scale.

This introductory chapter offers a frankly eclectic overview of Africa's past and the challenges ahead. It stresses the importance of contingency and choice alongside the evident structural influences on development. A tenet of the book is that it is necessary to recognise the social forces and economic constraints surrounding any political regime, but an understanding of the developmental outcomes requires that we also pay attention to the quality of institutions, the design of public policy, and the autonomous role of leaders.

Africa's colonial legacies

In *Leviathan*, Thomas Hobbes (1968) describes the nature of the state as a form of institution – as he puts it, an 'Artificial Man', defined by prominence and sovereignty, the authorized representative giving life and motion to society and the body politics. Crucially, Hobbes argues for a form of social contract by which individuals give up certain rights of '*self-government*', as David Held describes it, and in return are assured an improvement in their [*security*]. In this contract citizens confer a single authority – a sovereign – the right to control a definable territorial space and, in the process, the right to make and enforce such rules or laws as is deemed necessary in exchange for political, economic and military security. The contract between men and sovereign is carried out 'on the condition that every individual does the same' (Held 1983: 6). The result is the creation of a powerful sovereign, which cannot be limited in its authority since the sovereign requires considerable power to formulate laws, enforce agreements, ensure contracts: in other words, to bring order to previously natural condition of disorder.

However mythical the proposition of a mass opting into a social contract to create the state might sound, either for the imposition of minimal order or co-operative communal benefits, people have granted a central organ a monopoly of political authority and power. Reinforced by 19th and 20th century's concepts of ideology and nationalism, the state system has now become the most prominent unit of political organisation in the world; an organisation to which millions of people owe allegiance and for which many are prepared to die. Indeed, the psychological high of belonging has made it particularly satisfying to belong to a particular state and to be stateless is to enter a world of unimaginable misery and insecurity (Poku and Graham 1999 and 2000).

The imposition of this European notion of centralised power and authority, perhaps more than anything else, account for the fragility of the African continent in the modern world. The Congress of Berlin in 1884 offers an important starting point. It was there that the political map of modern Africa was drawn, not by African themselves, but by Europeans intent on staking out their claims to what James Mayall described as 'the last great land mass still awaiting enclosure.' To the colonisers the strategy was simple; whenever they occupied a piece of land they could legitimately integrate that territory into their empire. This extension of the European notion of sovereignty brought with it a near total compartmentalisation of political space in which there were very few uncolonised areas on the continent. Only 10 per cent of the continent was under direct European control in 1870, but by the end of the century only 10 per cent remained outside it.

By 1914, the political map of Africa was virtually complete. With callous disregard for the histories of their subject, colonial leaders grouped large number of diverse identities, ethnicities and cultures into new state; while at the same time separating nations with rich and unified histories into separate states. Superimposed over the continent were highly divergent and artificial geographical forms and the distortion of traditional social and economic patterns. For one, the physical map of Africa contrasts such sprawling giants as Sudan, Democratic Republic of Congo and Algeria with the mini-states of Djibouti and The Gambia. The Gambia for example, could fit into Sudan 240 times! Substantial diversity was and is also apparent in population size. Nigeria's population is now estimated at well over 130 million people, contrast with place like Guinea and Botswana with less than 2 million.

Unlike Europe, therefore, where nation-builders sought to replace the older empires with states comprising of some combination of cultural, linguistic, and patriotic unity, African states emerged from the authoritarian structures of their colonial past. The division of the Somali people of the Horn of Africa is a typical example. Previously united by a common culture but lacking a centralized authority, this classically segmented political system was ultimately subjugated and divided among four imperial powers: Britain, France, Italy and an independent Ethiopia. Regardless of whether one is sympathetic to past or current Somali demands to redraw the inherited colonial boundaries of the horn of Africa, or ultimately accepts the extreme methods of the military force, there is no question that the roots of these conflicts are at least partially the result of the manner in which Africans were drawn into world politics.

Total order in the Hobbesian sense, therefore, has thus been virtually impossible to achieve in Africa. Indeed, the biggest challenge to post-colonial leaders has been creating viable states. Various approaches have been tried to meet this challenge. In some states, the dominant traditional nation became the core of the new nation, as other ethnic groups were assimilated into it or marginalized. Wolof in Senegal, American-Liberian in Liberia, Hutu in Rwanda, Shona in Zimbabwe, Baganda in Uganda, and Amhara in Ethiopia were the key elements in defining the new nations as the cultural basis of the new state. In other states, an artificial creation was decreed and all traditional nations were dissolved in it; those who could or would not fit were excluded. The Ivoirité of President Henri Konan Bedie defined a new nation of essentially southern ethnic groups "native" to the land within Ivory Coast's boundaries and the rest were decreed non-nationals and non-citizens.

Consequently, many states in Africa are not able to claim the legitimate monopoly of force in the Weberian sense, both because the ostensible monopoly is contested and because its legitimacy is as well. In his chapter in this volume, William Zartman notes how there are large areas where security is challenged by both rebellion and internal lawlessness in Senegal, Guinea-Bissau, Liberia, Ivory Coast, Ghana, Nigeria, Chad, Sudan, Ethiopia, Somalia, Kenya, Uganda, Rwanda, Burundi, Congo, Angola, Zimbabwe, South Africa, and perhaps others, – a list that includes all of Africa's largest states. In all these states, though government is accepted, the political institutions through which its powers are exercised are treated with remarkable indifference by large sections of the citizenry. While this passive acceptance might not be problematic in other contexts (one often hears about the disenfranchised or disenchanted electorate in Western Europe and North Africa), in the African context it serves to deepen insecurities by alienating people from the apparatus of the state.

For these reasons and more, the parallelism between statism and nationalism has had a limited role in contemporary African history. Consequently, power does not rest in the legitimacy of public confidence and acceptance; instead, it resides firmly within political authorities. This has given rise to a position where individuals have greater attachments to their localities (or local communities) than to the overarching state. Hence, though the notion of the state is accepted, the political institutions through which its powers are exercised are treated with remarkable indifference. Until recently, multi-party systems have been replaced by single-party states, and in turn by military regimes, without raising much more than a flicker of interest from any but those who were immediately affected by the change. For the great majority, life simply goes on; and, while passive acceptance of this nature certainly has much to be said for it, it provides no assurance of political stability and no more than a resigned and probably temporary acquiescence in whatever policies the government pursues.

State effectiveness, therefore, has continually waned as a result of ongoing parochialisation of the public realm. Resources allocation by government and other state institutions has typically come to follow ethnic or religious lines. The segmentation of society that has followed has impeded the many reforms of the political structures that possibly could have enhanced Africa's ability to develop sustainably as well as exacerbating political tensions on the continent. The obvious manifestation of these political tensions is the litany of conflicts strung across the continent. Between 1970 and 2006, more than 42 wars were fought in Africa, with the vast majority of them intra-state in origin. In 2006 alone, 14 out of the 53 countries of Africa were afflicted by armed conflicts, accounting for more than half of all war-related deaths worldwide and resulting in more than 8 million refugees, returnees and displaced persons – see Figure 1.1.

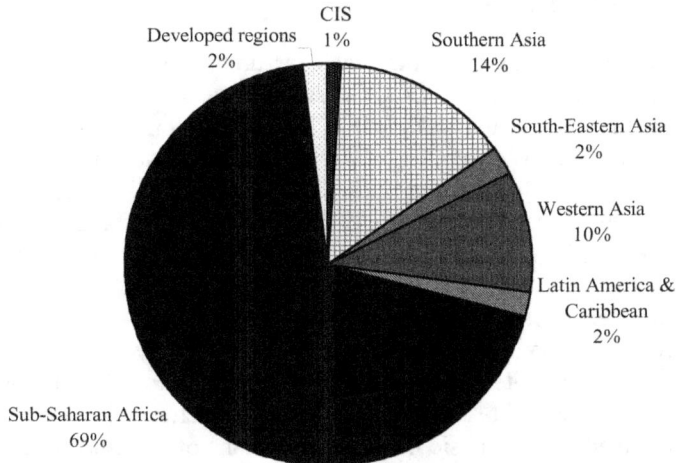

Figure 1.1 Deaths from Conflict 1994-2006, World Regions
Source: United Nations, 2005b

The parochialisation of the political realm has not only exacerbated the socio-political and economic disparities between and within African states, but crucially it has also played a central role in institutionalizing corruption. Due to an absence of effective structures with autonomy and strength to check corruption, the governing elite of most Africa states have engaged in high and sometimes egregious levels of corruption, increasingly diverting states resources for personal gains. In countries such as Nigeria, Sierra Leone, Democratic Republic of Congo, the Central African Republic, and Zimbabwe, corruption is so extensive that it is viewed as a way of life. Making or receiving bribes is considered a practical method for supplementing ones interest and achieving economic security far in excess of individual ability. An unpublished report from the United Nations into corruption in fifteen African countries suggest that nearly 40 per cent of annual government budgets are misappropriated by corrupt governing elite in the most affected countries (Poku 2005).

Across the continent, the motivation to earn income is strong, exacerbated by poverty and by low and declining civil service salaries. Opportunities to engage in corruption are numerous. Monopoly rents can be very large in highly regulated economies. In transition economies, economic rents are particularly large because of the amount of formerly state-owned property that is essentially up for grabs. The discretion of many public officials is also broad and this systematic weakness is exacerbated by poorly defined, ever changing, and poorly disseminated rules and regulations. Accountability is typically weak. Political competition and civil liberties are often restricted. Laws and principles of ethics in government are poorly developed, if they exist at all, and the legal institutions charged with enforcing them are ill-prepared for this complex job. The watchdog institutions that that provide information on which detection and enforcement is based – such as investigators, accountants, and the press – are also weak.

The crisis of post-colonialism

Ghana's first President, Kwame Nkrumah's, assurance in 1954 that, 'if we get self government, we'll transform the Gold Coast into a paradise in ten year' was one of his more extreme, but not markedly out of line descriptions of the fruits of African freedom. For him and his generation of African leaders, independence was a unique opportunity to prove in the words of Habib Bourguiba, Tunisia's head of Government in 1961, that 'the African was capable of running his own affairs; fighting his own battles and developing his own people.' For Nkrumah, the key was the control of the state; what he called the political kingdom. 'Seek ye first political kingdom' he exclaimed at independence, 'and all else will follow.'

As we celebrate Ghana's fiftieth anniversary, it is painfully clear that 'all else' has not followed'. African elites have failed to transform their 'political kingdoms' into 'paradises.' The inescapable image, therefore, is a picture of a people across the continent deprived of their basic needs in conditions of extreme adversity as state mangers and continental leaders fail to or seem incapable of advancing policies and programmes that would alleviate the plight of ordinary Africans (McGrew and Poku 2007). Prompting the late Claude Ake to conclude that, 'African leaders have presided over a pervasive alienation, the delinking of leadership from followers, a weak sense of national identity, and the perception of the government as a hostile force.'

Nowhere is the failure more apparent than in economic development. Black ruled Africa has fallen further and further behind the rest of the developing world. Today, the continent is the least developed in the world. According to the 2006 United Nations Development Programme (UNDP) data, some 80 per cent of the Low Human Development Countries – these are countries with high population growth rates, low income, low literacy, and low life expectancy – in 2005, were located in Africa. There are only ten African countries in the middle category – Algeria, Botswana, Egypt, Gabon, Libya, Mauritius, Morocco, Seychelles, Swaziland and South Africa; five of which have a combined population of just 4.6 million – Mauritius, Seychelles, Botswana, Gabon and Swaziland. The remaining 43 countries on the continent are in the low human development category. This, however, does not tell the entire story. There are 55 countries in this category, which means African countries account for a staggering 76 per cent of the category. Even more telling is that of the 30 countries with the lowest human development indices, 26 (or 87 per cent) are African.

The latest economic indicators from the African Development Report 2006 underline the extent of the continent's socio-economic condition. The Report's celebrated headline growth of 3.5 percent in GDP in 2005 compared to 3.2 percent in 2004 belies the systematic decline observable in real per capital GDP growth from 1.0 percent to 0.8 percent in the same period. In developmental terms, this means that the combined economies of Africa actually shrunk by 0.2 percent in the 12 months up to the end of 2005. To put this in context, all other regions in the world are already outperforming Africa, and efforts to redress this poor performance over the past two decades have not been successful. In 2004, for example, the average Gross National Product (GNP) per capita in the Organisation for Economic Co-operation and Development (OECD) countries was $28,086, compared with $528 in Africa (OECD 2004). This means that the industrialized countries are roughly 51 times wealthier than African states.

Assuming that the OECD countries could stop stretching this development gap further, and hoping that African economies could grow at an annual rate of 3.5 percent over the coming years, it would still take the continent some 135 years to reach today's level of wealth enjoyed by OECD countries.

An outcome of Africa's poor economic condition is an increase of poverty across the continent; with a fifth of the world populations, the continent is home to one in three poor persons in the world and four of every ten of its inhabitants living in what the World Banks classifies as 'a condition of absolute poverty.' More worrying still, Africa is the only region in the world where both the absolute number and the proportion of poor people are expected to increase during this millennium (UNDP 2004). Nearly half the population of Africa [300 million people] lives on less than 1$ a day: if current trends continue, by 2015 Africa will account for 50 per cent of the poor of the developing world [up from 25 per cent in 1990]. During the 1990s the region experienced a decline in GDP per capita of 0.6 per cent per annum, and because economic growth was highly skewed between countries, approximately half the total population is actually poorer in 2004 than they were in 1990. It is also the case that income and wealth distributions are extremely unequal in many countries, and with improved growth rates such inequalities are likely to increase rather than to diminish (World Bank 2003a).

Although it is currently fashionable to suggest that the economic troubles of Africa began with independence, this is not totally true. African economies performed relatively well in aggregate terms during the 1960s and early 1970s, and then between 1976 and 1978. During this period, GDP and exports grew at rates comparable to those in the other main developing regions and more rapidly in general than those in South Asia. Most notably manufacturing production rose at sustained rates, although from very low levels and in sectors such as food processing, textile, construction material and other simple consumer goods, that employed relatively unsophisticated technologies. This production effort was accompanied by massive expansion in primary education and significant mobilisation of domestic savings that raised the investment rations from 14 percent in 1963 to 20 percent in 1980 (World Bank 2003).

Similar progress was achieved in adult literacy and to a lesser extent in health care. In contrast and clearly disturbing was the performance of agricultural production, particularly for traditional food crops. Already in the 1960s the output of the latter was growing more slowly than population growth, which increased from about 2.4 per cent in 1960s to 2.9 percent in the 1970s and 3.1 percent in the 1980s.

In the 1970s a number of factors outside the continent served to compound the weaknesses of the prevailing development strategies. It begun when in 1973 the Organisation of the Petroleum Exporting Countries (OPEC) agreed to a dramatic increase in oil prices, it immediately affected the supply of foreign exchange of African countries. The price increase benefited a few of Africa's oil producing countries (Nigeria, Gabon, Angola and Congo), by increasing their supply of foreign exchange. However, it was an economic disaster for most African countries. It severely depleted their reserves of foreign exchange while simultaneously increasing their already heavy burden of debt as they attempted to continue to maintain imports of petroleum necessary for continuing their economic development plans.

Table 1.1 Selected Macro-economic Indicators, Sub-Saharan Africa and South Asia: 1963-1980

	GDP		Agriculture		Manufacturing		Export	
	1963-1973	1973-1980	1963-1973	1973-1980	1963-1973	1973-1980	1963-1973	1973-1980
Sub-Saharan Africa	6.0	2.8	2.2	0.0	10.7	10.2	16.9	-0.6
South Asia	3.7	4.3	3.4	2.4	4.1	5.2	-0.7	5.8

Source: World Bank (1989)

The impact of the oil crisis was compounded by a severe drought that stretched across the continent in 1972-1973. Hundred of thousands of refugees fled the drought-stricken areas, flocking to the cities or seeking new pastures, often crossing borders into other countries. Agricultural production decreased dramatically, and livestock starved to death. The affected countries required immediate supplies of imported food and food aid to prevent mass starvation of their population. This put a further burden on foreign exchange reserves and increased the debt of many countries. These mainly external factors in combination with domestic policy shortcomings resulted in a slowing of economic growth. A similar oil crisis in 1978 and declining world prices for the primary commodity exports of Africa, along with continued domestic policy deficiencies, led to a period of actual economic decline in the 1980s.

By the early 1980s, symptoms of Africa's economic malaise were evident almost everywhere on the continent. The returns on investment by organizations such as the World Bank were much lower in Africa than in other regions. It was – and still is – impossible to attract foreign private capital, either in investment or loans, and portfolio investment flows were negligible (see Table 1.2). The international price for Africa's government debt in secondary markets was the lowest for developing countries, reflecting the markets perception of the continent as uncreditworthy. The physical infrastructure, already poor, deteriorated from lack of maintenance, and the quality of government services declined, fuelling among other things civil discontent and corruption.

In pursuit of appropriate mitigation strategies, the World Bank and the International Monetary Fund (IMF) identified domestic policy weakness of African States as the main culprit in accounting for the continent's dire economic position. Based on this assumption, African governments were 'encouraged' to adopt Structural Adjustment Programmes (SAPs) as a crucial prerequisite to receiving vitally needed loans. The word 'encouraged' is used very loosely here, because in almost all cases, there was little choice on the part of the recipient states, but to follow the recommendations from the IMF and the World Bank.

Table 1.2 Foreign Direction Investment (as Percentage of Global FDI Flows) 1997-2006

Indicators	1997	1998	1999	2000	2001	2006
Developed Countries	56.8	69.8	77.2	79.1	80.1	
Developing Countries and economies	39.2	27.2	20.7	18.9	18.0	
Asia	22.4	13.8	9.3	11.3	11.2	
Latin America	14.9	12.0	10.3	6.8	6.8	
Africa	2.3	1.2	1.0	0.7	0.7	
Africa (as a percentage of developing countries)	5.88	4.63	4.72	3.78	3.87**	3.11**

Source: ADB Statistics Division and IMF; Note: * UCTAD data 2007 ** UNDP 2007

The nature of Structural Adjustment Programmes is well covered elsewhere and will not be restated here (Poku 2005). Our focus instead, is on the implications of the programmes on African people. Table 1.3 represents sectoral figures for the impact of SAPs on agricultural growth over a 20 year period. It is clear from the table that SAPs had very little impact on the sector. The more worrying observation is that the trend can be replicated across all the major indicators of economic growth. In almost all their evaluation reports (World Bank 1989, 1990, 1994, 1996, and 1998), the World Bank observed this trend, but attributed its causes not to the poor designs of SAPs, but to their implementation. In their words, 'no African country has achieved a sound macro-economic policy stance, and there is considerable concern that the reforms undertaken to date are fragile and that they are merely returning the continent to the slow growth path of the 1960s and early 1970s' (World Bank 1998:14).

Table 1.3 GDP Growth Under Adjustment – Agriculture-growth Rate (median) sub Saharan Africa, 1981-83, 1987-91 and 1992-97

	1981-1986	1987-91	1992-97
Large improvements	4.2	2.4	2.0
Small improvements	3.1	2.8	2.1
Deterioration	2.3	3.3	2.8
All Countries	3.1	2.8	2.2

Source: ADB and IMF

In truth, it is not clear whether the lack of effective implementation results from African government's unwillingness to undertake reforms (as the World Bank claims) or from the objective conditions of the economies not permitting the kind of adjustment being recommended. Despite two and half decades of adjustment policies, this debate remains large unresolved. The only certainty, however, is that SAPs often have an immediate and at time detrimental impact on the welfare of the poorest members of society, especially as they affect food prices, costs of education, and payment of medical services (see Table 1.4). Riley and Parfitt argue that the deprivations experienced by certain groups who 'have been deprived of their stake in society by some aspect of an austerity program that has moved them towards or below the poverty line' result in violence (Riley, S.P. and Parfitt, T.W. 1994: 140). For example, state employees who have been laid off become more critical of the regime and become actively opposed to the economic policies which they see as disadvantaging them. Thus, they argue that the overall result of such economic policies is often 'to destabilize the recipient states as key groups in the populace rebel against the combination of rising prices and declining real wages and public services' (Ibid., p. 140).

Table 1.4 Impact of Common Structural Adjustment Measures on Health Determinants

Intended Result	Policy	Common impact on the Poor
Reduced budget deficit, freeing up money for debt servicing	Reducing government expenditure	Reduced health, education and social welfare spending and the introduction of cost-recovery and user-fees put health care and education beyond the reach of many ordinary people. Public sector redundancies and salary freezes lead to fewer teachers and doctors.
Increased efficiency	Privatisation of state run industries	Massive lay-offs and increased unemployment with no social security provision push families deeper into poverty.
Increased exports, boosting foreign exchange reserves needed for debt repayment	Currency devaluation and export promotion	Cost of imports soar, including vital resources such as imported medicines. Moreover export prices fall because many countries are promoting the same exports under SAPs, so countries are still no better off.
Reduced inflation	Raising interest rates	Farmers and small companies can no longer afford to borrow money and are forced to reduce production or go out of business.
Increased efficiency in food production	Removal of price controls	Basic food prices rise putting even further pressure on already stretched household budgets.

Table 1.5 Circle of Decline and Vulnerability: The impacts of SAP on African Societies

Policy	Policy Response	Domestic Impact	Implications for the spread of HIV/AIDS
To reduce government expenditure	Introduce user fee for health services	Reduce access to health services; decline in general health of the population	Reduced awareness of health issues, including HIV/AIDS; poor general health; reduced treatment for opportunistic infections- particularly STDs
	Introduce user fee for education	Children, particularly girls, removed from schools; marginalisation of large section of population to informal sector like prostitution with associated risk	Reduced education; increased illiteracy; increased risk of HIV transmission due to poor educational knowledge. Particular vulnerability of women due to lack of formal education
	Decrease spending on health and education	Reduce quality and quantity of facilities; lack of equipment; fewer and less strained staff	Increased vulnerability to infection
	Public sector redundancies and wage freezes	Unemployment; staff shortages leading to reduced quality and quantity of education and health services	Increased vulnerability to infection
	Removal of price subsidies on food, fuel and other basic commodities	Reduced quality and quantity of food; declining calorie consumption per head	Poor health means greater vulnerability to infection, increased in informal sector activities with increased risk of HIV infection
	Reduced civil services	Reduced administrative capacity	Governments less able to promote AIDS prevention
To increase export earnings	Promote large export-orientated projects	Workers migrate to jobs from home; decrease food production; restructures domestic production patterns leading to decrease consumable food for domestic societies; rural to urban migration	Workers more likely to engage in risky behaviour with increased risk of HIV/ AIDS contraction; spreading of HIV through migration; returning migrants infecting local communities

Lipumba observes that the dominant 'opinion among African intellectuals is that structural adjustment programs are part of the problem rather than part of the solution' (Lipumba 1994). Certainly, SAPs have done little to foster the social, political and economic conditions that could contribute to the development of stable state-society relations in Africa and the creation of a stable social order. The promotion of exports for debt repayment and the cutting of public expenditure on welfare in a region where 100 million people are undernourished; where there is 1 doctor for 36,000 people, compared with 1 for 400 people in industrial countries; and where nine out of the ten HIV infected people worldwide reside, is tantamount to a scandal. One author has even referred to SAPs as a form of 'economic genocide.' When compared to genocide in various periods of colonial history, its impact is devastating. Structural adjustment programs directly affect the livelihood of more than 4 billion people (Chossudovsky 1996).

SAPs raise particular problems for African governments because they entail most of the factors that fuel the AIDS epidemic (see Table 1.5). The health of the poor is a particular case in point. A primary aim of adjustment policies has been to give more incentive to production in the rural economy. In Sub-Saharan Africa in particular most poverty is located in the countryside; raising the world market prices for tradable agricultural goods by reducing export taxes and devaluing the currency would, it was argued, increase rural incomes. The reality, however, has been different, rural producers have not been able to expand production of tradable goods (or switch production from one crop to another) because they lack the necessary infrastructure (roads and storage buildings for example) to bring their produce to market. In this respect adjustment policies have had the opposite effect because cuts in government expenditure are often the main reason why infrastructure is dilapidated. Moreover, a shift by rural producers away from food ('untradable') to non-food ('tradable') in response to policy stimulus have contributed to the decline in food production in sub-Saharan Africa, which is lower today than it was in 1980, with potentially serious consequences for nutritional outcomes.

At a time when up to 70 per cent of adults in some hospitals are suffering from AIDS-related illnesses—placing extreme pressure on health services—many African countries are still cutting health expenditure in order to satisfy IMF and World Bank conditionalities. For example, in Tanzania—where over half a million children are orphans as a result of AIDS (UNAIDS 2002) —the government spends only around $3.20 per person per year on health provision, a quarter of what the World Bank itself estimate is necessary to provide basic care (World-Bank 2002). The Tanzanian government spends in excess of three times more on debt servicing each year than it does on health care – see Table 1.6. Similarly, in Malawi where nearly 16 per cent of the population are either living with HIV or AIDS, where there is only one doctor for every 50, 000 people, government spending on health care was dwarfed by debt repayment by two to one – see Table 1.6.

The consequences of the continuing low levels of health expenditure in poor countries are apparent in a country such as Zambia – see Table 1.6. Some of the worst effects come through the implementation of user fees. In the face of declining expenditure on public services many countries have introduced user charges as a way to finance the health care system and deter unnecessary use. However, their effectiveness has been quite damaging. Evidence from several countries shows that they rarely raise significant levels of revenue for the health sector and have regressive effects in terms of equity. Studies from Nigeria, Zimbabwe and Algeria show that when user charges were implemented for maternity services the use of antenatal care declined and maternal mortality and emergency deliveries in hospitals increased. When the World Bank advised Kenya to introduce a user fee of US$2.15 for its STD clinics, attendance fell by 35-60%, a particularly worrying result as STD treatment is important to HIV prevention.

Table 1.6 Debt to Health and Education Profile: Selected African Countries

Country	Percentage of Population with HIV/ AIDS *	Percentage of Govt. Spending on primary education**	Percentage of Govt. Spending on Health***	Percentage of Govt. Spending on Debt Servicing 2006****
Malawi	15.5	15.8	14.5	34
Mozambique	13.0	20.2	11.1	57
Rwanda	8.9	9.2	9.8	32
Tanzania	7.8	25.4	14.9	42
Uganda	5.9	21.1	9.3	39
Zambia	21.5	14.6	12.6	62

Various sources: * (UNAIDS 2006) ** (World-Bank 2006), *** (WHO/UNAIDS/ International AIDS Society 2006) **** (UNDP 2006)

The future and Africa's renewal

In retrospect, Fanon's notion of renovating violence, that real freedom for Africans could be won only by destruction, true liberation only through fire, has proved to be an ultimate perfidy. Violence in Africa has begotten more violence. The outcome is the culture of corruption, brutality, destitution and despair. The many facets, of which, the authors in the volume write below. But there are increasing signs of positive changes across the continent. Political elite are growing increasing cognoscente of the realities facing the continent. They have, in the words of Nigerian president Olusegum Obasanjo, recognised that, 'an unjust international order will not change simply because of the euphony of their rhetoric.' As such, they have to stop blaming their problems on the legacy of colonialism; while acknowledging that their countries are bleeding from self-inflicted wounds.

The adoption of NEPAD and their commitment to improve economic and political governance, built on the substantial achievements of the last decade is some indication that changes are taking place for the better. Already 25 countries have voluntarily signed up for the African Peer Review Mechanism (APRM) and the process has begun with a number of reviews. Even beyond the formal processes of the APRM, there are encouraging signs that the African Union and regional bodies are beginning to assume greater leadership in settling continental problems - though the Mugabe's regimes continues to be a thorn.

The Commission for Africa and the resultant focus of the 2005 and 2006 Group of Eight industrialised countries meeting on Africa reflects a renewed international soul searching about how best to arrest the continent's underdevelopment. In all the unprecedented confluence of global and domestic (read African) forces bolds well for a continent which for so many decades had seemed hell-bent on self-destruction. Finally, the Africa renewal agenda espoused by the Lagos Declaration, over two decades ago, may well be in sight. Yet the task of arresting Africa's chronic underdevelopment will require much more than good well (however latent) from a fickle international community coupled with renewed enlightenment by African leaders notorious for their predatory instincts and their selective/amnesic approach to history.

This book is not intended to be a comprehensive survey of the political and economic problems of modern black Africa. It leaves out too many countries, too many wars and too many issues. Rather it is an attempt to show – through the combined experience of senior African civil servants and leading African scholars – what accounts for the failure of Africa's political kingdoms, the role of indigenous leaders in this failure and how to avoid mistakes of the past. Collectively, the chapters offer a reflective appraisal of the challenges facing contemporary Africa and point a positive way forward in the coming years.

Bibliography

Ake, Claude, "Sustaining Development on the Indigenous", Paper prepared for World Bank long-term perspectives study on Africa (December 1987).

Beissinger, Mark & Young, Crawford, eds., 2002. *Beyond State Crisis? Postcolonial Africa and Post-Soviet Eurasia in Comparative Perspective*. Woodrow Wilson Center.

Bratton, Michael and Van de Walle, Nicolas (1997). *Democratic Experiments in Africa*. Cambridge.

Buve, A., et al. 2001. "Multicentre Study on Factors Determining Differences in Rate of Spread of HIV in Sub-Saharan Africa: Methods and Prevalence of HIV Infection." AIDS 15, suppl 4, S5-S14.

Cornia, G.A. et al (1987), *Adjustment with a Human Face: Protecting the Vulnerable and Promoting Growth*, New York: Oxford Univesity Press.

Frantz Fanon, *Les Damnes de la terre* Maspero, Paris 1961.

Mayall, James, (1991) *The Hope and Fears of Independence*, in Douglas Rimmer (eds) *Africa 30 years on*, James Currey: London.

McGrew A. and Poku, N.K ed., (2007) *Globalization, Development and Human Security*, Polity Press: Cambridge.

Mukherjee, A. (1994), *Structural Adjustment Programs and Food Security*, Aldershot, U.K: Avebury.

Poku, N. (1996) "The Construction of Ethnic Identities in Contemporary Africa", in Neil Renwick and Jill Krause (ed) *Identities and International Relations*, Macmillan Press, London.

Poku , N. and David Graham (1999), *Redefining Security: Population Movement and National Security*. Greenwood, Westport.

Poku, N. and David Graham (2000), *Migration, Globalisation and Human Security*, Routledge, London.

Reno, W. (1998) *Warlord Politics and Africa State*, Lynne Rienner, London.

Tomasevski, Katarina (1995), "The influence of the World Bank and IMF on economic and social rights", *Nordic Journal of International Law*, Vol.64, pp.385-395.

Turshnet, Meredeth (1994), "The Impact of Economic Reforms on Women's Health and Health Care in Sub-Saharan Africa", in Nahid Aslanbegui, S. Pressmant, Gale Sumerfield (eds.), *Women in the Age of Economic Transformation*, Routledge: London, pp.77-93.

UNESCO (1996), *Trends and Projections of Enrollment, 1960-2025*, Paris: UNESCO.

UNCTAD (1999) *Global Trade and Africa: Policy Options for the 21st Century*. UNCTAD Review.

UNCTAD (2000) *FDI and Africa: Context and Opportunity*. UNCTAD Review.

UNDP 1999a. *Poverty trends and the voices of the poor*, Washington D.C.: World Bank, Poverty Reduction and Economic Management.

Wallerstein, Immanuel (2005), *Africa, the Politics of Independence and Unity*, University of Nabraska Press.

Weiss, Herbert and Carayannis, Tatiana 2005. "The Enduring Idea of the Congo," in Ricardo Rene, Laremont, ed., *Borders, Nationalism and the African State*, Boulder, Colo, Lynne Rienner.

World Bank (2000) *Africa Development Indicators 2000*, World Bank, Washington D.C.

UNDP (2006) *Human Development Report*, Oxford University Press, Oxford.

World Health Organization (2001), *Macroeconmics and Health: Investing in Health for Economic Development*, Report of the Commmission on Maroeconomics and Health, Who: Geneva.

World Bank (1996) *World Bank Annual Report 1996*, World Bank: Washington D.C.

World Bank (1997) *World Development Report: the State in a Changing World* Oxford: University Press.

World Bank (1996). *Poverty Reduction and the World Bank: Progress and Challenges in the 1990s*, World Bank: Washington, D.C.

World Bank (2000a) *Africa Development Indicators 2000*, World Bank: Washington D.C.

World Bank Operations Evaluation Department/Jayarajah, C., Branson, W. and Sen, B. (1996a) *Social Dimensions of Adjustment: World Bank Experience 1980-93*, World Bank: Washington D.C.

Zartman, I William, ed., 1997. *Governance as Conflict Management: Politics and Violence in West Africa*. Brookings, Washington DC.

Zartman, I William (2005a). *Cowardly Lions: Missed Opportunities to Prevent State Collapse and Deadly Conflict*, Boulder, Colo, Lynne Rienner.

Ziegler, Jean (2001), *Economic, Social and Cultural Rights: The Right to Food*, Report by the Special Rapporteur on the right to food, Commission on Human Rights, Fifty-seven session, Economic and Social Council, E/CN.4/2001/53.

Chapter 1

The African State

I William Zartman

The African state is an elusive target for a single-focused analysis, and yet it is that elusiveness that is key to its complex nature. To begin with, there is no single accepted definition of a state in general. "The state is on the active agenda of essentially contested subjects." (Walker 1995, 27) In addition, the "state" in Africa is a moving target, developing—or underdeveloping—like everything else on the continent, so that the state of the state differs not only from the pre-colonial to the colonial to the post-colonial periods but also from the immediate post-independence to the present periods. Furthermore, as in so many areas where Africa is subjected to undifferentiating generalities, there is no African state but 50 of them, similar perhaps but never the same. Finally, Africa is or has been the home of the largest number of collapsed, as well as failed and failing, states, raising the question whether a collapsed state still a state or falls outside the category, and where in the spectrum of failures should be line of inclusion be drawn? The purpose of this chapter is to evaluate the multifaceted thing called a state in Africa by its several characterizations, leading to a brief note about what can be done, from he outside, to help it come closer to its ideal types.

State is here defined as the authoritative political institution that is sovereign over a recognized territory (Dawisha and Zartman 1988, 6-7), similar to the international law characterization as a body of people occupying a definite territory under a sovereign and recognized government, or Weber's (1946, 78) definition as "a human community that (successfully) claims *the monopoly over the legitimate use of physical force* within a given territory" [italics and parenthesis in the original]. Despite difference is details and emphasis, the classical components are territory, people, and governance, and these will be used to organize the following discussion. But first, a word on the moving target.

The State in Evolution

Whatever the nature of the proto-states before colonization, the African states that saw independence for the first time in the 1960s and 1970s were new, colonial creations. Nationalist elites were given a framework to fill, and they did so with proto-parties organized as anti-colonialist or national liberation movements (Zartman 1966, 1997). Territory was delimited on a map and accepted by the Organization of African Unity (OAU), with a few exceptions; people were represented and administered officially by party-governments. Yet all of these elements were only approximations: Boundaries were demarcated in only 3 out of every 5 cases and the writ of the government often did not reach them; populations crossed borders at will to live in and identify with transborder communities; and nationalist elites were uncertain whether they were replacing the incumbents in the colonial institutions or the institutions themselves. In an ironic reversal of nationalism, it was the international community that maintained the external appearances of an often-virtual state (Jackson 1990): Absent a positive definition of what their nation was, African elites agreed on what it was not—the Foreigner, just as in the absence of a fully functioning state, it was the international community that asserted its sovereign existence.

Independence brought an extraordinary opportunity to establish a social contract to underwrite the state, but it was severely flawed, consistent with the condition of nationalism and sovereignty. The contract had two sections, external and internal. It was above all an agreement between nationalist elites and the departing colonizer to receive a successor state and maintain it with as much continuity as possible (Zartman 1964, Khadiagala and Rothchild 2005). Less explicitly, it was also an agreement among the nationalist elite on the allocation of rules, roles and shares in the Golden Eggs of independence, not an agreement involving the body politic as the idea of a social contract implies. Highly explicit was the notion that the nationalist movement turned single party incarnated the nation in its social, political and economic form; deeply implicit was the promise that the nationalized state would provide the population with the benefits that the colonizer had enjoyed and more, through jobs and services; when the Golden Eggs ran out, the Goose was nationalized and distributed (Addison 1995, 55-57). But no popular accountability was provided. The only accountability was to the military and the replacement of nationalist elites by their military only locked the closed door of accountability.

When the Goose ran out in turn, the nation demanded accountability of the state. Indirect taxation of agriculture, rent-seeking, corruption and poor management, overindebtedness, and falling terms of trade invalidated the old contract (Addison 1995). The collapse of ideological supports for party-state monopolies at the end of the Cold War and their replacement with notions of political and economic competition set the stage for new terms. However, full political and economic participation and political and fiscal accountability has taken hold, even imperfectly, in only a few places (Zartman 1997, 36-48). Instead, the second wave of democratization of the 1990s petered out in most of the continent, leaving only unsubstantiated forms of accountability and a population repeatedly disenchanted and alienated by rent-seeking elites. Instead of serving as the manager of conflicts and the arbiter of demands among various demand-bearing groups in society, the state has become the source of conflict with such groups and the repressor of their demands.

In the first decade of the new millennium, the appearance of a new social contract is still a development in waiting. Accountability that had appeared in many states in the 1990s then stagnated in either a Tweedledee-Dum alternance or a one-step progression from a single-party to a dominant party (*un parti quasi-unique* in French-speaking Africa). Often, a, ethnic or atavistic rebellion made the system a biparty or "quasi-federal" state. Nations fractured into acephalic segmentary systems where none had existed before. Inefficiencies and structural adjustment limited state functions and state capacities. A third wave of state collapse has not materialized but widespread state failures had occurred. These conditions will be assessed in the following sections. Yet the African state continues to exist, perhaps held together in the end by a lack of alternatives.

A State of People

Whether referred to as a political institution, a body of people or a human community, the state stands in a particular relation to its population, generally expressed as its Nation. However, its inherent definitional ambiguity is not tamed thereby, for Nation-State has two distinct meanings, both ideals only approximated in various degrees in reality. It can refer either to the notion of popular sovereignty developed in the French Revolution to replace the then-current notion of monarchial sovereignty, or to the coincidence of the "imagined community" of the Nation with the political institution of the State. Both meanings are elusive in Africa.

Popular sovereignty was both the goal and the expression of the nationalist movement that took or received independence from the colonial authorities. The opposition is well expressed in the French expression of the time, which contrasted the *pays réel* of the nationalist against the *pays légal* of the colonizer. Since the nationalist movement was the self-proclaimed incarnation of the nation, its takeover *ipso facto* created the Nation State. When the nationalist movement turned into a single party (because there was only one nation in one state), first under a civilian and then under a military regime, it represented the institutionalization of popular sovereignty, much in the same way that popular sovereignty was originally instituted as the national will in the French Revolution. However, it gradually became evident to African people that this first wave of democratization was truncated, a case of "delegative" rather than "representative" democracy (O'Donnell 1992; Weffort 1993; Cohen 1995) since it provided a means for nationalist elites to come to power but not for the nation to hold the accountable for being there; they could be replaced only by other nationalist elites whose representativeness was by revelation, not by any exercise of popular sovereignty by the people they claimed to represent.

As of the middle of the first decade of the 2000s, the number of Black African countries holding free and fair, effective[1] multiparty elections is small. Although there can certainly be debates over individual cases, arguably they include Sierra Leone, Ghana, Benin, Liberia, Mali, Mozambique, Nigeria, Senegal, Kenya, Tanzania, Malawi, South Africa, Lesotho, Swaziland, Namibia, Botswana, and Zambia; even in a quarter of these, alternance has not yet occurred under the current system and in another quarter are essentially no different in their policies or practices than their predecessors. It must be quickly noted that none of these indicators—elections, alternance, policy change—assures democracy and popular sovereignty. Elections can be controlled and guided, especially when they pit seasoned old autocrats against new and inexperienced democrats, but the body politic may also simply be satisfied with policies and even policymakers or sincerely prefer the incumbents

---

1 "Effective" meaning where several parties have an objective chance of coming to power or represent a sizable opposition in parliament.

to the opponents. Furthermore, party machines are to be considered a hallmark of democratic competition, as long as they operate in open competition and are not simply the control mechanism of the incumbents. It takes a bundle of these characteristics to constitute free and fair, effective multiparty expressions of popular sovereignty in the state.

On the other side of the definition, it would be a confusion of terms to assert that popular sovereignty is a necessary element in the existence of the state. Although they offer mo way to substantiate their claims to represent the nation, Faure Gnassigbé, Denis Sassou Nguesso, Robert Mugabe, or Idriss Deby do run a state in Togo, Congo, Zimbabwe, or Chad, respectively. Even without the controlled elections that each of them ran, the sovereign institution over which they presided contained a recognized government, was authoritative over a definite territory, and claimed the monopoly over the legitimate use of force, as their repressed opponents would be the first to admit. As in the case of Weber's definition (as is usually overlooked), the operative word is "claims:" those who run the state claim to represent the popular will.

In the second meaning of Nation-State, the coincidence of the popular community of historic identity and the sovereign political institution is also asserted as an inheritance of the nationalist movement. Not only was the nationalist movement an incarnation of the *pays réel* and the popular will; it also claimed to incarnate the nationals of the country in opposition to the foreign colonialists.[2] In fact, in most cases, the national identity was only negative, as stated: The people were self-decreed nationals of their country because they were not Europeans, not because of any common characteristics that distinguished them from their neighbors and held them together. The real nations of the new state were the traditional nations, tribes or ethnic groups, who did claim a common history, mythology, language, customs, and other characteristics associated with "imagined communities" (Anderson 1991). Indeed, in one of the few purportedly Nation States—Somalia—it became clear that it was the presence of an external enemy—Ethiopia—that kept the country together, and in two others—Rwanda and Burundi—the nation by all the common characteristics contained murderous cleavages.[3] Thus, the Nation-State claim posed a challenge to the new nationalist elites, that of creating a new Nation to go with the State.

Various approaches were tried to meet the challenge. In some states, the dominant traditional nation became the core of the new nation, as other ethnic groups were assimilated into it or marginalized. Wolof in Senegal, American-Liberian in Liberia, Hutu in Rwanda, Shona in Zimbabwe, Baganda in Uganda, and Amhara in Ethiopia were the key elements in defining the new nations as the cultural basis of the new state. In other states, an artificial creation was decreed and all traditional nations were dissolved in it; those who could or would not fit were excluded. The *Ivoirité* of President Henri Konan Bedie defined a new nation of essentially southern ethnic

---

2   Perhaps the most important—and often unnoticed—gift of the nationhalist movement in South Africa was the early decision that it was not an anticolonialist bvut an equal rights movement and that the South Africa whites were Africans too.

3   The cohesiveness of the Nation in the other three cases—Botswana, Lesotho, and Swaziland—is yet untested.

groups "native" to the land within Ivory Coast's boundaries and the rest were decreed non-nationals and non-citizens. President Mobutu Sese Seko of Zaire (named Congo before and after his reign) instilled a Zairean identity among the many ethnic groups of the Congo that was so strong that it outlived both him and the change of name of his (and their) country back to Congo again (Weiss and Carayannis 2005). John Garang, eventually Sudanese vice-president, struggled mightily all his life not only to give dignity and respect to Southern Sudanese identity but also to create a single overarching identity to a Sudanese nation within a single state. In Tanzania, where none of the 340 ethnic groups is large enough to hold a dominant position, nationalist elites strove to forge a Tanzanian nation.

The irony of these efforts is that their major effect was to arouse divisive reactions among the excluded or the dissolved ethnic groups. Their natural reaction was accentuated when the resources of the state diminished under the weight of the fiscal discipline, energy crises, and falling terms of trade of the mid-1980s into the mid-1990s. When Casamançais in rebellion talk of "the Senegalese," they mean people in Dakar. Official efforts to enact *Ivoitite* pushed excluded Northern Muslims in Ivory Coast to rise in armed rebellion in 2003. Intensified policies to make Sudan an Arabic-speaking Muslim nation brought Southern Sudanese to fight to become full Sudanese since 1955 (with a decade interlude 1972-82), pausing for agreements with the North in 1972 and 2005 that Khartoum has not implemented. The Banyamulenge in eastern Zaire rebelled against their exclusion from Zairean citizenship, leading to the overthrow of Mobutu in 1996 and the War of Zairean Succession over the subsequent decade. The southern Ewe minority that defined the Togolese nation at independence was soon overthrown by the excluded northern Kabye minority who have run the state for over four decades, excluding the Ewes and others in their turn. The majority Hutus who defined the Rwandan nation since before independence were overthrown by the Tutsi minority they had exclude and against whom they committed the 1994 genocide in their last, futile attempt to hold on to power. Siad Barre, who took over power over the Somali nation in 1969 and decreed that there were no tribes, reduced the representatives of that nation to his Marehan-Ogadeni-Darood (MOD) clans and so was overthrown by other, excluded clans, some of them then seceded to declare their Somaliland in the northwest and Puntland in the northeast independent, while the rest of the state was destroyed by contesting Hawiye subclans. There is scarcely an African state where attempts to define a new nation have not produced rebellions by the excluded.

It is unclear how population fluidity affects the state, but the state is a leaky container for its population in Africa. Out off 500 million Sub-Saharan Africans at the turn of the millennium, 3.3 million were refugees and another 14 million were internally displaced (IDPs) (USCR 2001). Sudan, Burundi, Sierra Leone, Somalia, Congo, Eritrea, and Liberia each suffered population losses between 500,000 and 100,000. The oft-repeated assurance that many of such population merely moved next door among their own people on the other side of the border does nothing to reinforce the hold of the state over its people, their allegiance and their identity. On the other hand, the guestworker phenomenon is widespread in Africa, laying the ground for serious frictions the more the notion of national identity and the efforts to build a State Nation are emphasized. Foreign populations from neighboring countries have made possible the economic growth of such disparate states as South Africa and Ivory Coast. The danger is seen in notable expulsions of foreign Africans— such as the 200,000 evicted from Ghana in 1969, the 3 million from Nigeria in 1983, of hundreds of Senegalese and Mauritanian traders and farmers from each other's country in 1989, and uncertain numbers from Ivory Coast in the early 2000s, showed state control over its own labor market and the destabilization of its neighbors'.

Clearly the African state is less a Nation State than it was—or at least purported to be—nearly half a century ago at independence, despite or because of efforts to make it so. In many cases, the state claims to rule over a defined territory but in fact rules only a large part of it and the people in that part, while in another part another group contests its right not just to rule the land but also to speak for the nation. Yet few of these rebellious groups are secessionist, and many of those few are protesting neglect rather than asserting separateness, as discussed below; they do not contest the territorial unity of the state but its national unity. "It is not our state, and we live in its territory too." On either count, as an expression of popular sovereignty or cultural identity, the state in Africa is not or has yet to become a Nation-State. It remains an authoritative political institution, ruling over some of its people by some of them.

A State of Functions

A more comprehensive way of looking at the state is as an institution. Much of the current analysis of the African State examines its functional capacities. In particular, the recent literature on failing states focuses on shortfalls in its capabilities; states are said to collapse "because they can no longer perform the functions required of them to pass as states" (Zartman 1995, 5). Again, there are two different ways of conceptualizing these functions and measuring state performance—as output capacity and as conflict management.

Jeffrey Herbst (2000), who has written the very best book on the state in African, discusses major functions of the state, of which a number of particular significance can be highlighted, including taxation, security, and money, among others. States' eyes are always bigger than their treasuries, but African states are forced to have both small eyes and smaller purses. Although data are incomplete and state performances often vary widely, African states depend heavily on taxes on foreign trade (tariffs) and transactions for state revenue—nearly 40% of revenue or more than twice the levels of other low and middleincome areas of Asia and the Americas. On the other hand, domestic producer taxes (income, profits, capital gains) have been declining to less than 25% and consumer taxes (sales, value added, excise) follow the same pattern. The gap is made up by foreign aid, borrowing and deficit financing, all areas in which the African state excels. As a result, state resources are low, against the high needs of development.

Security is also below needs; many African states are not able to claim the legitimate monopoly of force, both because the ostensible monopoly is contested and because its legitimacy is as well. As noted, there are large areas where security is challenged by both rebellion and internal lawlessness in Senegal, Guinea-Bissau,

Liberia, Ivory Coast, Ghana, Nigeria, Chad, Sudan, Ethiopia, Somalia, Kenya, Uganda, Rwanda, Burundi, Congo, Angola, Zimbabwe, South Africa, and perhaps others, a list that includes Africa's largest states. In many of these cases, rebel forces contest the legitimacy as well as the effectiveness of state security forces. As a result, states have often had to reach high and low to augment their own meager capabilities. They reach low to militias, such as the Jeunes Patriotes in Ivory Coast or the Kamajors and Civil Defense Forces in Sierra Leone, Ninjas in Congo-Brazzaville, janjaweed in Sudan, civil defense forces in Zimbabwe and AliR in Congo who serve as "official rebel armies" to enforce partisan security and impose their own law and disorder. More officially, states reach high to farm out security to private and public mercenaries at great cost to their own functional legitimacy (Reno 1998). Private mercenaries include such companies as Executive Outcomes, Sandline International, Military Professional Resources Inc, and others. Public mercenaries include the proliferation of UN Peace-Keeping Operations (PKOs) operating in Africa—in Ivory Coast, Congo, CAR, Ethiopia and Eritrea, and Sierra Leone, the African Union's PKO in Sudan, and regional PKOs such as the Military Observer Groups (ECOMOGs) of the Economic Community of West African States (ECOWAS) in Liberia, Sierra Leone, Ivory Coast and Guinea-Bissau. With friends like this, it is hard for the African state to claim a monopoly on the provision of security, even—or perhaps especially—since these forces are contracted by the incapable state itself.

Fiscal authority is a state function that is lacking, or at least shared, in fifteen of Africa's states. The Africa Financial Community (CFA) shares its authority with the French Treasury. However in other countries, simply security conditions led to the informal incorporation of a part of the country into neighboring states' currency zones, as in Congo, Somalia, and Liberia.

Many other functions could be examined. They would bear the same message, that the African state is frequently hard-pressed to meet its job description but that it is trying, often enlisting the support of other states and populations at a cost to its own autonomy. If they did not have credible pretensions at being a state, others would not come to their aid, as the plight of Somaliland, Puntland, and the Sahrawi Arab Democratic Republic illustrate. For all its importance in buttressing a virtual status, this aid is temporary, an external protectionist effort until the infant industry can assert its own sovereignty. Admittedly the pump-priming or stop-gap has lasted a while, or at least longer than expected. The trade-off is evident and will be revisited at the end of this chapter.

The other conceptualization of the state is as a conflict management mechanism. The state, as social contract theorists indicate, is created to provide security by managing conflict, either by repressing it or by dealing with it in more creative ways through "normal politics." Society is made up of groups of all kinds bearing demands of all kinds, all necessarily in conflict with each other, that is, they cannot all be satisfied at the same time. Thus there are two forms of conflict to be managed, between the groups themselves and between their demands. The state is not the only conflict manager, although that is its main internal task. The other conflict manager is civil society, and a well-functioning society handles many of its own conflicts without state interference. If it is the only handler, it is an acephalous society, as exist in some traditional Africa nations; if it has no role, it is a deficient society in a totalitarian state, scarcely a danger at present given the state of the African state, as is being discussed. Optimally, there is a balance between the two levels. If the state does not do its job either society has to increase its role or conflict and anarchy begin to take over; if society does not do its job, the state has to step in or risk exacerbation. In addition, there is occasion for conflict between the two levels, a major characteristic of the land ownership issue that will increasingly bedevil African states and societies (Herbst 2000, 173-197).

Whether it acts as a neutral arbiter between groups or a rulemaker between demands, a state's role is to manage conflict (Zartman 1996, 1997). Demand-bearing groups were a distraction to single-party states and a nuisance to military regimes, and were generally coopted or repressed. Since the even partial liberalization of political systems after 1990, such groups have increased in numbers, bearing both achievemental (labor, student, human rights) and ascriptive (ethnic) demands. Cooptation is less directly available than when such groups could be made party auxiliaries but state control is still possible; if not, repression is a ready option. In the process, states have moved from the role of arbiters in conflicts between groups to targets of conflicts with groups, further reducing their availability to act as arbiters in a vicious circle effect. The underlying grievance was that monolithic governments, whether civilian or military, were not able to resolve conflicts in demands from the increasingly pluralistic and disappointed population. Thus another contributor was the sudden disrepute of socialist and single-party regimes, beginning with the Soviet Union, although this development so closely paralleled the evolution of attitudes in Africa that it is hard to establish a cause and effect. Similarly, ‹although the growing procedural demands echoed the pressures of the international financial institutions—World Bank, Monetary Fund, and private sector—for economic openness, accountability and competition, those pressures were generally so unpopular in Africa, even or especially when finally adopted by the governments, that they might have been predicted to undermine the development of political openness and competition. That they did not is testimony to the strength of grassroot demands for debate and participation. Instead, austerity measures required by the IMF often served as the trigger for popular uprisings against the corrupt authoritarian regimes that enacted them, creating a particularly difficult dilemma for the resulting democratic regimes. In sum, conflicts increasingly gravitated from group vs group to groups vs government.

The balance sheet is hard to draw up, because conflicts successfully managed are dogs that didn't bark. Dogs that stopped barking are notable in the continent: peace agreements with the Mozambican National Movement (Renamo) in 1992, the Tuareg rebellions in Mali in 1997, the Casamance Democratic Forces Movement (MFDC) in 2005, the Movement for Congolese Liberation (MLC) and the Congolese Democratic Rallies (RCDs) in 1999, the Hutu and Tutsi rebels in Burundi in 2004, the National Union for the Total Independence of Angola (UNITA) in 2002-2005, and the Sudanese Peoples Liberation Movement (SPLM) in 2005 are notable achievements in restoring state unity, even if the proof of the pudding has yet to be found in the implementation in some cases. Equally notable is reassertion of state capabilities in dealing with a number of state-building issues and demands in the preparation of elections in Mozambique and South Africa in 1994 and in Congo in 2006. Such actions are not a new trend, but they are underreported and need recognition, as evidence of a functioning state.

But the dogs of internal war barked viciously in the oil delta of Nigeria, the genocide sites of Rwanda and Sudan, the War of Zairean Succession and the associated local land and ethnic conflicts in Eastern Congo, the chieftancy riots in northern Ghana, the internecine battles in the collapsed Somali state, the renewed rebellion in Chad, the land and participation protests in Ivory Coast, and many others where the state did not serve as the authoritative arbiter between conflicting groups.

The state's other main task is its external obligation to manage conflict with its neighbors and more distant peers. Here the African state has been more successful, although paradoxically in part because of its weakness. In general, the state is too weak to threaten its neighbor and its neighbor is too weak to be a tempting target for conquest. Why take one's neighbor's territory when one can benefit from what is in it—natural resources, sanctuary, market outlets—without the burdens of ownership? But there are also normative reasons for the successful provision of external security. African states have learned to be comfortable with their boundaries, and have Africanize their colonial territorial inheritance through a number of conflict management mechanisms—pan-African declarations in the Organization of African Unity (OAU), treaties and diplomacy, minor rectifications, demarcation (Zartman 2006). They have also used war to Africanize their boundaries, learning in the process that military attempts to change boundaries have all failed without exception; it is not worth trying.[4] Neighbors' involvement in internal conflict is another matter, again testifying to state weakness. With the exception of the Ethiopia-Eritrea war, however, African states have functioned effectively, for negative as well as positive reasons, in managing external conflict.

The State of Demands

A notable evolution of significant proportions is the change in the nature of demands imposed on the African state since independence and particularly in the last decade. The nationalist movement was one of procedural over substantive demands: Self-government predominates over material satisfactions, independence over welfare, or at least is the precondition for welfare. If the first decade of independence in the 1960s was a period of optimism over the assumed prospects of development and the satisfaction of substantive demands by African states, the opening of the fourth decade of the 1990s revived optimism over the assumed prospects of Africa's second wave of democracy and the rise of procedural demands, even though those demands were deeper and more serious for the state than mere expectations of benefits. Substantive demands are demands for the receipt of benefits; procedural demands are demands for participation in their allocation and distribution, and hence pose the

---

4   Boundaries between existing states are referred to here. Even the Eritrean case of introducing new (actually old) boundaries through the creation of a new state is a singular exceptions after 30 years of enormous and costly effort, and the subsequent border war is to establish rather that change a boundary, also after extraordinary and costly effort.

question of the organization of the state. A decade later, the pressures for procedural change in the nature of the state have produced half-results at best, a better record than the previous expectations of development but an only limited achievement nonetheless. It is important to an assessment of the African state to consider whether the half-results are nonetheless one decade's step toward gradual fulfilment in the longer run or whether they mark a resting place and the stagnation—or even pause for reversal—similar to the development curve.

Stocktaking should begin by noting why the procedural demands arose, half a century after the original procedural demands for independence had appeared. Governments are not states, but governments—and, in their collective designation, regimes—run states. The stifling of substantive demands by single-party civilian and military regimes over the first decades of independence led to pressures for participation in the conflict management process itself, and they rose for simple, straightforward and right reasons: popular dissatisfaction with centralized, monistic, controlling governance coupled with government willingness to open demands and participation to the political marketplace (Zartman 1997). The change came at the beginning of the 1990s rather than before for reasons of both demand and supply: While the partial effects of development had produced pluralization and new groups with demands for pieces of the national pie, the world economic recession meant that the pie was shrinking and monistic governments were called to account for their stewardship. The world context reinforced the second part of the equation in three ways—by withdrawing economic resources, by imposing constraints for fiscal discipline, and by providing full examples of the illegitimacy of centralized political and economic control from the communist world.

A second element was the availability and emboldening of pluralistic actors ready to take up the procedural issue of Who governs? On one hand there was the continuing insecurity of the military concerning its legitimacy as ruler, particularly in English-speaking countries. After some slow learning, the African militaries appeared to have become convinced that governing is not their business, not rewarding, not safe, and not legitimate. Clinching examples ranging from Sani Abatcha's Nigeria to Johnny Koromah's Sierra Leone vying for worst case positions in the mid-1990s provided lessons that doubtless deterred militaries elsewhere from taking power. On the other hand, the human rights movement Leagues (Ligues des Droits de l'Homme) and chapters (Amnesty International) began to be set up as institutional expression of the concerns of groups and individuals with a social basis and a supportive set of their own substantive demands, including lawyers with an interest in cases and causes, professors concerned about open debate, and businessmen looking for discussions on alternative economic systems. In this situation, ethnic groups become increasingly functional, providing clientele for parties, voters for elections, and specific demands for participation.

The third element involved the development of social organizations around the issue of employment, underscoring the failure of the state to fulfill the task of meeting substantive demands for which it claimed a monopoly of responsibility. Student fortunes took a peculiar twist after the mid-1980s that turned them from restive targets of party government organization to the avant garde of the pluralist opposition. As the economic fortunes of African states declined in the mid-1980s, the guarantee of employment given to students faded away and urban streets became filled with unemployed graduates, trained to know more than government incumbents but blocked by the same incumbents from putting their knowledge to work. The effect of lessened demand was in turn to reduce the supply, of graduates but not of unemployed; youth dropped out of school and college, since their efforts gave them no jobs, but dropped into the petty trades of the unemployed—windshield washers, parking attendants, sunglass salesmen, and so on. They thus became available for political employment as demonstrators and then rebel thugs—Sierra Leone's lumpens and Ivory Coast's young patriots (Kendell 2005), while their brothers and sisters who stayed in school became ipso facto a demand-bearing group for change.

Even those who did achieve government employment for their efforts then constituted the other already mobilized group—the labor unions—that also shifted its position toward the end of the 1980s to become a force for pluralism and political change. Formerly organized, however restively, under party government control as a source of support for the monistic system, organized labor became the immediate target of government reform when structural adjustment programs were adopted under the pressure of the international financial institutions (IFIs), the US and eventually even the EC. Up to this point, labor had been held in control by rising salaries and bloated bureaucracies, but when these means of cooptation were no longer available, unions turned to bite the hand that no longer fed them, calling for accountability from the governors. Underlying the unions' complaint against structural adjustment austerity was the deeper complaint that it had been decided without their participation.

An additional demand-bearing group with its own needs and interests was also involved in making procedural demands, called the incumbents. Enjoyment of the perquisites of office (time at the trough) and fear of retaliation for mismanagement (as Rawlings and Doe did to their predecessors), as well as the normal politician's belief that he alone has the answers and needs just a bit more time to make them stick, worked to lower the interest of incumbents in Nigeria, Senegal, Cameroon, Gabon, both Congos, Togo and elsewhere in practicing democratic alternance. Incumbents and challengers alike have not yet learned or have no grounds to believe that losing an election is not permanent and fatal; indeed, in some places, they have learned the contrary. When new rules of participation were inaugurated in response to procedural demands, no one was better practiced and more capable at winning elections than the old incumbents, who managed to beat the democratizing movements at their own game and reverse the momentum in a number of states.

There was clearly a fork in the road, and an open contest over which of the two paths would dominate the evolution of each country and provide the decisive demonstration effect for its neighbors. As in the 1960s (later for southern African states), the focus on procedural demands for greater participation in governance in the early 1990s was an exceptional phase expected to last only as long as the governance issue was not settled. But that phase could be a long time, particularly if the various national attempts to settle the issue were not reasonably well synchronized. Events in key exemplar states that have made the evolution slow and uncertain need to be recalled in perspective. In West Africa, the reversal of the results of the Democratic Party election in Nigeria in June 1993 and the Abatcha interlude meant that democratization had to await the 1999 election of Olasegun Obasanjo to begin. The opening of the political system to competition in Ivory Coast began seriously only after President Houphouet Boigny's death in 1993, was restrained by his successor Henri Konan Bedie, and then gradually ground to pieces in the coups and controls that began in 1999. It was the smaller neighbors such as Benin and Mali that led the way earlier in the decade and have held the course; the last incumbent reelections of the dominant party in Ghana and Senegal in 1992-1993 gave way to alternance in the next elections in 1996 and 2000, respectively.

In Central Africa, the reversal of the political opening in the 1990's Third Republic in Zaire led to Mobutu's overthrow in 1996 and the decade-long War of the Zairean Succession "ending" only with the 2006 elections. In East Africa, the overthrow of the communist military derg in Ethiopia in 1991 brought in a new single-party regime that could not control the oppositional reaction in multiparty elections in 2005. Multiparty elections under extreme international pressure on Kenya in the 1990s finally brought the opposition to get its act together and win in 2002, and then to act with the same control and corruption as its predecessors. This was the same pattern followed in Southern Africa in Zambia and Malawi. In Mozambique a notable international effort to end the civil war brought multiparty elections in 1994 and thereafter that perpetuated the former single party's role as a dominant party; similar efforts a decade later in Angola produce the same results, replicated viciously in Zimbabwe despite international pressure. Finally, extraordinary efforts to end the conflict in South Africa brought in a new state system with the formerly banned opposition taking power as the dominant party, for the foreseeable future.

Four patterns are evident. One is the emergence of dominant party systems, in which opposition parties serve as safety valves, unlikely to come to power. This is Botswanan democracy, much touted for its freedom but far from the test of alternance frequently proposed (Stedman 1994, Bauer and Taylor 2005). Three evolutions are possible from this situation—a step in place, a step forward, and a step backward. The first is of course continuance of one-party dominance, if the opposition is content to complain in its impotence, and the government is comfortable enough in its omnipotence to bear the complaints, as in Namibia, Tanzania, Mali and Mozambique. The second is the return to single party dominance in essence, when opposition the complaints become telling and annoying enough for the dominant party to shut them up, repressively or cooptively, as in Togo, Uganda, and Ethiopia. The third is that the complaints finally gather resonance and the opposition wins, someday, as in the Senegalese, Zambian and Malawian evolution. Only the third presents a restructuring of the nature of the state, and then with qualifications, as the second pattern indicates.

The second pattern, an evolution from the first, limits the degree of change even when alternance occurs. Either the opposition coming to power ends up acting with the same corruption, cronyism, and control as its predecessor, or it is replaced by the predecessor after a single turn and the reality of change in the nature of the state is over. The first was the evolution of Senegal, Kenya, Zambia (Lire de haut en bas 2006); the second in Benin benevolently, and Congo-Brazzaville violently. Although the Somali experience is likely to remain unique, it has lessons relevant to this discussion (plus others to be elaborated later): if an Islamic state such as promised by the Conference of Islamic Courts will occur because the population is tired of the corruption, infighting and ineffectiveness of the warlords and transition governments, it too will be as much a single party regime in a delegated democracy.

The third pattern, partially overlapping some of the other two, is the category of unreconstructed authoritarian regimes embodying the ethos of the previous civilian and military single-party regimes with only symbolic nods to the rising procedural demands, including, variously, Guinea, Togo, Congo-Brazzaville, Gabon, Chad, Burkina Faso, Rwanda, Eritrea, and Angola, a motley assortment. The fourth category includes some arguably promising unknowns whose seemingly positive multiparty experience is recent enough to warrant suspended judgment, including Sierra Leone, Liberia and Congo.

The relation of such a categorization to the nature of the African state is complex. From this summary, it is hard to assert a winning dynamic in any of Africa's regions that would tip it in the direction of full satisfaction of procedural demands for meaning participation in the state. The dominant party system, the first pattern, and its evolution, the second pattern, are functionally little different from the single party system, only that the latter has the softening feature of a safety-valve opposition to relieve pressure on the dominant/single party. The ensuing model of the state is then one of an authoritative institution supported by a vertical column of the population, heavy at the top and charged with its own justification and legitimization rather than being emergent and supported from the base. Those not in the column are excluded from the system of allocating benefits and excluded from the allocation of benefits as well. An excellent study by Kayizzi-Mugerwa (2003) shows that African states privatized" only when the [politicians] were sure that the benefits to themselves and their supporters exceeded the costs, including loss of rents, of denationalization" [p 250] despite the opposition of "the local middle class" [Museveni 1993] and public opinion in general. When elections are not decisive, open, programmatic contests, private interests take over. "[R]egimes have sought to protect the interests of a narrow stratus of state elites and have regularly been willing to inflict austerity on the population" (Van de Walle 2001, p. 16), a situation that the evolution from single tp dominant party regimes, with or without alternance, has not changed. As an institution responsible to its stockholders, the state is above all beholden to its board of directors and only secondarily to its other shareholders.

Of course, this picture depends on the assumption--or the evidence--that the single/dominant party is a weak mobilizer, involving a limited column of supporters in a passive role, a description that generally obtains across the continent. One result of this situation is the outbreak of two types of endemic conflict, both of them voicing the complaint of the excluded. One is a centralist conflict for power without any program to distinguish rebels from government. This is the time-at-the-trough phenomonen, where one group-often without any ascriptive or other distinguishing characteristic than simply being excluded-seeks to replace the other in the seat of power without any clear ideological or programmatic difference. The conflict bears no procedural demand; it simply voices a substantive demand for me rather than for you. Thus rebellions such as the RUF in Sierra Leone or Renamo in Mozambique were not ethnic revolts, and their programmatic elements were tenuous.

The other is a regional or ethnic revolt for self-determination, voicing deeply procedural demands to take the governing process into its own hands because those in power have shown that they cannot be trusted to allocate benefits fairly. Such are the rebellions of the Democratic Forces Movement in the Casamance in Senegal, the New Forces in the North in Ivory Coast, the Acholi through the Lord's Resitace Army (LRA) in Uganda, and the rebels in Darfur and Beja in Sudan, among others. Still others bridge the two categories; they are not content to seek self-determination for their region but rather want their turn to govern everyone (as in the first type) but for the defense of their own ethnic group. Such were the Tutsi of the Rwandan Peoples Force (RPF) and now the Hutu of the Democratic Forces for the Liberation of Rwanda (FDLR).

The frustrated shift from substantive to procedural demands in the 1990s has meant that that nature of the African state is still uncertain at a crucial junction. At the beginning of the shift it was torn between the pressures for change and the obstinate reality; in the middle of the first decade of the 2000s, pressures remain in violent conflicts but have slumped into alienation and disinterest in the general public. The demands for pluralization, accountability and participation have produced results in form but not much of a change in the nature of the state, from a delegated to a participatory democracy.

The State of the State

The African state has a long way to grow. That is scarcely surprising, when one compares its less than half a century of existence with the centuries that it took post-colonial states in the Americans, let alone post-monarchial states in Europe, to reach their current condition. But patience alone may not be a satisfactory answer before the meanwhile is evaluated. Is there an African state now? Where is it headed? Is its trajectory similar to that on the other side of the Atlantic? And then, what is the alternative?

No one doubts that the African state is held together by powerful international forces—recognition of status and borders, norms of sovereignty, international organization membership, international law, legal domestic authority. None of these is absolute, even among the most developed states, so African state weakness needs to be evaluated relatively.

A similar judgment needs to be made about the Nation-State. In either meaning and any case, state-building is a continual work in progress, anywhere. The norm of popular sovereignty was posited at independence and the renewed demand for popular sovereignty has been reposed since the 1990s. Elections, contested or not, free and fair or not, are the norm and the practice throughout the continent, and once they occur the pressure is on for them to be contested and free and fair. There is no democracy in this world, anywhere, only democratizing states, and once the process is forgotten, the goal fades, in Africa as elsewhere. Against this general background, the trend in Africa has been to move from single to dominant party states, and when the dominant party becomes so alienating that the leading opposition party effects an alternance, the trend is for the new winner to act similarly to its predecessor. Mali,

Burkina Faso, Togo, Nigeria, Liberia, Sierra Leone, Rwanda, Burundi, Uganda, Congo, Congo-Brazzaville, Gabon, Cameroun, Zimbabwe, South Africa, Namibia, Mozambique, Angola, Botswana, and Tanzania present various versions of the first stage; Senegal, Benin, Kenya, Malawi, Zambia, and arguably Rwanda and Uganda are in the second. The other states have their own idiosyncratic trajectories. The trend is forked: toward apparent norms and practices of accountability (just as independence meant the adoption of the norms of self-government), but also toward frequent disenchantment and alienation from political participation.

Similarly, the building of a new national identity has its two sides. Nationalist enthusiasm has waned, perhaps in large part because there are few effective external enemies against which to rally the nation (Herbst 2000, 112-116); anticolonial unity has passed and neighboring states do not provide a rallying war cry, with a few exceptions, as already discussed. Ethnic revolts challenge national identity as a uniting principle behind the state. Yet people know who they are and are not, and states are able to enforce it, even if with divisive impacts. Nation-building too can be a long process, sometimes quite independent of state-building. State attempts to formalize a definition of a nation in Africa have tended to be counter-productive. But when Senegalese, Sudanese, Ivorians, and Congolese finally come to a consensus on what it means to be a national of their state, their state will also be strengthened as a result. It is however, noteworthy, that nether the Casamançais, nor the Southern Sudanese, nor the Northern Ivorians, nor the eastern Congolese—like many other nationalities elsewhere—are united among themselves about who they are.

It is hard to foresee a dramatic turnaround in state capabilities. Statesmen could act more statesmanlike in managing conflicts among internal groups and demands, and arguably responsible state-building has improved in Nigeria, Mozambique, Congo, and Mali. But resources are likely to remain limited for the foreseeable future, and recent windfalls have not been used to build a responsive state in Chad and Angola, among others. Foreign aid has been notoriously ineffective in building states and their economies (Lancaster 1999), although there is no control case to measure the situation in the absence of aid. Nor is there any assurance that foreign economic aid or peacekeeping forces are not habit-forming crutches for infant states, much like protectionist tariffs for infant industries, rather than true pump-primers; again, the swim-or-sink school that opposes aid has not found an acceptable example. In sum, African states will have to continue to muddle through with inadequate resources and a little help from their friends; they may swim awkwardly but they stay afloat.[5]

State collapse (as opposed to mere failures) is probably the best definition of sinking, and it has lessons for the African state, which provide some of its clearest cases. Many of the states that have undergone collapse in the past—Chad, Ghana, Sierra Leone, Mauritania, Liberia, Congo—have reengaged in the process of rebuilding, often with dramatic success such as in Ghana. State collapse is not fatal; the body politic, essentially on its own with sometimes a little assistance from outside, has felt the need for a state of its own and reasserted control over its affairs. The exception that proves the generalization is of course Somalia, a particular

---

5   The title of the Georgetown University symposium on the African State in Transition in 1985 was "Fluctuat nec Mergitur?".

obdurate case where the disappearance of a strong neighbor as the traditional enemy and the presence of a segmentary system make reinstatement more difficult. But the case of Somalia has several lessons, as already noted. It shows conclusively that the state has no functional substitute and that in its absence, multiple functions are simply not performed. It also shows—as have Congo, Liberia, and Sierra Leone—that, the power vacuum does have beneficiaries who take advantage of the absence of legitimate authority, law and order for their own ends. Finally, it shows—as has Afghanistan—that given enough time, forces will arise with popular support to impose a more authoritarian version of a state to replace the anarchy of collapse. It is worth noting, even if not yet conclusive, that the previous rounds of state collapse in Africa around 1980 and around 1990 have not been followed by a third, and that the cases to watch have not materialized (Zartman 1995, 2-5).

It has been noted that weak states have been held in place by weak neighbors; they have also been held in place by weak alternatives. As the Somali case shows, there is no substitute for a state, and putative substitutes simply turn out to be states too. It has been suggested that giving aid to regional organizations, decertifying old states (as political punishment, according to the cases), and recognizing new nation states, would constitute alternatives within the current state system (Herbst 2000, 262-269). But these do not provide alternatives, and in the last case merely add to the list of weak claimants on sovereignty without improving their capabilities. "Decertification," presumably to make the targets ineligible for aid, compounds weakness and carries the assumption that ensuing collapse and rebirth is better than middling through. Aid to regional organizations (of states) is an important proposal that can increase member state capacities with economies of scale and cooperation.

The fact is that there is no substitute for a state and none has been proposed, no institution that can fulfill the functions that a state is created to provide (Herbst 2000, 269-273; Ottaway, Herbst and Mills 2004; Ghani, Lockhart and Carnahan 2005). Reducing parts of Africa to Somali status would be to make it even more difficult for those areas to overcome the weaknesses that brought on the punishment to begin with. There is nothing uniquely African about the African state and its weaknesses; it is just a work in progress, trying to achieve a sovereign reality at a time when other who are already there are struggling with new problems of globalization and permeability. This is not a new challenge; it was faced by the fledgling United States, the developing states of Latin American, and the post-colonial states of Asia, each in their time. Current experience shows that contemporary conditions do not outmode the state but rather add new layers of players and interactions to complicate its tasks and make it more necessary than ever.

What then does state-building (the real meaning of the misused term "nation-building) mean for outside states in the current context? In dealing with state collapse and deadly conflict, perseverance in mediation and convocation efforts, monitoring of implementation measures and reestablishment of conflict-management institutions, are crucial components of third-party activities, all elements in state-building (Zartman 2005a, chaps 8 & 9). The African experience shows clearly the importance of foreign actors—other states and the IFIs—is bringing both economic and political competition and accountability into African state practices, even if the measures adopted are only halfway steps. More broadly, the establishment of standards, norms and regimes in these and other matters is influential in setting criteria for performance that can help prevent debilitating conflicts later on (Zartman 2005b), even if not met fully by African (and other) states. For all its continuing imperfections, the standards embodied in the New Economic Partnership for African Development (NEPAD), following Obasanjo's Conference on Security, Stability, Development and Cooperation in Africa (CSSDCA), show the effect of such norms (Deng and Zartman 2005), as indeed does the support given to the rise of procedural demands by the world context at the end of the Cold War.

Such activities carry with them the concomitant danger that they accentuate accountability to foreign agencies rather then to domestic participants. The African record shows both the positive and negative aspects of this effect. It also shows the need for the two to work together. Foreign events and pressures aided a shift in African demands, and local demands can use foreign pressures to their benefit. Democracies cannot make others democratic, but they can help others make themselves democratic and others can exploit that help. African criticism of CSSDCA because it drew inspiration from the Conference (now Organization) for Security and Cooperation in Europe, for example, missed an opportunity.

Might it not be the ultimate irony that when the African state finally gets there, the world system may no longer be there? The danger is not great. If there is international state system, there are many types of states at different levels of development within it, a diversity that is likely to continue as states and system evolve. Africa states are evolving too, both in their relations with the other states at various levels of development in the system and in regard to their internal nature and functions toward their own societies.

References

Bauer, Gretchen and Taylor, Scott 2005. *Politics in Southern Africa: State and Society in Transition.* Lynne Rienner, Boulder, Colo.

Beissinger, Mark and Young, Crawford, eds., 2002. *Beyond State Crisis? Postcolonial Africa and Post-Soviet Eurasia in Comparative Perspective.* Woodrow Wilson Center, Washington DC.

Bratton, Michael and Van de Walle, Nicolas 1997. *Democratic Experiments in Africa*, Cambridge University Press, Cambridge.

Cohen, James 1995. "Quelles démocracies? Perspectives critiques sur les transitions démocratiques en Amérique latine," *Revue internationale de Politique comparee* II 2:356-72.

Dawisha, Adeed and Zartman, I William, eds. 1988. *Beyond Coercion: The Durability of the Arab State*, Croom Helm, New York.

Deng, Francis et al 1996. *Sovereignty as Responsibility.* Brookings, Washington DC.

_____ and Zartman, I William, 2005. *A Strategic Vision for Africa: The Kampala Movement*, Brookings Institution, Washington DC.

Ghani, Ashraf, Lockhart, Clare, and Carnahan, Michael, 2005. "Closing the Sovewreignty Gap: An Approach to State-Building," London: Overseas Development Institute, Working Paper 253.

Herbst, Jeffrey 2000. *States and Power in Africa: Comparative Lessons in Authority and Control*, Princeton University Press, Princeton.

Kayizzi-Mugerwa, Steve 2003. "Privatization in Sub-Saharan Africa: On Factors Affecting Implementation", in Kayizzi-Mugrwa, Steve, ed., *Reforming Africa's Institutions: Ownership, Incentives, and Capabilities*. UNU, New York.

Lancaster, Carol 1999. "Aid Effectiveness in Africa: The Unfinished Agenda," *Journal of African Economies* VIII 4:487:503.

O'Donnell, Guillermo, 1992. "Delegative Democracy?" University of Notre Dame, Kellogg Institute for International Studies, Working Paper 172.

Ottaway, Marina, Herbst, Jeffrey, and Mills, Greg, 2004. "Africa's Big States: Toward a New Realism," Washington: Carnegie Endowment for International Peace, Policy Outlook paper.

Reno, William 1998. *Warlord Politics and African States*. Lynne Rienner, London.

Rothchild, Donald and Olorunsola, Victor, eds. 1983. *State vs Ethnic Claims: African Policy Dilemmas*, Westview Press, Boulder, Colo.

US Committee on Refugees 2001. *World Refugee Report*. USCR.

Van de Walle, Nicolas 2001. *African Economies and the Politics of Permanent Crisis, 1979-1999*, Cambridge University Press, Cambridge.

Villallon, Leonard A. 1995. Islamic Society and State Power in Senegal: Disciples and Citizens in Fatick, Cambridge University Press, Cambridge.

Walker. R.B.J. 1995. "From International relations to World Politics," *The State in Transition: Reimagining Politics Space*, Boulder, Colo, Lynne Rienner.

Weber, Max 1964. "Politics as a Vocation," in H.H. Gerth and C Wright Mills, eds, *From Max Weber.* Oxford (Galaxy).

Weffort, Francisco, 1993. *Cual democracy?* San Jose: FLACSO.

Weiss, Herbert and Carayannis, Tatiana 2005. "The Enduring Idea of the Congo," in Ricardo Rene, Laremont, ed., *Borders, Nationalism and the African State*. Lynne Rienner.

Zartman, I William 1964. "Les relations entrs la France et l'Algérie," *Revue française de science politique 6:1087-1113.*

_____ ed., 1997. *Governance as Conflict Management: Politics and Violence in West Africa*, Washington DC, Brookings.

_____ 2005a. *Cowardly Lions: Missed Opportunities to Prevent State Collapse and Deadly Conflict*, Boulder, Colo. Lynne Rienner.

_____ 2005b. "Measures of Prevention," in Chesterman, eds, *Making States Work* UNU.

Chapter 2

The Post-colonial African State: Issues of Citizenship and Subjectivity

Lawrence Flint

As aspects of identity, citizenship and subjectivity are issues of increasingly varied interpretation in contemporary society, not least among academic and governing circles in the postcolonial world. This is especially so in the light of increasing trans-national mobility and flexibility, the creation of diasporic communities across the globe, and the supposed blurring of the borders of the nation-state and diluted notions of sovereignty. Particularly in the developing world, or more accurately, in the developed world's perception of the developing world, there is concern and frustration over the apparent failure of people to sufficiently absorb, recognise and wear the badges of a specific brand of citizenship and subjectivity, that is, that of the postcolonial state.

This is most particularly the case in Sub-Saharan Africa where decades of regionalised armed conflict, corrupt governance, declining measures of human development and economic decline have convinced a sceptical outside world that what Africa needs most is 'good governance'. In large part, this is parlance for the imposition of liberal democracy *à la mode* Western Europe and the United States. There exists, in the corridors of western power, particularly in the United States and Great Britain, a defiantly entrenched conviction that the adoption of the liberal democratic political creed is an all-embracing panacea. This, it is proposed, will put an end to local conflicts and inter-ethnic strife, reduce poverty and put post-colonial states on the road to economic and social development whilst remaining 'good friends' in the global war on terrorism.

An intrinsic component of this grand prescription for the developing world is the theory that 'good governance' or, rather, the adoption of the liberal democratic ethos, will encourage African people to become good citizens and subjects of post-colonial African states, thereby reducing the tendency for them to protest or behave in other non-conformist ways that elide respect for state institutions. It is through these institutions that western powers, in particular, prefer to channel their influence, not least because such institutions were imposed by those very same powers as servile, infant images of themselves as formal colonialism drew to a close in the mid-to-late twentieth century. Thus, the world saw the creation of the French African Community under the patrimonial tutelage of Charles de Gaulle, and the British Commonwealth.

This is not to say that western powers do not simultaneously channel influence through other powerful conduits such as international NGOs, many of whom are often at odds with governments in Africa. This dynamic has increased dramatically during the last half century or so since independence as many Northern states have sought to lessen their responsibility to Africa in the form of direct intervention. Instead, many opt to externalise aid and development efforts to non-governmental agencies that can operate more cost-effectively and, equally importantly, shoulder the burden of accountability.

Newly created states, despite the paucity of knowledge, skills and experience bequeathed to them by departing colonial powers, were seen as comprehensible, while concomitantly manageable and malleable organs of power that would, hopefully, enable the realisation of neo-colonial benefits in realms such as trade and geopolitical influence. Meanwhile, it is debatable as to whether that aspirational dynamic has changed much in the first decade of the twenty-first century. In the late 1960s and 1970s, many African states became far from democratic, as governments struggled to retain power in the face of disaffected populations and economies floundering under the pressure of worsening terms of trade, weak currencies, increased prices of inputs, and lack of investment. Significantly, no great pressure was brought to bear by ex-colonial powers and international institutions to democratise during this era of autocratic power. Meanwhile, praetorian military regimes and idiosyncratic leaderships in new states struggled to assert their sovereignty over populations which, apart from those living in the major urban centres, had little knowledge or empathy with western-educated nationalist leaders and urban elites. The latter, it appeared, had little in common with and regularly appeared to look down on those living in communitarian, 'unmodern' societies both in the countryside and in urban areas.

In fact, nationalist leaderships in newly independent African states tended to be suspicious of traditional political communities, usually castigating them as undemocratic, self-seeking and anachronistic. At best, traditional leaderships in the rural regions were treated in the same way as they had been under formal colonial rule. That is, as default intermediaries in the struggle to assert some sort of sovereignty over peoples and lands that continued to exist in a world permeated but uncontrolled by the market forces of global capitalism upon which the democratic ethos was built. State power in postcolonial Africa remains firmly entrenched in the capitals and main urban centres, despite the current rhetoric of decentralisation and deconcentration. Yet, up to the end of the twentieth century at least, most Africans lived, not in the urban centres, but in the countryside where the influence of communitarian style hierarchies of traditional power remain as pervasive nuclei of influence and culture. Unsurprisingly, perhaps, enthusiastic subscription to ideas of state citizenship and subjectivity, particularly in rural areas, is hard to find except in regions where the dominant ethnic group also happens to be influential in national government. In this mindset should be borne in mind the context of state institutions that appear unable and/or unwilling to initiate development in the form of infrastructure and social welfare.

Such disenchantment at the rural level is quickly communicated to urban centres as most rural African families have previously sponsored at least one family member to migrate to the urban centres in what represents a high investment. Indeed, partly due to disillusionment with dreams of modernity in the urban areas, and partly to the tendency of most African cities to exist in a parasitic relationship with their rural hinterlands, urban-rural linkages are remarkably robust despite poor communications. Add to this the dynamic of armies of 'unmodernised' populations increasingly on the move from rural to urban locations and one can begin to understand regimes and state apparatuses based in the capital cities of Africa that have shunned or paid lip service to ideas of liberal democracy as the short route to loss of power, wealth and influence.

The current western insistence that African states should adopt liberal democracy as an all-embracing politico-economic *modus operandi* may seem, at first glance, to be surprisingly simplistic and naïve, given that western institutions of government possess a far from simple history of state formation, where the adoption of contemporary articulations of liberal democracy is a notably contemporary dynamic. Any doubt concerning the deep-rootedness of such prescriptive notions in western governing circles, however, is rapidly dispelled when confronted with the evidence of enforced regime change in Iraq and Afghanistan. It is further entrenched through the insistence of the International Financial Institutions (World Bank and IMF) and western donor countries that there be evidence of liberal democratic modes of 'good governance' – even if the reality is implicitly cosmetic – in order to qualify for financial assistance on which many developing world states have come to rely in umbilical-style dependence. It follows that with such a dependency relationship, the weaker partner feels constrained from pointing out the hypocrisy of a prescription that appears to overlook abuses of its own ethos when there are vital resources at stake or where the practice of liberal democracy results in the formation of governments not in the interests of the prescribing agency as has been the case with Iran and Palestine.

Thus, lack of adoption and adherence to the liberal democratic creed, implicitly embodying state citizenship and subjectivity, apparently impinges on the legitimacy of the postcolonial state, devised by the ex-colonial powers and premised on their own ideas of 'modernisation'. This 'modernisation' can be understood as the enduring dilemma of abandoned discourses of overt formal domination and the struggle for neo-colonialist politico-economic exploitation. But, of course, no amount of arm-twisting, be it from struggling developing states or, indirectly, from external agencies, can force local people to respect and commit themselves to notions of identity associated with institutions that they neither respect nor have experience of, and invariably view as impotent or predatory and threatening. In this scenario, state citizenship becomes a default imposition, accepted as unavoidable in order to access basic capabilities such as employment and mobility and to negotiate the strictures of everyday life, including justice and suffrage. And yet, many Sub-Saharan Africans see themselves primarily as citizens of other entities, often non-state oriented, extant either prior to European colonialism or as a result of colonialism. Concomitantly, there are other mostly pre-existing realms of citizenship that now require to be taken into consideration; some are only newly recognised in the West and have more to do with culture and are oblivious to state-based citizenship.

Meanwhile, there remains palpable and enduring frustration that the nation-state project, itself a discourse of the dominant liberal democratic political ideology and central to the operation of the capitalist world economy, has not resulted in the appearance of a patriotic citizenry in much of Africa, demonstrating loyalty and obligation to post-independence national governments. This frustration derives from the premise that the efficient functioning of the world economy is dependent on a world system as described by the Marxist theoriser of social change, Immanuel Wallerstein, of so-called 'nation-states' freely interacting in an imaginary multinational politico-economic arena which Taylor refers to as the inter-state system. (Taylor, 2000; 153)[1] That a large majority of these 'nation-states' are the artificial creation of a few European states, with a particular hybridised history of political and economic development, tends to get lost in the search for a kind of global uniformity conducive to the interests of the core states of the world economy.

In fact, many governments in the developing world are either within their own borders or in the wider diaspora, respected by their putative citizens as institutional icons providing rights and responsibilities corresponding to traditional conceptions of citizenship. They do not appear as virtuous arbiters of moral and political behaviour. Nor, concomitantly, are they perceived to be promoting economic and social development in the form of what the World Bank likes to euphemistically call 'basic capabilities' or the wider interests and aspirations of the 'nation-state' and its subjects. Herbst explains this phenomenon in the context of incomplete state formation, a project left unfinished by colonialism, leaving post-independence African states vulnerable to 'state failure', where governments are unable to effectively control their territories. (Herbst, 2000; 254)[2]

Citizenship in the Realm of Identity

Citizenship and subjectivity, while traditionally associated with state formation, are intimately related to other aspects of identity, particularly nationalism (a state being composed of a conglomerate of nations or, more rarely, a single nation), ethnicity, culture and race. The latter three are often conflated or spoken of as one phenomenon, referred to variously as 'tribalism', a colonial construction, or tradition, both treated as comparatively more significant in Africa, a continent invariably perceived as stuck in the transition from 'tradition' to 'modernity'. Tradition here, in the jargon of the 'modernisation' theorists of the 1950s and 60s and a surprising number of influential thinkers today, is interpreted as a negative euphemism for backwardness. Tradition also refers to the idea of community as the hegemonic expression of identity as opposed to the individual and, in this parlance, community is seen as local and vertically structured with its members sustaining their existence through collective effort in the interests of the community or 'greater good'.

Modern, meanwhile, suggests an associative stage reached by some unilinear process of economic and social development first seriously promoted by the

---

1 P.J. Taylor *Political Geography: World-Economy, Nation-State and Locality* (Prentice Hall, Harlow, 2000), p. 153.
2 J. Herbst, *States and Power in Africa: Comparative Lessons in Authority and Control* (Princeton University Press, Princeton, 2000), p. 254.

modernisation theorists of the mid-twentieth century.[3] Here the individual's productive effort is aimed more at the sustenance of the self and the self-image in a more broad-based, horizontal or associationist community where specialisation of production and social expression becomes a norm. State nationalism, that is identity expressed as that of a state embracing multiple nations, ethnies and traditional communities, also becomes a norm. Meanwhile, in the contemporary so-called developed world, by comparison, the transition is said to have moved on from tradition to modernity and is now in a new phase, that from modernity to post-modernity. Here, the individual or 'self' attains even more agency as an economic and social actor, flexible and chameleon-like in nature, crossing politico-economic and socio-cultural borders at will blurring the boundaries of these socially constructed entities in the process. By so doing the actor enters into new cosmologies known variously as transnationalism, cosmopolitanism and diaspora, suggesting new communities into which to invest notions of identity and citizenship. The flexible and sometimes ephemeral nature of this type of community relates directly to the accumulative and lifestyle activities of the individual as these form the basis of existence in such communities.

The question then arises as to whether an apparently rigid construction such as citizenship, hitherto so closely associated with the state, has a place in either 'traditional' or postcolonial society. First, one must consider the apparent mutability and immutability of different aspects of identity. Du Gay, Evans and Redman suggest that notions of identity are 'more contingent, fragile, incomplete and thus more amenable to reconstruction than was previously thought possible'. (Du Guy, Evans and Redman, 2000; 1-2)[4] This is a generalisation, in that it implies that identity is intrinsically vulnerable to change, which is not always the case. Race, for example, is an aspect of identity very difficult to escape from or alter. Other writers such as Geertz, Van den Bergh, and Grosby assert that there are certain vertical aspects of identity, sometimes referred to as 'primordial ethnicity', that are largely immutable. (Geertz, 1973; 259-260; Van den Bergh, 1978; 401-411; Grosby, 1994; 164-171)[5] These include geographical origin, language of upbringing, parentage and race, a collection of cultural defaults while there are other, more mutable or transferable elements, classed as horizontal or instrumental such as those related to wealth creation and consumption. This assumes an unchanging and accurate self-perception sometimes expressed in the context of 'primordialism'.[6]

---

3 Such as W.W. Rostov, *The Stages of Economic Growth: A Communist Manifesto* (Cambridge University Press, London, 1960) and Talcott Parsons, particularly *The Social System* (Routledge and Kegan Paul, London, 1951), *Structure and Process in Modern Societies* (The Free Press, Glencoe, Illinois, 1960).

4 A theme pursued, for example, by Du Gay, Evans and Redman in *Identity: A Reader* (Sage, London, 2000) pp. 1/2.

5 C Geertz, *The Interpretation of Cultures* (Fontana, London, 1973), pp. 259-260, P. Van den Bergh, 'Race and ethnicity: a sociobiological perspective', *Ethnic and Racial Studies*, 1, 4 (1978), pp. 401-411, S. Grosby, 'The verdict of history: the inexpungeable tie of primordiality – a response to Eller and Coughlan', *Ethnic and Racial Studies*, 17, 2 (1994), pp. 164-171.

6 Discussed at length by A.D. Smith in his *Nationalism and Modernism* (Routledge, London, 1998), pp. 146-159.

In reality, not only do individuals experience confusion over the nature of their 'primordial' origins, for instance in the case of children of mixed race or mixed nationality parents, but they are also likely to alter what is, in any case, a largely imagined origin. An example is the case of white South Africans who grew up during the last two decades of the apartheid era believing, as they were taught, that they were white Europeans and are now, in the post-apartheid twenty-first century, attempting to re-invent themselves as 'Africans' and members of the 'rainbow nation' by virtue of their place of birth and in order to don a new sense of collective citizenship, subjectivity and acceptability in a society now dominated, politically at least, by non-whites. Even issues such as race and colour can be obfuscated and subject to interpretation when people attempt to describe their identity. Examples are the 'white' and 'black' Moors of Mauritania and the insistence of many African Zanzibaris who call themselves 'Arabs'. In both of these latter examples, perceived colour and race have potential impacts on a person's status and prospects, thus conflating and blurring the boundaries of what Lake and Rothchild consider to be exclusively primordialist and instrumental components of ethnicity.[7] (Lake and Rothchild, 1998; 5)

It would, meanwhile, be fair to propose that there are aspects of identity associated with birth, blood, race, ethnicity, class, language and personal or group pasts that, while subject to interpretation, social reconstruction and the agendas of translators, historians and editors, prove more permanent than those elements concerned with wealth or accumulation. Yet it would also be fair to suggest that such aspects take on more importance in the somewhat dynamic overall sense of identity when other, more mobile, associative layers are peeled off or where they have never been prominent. This is especially so with members of groups that, today, feel excluded from power and decision-making yet were part of strong centralised polities in the pre-colonial past whose status and power were preserved or even elevated as part of colonial 'indirect rule'. Such alienated people perceive themselves to be worse off in terms of wealth and power in the post-independence era than they were in the pre-colonial and/or colonial era. They tend to feel little empathy with the post-colonial states in which they now subsist and which are perceived to provide few, if any, benefits of membership.

Meanwhile, individuals and groups may vary the criteria by which they determine membership according to the ruling social, political or economic climate. Thus, people who see themselves as ostensibly Yoruba or Hausa before they emigrate or take up residence elsewhere, take on more prominent notions of 'Nigerianess', blackness or Africanity when outside of the African continent on account of the need to seek wider group membership in arenas of xenophobic and other political or socio-cultural discrimination. Alternatively, for a Zambian Lozi in Europe, to articulate oneself as Lozi would have no meaning to the target audience who would know of no such people or ethnicity, but might be aware of Zambia and certainly of Africa which provide convenient 'pigeonholes' in which to locate for acceptance. In

---

7   D.A. Lake and D. Rothchild, 'Spreading fear: the genesis of transnational ethnic conflict' in Lake and Rotchild (eds.), *The International Spread of Ethnic Conflict* (Princeton University Press, Princeton, 1998), p. 5.

this example, Zambianess becomes a convenient default identity for others to relate to even though the average Lozi feels comparatively little sense of Zambianess at home. At all times, people aspire to membership of some kind of political or cultural community, the tendency in the developed world being more to a plural, associative identity with multiple ephemeral layers than to a more simplistic and less mutable primordialist one. This is surely due to the fact that the human species is a sociable one, where emotional stability, personal success and status are accredited by and dependant on the appraisal and evaluation of other group members. As Mbiti puts it 'I am because we are, and because we are, I am'[8] (Mbiti, 1974; 14)

Eligibility for membership is premised on acceptance by or within a group which is surely central to all notions of citizenship and subjectivity in that the individual cannot consider the latter two notions in the absence of acceptance and membership except where membership cannot be denied, as in the case of certain aspects of so-called primordial ethnicity. Thus, for a group member living outside of the confines of an imagined homeland but within the borders of a post-colonial state that offers neither the benefits nor even the offer of membership (for instance, voter registration in many African countries is an elusive dream), there is an understandable recourse to the introverted 'ethnicity of the group'. There is also a perceived need to display that mode of membership to the dominant host community so that one can at least be defined as belonging to some political or cultural entity, even if not respected. Thus, the polarities of total mutability of identity, and the supposed unchangeability of primordialist ethnicity are too absolutist.

Citizenship, then, is intimately linked to other aspects of identity such as ethnicity, tribe, race and gender, discussions of which entail questions of rights and obligations central to the citizenship debate. What is surely needed, then, is a clear understanding of what is meant by 'citizenship' lest it becomes as vague and variedly understood as a term like 'development'. Having defined the term it needs to be asked what people consider relevant in terms of their citizenship, why they choose to be considered as citizens of a particular community such as a state, and why an entity such a community would want people to become its citizens and subjects. A third issue is how citizenship can be understood in non-state contexts; specifically, whether there are concepts of citizenship applicable to other forms of membership such as faith or other socially constructed entities like culture and tradition. If so, how important and relevant are these other modes of citizenship? A fourth issue, directly affecting the subject matter of this chapter is the idea that citizenship is thought of in different ways in different parts of the world, the biggest gulf in perception being between the developed core countries of the world economy and those parts most recently emerging from European-style colonialism such as most of Sub-Saharan Africa.

---

8   J.S. Mbiti, *African Religions and Philosophy* (Doubleday, New York, 1974), p. 14 in J.A.M. Cobbah, 'Toward a geography of peace in Africa: redefining sub-state self-determination rights' in R.J Johnston et al., *Nationalism, Self Determination and Political Geography* (Croom Helm, London, 1988), pp. 70-86.

Construction of Citizenship

A considerable stir was caused when the late Lozi Litunga (King) Ilute Yeta IV visited offices in a Lusaka suburb in 1998 and Lozis in and outside the offices were throwing themselves to the ground, clapping and showing traditional obeisance to their leader, People of other groups were shocked. Even today, Bemba and Nyanje friends speak of the occasion. Many are dismissive and say it shows how out of date Lozis are. Some say it shows that the Lozi only respect their own anachronistic tradition and culture; it further demonstrates why a Lozi must never be allowed or trusted to become President of Zambia because this would result in a transfer of power and wealth to Barotseland, their homeland in western Zambia. One said, 'who do they think they are to do that in my street in my town, why do they think they are so special?'.

Others, meanwhile, are more cautious and honest enough to talk of the admiration they felt that the Lozis retain some undefined 'African' citizenship that goes back in time that others had lost. Another said,' At least these Lozis know their place. If we still had that kind of respect in our society, we wouldn't have to put up with crime and politicians who do everything for themselves and nothing for us.' Here the implication is that the way that Lozis identify themselves with their iconic mystical institutions has knock-on effects for positive human behaviour. To be Lozi, in this sense, implies responsibility to demonstrate respect and other codes or badges of behaviour that are indelibly associated with being Lozi. These behavioural components are part of the obligations of being social subjects in a communitarian sense.

Citizenship and subjectivity are much-debated topics in academic as well as political circles in the contemporary era.[9] Defining and understanding these critical concepts, however, has proved as difficult as with other such famously vague and all-encompassing terms as 'development' and 'identity'. Citizenship and subjectivity often appear like two sides of the same coin but both terms are highly contested in their meaning and significance. In the developed and developing worlds alike, although for different reasons, these ideas have tended to become blurred and conflated with other issues of identity as well as with nationalism, transnationalism, cosmopolitanism, ethnicity and tribalism. In the era of globalisation when boundaries and borders are becoming increasingly flexible, mutable and uncertain, there seems to be an ever more urgent need to know exactly who we are and what we perceive we belong to or are members of.

If one is to understand citizenship according to the dictionary definition, in the developed world it is directly related to the state. To this keyword might be added membership, belonging, protection, rights and obligations. A state must have citizens in order to confer rights and duties, entitlements and responsibilities because, in order to be able to carry out its functions, a state requires a citizenry

---

9 See N. McAfee, *Habermas, Kristeva, and Citizenship* (Cornell University Press, Ithaca, 2000), Pal Ahluwalia, *Specificities: Citizens and Subjects Citizenship, Subjectivity and the Crisis of Modernity* (Routledge, London, 1999), K. Canning and S.O. Rose, 'Gender, citizenship and subjectivity: some historical and theoretical considerations, *Gender and History*, 13, 3 (2001) amongst others.

to govern and take part in government, not least in order to provide the resources a state requires to operate. Key here is the idea that a citizen of a state expects the responsible government of that state to provide something, a set of services perhaps, or a sufficient say in who runs that state. A citizen might also expect a set of laws to protect him or her from unjust treatment by other parties, whether citizens or others, organisations or the state itself. Other expectations might involve the provision of education and healthcare facilities, communication links such as roads, railways and telecommunications, a financial system including a central bank, institutions of law and order such as a police force and a judiciary, and a military that protects the borders of the state and its citizens/subjects from violence at the hands of each other or of external forces.[10] (Bartkus, 1999; 33)

Another important aspect is the ability to elect, re-elect or change the government of the state in order for that government to represent the hopes and aspirations of a majority of the citizenry. Although in the developed world an increasingly small percentage of the electorate actually vote at elections due to so-called 'voter-apathy', in most of the developing world, and particularly in Africa, freely-held elections usually attract as many voters as are registered. This is a right as is the conceptual expectation of human rights, the idea that a citizen is entitled to be treated fairly and justly by and within the borders of a state regardless of class or position in society, and that the state will actively seek to protect the citizen from bad treatment at home or abroad. Concomitant with the above, then, a state must also have a constituency (a population of citizen-subjects) and a clearly defined territory to govern, with clearly demarcated borders to defend. Thus the expectations of a citizenry can be roughly divided into provision of services and rights.

Meanwhile, a citizen must expect to behave as a subject, to owe allegiance and to give something in return for these expected entitlements. This might include taxes on earnings, military or community service of some kind, jury duty and subjection to the rule of law if laws set by the state as moral agency are broken. A citizen is also expected to make some show of allegiance to the state. This may be at an oath-swearing ceremony or by being expected to be able to read, write and speak the national language or by proving knowledge of the culture of the country concerned (this is of increasing importance in the West). Meanwhile, some states do not allow citizenship of other states simultaneously. In order to be a citizen, one must also be a subject although the reverse is not necessarily true – citizens expect to be full members of the political community whereas subjects may not be, as in the case of asylum seekers who obtain residence rights as refugees but little else. Clarke illustrates the distinction by describing the citizen as a 'free subject'. (Clarke, 1994; 14)[11] Thus citizenship, the entitlement to rights and obligations, and subjectivity, involving just the obligations in return for the right to remain in the state's territory, run hand in hand in terms of the state. This is not necessarily the case in non-state citizenship as will be discussed below.

---

10 V.O. Bartkus, *The Dynamic of Secession* (Cambridge University Press, Cambridge, 1999), p. 33.

11 P.B. Clarke, *Citizenship* (Pluto Press, London, 1994), p. 14.

These state concepts of citizenship and subjectivity, as discussed, may seem somewhat simplistic and applicable more to the advanced states at the core of the world economy where liberal democracy is the ruling and accepted political ideology. State citizenship is an essentially Western concept[12] (Heater, 1990; 128) therefore, can only really be expected to flourish to any great extent where European-style political institutions have become deeply embedded and where capitalist economic processes are operating in the arena of the global market sufficiently for a majority of the citizenry to feel that the state is providing some sort of stage worth acting on. Isin says that there are two fundamental perspectives to the traditional western view of citizenship, one that sees the world split into two civilisational blocs, one rationalised, secularised and therefore, modernised and the other, 'irrational', religious and therefore traditional. The second perspective sees citizenship as all-embracing, harmonious and fraternal, espousing ideas of equality and liberty and of the citizen as secular and universal, lacking tribal loyalties.[13] (Isin, 2002; 118)

But there are other aspects to the western or northern notion of citizenship that distinguish it from how people in the ex-colonies or 'South' are likely to view the concept. The word citizen derives from cité and sein and literally means 'to be of the city', implying expectations and rights accorded to city dwellers who considered themselves to be more acculturated and civilized than their rural counterparts. (Isin, 2002; 5-6)[14] Thus, city dwellers in Ancient Greece and Rome and later in Western Europe, distinguished themselves from feudal overlords and rural dwellers who were considered as pagan, uncivilized and unworthy of rights. In this way, culture, or lack of it, becomes an arbiter of citizenship. Citizenship, therefore, becomes at once an exclusionary as well as an inclusive category, contrary to Dahrendorf's assertion that, 'Exclusion is the enemy of citizenship'.[15] (Dahrendorf, 1994; 17) By implication, it is synonymous with urban living and modernity and, indeed, most people living in Western Europe and the United States today live an urban lifestyle, even those living technically in the countryside.

Meanwhile, conventional European and American-style citizenship, so closely associated with the authority of the state has been undergoing some modification since the 1980s, corresponding to the dynamics of globalisation where the physical and subjective boundaries of the state are perceived to have become less clearly defined and politicised, and citizenship more personal and commoditised. The basic premise of citizenship has become a seriously contested issue as different mediating social and cultural influences dispute the basis upon which citizenship is articulated. People are no longer considered to be the rational beings that Weber thought of, acting according to the Protestant capitalist ethic or, indeed, as individual

---

12 D. Heater, *Citizenship: The Civic Ideal in World History, Politics and Education* (Longman, London, 1990), p. 128.

13 E.F. Isin, 'Citizenship after Orientalism' in E. Isin and B. Turner (eds.) *Handbook of Citizenship Studies* (Sage Publications, London, 2002), p. 118.

14 E.F. Isin and B.S. Turner 'Citizenship studies: an introduction', in E. Isin and B. Turner (eds.) *Handbook of Citizenship Studies* (Sage Publications, London, 2002), pp. 5-6.

15 R. Dahrendorf, 'The changing quality of citizenship' in B. Van Steenbergen (ed.) *The Condition of Citizenship* (Sage, London, 1994), p. 17.

maximisers of self-interest according to neo-liberal theory. (Rose, 2001; 2)[16] Nor are they considered to be social in the manner of post-World War II social government in Europe or indeed to be psychologically mobilised by unconscious forces. (Rose. 201; 2)[17] In this broader arena, in which citizenship is defined more as a social process where the emphasis is more on norms, practices, meanings and identities instead of legal rules; (Isin and Truner, 2002; 5-6)[18] religion, race, gender, sexual orientation, economic status, ecology, diaspora, and cosmopolitanism, can affect the citizenship status of an individual.

It is also now quite possible for two or more modes of citizenship to be considered simultaneously applicable. Thus, an individual might consider him or herself to be a 'citizen' of the 'Nation of Islam' as well as a Nigerian or a Rastafarian as well as a citizen of Barbados, or to be a Green Activist or Friend of the Earth *and* as British or French, Basque or Catalan. Each category creates its own physical and metaphysical spaces where members can act. Each provides some sense of warmth of membership whether it is spiritual protection or unity of purpose. However, one may also divide all of these more flexible modes of citizenship into two camps, ones that can be changed and ones that are unchangeable or primordial. The latter are becoming less in number but, for example, being white, male and born in the UK are categories that are barely mutable. Being British or holding to a certain faith, a certain sexuality or any sort of philosophical, political or economic persuasion are all becoming increasingly flexible and the speed with which we can change our identity is increasing also.

Personal identity in developed countries thus becomes increasingly ephemeral and chameleon-like in nature; as citizenship is a tool of identity so the conception of citizenship must also become more malleable. It is shaped by Lash and Urry's 'signs and symbols' where personal branding allows individuals to mark themselves out from one another[19] (Lash and Urry, 1996) where transnationalism and cosmopolitanism become the norm. One 38 year-old Muslim male colleague I interviewed in 1999 explained that he was born and brought up in Mali, then spent 3 years in Senegal and eight years in France in education and since then, 14 years based in the United Kingdom (UK) where he now holds citizenship status but has worked on and off in several different countries as a development analyst. This colleague explained that in terms of imagined citizenship it was hard for him to define any particular prominent modality, except in terms of the Muslim faith which has remained a cultural constant throughout. Much has to do with personal circumstance while the boundaries of any fixed sense of identity become more blurred and mutable. The status or importance of different modes of citizenship is also flexible according to the priorities of the day.

---

16 N. Rose, 'Community, Citizenship and the Third Way' in D. Meredith and J. Minson (eds.) *Citizenship and Cultural Policy* (Sage, London, 2001), p. 2.
17 Ibid.
18 Isin and Turner, 'Citizenship studies...', op. cit., p. 4.
19 S. Lash and J. Urry *Economies of Time and Space* (Sage, London, 1996).

A further factor at play here is that layers of citizenship can be overlapping and fluctuating in prominence, depending on self-image in juxtaposition with the various social, cultural, political and economic dynamics exerted on or being exerted by the person or group at any one time. As already implied, most are also 'peelable' and replaceable. Each must bestow rights and obligations agreeable to the holder. This flexible conception of citizenship then, is a post-modern or post-Fordist version applicable surely to those places where post-modern, post-Fordist modes of societal dynamics and economic regulation are seen to operate i.e. in the advanced economies of Europe, North America and Japan. As will be argued, however, flexible citizenship is a concept that is not confined purely to the core countries of the world economy where the most advanced economies cohabit. In the developing world also, citizenship is articulated flexibly, though for reasons not associated with any sense of having transcended the modern. Ong suggests that the observable flexibility of citizenship seen today is a product and condition of late capitalism.[20] (Ong, 1999; 240) However, arbiters of citizenship have been metamorphosing since societies first started centralising. The pivot of change, it is argued here, is economic development or underdevelopment and processes of physical or cultural change that relate to factors such as environmental change and migration which can be due to a variety of factors.

The State in Africa as Problematic

Moommen claims that it is not possible to articulate citizenship without a state or nation-state as the arbiter of context and content, asserting that any attempt to define citizenship without the state as foundation is meaningless and empty. (Moommen, 223-229)[21] But this idea is too reactionary as it insists on the Western-style state as the prime arbiter of citizenship and effectively rules out other types of political or cultural community as illegitimate. It denies the application of the concept of citizenship to a large proportion of people in the developing world who do not live in a country controlled by an effective state in the western sense. If citizenship is to be judged from a western perspective, then non-western societies would appear to perform poorly in relation to indicators such as western-style human rights and universal suffrage; but this would not diminish their ability to distribute rights and obligations and the ability of their populations to articulate feelings of membership commensurate with citizenship.

To follow Moommen's logic then is to give citizenship too narrow and inflexible a set of parameters and indulge in colonial-style thinking. Citizenship, like all modes of identity, is located largely in the imaginary. Stevenson says that this imaginary is a 'social and historical creation and serves to remind us that society must always create symbolic forms beyond the purely functional' (Stevenson, 2003; 5).[22] The

---

20 A. Ong, *Flexible Citizenship: The Cultural Logics of Transnationality* (Duke University Press, Durham, 1999), p. 240.

21 Moomen., op. cit., pp. 223-229.

22 N. Stevenson, *Cultural Citizenship Cosmopolitan Questions* (Open University Press, Maidenhead, Berks., 2003), p. 5.

power to construct oneself as a citizen or subject is a metaphysical force; as Castells asserts, 'The sites of this power are people's minds'. (Castells, 1997; 359)[23] In all of the communities suggested above as likely candidates for flexible citizenship, it is surely the case that most are imagined because, as Anderson points out when talking about nations, 'members of even the smallest nation will never know most of their fellow-members, meet them or even hear of them, yet in the minds of each lives the image of their communion'. (Anderson, 1991; 6)[24]

Clearly, people living in sub-Saharan Africa, where nations with a clear idea of homeland preceded the arrival of colonialism and the European concept of the state, also experience feelings of citizenship and these feelings may or may not be attributed to a state. However, the European experience is not a good guide to citizenship modalities in Sub-Saharan Africa. (Herbst, 2000; 233)[25] People mostly become citizens of a state by default, that is to say, by being born in a certain territory nominally controlled by a state within borders defined by a departed exogenous power. Yet the state may be a failed state, unable to offer basic social services and entitlements such as a passport, or collect taxes, or only able to enforce its sovereignty very weakly from the centre as is the case in the Democratic Republic of Congo and Somalia. Thus, to consider the only use the state to construct modalities of citizenship is too arbitrary and ignores the fact that such constructions are still within the realm of the imaginary.

Another way of explaining the very different ways that people in the developed and developing worlds regard the state is through history, or rather dissimilar roles in the same history. Contemporary European states were mostly formed after the overthrow of monarchical or colonial regimes or by the merger of smaller states whose existence had become unrealistic, as in the case of the early nineteenth century German Confederation of states. Revolutionaries espoused a mix of liberal, republican, and, later, Marxist (proletarian) values in defining ideological underpinnings of new states. Key to these revolutionary processes was the concept of mass action. However, such ideologues also had to be pragmatic and careful not to threaten the new regimes that had come into existence. Thus, revolutionaries had to adapt their ideas to prevailing ethnic, racial, religious, gender and class sensibilities. These new European states were then, in part, the result of a certain set of historical processes that formed an evolutionary path. They were also imbued with what R.M. Smith refers to as 'constitutive stories' of ethnie, race, religion, gender, culture and class in order to define national identity upon which citizenship status could be defined. (Smith, 2002, 109)[26] Even the United States shares this type of political history although the resulting post-revolutionary state became polyethnic (not dominated by one ethnic group) and lacked the same historical emphasis on class.

---

23 M. Castells *The Power of Identity* (Blackwell, Malden, Mass., 1997), p. 359.

24 B. Anderson, *Imagined Communities: Reflections on the Origin and Spread of Nationalism* [Revised Edition] (Verso, London, 1991), p. 6.

25 J. Herbst, *States and power in Africa: Comparative Lessons in Authority and Control* (Princeton University Press, Princeton, NJ, 2000), p. 233.

26 R.M. Smith, 'Modern citizenship' in E.F. Isin and B.S. Turner (eds.) *Handbook of Citizenship Studies* (Sage, London, 2002), p. 109.

In Sub-Saharan Africa by contrast, new states were formed in the twentieth century at the behest and timing of European colonial regimes, nationalist agendas and the will of dominant neo-colonial regimes such as the USA and USSR. These new states took the place of the colonial regimes whose histories were based in Europe, not Africa. Meanwhile, colonial regimes had themselves only partially deconstructed the political communities they found on arrival in Africa. In rural Africa, which constituted most of the continent and its people, pre-existing political communities including thousands of nations, primitive states and mere ethnies, were simply overlain, either within the same colony or divided by new colonial boundaries. Thus, when colonial regimes made way for new nationalist states that attempted to form states based on the artificial land borders of departing colonialists, the governments of these new states were faced with multifarious political communities whose ethnic, racial, religious and cultural underpinnings had not been modified since the pre-colonial era. Separately, these pre-colonial political communities all had history and 'constitutive stories' that were firmly entrenched.

Meanwhile, the ability of new African states to produce 'constitutive stories' was severely constrained by lack of revolutionary process that had led to their coming into being. There was little evidence of mass action, except in the case of wars of liberation such as those in Angola, Mozambique, Zimbabwe and Namibia. But even in these cases, after independence ethnic and class divisions rapidly split any overwhelming sense of unity in the new state. New nationalist leaderships were usually formed from an educated elite minority base that gained its ideological values from urban, industrialised Europe and America and found it hard to value the largely communitarian and non-urban 'constitutive stories' of the many political communities inherited by the post-colonial state. Thus, these new states have suffered from a paucity of history or, at least, of evolutionary historical processes and have often tried to construct 'constitutive stories' such as those associated with a 'freedom struggle' that are inappropriate to large sections of the population who did not participate in or understand such dynamics although they were all impacted by them. In such situations, people, particularly in the rural areas, received or are 'subjected' to citizenship that they have not chosen and are not convinced of the value of, simply because they or their community happen to live where a new state was born. As R.M. Smith asserts, 'Even today... most people acquire their political citizenship through unchosen, often unexamined, hereditary descent, not because they explicitly embrace any political principles....' (Smith, 2002; 110)[27]

Another major factor in the inability of the state, in Africa at least, to manifest itself as an attractive citizenship option is not hard to locate. It lies in economic poverty, the inability to offer services, economic development and the trappings of modernity to more than a sliver of the population, just enough to keep a government in power. If the maxim is correct that social development follows in the trail of economic development, and vice versa, then it also follows that state-related citizenship rights as part of political development will be elusive in the absence of economic development.

---

27 R.M. Smith., op. cit., p. 110.

Thus, while African states are held in dependence and in economic subordination to the developed core of the world economy and remain bereft of institutional capacity, and while the decision-making capacity to make changes to this status quo are located largely outside of the borders of the African state, it is difficult to see how that same state can manifest itself as an attractive citizenship option to the marginalised masses be they in the rural or urban arena. Meanwhile, it would not be true to assume disillusionment with the state as normative and universal across Africa. As Miles and Rochefort discovered, Hausa villagers on the Niger/Nigeria border 'do not place their ethnic identity as Hausas above their national one as citizens of Nigeria or Niger and express greater affinity for non-Hausa co-citizens than foreign Hausas' (Miles and Rochefort, 1991; 401)[28] and this in spite of an underdeveloped economy. Colonialism imbued this sense of difference, however, as Hausas differentiate themselves according to European language.

The apparent inability or unwillingness of many Africans to take on European-style citizenship is also because the state in sub-Saharan Africa, sometimes deprecatingly referred to as the 'Fourth World' (comprising the world's poorest countries), is, with few exceptions, a poor parody of its 'First World' counterpart on which it is modelled. The African state network is, like most African economies, still essentially held in subordination to Europe, the United States and the International Financial Institutions (IFIs). The ability to act decisively in the interests of the majority of the citizenry is severely constrained by this subordination which, in turn, is borne out of politico-economic dependence, a legacy of colonial and neo-colonial domination. This makes African states, existing as they do in some kind of post-colonial torpor, vulnerable and unattractive citizenship options.

The use then, of the state or nation-state as the only arbiter of citizenship fits the developing world, particularly Sub-Saharan Africa (with the possible exception of South Africa), even less than it does the developed. (de Boeck, 1996; 93)[29] This is in spite of the fact that Europe is, historically at least, responsible for the creation and maintenance of what is euphemistically referred to as 'Africa' and the state network therein. The rationale for this is that the history of the contemporary state in Africa is, in fact, a by-product and reaction to dynamics in the history of the political economy of Europe and America and not based on pre-existing political communities and societal structures.

In addition, the political ideology of liberal democracy, so crucial to the operation of political economy in Europe and the rest of the core of the world economy, where nation-state-based citizenship is strongest, is only recently arrived and weakly embedded in Africa. Indeed, colonialism, experienced by all African peoples in one form or another,[30] in its formal mode, was an alien, authoritarian

---

28 W.F.S. Miles and D.A. Rochefort, 'Nationalism versus Ethnic Identity in Sub-Saharan Africa' *American Political Science Review* 85 (1991), p. 401.

29 F. de Boeck, 'Postcolonialism, power and identity: local and global perspectives from Zaire' in R. Werbner and T. Ranger, (eds.) *Postcolonial Identities in Africa* (Zed Books, London, 1996), p. 93.

30 Including, it would be argued here, Liberia, which experienced unofficial or indirect colonialism through the delivery of Americanised freed slaves who rapidly formed an elite

patriarchy controlled from a remote power base where rights applied to the selected few on completely illiberal, undemocratic principals and obligations, were applied to everybody else, particularly the indigenous populations. Such an experience was hardly good preparation coming, as it did, immediately ahead of the independence era when new African states were suddenly expected to don the mantra of liberal democracy.

This does not, in any case, imply that citizenship and democracy are natural bedfellows; indeed, I would argue this is rarely the case. Nor does democratisation necessarily lead to a fairer and more effective working of the capitalist free market, economic development and the realisation of the modernist dream including liberal or republican citizenship rights. As Kelsall says, where liberal norms are only weakly institutionalised and where people find it easier to work in vertical rather than horizontal networks, democratisation 'may lead to increased competition of a most illiberal kind'. (Kelsall, 2003; 55)[31] Meanwhile, the modalities of African self-identification continue to be largely communitarian and cultural. This is not to say that urban or associationist identity does not exist. Clearly, there are substantial changes which take place to a person's sense of self and other when adapting to the African urban environment. However, there remains a dominant communitarian core, which is unsurprising as Africa has been constrained from undergoing agricultural and industrial revolutions Europe-style, together with the concomitant social revolutions one would expect from these economic dynamics.

In many African countries, the idea that governments and their institutions are in existence to serve the people is treated with apprehension and suspicion at best, and cynicism and contempt at worst. Individuals tend to consider themselves to be citizens and subjects of more than one socio-political community and these communities are more communitarian and less associationist in nature, although they can be just as 'peelable'. Thus, people often consider themselves to be of their ethnic groups or tribes (which may cross national boundaries) first and of the postcolonial state second. Religion, which also knows no national boundaries, becomes another major identifier, articulated by lifestyle, mode of worship, type of church building and the appearance of the followers of each faith when engaged in religious activity. Thus, the streets of an average town in eastern or southern Africa is likely to be adorned with smartly dressed people wearing the colours of their respective faith, scurrying in different directions to different places of worship, often to spend a whole morning or entire day engaged in services and cultural activities associated with the church Indeed, people are often defined, firstly by their ethnic group and secondly by their church.

Physical boundaries have also been poorly identified with in Africa because, as Herbst points out, before formal European colonialism, power was exercised more through the control of people than land as land was in abundance but people over whom to have influence, were not. (Herbst, 40,232)[32] This notwithstanding, Herbst

---

layer of society based at the coast around Monrovia.

31 T. Kelsall, 'Governance, democracy and recent political struggles in mainland Tanzania' *Commonwealth and Comparative Politics* 41, 2 (2003), p. 55.

32 Herbst, *States and power in Africa...*, pp. 40 and 232.

is too absolutist and categorical when he says that African boundaries in the past were not designed to regulate the movement of people. (Herbst, 232)[33] In the case of the Lozi of Zambia, before, during and after the 'Makololo interregnum',[34] use was made of the Zambezi and Chobe/Linyanti/Kwando rivers and their swampy environs; the various sentinels were placed at strategic locations along these rivers precisely to monitor and regulate the flow of people into and out of southern Barotseland.

Due to paucity of resources, the state, often dominated by one ethnic group, is perceived to reward only its own clients, leading to what is locally referred to as the tribalisation of politics. To do so, however, the capital city, where the modernistic seat of power lies, must also be taken over in differential respects associated with the ruling group. In Namibia for example, the Ovambo group have successfully taken charge of state politics based in Windhoek despite the fact that the Ovambo homeland is located in the far north of the country and in Angola. Strength of numbers was a factor here, as was language. In Namibia, Oshiwambo soon started to be heard on the streets of the townships of Windhoek while, at independence, the national language was English, a language that the other large ethnic groups of Namibia, such as the Herero and Nama, had never spoken (being largely educated in Afrikaans by edict of the South African colonial regime). Thus when Lozis in the Caprivi region of Namibia consider the organs of government, they tend to think of Oshiwambo-speaking Ovambos, and peoples from other regions speaking Afrikaans, bent on holding key positions of power and subjecting Caprivians to their will. Meanwhile, Silozi-speaking Caprivians exposed, even by South Africa, largely to English as the colonial medium of communication.

Zambia is another example of this phenomenon where the Bemba are perceived by other groups to have achieved dominance in top-level government positions in the civil service. It has been difficult, therefore, particularly for large groups such as the Lozi, with their own national history, to feel and display feelings of allegiance to the Zambian/Bemba state. Despite nationalist political awakening during the colonial era, in most of Sub-Saharan Africa State nationalism has failed to permeate communitarian group identity or sub-nationalisms. Put simply, the nation-state has failed to materialise. The difficulty in postcolonial Africa has been in determining whether citizenship or subjectivity are uppermost in the minds of local people when they think of the state. This is because the state is perceived to make many demands upon its population but fails to provide or guarantee adequate public services, human security, and rights to more than a select few of its population. It also largely fails to provide an economic platform where the individual can expect to find opportunities to make personal gains. The fault for this state of affairs is invariably placed at the foot of the national government which is seen as inept, corrupt, predatory and indulging in patron-clientage. For groups like the Lozi, who believe that the state has been deliberately withholding development, the state is even seen as colonialist in behaviour. This is ironical, given that the state in Africa, struggling to break free from the colonial legacy of lack of institutional capacity and training, also feels

---

33 Ibid., p. 232.
34 Makololo interregnum – period of occupation during the mid nineteenth century by a horde led by a Sotho clan.

itself locked into postcolonial dependence on a global politico-economic system from which it cannot break free.

All this still does not mean that citizenship is not evident in Africa, particularly in the postcolonial era. On the contrary, the basic tenets of citizenship, namely, membership, belonging, exclusionary identification, the potential for inclusivity, personal branding, rights, and obligations, are all enthusiastically subscribed to but in ways other than allegiance to a state. People in the developing world have an equal if not more urgent need of membership of social entities that will provide and protect. But the premise upon which notions of citizenship are based is so different, for example in the behaviour of political communities, modes of production, and of distribution of power and wealth. As already stated, this is due to different histories prior to the arrival of the world economy and different histories within it. A closer look at the trajectory of African political development is perhaps appropriate here.

Historical Trajectories

Certainly before the coming of Europeans, Africa consisted of thousands of polities and political communities which, for convenience, may be referred to as tribes. Many of these polities were nations, in the sense that several groups had coalesced or been subsumed by one dominant group but all of whose constituent parts now recognised a shared sense of identity and solidarity in a shared homeland. Some nations, such as the Lozi, had even transcended into early forms of state in that the national identity had become collective, spanning a number of ethnies, united within one political community governed from a centralised institutional apparatus. In the case of the Lozi, King and state existed in tense co-habitation with one another. The properties of citizenship, as described above, existed in many of these nations even though the state may have been primitive in form and lacking in democratic practice with an economy that was dominated by the centralised polity and not by the market. Society was, by nature, then, communitarian and stratified according to class.

With the arrival of colonialism, authority over Africans was in varying degrees of direct and indirect rule. Direct rule usually involved the breakdown of traditional structures of power and authority which were replaced with rule by white European administrations whose officers were sent out from the metropole. Direct rule did not spread widely to the countryside excepting if there existed valuable mineral resources such as in the Copperbelts of Zambia and Katanga or concentrations of white European settler-farmers such as in the highlands of Kenya, Natal, the central highlands of Namibia and Southern Rhodesia. However, it was in urban areas, particularly the colonial capital cities, such as Dakar, Lusaka, and Nairobi that direct rule was mostly exercised.

Indirect rule was most often found in the rural areas that Europeans did not consider suitable for farming and settlement, where no substantial resources, such as minerals, were located, and where the colonial administrative machine found it hardest to permeate due to the paucity of resources. It was also where there were traditional or customary rulers and authorities who could be authorised and relied upon to maintain order and allegiance to the metropole in return for leaving these indigenous and localised structures of power undisturbed. As Mamdani makes clear in his 'Citizen and Subject', in non-settler colonies, colonialism reinforced and promoted a form of 'customary' power, that is, traditional authority, although this was always subordinated to colonial state rule in order to effect 'indirect rule'. (Mamdani, 1996; 21-23)[35] Indirect rule had definite advantages for colonial regime: it was cheaper to administer and had the effect of boxing African people into discreet ethnic or 'tribal' units maintained by African leaders whose interests were also served by emphasising and maintaining tribal mentalities among their peoples. Ranger describes ethnicity as a great colonial 'invention' which involved ascribing monolithic identities. (Ranger, 1996; 274)[36] According to Vail, these were key in preventing the appearance of de-tribalised natives of whom white colonialists were deeply suspicious. (Vail, 1993; 11-12)[37] Meanwhile, in Zambia, as in most of Africa during the colonial era, a mix of direct and indirect rule prevailed.

Where Lugardian indirect rule was most prominent, a local oligarchy was often subsumed and made reliant upon the metropole. It was through these autocratic but mostly respected organs of power that the will of the colonial administration was imposed. In some cases, such as the Lozi of Barotseland and the Baganda of Uganda, the internal political structure of the nation was left virtually untouched except that traditional rulers were now answerable to a narrow, white, elite layer of authority. This authority was invariably located in a remote European-style new urban place such as Lusaka, or an adapted African urban place created for colonialist economic expediency. So long as value, usually in the form of taxes combined with migrant labour, was seen to be exacted from these rural regions, the colonial administration exempted itself from the need, impetus or expense of extending formal colonialism to peoples and regions not deemed economically viable.

Thus, through the co-operation of traditional leaderships, colonial regimes were able to withhold modernising influences applied in the colony area from other parts of the country, sowing the seeds for future mistrust and inter-group rivalry. This is at the root of much of the inter-ethnic rivalry in Nigeria, where first Yorubaland in the south-west and then Iboland in the south-east benefited from educational, professional and commercial opportunities while in the north, which received none of these, Britain found willing allies for their system of indirect rule in the Fulani emirs. (Bartkus, 98)[38] That traditional rulers and colonial overlords seemed able to co-exist and co-operate so well can be ascribed to the fact that both existed as the most powerful echelons of their societies, which were highly stratified by class. Both were used to occupying and articulating power and status.

---

35 M. Mamdani *Citizen and Subject: Contemporary Africa and the Legacy of Late Colonialism* (Fountain Publishers, Kampala, 1996), pp. 21-23.

36 T. Ranger, 'Colonial and postcolonial identities' in R. Werbner and T. Ranger, (eds.) *Postcolonial Identities in Africa* (Zed Books, London, 1996), p. 274.

37 L. Vail, *The Creation of Tribalism in Southern Africa* (James Currey, London, 1993), pp. 11-12.

38 Bartkus, op. cit., p. 98.

The same dichotomous power relations between urban and rural populations continued when colonial rule gave way in the second half of the twentieth century to rule by African nationalists from the urban centres; they also inherited from the departing colonial regimes whatever institutional capacity was left behind, The towns, cities, and whatever industrial development existed, were much easier to imbue with republican and African nationalist sentiment. Urban populations could more easily be de-racialised and democratised. Here we can equate 'democratise' with the taking on of citizenship along the lines of the Greek city-states where those in the countryside were considered as backward and less developed. Urban bias quickly set in, encouraged by the modernisation thinkers and strategists of the day and as the new governments also realised that their constituencies lay in the towns and cities. Meanwhile, in the rural areas, most of which the colonialists had not bothered to penetrate (with the obvious exception of settler agricultural areas) or had kept under control using the sway of traditional leaderships, contestation over political allegiances soon began to emerge.

As in the case of the Lozi, sharp differences soon emerged between the all-encompassing ideals of nationalism and the threat that this posed to traditional leaderships and authority. Nationalist politicians encountered difficulties in mobilising rural people and their leaders through dynamics such as de-racialisation, which was rarely an issue in the countryside, and democratisation, which was perceived as threatening the status quo of traditional authorities. This sometimes resulted in outright conflict or it simmered beneath the surface amid an atmosphere of suspicion and innuendo. Traditional leaders were portrayed by the nationalists as backward and reactionary, holding up the spread of modernity to the rural masses. The former colonial powers mostly supported the new nationalist governments; they left former polities that they had used to their advantage in indirect colonial rule at the mercy of nationalist regimes that felt little empathy towards traditional rulers.

When disillusionment set in after the dreams of modernisation had failed to materialise and as political power rapidly became more authoritarian and less accountable in the 1970s, leadership became more autocratic and idiosyncratic. This opened up the possibility of co-operation between holders of power in the cities and in the countryside in alliances of convenience. As many of the new rulers came from the military, this type of alliance was acceptable as no particular political ideology was being employed other than the struggle to hold on to power. New patron/client relationships evolved that replicated, in many respects, the indirect rule style of relationships that existed in colonial days. In Zambia, in the infamous Barotseland greement (1964), Mwanawina, the Lozi king, was forced into signing away his kingdom to an independent Zambia by a combination of threats of excommunication by the British government and by the sudden unpopularity of the traditional elite which had been made to appear self-serving and elitist by the British colonial regime. With his death, the kingship was co-opted by Kaunda who hung on to power through one-party rule from 1973 to 1990.

As economically bankrupt African states seemingly 'redemocratised' in the 1990s in accordance with the conditionalities of the World Bank, IMF and other lending authorities through such programmes as Structural Adjustment, the ability of these states to impose sovereignty and order in the rural areas became ever more difficult. This was due to the compulsory cutting back of the state and reductions of spending on social upliftment programmes, such as health and education, which would have given the state legitimacy in rural areas. For regions such as Barotseland which had suffered underdevelopment during both the colonial and post-colonial eras, this led to even more dissatisfaction with the state and, even though traditional authority could not fill the modernising gap left by the moribund state, it could at least provide a cultural and communitarian hearth in which people could bask in the glow of history, heritage and familiarity.

Citizenship Construction in Sub-Saharan Africa

In the communitarian version of citizenship, it is participation and group identity which is recognised and emphasised. Delanty claims that these take precedence over rights and duties (Delanty, 2000; 23)[39] although in the case of most African groups, rights and duties are part of citizenship but not in the western state sense. Thus, in the contemporary era, the state capitals and other main urban areas continue to enjoy the lion's share of available development. Meanwhile, many rural societies, which have hardly been penetrated by the state and by processes associated with modernisation such as democratisation, which distributes citizenship rights and provides new means of inclusion and exclusion, languish in unequal underdevelopment.

Citizenship entitlements, such as voting rights, become seriously contested as governments, whose clutch on power has become precarious, seek to withhold such rights from those suspected of harbouring alternative political allegiances. This is the situation currently prevailing in Zimbabwe. Citizenship thus becomes a seriously contested issue as different mediating social influences dispute the bases upon which citizenship is adjudged. As with the citizens of the advanced economies of the North, who are experiencing the flexible processes of post-modernity, people in sub-Saharan Africa are also articulating their citizenship in a broader arena in which multiple layers of citizenship are bought into, but in which nation-state citizenship achieves a much lower ranking. Thus citizenship discourse surrounds issues such as ethnicity or tribe, religion, and community. Citizenship is defined more as a social process where the emphasis is on norms, practices and meanings. In the case of tribe, in many cases this can be interpreted as nation. For the Buganda, Lozi and Wolof nations for example, the citizenship arena is easier to define as there is a clearly delineated homeland territory and these groups have long been able to transcend Oommen's conception of ethnie into nationhood.[40]

In the developed economies of the North alternative articulations of citizenship are sought out as the nation-state evolves and adapts to new technological and regulatory developments in the ever-dynamic global world economy. In Africa, they are sought

---

39 G. Delanty, *Citizenship in a Global Age: Society, Culture, Politics* (Open University Press, Buckingham, 2000), p. 23.

40 Oommen states that the ethnie becomes a nation when it can relate to a defined territory and reverts from nationhood into an ethnie when this conditionality is lost, for instance after displacement – T.K. Oommen, *Citizenship, Nationality and Ethnicity: Reconciling Competing Identities* (Polity Press, Cambridge, 1997), pp. 16-17.

out because of the failure of the state to deliver the trappings of modernity and nation-statehood promised at independence. It is also due to a feeling of impotence as people, particularly away from the cities, feel they are unable to change the status quo that they know is responsible for their unequal impoverishment in the world. This leads to low morale and feelings of loss and exclusion, felt even more keenly because the global media and telecommunications now permeate the remotest corners of less-developed countries and demonstrate to the populations how badly off they are in comparison to peoples in other parts of the world. Whereas citizenship and subjectivity might be expected to offer opportunities for improvements in standards of living in the North, in many African states they are often absorbed by people as part of a survival strategy. Thus, a person might primarily subscribe to citizenship of a tribe or group offering protection, food, or some form of power and/or wealth regardless of ethnicity or place of birth.

Equally, religions, such as Islam in the Sahelian regions or, in the case of Barotseland, the New Apostolic faith, may offer spiritual protection and even opportunities that a state government that is too often seen as a predatory interest group fails to offer. Belief systems also offer rationalisations and explanations to poor people for their plight (the will of God), and may even offer themselves as vehicles for protest at the unequal treatment of the marginalised (for example, as catholic priests in Latin America have often been prepared to stand up to autocratic and praetorian regimes on behalf of local protest groups).

By implication here then, cultural citizenship in this flexible sense is something to be aspired to. The sorts of conditionalities concomitant with citizenship in the North are not replicated here. Instead, the right to be able to call oneself and be recognised as Lozi may be an honour that is either endowed at birth or awarded or bought about in the course of living.

For the state in Zambia, what seems to be occurring is the emergence of feelings of post-coloniality and helplessness on the part of the state and its supporters. It is undoubtedly true that the Zambian state has demonstrated ethnic nepotism in the past, in terms of appointments and apportionment of services and development. But this is surely an inevitability in a political economy that finds itself unable to deliver 'basic capabilities' for the majority of the population. It is very difficult for a political party in government to project itself and the state as an attractive option for citizenship when it finds itself having to reduce and ration out the provision of services and human security and where decision-making power is constantly being eroded by the dictates of the IFIs and international NGOs. Certainly, the locus of power in African countries, once located in the capitals of European colonial powers, now seems to have shifted, to differing extents, to locations such as Washington D.C. instead of the capitals of the African countries themselves. Empathy amongst the marginalised and impoverished populations of Africa for their hapless governments is, however, very limited as it is difficult to see the constraints they work under from below. As in the case of the Lozi and the Barotseland Agreement, there are often individual experiences that have led marginalised groups to mistrust the state.

Meanwhile, for groups such as the Lozi in Zambia and the Ovimbundu in Angola, remote from any of these centres of power, there is a feeling of peripheralisation and exclusion, a kind of 'fourth worldism' that, in turn, generates an introversion to culture and community. Implicit here is the attraction of the past, to a history constructed to provide a warm and attractive cushion against the frigidity and impotence of the state. For the Lozi and the Ovimbundu, there is no sense that the state offers anything other than burdensome and enforced subjectivity. There are few perceived benefits deriving from this subjectivity. Lozis feel instead that they are not trusted and today face a 'glass ceiling' when attempting to climb the ladder in the public sector, due to a perception that they received favour in the past from the colonial regime. This is not to say that some Lozis are not recruited, but there are other ways in which the state shows its distrust and ambivalence to a people. For example, it would be almost impossible to find a Lozi policeman appointed to work in the Office of the President, the Zambian state intelligence agency in western Zambia, or as an immigration officer on the borders of western and south-western Zambia, adding to the negative perceptions held by local people.

In addition, the state's control of violence has been insufficient in the past to prevent incursions of armed and lawless people from Angola and elsewhere, causing havoc for local people. In these cases, it appears to local people that the Zambian government is more interested in its relationship with the Angolan government than with protecting local people from abduction, rape, killing and plunder by foreigners. 7[41] Furthermore, it is still within the living memory of many of the older generation of Lozis that the Zambian state under the tenureship of President Kaunda licensed a war between foreigners (the freedom struggle between SWAPO and the South African Defence Force) to take place on Barotse soil in the 1970s leading to the terrorising, death and displacement of thousands of local people. Meanwhile, in his discussion on public education and nationalism, A.D. Smith asks whether people of a non-dominant ethnic community would be prepared to die en-masse for the *patrie en danger* just because they have been taught that they are citizens of the state. (Smith, 1998; 38-39)[42] In the case of the Lozis, the answer here would at once be ambivalent and paradoxical. On the one hand, many Lozis would not feel patriotic fervour for the Zambian state, while, on the other, in the context of prevalent poverty and underdevelopment and the fact that soldiers are likely to be paid a reasonable wage and receive other perceived perks, many Lozis would probably enlist. As stated by a company worker:

> I would willingly join the army or air force and wear the Zambian uniform, just as I would be a prison officer or a policeman or special agent. This is because I am poor and

---

41 7 An example being the reaction of the government of President Chiluba in November 2001 following incursions first by rebel UNITA soldiers and then Angolan government soldiers into the Shangombo district of Western Province leading to the deaths of 7, the rape of 14 women and abduction of 103. Chiluba spoke only of regret and hoped for closer collaboration between the two governments of Zambia and Angola 'to avoid further misunderstandings' and to 'improve their relations'. Info taken from the Times of Zambia November 23rd 2001 <http://www.times.co.zm/news/viewnews.cgi?category=2&id=1005939860> and Zamnet News Service November 26th 2001 <http://www.zamnet.zm/newsys/news/viewnews.cgi?category=2&id=1006407947>

42 A.D. Smith, *Nationalism and Modernity: A Critical Survey of Recent Theories of Nations and Nationalism* (Routledge, London, 1998), pp. 38-39.

my family spends most of the year hungry. But I would not do anything to endanger my people, my Chief or the Litunga. That is for Lozis. I am a Lozi first and foremost even if I am wearing a Zambian uniform.[43]

Here, economic realities can overlay feelings of disenchantment and exclusion although few feelings of nationalist fervour or pride would result, which helps to explain the often apparently lacklustre and unenthusiastic performance of many African armies.

Meanwhile, Lozis still feel the need for some sort of citizenship to buy into, and this takes the form of group membership of a socially constructed warm and inviting past, a feeling of solidarity with those who share affiliation to myths of past power and wealth. It is then, as afore-mentioned, a cultural and communitarian style of citizenship that Lozis are expressing in the contemporary era, whereby the gaze turns inwards to gain sufficient protection to endure the alienation and misunderstanding of the outside world. Most do accept they are also Zambian, if only by default. It does not help that so few, particularly in Western Zambia, are able to get onto the voters' register and indulge in some kind of participation in electing representatives to the state's decision-making bodies.[44] However, low morale and disillusionment of marginalised peoples in African states does not rule out the potential for the state to generate feelings of patriotism if only because of the location of the state in the world system. Thus, when the Zambian football team is playing against other countries, Lozis in Western Province enthusiastically cheer the Zambian team. This could be interpreted as a default expression as there is no Barotseland team and no feelings of loyalty exist to other African states. However, human insecurity and economic hardship breed strange bedfellows and loyalties can be very flexible in such situations, as the example of military enlistment demonstrates. It is also remarkable how fluid and flexible notions of identity can become when economic development and globalisation stray into previously remote areas, particularly if these are close to borders.

Conclusions and Policy Implications

This chapter would not serve its purpose in a book of this nature without relating the foregoing contextual analysis to a glimpse of the route map for policy and practice in the decades to come for a continent poorly served by effective governance (not to be confused with the western influenced term 'good governance').

---

43 Muyunda Nasilele, 30 year-old water company worker of Mongu, interviewed 21-10-2002.

44 The writer witnessed the endless queues of people lining up outside a small building in Mongu in September/October 2002 in the hope of registering on the electoral role ahead of Zambian elections held in the following December. Many had travelled long distances to get to these registration points yet were jostled by police and security, often only to return home disappointed. There are clearly large numbers of rural people classed as Zambians who are unable to participate in the basic processes associated with state citizenship.

The African experience to date has produced a post-coloniality that indelibly imbues contemporary conceptions of identity such as citizenship and subjectivity. There are palpable feelings of a job left undone, of failed dreams of modernity, of frustration at the incompletion of the nation-state project, of self-serving 'tribalised' governing apparatuses and of an uncaring, pejorative and xenophobic outside world that subjugates and alienates the majority of Africans from their rightful place at the table of human and social development. In short, there is a lack of pride, trust and confidence in that most visible of institutions of Africa, the postcolonial state. There are exceptions of course and it would be contentious to start naming any here.

This chapter argues that a vibrant sense of citizenship and subjectivity are present in Africa and are indeed vital to the human spirit for a collective, sociable species where a hierarchically ordered system of membership is intrinsic to society. The context in which membership is structured in Africa differs, however, from the conventional western one after which the term citizenship was coined. Due to the alleged failure of the state to access and disseminate the dreams and fruits of a certain version of modernity as perceived through the lens of global medias now intruding into the consciousness of Africans as never before, state-centred citizenship is endured by default. Morale in this state-centred citizenship is low and this, in turn, affects the enthusiasm of the holder to engage in representative and productive tasks that are associated with the state.

Meanwhile, proactive brand-conscious citizen/subject style membership is articulated more through cultural and belief systems that intrude into the political realm both at a local and regional level, crossing state borders at random. These systems, like nations and states, indulge in inclusion and exclusion and are able to both mediate and militate in the formation and articulation of political communities, particularly where the authority and sovereignty of the state is weakest. In part, the production or re-emphasising of these systems of identity, most of which pre-existed the postcolonial state, can be seen as a reaction to the failure, exclusion, impotence or predation of the state.

Another outcome of this state of affairs is the out-migration of talent and skills from Africa to exactly the locations that are the cause of the continent's peripheralisation. This migration comprises the most productive and most educated, and most resourceful members of the community, in a loss to Africa comparable with that associated with the scourges of the Trans-Atlantic Slave Trade and HIV-AIDS, taking a comparable toll of the brightest and the best. Another outcome, as analysed in this chapter, is the way in which local people identify themselves variously but rarely primarily in terms of state citizenship and subjectivity.

In Africa, meanwhile, nobody is quite sure who to blame most for what are seen as unfair outcomes. That said, it is state governments who are the first target of most people's wrath for the inequalities that, with the advent of advanced telecommunications, are all too easily perceived. State governments get bad press from all sides above and below, from western governments, IFIs and NGOs, from supra-national institutions such as the United Nations and the European Union, from external and internal medias, and from frustrated local people, the very constituency of governments. Even those who do best from African state governments, including those who have been part of government or whose interests have been served well by government (mostly urban elites), usually have little good to say.

Meanwhile, it does not help that in this time of crisis over the future of planet earth, African peoples and their governments, struggling to assert themselves and provide some semblance of economic and social development, are being lectured as to what policies and practices to adopt and adhere to in order to mitigate and adapt to global environmental change such as climate change. Of course, the anthropogenic causes of climate change, which threatens the well-being of us all, lie wholly in the countries of those doing the lecturing to Africa.

How then, out of this morass of negative pasts and presents can a positive future be imagined that reflects the necessary care and respect due to African people? Presidents Mbeki, Obasanjo and Wade, together with other African leaders, welcomed in the twenty-first century as the century of Africa, heralding an African 'renaissance'. The New Partnership for Africa's Development (NEPAD) and a rejuvenated African Union (AU) were supposed to reflect and direct this optimism. And yet the rhetoric so far has been little else but that, articulated through vague aspirational targets associated with the equally vague and aspirational Millennium Development Goals These have been accompanied by little in the way of achievable plans or properly funded projects that have the enthusiastic support of all stakeholders including the much elided and much misunderstood mass of the population. The gross inequalities and lack of opportunities that perpetuate low morale, poor productivity, out-migration and lack of association with and pride in national identity are still in place and continue to widen.

The answer then must lie from within. Whilst African communities, be they states, nations, ethnic groups, urban or rural, try to compare and contrast themselves with their peers elsewhere, particularly in the west, the result is likely to be a continuation of the current malaise and disillusionment. In order to do better, an individual must feel good about him or herself. The same surely applies to political, cultural or economic communities. And, given that the state is likely to be the most influential stakeholder among the other types of community mentioned, the need for positivity must start in that institution.

Nevertheless, while it is true that the state in Africa has certainly not been a helpful tool in economic or social development, it is also the most likely tool for motivating and catalysing such development in the future.

The barriers are all too clear – low skills, poor training, ephemeral tenancy of holders of influential policy-making posts, inappropriate selection criteria, inadequate funds from within (fiscal collection), external pressure on policy making that is not often related to internal needs to name but a few. The current barrage of 'capacity-building' components to development projects aimed at developing world governments do not help. This is partly because they are largely uncoordinated and have different, often competing, agendas. It is also because most are funded and, despite all the 'bottom-up' and 'grassroots' rhetoric, directed by Northern agencies and donor bodies that still aim to mould institutions in the image of themselves. Capacity building is so often aimed at governments and policy-making bodies that donor and Non Governmental Organization bodies realise *have to be negotiated* in order to execute projects and programmes do not help the situation. This is different from specific capacity building in governance which should become a main plank of activity, directed by the stakeholders in governance with help from those who have the experience and skills to train and teach but whose aspirations, agendas and interests ,coincide with those of the most important stakeholder, the populations served by governance institutions, be they supra-national (such as the AU), regional (such as the Economic Community of West African States (ECOWAS) and Southern Africa Development Community (SADC), national or local.

In stressing this imperative, it is accepted that strong, effective and representative governance is key to social and economic development from which human development is likely to ensue. However, in order to become proactive agencies of progress, institutions of governance have to be seen to be in possession of sovereignty and authority and able to make decisions on behalf of their constituents. The current climate of domination by external powers in policy and decision-making will not relieve the increasing inequalities that are a root cause of dissatisfaction and low morale in contemporary Africa. This is not a recommendation for autocratic dictatorship. Neither does it say that liberal democracy, described here as a western centric ideology attached to the functioning of the capitalist world economy, is wholly inappropriate for Africa. Africans love voting when given the chance and when they believe there is something worth voting for.

A start in the process is the acceptance, both internally and externally, first, that much, though admittedly not all, of what is wrong with the postcolonial state in Africa is as a result of its inputs, both past and present. This, then, is the realisation that the expectations, particularly of state governments in Africa, did not and have still not taken into account what was left behind at independence and what have been inputs in the half century or so since. These inputs include policy-making skills and experience in governance. Institutions of governance are not built overnight and cannot be created by politicians whose tenancy in their positions is likely to be short. In the European model, there is normally a permanent functioning civil service that actually processes the work of governance and advises politicians of what is possible and what is not. This is where the experience and skills really lies. In Africa, even where a strong civil service exists such as Botswana and Senegal, such a body of experience is lacking and is prevented from forming by economic constraints, partly imposed from outside.

The second acceptance is that Africa, particularly Sub-Saharan Africa minus South Africa (which is fast becoming a new neo-colonial force in its own right across the continent) and its people have never been given access to a level playing field in any field. Politically, economically and socially, Africa and Africans have always had to fight against unfair barriers and a pejorative and xenophobic treatment not just from the usual white Europeans and Americans culprits but also from other Africans who share a sense of otherness and lack of confidence in their own achievements and potential. This is a condition of post-coloniality which exists as a mindset, a construct that encourages belief in the idea that Africans don't do things as well, fall out unnecessarily, and aren't as industrious as their Northern counterparts. The point of significance is that the erroneous perceptions described here are not just those held by outsiders but also by Africans themselves. This lack of confidence, imbued so indelibly during colonial times has to be expunged with alacrity if Africa is to gain its rightful place on the geopolitical and socio-economic map of the world.

Chapter 3

Liberalization, Democratization and Political Leadership in Africa

Edward Kannyo

Most of the first 40 years of African independence have been marked by missed opportunities in the political, economic and social realms. Political authoritarianism and even state terrorism, economic decline and civic violence have blighted the hopes of the independence movements of the late 1950s and early 1960s. One of the major explanatory factors is the POOR political leadership in the continent during the early part of that period. Over 20 years ago, Rosberg and Jackson (1982) classified the prevailing African personalist leadership into three categories: (a) 'princes,' (b) autocrats, (c) 'prophets,' and (d) tyrants. The 1980s and 1990s witnessed the emergence of a new generation of leaders promising to move away from the old political style of leadership. But while under the 'Third Wave' of the 1980s in most states there is now a larger degree of freedom of expression and political pluralism, very serious limits remain on the exercise of basic civil and political liberties. Leaders who came to power on the wings of popular democratization movements have sought to restrict freedom in order to ensure their continued tenure in office. And for those outside elite circles, general political arbitrariness and insensitivity to the economic and social needs of the average peasant and worker have continued.

In the realm of governance, there has been much less progress towards 'good governance'.[1] Venality and other types of abuse of power for personal gain remain very serious problems. Power remains concentrated in the hands of the executive that usually intervenes in all aspects of governance. As van de Walle (2003:310) points out:

> Throughout the region, power is highly centralized around the president. He is literally above the law, controls in many cases a large portion of state finance with little accountability, and delegates remarkably little of his authority on important matters. In most countries, the presidency emerges as the dominant arena for decision-making, to the point that regular ministerial structures are relegated to an executant's role.

Autocrats, tyrants and prophets may have left the stage, in most cases, but princes under democratic guise are very much in evidence.

The first part of this chapter briefly reviews the experiences of selected countries in introducing or sustaining political regimes essentially based on the

---

1 "Good governance" has been generally defined as coherent policy formulation, effective public administration, and limited corruption (Alence, 2004).

liberal democratic model. One criterion for selection is that they these ountries are significant examples of cases where there were high hopes among people in and outside Africa of creating democratic societies on the continent. Senegal is included because, alongside Botswana and Mauritius, it has long enjoyed the reputation of being the longest-lived liberal regime in the region. The rest of the chapter provides a theoretical framework that relates political leadership to the political, social and economic legacies inherited at the time of decolonization. Finally, the discussion concludes on prospects for further liberalization and democratization.

Selected Country Experiences

Uganda

Following his accession to the presidency in 1986, Yoweri Museveni was hailed as an example of a new generation of serious and relatively young African leaders who promised to implement policies that would more effectively push their countries in the direction of development and democratization.

Beginning with an uncertain political mandate in 1986 resulting from a successful guerrilla campaign that overthrew the last of a string of repressive regimes, Museveni and the National Resistance Movement (NRM) proceeded to build grassroots representative political institutions. Initially, they were based on very limited competitive electoral processes. Subsequently, largely in response to domestic and international pressures, more genuinely competitive elections were gradually introduced at the presidential, parliamentary and local levels. In spite of these changes, until recent constitutional changes, the regime had been described as 'semi-authoritarian'. It was characterized by the restriction of political expression within the NRM, selective suppression of freedoms of expression and political choice, arbitrary arrest of political opponents, and curbs on the exercise of other important forms of civil and political rights (Aili M. Tripp, 2004; Oloka-Onyango, 2004).

In 2005, the NRM-dominated parliament removed the two-term limit on the presidency that had been written into the 1995 Constitution. Without it, Museveni would not have run in the scheduled 2006 presidential elections. In part, and as a kind of *quid pro quo* to the opposition, for the first time since 1986 the political system was opened up to full-fledged multiparty competition.

In February 2006, Museveni faced Kiiza Besigye, the leader of the Forum for Democratic Change (FDC), who had also challenged him in the 2001 presidential elections that were held without official party platforms. Unlike these earlier elections, which had been marred by intimidation and violence against the opposition, in 2006 overt intimidation and violence were much less evident. However, a major blow against fair electoral contestation was delivered when Besigye was arrested on charges of rape and treason shortly after he returned from self-imposed exile to lead the FDC. He spent a good part of the short time he had for campaigning either in prison or going back and forth to civilian and military courts. Officially, the elections resulted in a Museveni victory with 68% of votes cast.

One of the ominous political developments just before and after the election was the sudden public appearance of an apparently secret armed military unit which interfered with actions of the High Court in the course of Besigye's trial. By April 2006, it was not entirely clear whether the competitive multiparty elections represented a giant leap forward in the process of liberalization and democracy or an illusory and temporary impression of progress. Intimidation of opposition leaders and supporters continued after the elections in spite of the legal opening to multiparty competition.

Zambia

Zambia is one of those African states that went from a civilian authoritarian to a pluralist regime without the violence of a military coup or civil strife. After some 27 years of autocratic but relatively benign rule by Kenneth Kaunda's United National Independence Party (UNIP), internal and external pressures led to the first presidential and parliamentary multiparty elections in 1991. The new opposition Movement for Multiparty Democracy (MDD) won the elections and its leaders, Frederick Chiluba, assumed the presidency.

In the next five years, the country enjoyed greater political liberties. However, the MMD regime was marked by economic and political abuses of power. An observer stated that 'development policy remains, too often, contingent upon how government plans overlap with personal enrichment projects' (Venter, 2003: 5). There were also reports of extra-judicial killings, torture and harassment of the independent press and opposition parties. Political choice was restricted when a new Constitution was introduced in 1996 before the presidential and parliamentary elections, with provisions that prevented former President Kaunda from standing for the presidential election on the grounds that his parents were not born in Zambia.[2]

In addition, the regime attempted to restrict the constitutional role of the judiciary. In 1996, it proposed a set of constitutional amendments including a provision that every act passed by the National Assembly would be presumed constitutional and not subject to judicial challenge or probe. The proposals also aimed to increase the power of the president to remove High Court and Supreme Court justices. Strong opposition from various political forces, civil society organizations, and foreign donors compelled the regime to abandon these proposals (Von Doepp, 2005).

Chiluba won a second term and an MDD parliamentary majority in the 1996 elections. However, observers were critical of aspects of the conduct of the elections such as the ruling party's use of the state apparatus to its partisan advantage. Political opponents were harassed and doubts were expressed about the voter registration process itself (Venter, 2003: 8).

Towards the end of his second term, which was to be his last under the 1996 Constitution, Chiluba and supporters attempted to amend it to enable him TO run for a third term. This move was eventually defeated by opposition from within and outside his party. The 2001 presidential elections produced the anomalous result of a winning MMD candidate, Levy Mwanawasa, winning only 28.7% of the total

---

2   They were born in Malawi.

vote in a crowded field of 11. In the parliamentary elections, the MDD won only 69 of the 150 seats. Some foreign election observers doubted the honesty of the entire electoral process. Since the country's constitution does not provide for run-offs to ensure a majority poll, the new government could only rule by forging a coalition with co-opted opposition forces.

An observer of Zambian politics has suggested that during its two terms of office, the MDD 'has appeared to be more interested in consolidating its hold on power than in consolidating democracy,' (Simon, 2005: 206). Attempts to suppress opposition activities have continued under the Mwanawasa presidency. Amnesty International's Annual Report (Amnesty International, 2005) covering the year 2004 highlighted cases of arbitrary detention or harassment targeting members of the opposition and civil society leaders, journalists and even members of parliament. Opposition activities were curbed through the denial of police permits to hold rallies.

Malawi

In the early 1990s, Malawi shed off one of the longest-lasting authoritarian regimes in Africa. Hastings Kamuzu Banda had ruled the country with an iron fist through his Malawi Congress Party (MCP) one-party regime between 1966 and 1994 (Ihonvbere, 1997). In that year, Bakili Muluzi was elected president in the first multiparty elections. This appeared to open a new dawn of liberalized democratic politics. Ten years later, there were very serious questions about the extent to which the new regime was committed to truly competitive elections, including the possibility of accepting defeat at the polls.

Muluzi's United Democrat Front (UDF) did not win an absolute majority in the presidential or parliamentary elections. Its tenure was therefore potentially precarious. It resorted to the use of various means including cooptation of opponents through patronage. Concurrently, sticks were wielded. Opponents were subjected to thuggery during electoral campaigns and steps were taken to weaken the economic resources of the political barons of the Banda regime who were the leading opponents of the UDF (VonDoepp, 2005). As in Zambia and other countries, Muluzi tried to amend the constitution to remove the two-term presidential limit so as to continue in office but the attempts were defeated by opposition within and outside the regime. In 2004, the UDF presented another presidential candidate, Bingu wa Mutharika, who won in a three-way race.

The Mutharika presidency has continued some of the anti-liberal and anti-democratic practices of the previous regime. The United States State Department's Annual Human Rights report for 2005 (US, Department of State, 2006) highlighted the arrest of a man for making derogatory comments about the president at a gas station in Blantyre. The report also noted other instances of political repression, as follows:

On September 16, police arrested former DPP Vice President Gwanda Chakuamba for statements he made at a political rally after leaving government, in which he allegedly referred to the president as a "brute" and a "drunkard." Chakuamba was charged under the Protected Emblems and Names Act with insulting the president. Capital Radio, which conducted live coverage of the rally, challenged the legality of the act; the case was still pending at year's end. On March 15, journalists Raphael Tenthani and Mabvuto Banda of the independent newspaper *The Nation* were arrested for allegedly violating the Protected Emblems and Names Act. The journalists had written articles alleging that the president had moved out of his residence for fear that ghosts haunted the building. They were charged with publishing information likely to cause public alarm and were released after 24 hours. The charge was later changed to publishing information likely to insult the president. Although Tenthani and Banda were not prosecuted, the president demanded an apology and a retraction of the story. Neither journalist complied with the demand; there was no court action by year's end.

In 2006, the media continued to be subjected to intense pressure. In May, the general manager of Blantyre Newspapers Limited (BNL), and one of his reporters were charged with criminal libel for writing 'negatively' about Health Minister Hetherwick Ntaba. The article in question alleged that the minister was implicated in an audit report for failing to account for public money (Media Institute of Southern Africa, 2006).

Senegal

Senegal stands out as one of the few African countries that have maintained a liberal political system following some ten years of benign authoritarian rule after the acquisition of independence in 1960.[3] Nonetheless, there have continued to be restrictions on freedom of the press. An example occurred in July 2004 when the owner and managing editor of a private newspaper was imprisoned under a national 'security' provision for writing articles alleging executive interference in the judiciary and corruption in the customs service. He was charged with publishing 'false news' and printing 'secret government documents', both criminal charges under a law (article 80 of the penal code) that criminalizes acts deemed to 'compromise' public security or cause 'serious political disturbance'. In May 2006, the case was dropped on procedural grounds. Some 20 'criminal defamation' cases are brought against journalists every year although they do not normally result in imprisonment. Nevertheless, some Senegalese journalists have stated that the mere existence of the laws has a chilling effect on the media and inhibits a free press (Arieff, 2005).

Nigeria

Nigeria's current civilian constitution has to date been the most successful in the country's history. It is based on a liberal democratic model that presumes basic civil and political rights. For the first time in the country's history, a civilian government completed its first four-year term in 2003. Olusegun Obasanjo was re-elected for his last term that should end in 2007.

---

3 The liberal democratic regime was transformed into a benign authoritarian one-party regime shortly after the acquisition of independence in 1960. Beginning in 1976, the regime gradually returned to the pluralist model.

The civilian pluralist political regime has not fully guaranteed the basic rights of ordinary people who continued to be threatened by communal violence, armed criminals and low-level insurgency in the oil-producing Niger Delta. Freedoms of the press and expression continued to come under attack from the government. In early 2006, the National Broadcasting Commission suspended a radio station's broadcast operations on the grounds that, during a call-in show, guests and callers had made 'unguarded comments that violate provisions of the Nigeria Broadcasting Code'. Following protests by journalists and advocates of press freedom, the suspension was lifted. It was believed that the real reason for the attack on the station had to do with discussions of the apparent quest by incumbent President Obasanjo to arrange to have the country's constitution amended in order to allow him to run for a third term (Committee to Protect Journalists, 2005).

Zimbabwe

For a while after the attainment of independence under an African majority government that had won competitive multiparty elections at the end of a bitter anti-settler guerrilla war, Zimbabwe was regarded as an example of an African state that was succeeding in implementing the liberal democratic model. Within a few years, it began a slide into violence, brutal authoritarianism and economic decline.

Under the personalist leadership of Robert Mugabe, the governing ZANU-PF has all but eliminated the scope for meaning political opposition and dissent. Intimidation, bans on demonstrations, assault, assassination attempts and arraignment on 'treason' charges has been the fate of leading opposition figures (Maltz, 2006). The regime's cruel exercise of arbitrary power reached a new height in 2005 when it expelled thousands of poor people from the capital city, Harare, and other urban areas and demolished their houses and shelters. As a result of what was dubbed 'Operation Murambastsvina'[4] an estimated 700,000 people were left homeless. As justification for this measure Mugabe was reported to have said: 'We have rejected the scandalous demand... that we lower our urban housing standards to allow for mud huts, bush latrines, and pit toilets as suitable for the urban people of Zimbabwe and for Africans generally' (Cited in Kapp, 2005:1151).

Neo-Patrimonialism as a Theoretical Construct

Why have so many of the 'Third Wave' African leaders disappointed the great expectations that were aroused by the promises of democracy? The explanation is to be found in a number of interrelated aspects of the African pre-colonial, colonial and contemporary sociological and political structures. A big part of the explanation lies in the continued prevalence of neo-patrimonial political culture and processes, the relationship of state power to capital accumulation, and the anti-liberal and non-democratic historical legacies. In addition, all too many leaders have succumbed to the lures of unbridled power and glory.

---

4   Variously translated as "Restore Order" or "Clean up the Garbage".

The term 'neo-patrimonialism' has been used to describe an interrelated set of phenomena whose common characteristic is the preeminence of personal relations in administrative and political processes. It is a modification of the Weberian ideal type of personalistic government that is contrasted with the bureaucratic model. As Brinkerhoff and Goldsmith (2004: 166) put it:

> Patrimonial administration is closely associated with clientelistic politics, for administrative jobs are among the choicest plums a boss or patron can offer his protégés. Treated as a type of income-generating property, such jobs are more valuable than the equivalent posts in a state that has carefully circumscribed job descriptions.

Patrimonialism has been identified in a wide variety of settings, from traditional to semi-traditional to more modern and industrialized Western societies and in different parts of the world. One observer of the Dominican Republic has highlighted strong presidentialism, personalistic parties and weak electoral and judicial institutions as integral parts of neo-patrimonialism in the 1990s (Hartlyn, 1994). The political regimes of Syria, Iraq (under the Baathists), Libya and Tunisia have been discussed in terms of neopatrimonialism (Brownlee, 2002). The concept has been extended to the analysis of some successor states of the Soviet Union. Van Zon (2005: 19) for instance, has suggested that Ukraine exhibits the main characteristics of a neopatrimonial state and society such as an intertwining of polity and economy, sharp separation of state and society, a cult of power, the absence of the rule of law and 'a sharp distinction between formal rules and the de facto functioning of the state apparatus'.

It has been suggested that in the underdeveloped world, personal rulership is probably the dominant form of government: 'In fact, some of the new states are, properly speaking, not states at all; rather, they are virtually the private instruments of those powerful enough to rule' (Theobald, 1982: 549). Under these systems, although the state formally operates on the basis of modern bureaucratic norms, the reality is that power is held and exercised as a personal possession and is used to create and cement a network of hierarchical personal relations extending from the leader (president, prime minister, king, etc) to local leaders and communities.

As far as African experiences are concerned, over a decade ago Bratton and Van de Walle (1994) stipulated that neo-patrimonialism was 'the distinctive hallmark of African regimes' (458). In these societies, patron-client relationships are woven out of a number of ascriptive and associational networks. These include personal, clan, ethnic, linguistic, regional and political-ideological associations. The patterns are complex, cutting across each other. It is the ascriptive bases of these networks that are often superficially described as 'tribalism', ethnicity, regionalism or religious sectarianism.

Writing about Cameroon, Charles Fonchingong (2004: 45) has stated that those in power are inclined to share it with a very small coterie of collaborators: 'Often, the state is effectively privatised in the control of this small group, whose most powerful members are usually drawn from the leader's community, religious faith, geographical region or ethnic base.' The general effect of neo-patrimonialism in the country is a society marked by ethnocentrism, clientelism, corruption, bribery, regionalism, nepotism and other tendencies that undermined economic growth, prospects for liberalization and democratization and respect for human rights.

Like all traditional societies, patrimonialism was the dominant mode of pre-colonial governance. The limited bureaucratization of the African administrative and social institutions and partial incorporation into the modern economic and class structures have enabled patrimonial values and practices to survive. A visit to any African minister or senior government official's office gives one the impression of a mini monarchical court full of supplicants looking for all kinds of favors. In different ways, this scene is duplicated wherever powerful people who control financial and other resources are accessible to the public. This does not take account of what must necessarily be clandestine encounters between the patrons and clients who have rewards to give to the former.

The centrality of the African post-colonial state has enormous significance for the persistence of patriamonialism and the weakness of liberal democratic foundations. The colonial state was from the beginning the main agent of economic and social infrastructural development. In the post-colonial era, there was no alternative but to continue and even expand the leading role of the state through various forms of state capitalism. Not surprisingly, holding political power and bureaucratic employment, particularly at the higher levels, became the shortest path to wealth and 'the good life'. Even for those who sought their fortune in private enterprise, connections with the state are vital. It provides contracts, trading licenses, access to foreign exchange (before the economic liberalization of the 1980s and 1990s) and other scarce resources. Connections and influence are translated into economic assets and opportunities. It has been pointed out, for instance, that Nigeria's private sector depends on the government for patronage: 'Most of the private sector businesses, such as banks, airlines and construction companies, are either owned by public servants, serving or retired, directly or indirectly' (Shehu, 2004:77).

From the 1990s, the International Financial Institutions and Western governments pushed for the privatization of state and para-statal enterprises that were involved in production, distribution and service activities. The aim was to minimize the opportunities for patrimonial abuse and also promote a private sector that would increase opportunities for the growth of a vigorous civil society. However, in the short run at least, the processes of privatization themselves fed into patrimonial mechanisms.

A study of the Ugandan experience with privatization in the 1990s demonstrated that government personnel:

> used their considerable discretion to favour those with whom they had close political and kinship connections. They also turned a blind eye to various irregularities...especially when close ethnic and political loyalists were acquiring public companies (Tangri and Mwenda, 2001, 127).

Parliament and the media denounced these practices and forced the resignation of some of the ministers who were most directly implicated. After a year or two, two of them were re-instated into the government without any explanation regarding their previous censure. One of them is the brother-in-law of President Museveni.

Patrimonial politics is accentuated in states which are dependent on mineral resources. These economies make it easier for leaders to ignore rural and other sectors of the economy and concentrate on controlling and acquiring substantial amounts of the mineral rents. Gold, diamonds and similar resources produce limited upward and downward linkages. Even the oil sector's multiplier effects can be limited when the regime does not take trouble to create associated chemical and other industries.

In 2006, oil exports accounted for 20 percent of Nigeria's GDP, 95 percent of foreign exchange earnings, and about 65 percent of its budgetary revenues. By 1999, it was estimated that up to US$107 billion of the country's wealth was held abroad.[5] Former military dictator Sani Abacha is reported to have salted away an astounding US$13 billion in 42 accounts during his four years in power (1996-2000) (Malgwi, 2004).[6] In 2005, Nigeria's GDP per capita was estimated to be US$1,000. In 2000, some 60 percent of the population was deemed to be living below the poverty line and other estimates put the figure as high as 70 percent.

One observer has suggested that the following conditions sustain corrupt practices in Nigeria: a poor reward system; lack of economic opportunities for individuals; pressures of the extended family system; the oil industry 'providing the most lucrative and immediate opportunity for illicit enrichment by the privileged elites'; laxity in moral codes; inefficient law enforcement; tendency to dictatorship 'as a carry-over of the prolonged military administration.' He argues that 'All these create a vicious cycle in relation to corruption' (Shehu, 2004: 69).

The Republic of Congo is another example of an oil-dependent economy where patrimonial behavior has created opportunities for venality and abuse of power for personal economic gain. The Sassou Nguesso regime came to power as a result of a brief civil war that ended the country's democratic experiment between 1992 and 1997 (Clark, 2005). It has since reportedly continued the practice of diverting large amounts of national wealth into the hands of the leaders and their clients. Blurring public and private assets, the regime has used offshore shell companies to sustain venality in the country's key economic sector. An estimated one third of the country's oil income appears to be unaccounted for in its budget (Global Witness, 2005).

In typical patrimonial fashion, in 2005, the head of the state *Société Nationale des Pétroles* (the National Petroleum Company-SNPC), a close advisor to President Sassou Ngouesso, IS the majority shareholder in the African Oil and Gas Corporation (AOGC) and owner of other oil companies which engaged in oil purchase and sales business with the SNPC. It is also worth noting that the head of *Cotrade*, a subsidiary of SNPC that is charged with marketing the country's oil, is the president's son (Global Witness, 2005).

Angola suffered from the ravages of some 27 years of civil war starting just before the end of Portuguese imperialism in 1975. It has enormous wealth in land, water, oil and diamonds. Under the regime of the *Movimento Popular de Libertação de Angola* (the People's Movement for the Liberation of Angola-MPLA) since 1975, José Eduardo dos Santos has been president for most of that period. Since the achievement of independence, the country's resources have been lost through warfare

---

5 Not all of this wealth is necessarily the fruit of illicit and illegal activities.
6 Some sources give a lower figure of around $5billion.

and massive corruption. One observer has noted that oil revenues 'disappear into a "Bermuda triangle" comprising the state oil company SONANGOL, the presidency and the Finance Ministry, never to reappear' (Munslow, 1999: 552). More recently, it has been reported that more than US$1billion in oil revenue is lost every year. These funds are controlled by SONANGOL and the president' office. Much of the money is deposited in secret offshore bank accounts (McMillan, 2005: 159). The sad irony is that until recently, the MPLA defined itself and was seriously perceived as a Marxist-Leninist party.

Other Explanatory Factors

One consequence of European imperial rule in Africa was the creation of centralized states that generally enjoyed a monopoly of modern weapons. This sharply contrasts with the pre-colonial period when more evenly dispersed possession of military and civilian technological capabilities served as a brake on the exercise of arbitrary power even in relatively centralized despotic states like Buganda (Wrigley, 1996). Rebellious princes or governors would have access to the same types of weapons that the rulers had. The creation of military and police forces equipped with modern weapons has meant that small groups of people can now dominate a state and even terrorize it for long periods of time. The experiences of Idi Amin in Uganda and Macias Nguema in Equatorial Guinea in the 1970s readily come to mind.

Centralized monopoly of the means of destruction has been successfully challenged by opposition forces in a number of countries. Chad, Uganda, Ethiopia, Eritrea, Liberia, Congo (Zaire), Rwanda, Sudan and Ivory Coast are some of the more prominent cases. Quite often, these challenges have been motivated by ethnic, regional or religious concerns and have resulted in prolonged and indecisive civil wars.

Patrimonial practices are also reinforced by pre-colonial traditions of deference GIVEN to rulers such as kings, and chiefs, elders, men, nobles, priests and the like by commoners, subjects, women and the 'laity'. This deference was reinforced by the colonial regime. Under indirect rule, deference was demanded not only under the traditional cultural norms but also the new political structures. Governors, colonial administrators, foreign missionaries and all those who exercised authority over the subject peoples tended to demand servility in their relations with africans. These practices have been carried over to the post-colonial era. Any one who visits government offices is struck by the awe with which the Ministers, Permanent Secretaries and other senior official are held. The waiting rooms of Ministers, Senior Army officers and all people who hold power are often filled with supplicants looking for various kinds of personal favors. These favors are extended through the use of public resources whether it is money, scholarships, a note to another official who can provide a valuable service or a useful telephone call.[7]

---

7 Hansen's (2003) fascinating description of the visit of a Cameroonian Minister to his home region, including the grant of an undisclosed sum of money in cash to a leading local community leader, illustrates the feudalistic relationship between power holders and ordinary citizens.

This deferential culture creates role expectations which even the most secular- and high-minded find difficult to resist. It also increases the stakes of political power at all levels of society and the temptation to blur the lines between public and private authority and resources. From the perspective of democratization, it is an obstacle because it makes it harder to generate the ethos of equality and political efficacy that are necessary for a democratic polity.

Another significant obstacle to liberalism and equality—a basic assumption of democracy—is patriarchy and the related gerontocratic elements in many African cultures. Where equality is denied in such a fundamental sphere of inter-personal relations as gender, it is likely to encourage the persistence of inequality in other spheres (McFadden, 2005). Nearly 20 years ago, Parpart (1988: 218) pointed out that the most important consequences of female underrepresentation occurred in the economic and legal spheres. In spite of formal political rights and equal access to education, a gender-biased mixture of colonial and customary law still operated, especially in matters relating to land, marriage, divorce and inheritance.

In spite of the new reformist currents currently blowing across the continent, the issue of women's equal access to property, particularly land, remains contentious in many African states. The issue is directly tied to the cultural and normative challenge of redefining gender relations. This fundamental change is resisted even by those who have otherwise been revolutionary.[8] It is nevertheless undeniable that women have made remarkable progress in political and social representation. There are significant numbers of women in cabinets, parliamentary and other representative bodies, managerial and professional positions. In 2005, Ellen Johnson-Sirleaf became the first African woman to be elected president in a direct election in Liberia when she beat a male opponent.[9] On the other hand, as in other Third World regions, women who have achieved leadership positions and recognition have generally been highly educated middle class women. In a sense, their class status and personal qualities have trumped their gender as disabilities in patriarchical societies. The overwhelming majority of peasant and poor urban women do not have these resources and levers that can hoist them into male-dominated powerful positions.

The examples discussed above reflect a number of crucial obstacles to the political and social development of the African continent. One such is weak civil society which does not provide an effective countervailing force to power holders. Then also there is the continuing role of the state as the main instrument of the accumulation of wealth and a patrimonial political and social culture that largely prevailed in pre-colonial social formations, was sustained during the colonial regime by partial economic and political modernization and political authoritarianism, and has been strengthened in the post-colonial era. Civil society is understood in this context to refer to modern organized forces that are not directly political which

---

8   McFadden (2005: 12) quotes President Robert Mugabe warning Zimbabwean women who were demanding equal access to land ownership against "such 'culturally unacceptable' demands".

9   It is worth noting that although women had come into executive positions in Europe, Asia and Latin America, in most of those cases, they were chosen in parliamentary systems where the vote was not national.

have the potential to provide the sources of legitimacy for the political, social and economic institutions. The weakness of civil society stems from the economic underdevelopment of society.

Important aspects of globalization have accentuated the problem of neo-patrimonialism. Contemporary communications technology has created a global consumer culture dominated by images of the affluent West. Elites in Africa and elsewhere increasingly measure their economic success in terms of the lifestyle of the rich in North America and Europe. African and other Third World cities are clogged with luxury cars whose owners often live in mansions equipped with the latest entertainment and communications technology available on the world market. In order to afford this lifestyle, one must find resources outside the official regular wages. This is a major catalyst of venality and a contributor to patrimonial politics.[10]

Abuses of Power: Nature and Causes

The term 'corruption' is often used to describe a broad range of activities involving the direct or indirect use of public authority or power. It evokes normative judgments that vary with context and culture. in this discussion the broader concept of 'abuse of power' is preferred because it avoids the narrowly moralistic connotations of the term 'corruption' and focuses on the more general behavioral and causal aspects of this pathology. The idea of abuse of power is not itself devoid of normative connotations but the standard of judgement is simpler and essentially empirical. It refers to any political and administrative behavior that is designed to benefit office holders in ways that violate the public interest as defined in constitutional, administrative and political norms of democracy and social justice. Such behavior would range from venality through nepotism to discrimination based on ascriptive characteristics to various forms of blackmail.

Abuse of the public charge is universal and situationally ubiquitous. The difference is that in some societies, it operates at higher levels and does not directly affect the citizen. In others, like the United States, where most of the economy is in private corporate hands, a lot of the venality takes place within the corporation or in its contractual relations with the state at different levels.

In Africa and other Third World societies, it is not only ubiquitous but infuses all aspects of public life from the lowest to the highest level. It is not only politicians and bureaucrats who solicit bribes to perform a service. The gatekeeper outside a government or parastatal agency premises will demand money or some other 'reward' for letting in people he deems to be ordinary citizens without the power to punish this abuse. He almost certainly suspects that the visitor is looking for some illicit favors from the political and bureaucratic barons and baronesses. Petty functionaries

---

10 McSherry (2006) has pointed out that tiny oil-producing Equatorial Guinea's President Teodoro Obiang Nguema bought a multimillion dollar mansion outside Washington, D.C. "His son Teodorin has become a regular in Manhattan, Hollywood and Paris, where he is famous for driving his many fancy cars up and down the Champs-Elysees (sic)," (26).

will demand a bribe to put a passport application on top of the pile that some senior official, possibly a minister, must sign before it is issued. The examples are endless.

All these forms of abuse thrive best when there is limited political accountability. The roots are primarily to be found within the societies in question. However, there are also international dimensions. The more dramatic and lucrative forms of venal corruption involve dealings with foreign investors, service providers and vendors of multi-million (US) dollar goods and services. Foreign, particularly Western economic interests are often complicit in the illicit diversion of economic resources from the continent.

A major factor in the sustenance of patrimonial and unaccountable governance stems from the impact of financial flows into the continent—generally defined as 'foreign aid'.[11] This aspect of post-World War II and post-colonial international politics has been critiqued from different angles (Easterly, 2006; Calderisi, 2006). From the point of view of patrimonialism and misgovernment, at least two negative consequences for good governance flow from the availability of these resources. The incentive on the part of political elites to invest in the countries' resources in order to facilitate the extraction of taxes is made less urgent. The second and related effect is to enable the political and bureaucratic elites to engage in profligate expenditures and personal conspicuous consumption at public expense. Infusion of foreign funds reduces the possibilities of revolts by unpaid civil servants or security forces.

Examples of wasteful expenditures on the political and bureaucratic elites abound. For example, in 2006, members of the Kenyan Parliament decided to increase their monthly travel allowances from US$3,500 to US$4,800.00. Since the elections of 2002, which led to the first transfer of power from the incumbent to the opposition coalition, the parliamentarians have increased their monthly pay from US$5,600 to $7,000, excluding allowances.[12] In 2005, Kenya's GDP (PPP) per capita was estimated to be US$1,200. In neighboring Uganda, in 2006, the 317 Members of Parliament were each set to receive a monthly package of salary and allowance of approximately US$6,000 per month (Mutumba, 2006). A Ugandan has observed that being a Member of Parliament is one of the best jobs in the country.

In March 2006, in the course of investigations into the illegal diversion of funds donated to Uganda by the Global Fund to Fight AIDS, Malaria and Tuberculosis, it was revealed that some Shs.42 million (approximately US$23,000) was used to pay a former minister's hospital bill in a Kenyan hospital. The expenditure was authorized by the Minister of Health who stated that he had received a directive to effect the payment from the President and had no apologies to give for his decision

---

11 The term "foreign aid" is misleading because it suggests an altruistic activity that is presumed to benefit the country at the receiving end. However, this assumption is often brought into question in concrete cases when the "aid" involves purchase or donation of weapons that, at best, benefits a small segment of the population; when loans are counted as aid; when aid is used to prop up dictatorial regimes for the strategic interests of the giver; and when it is directed to inappropriate schemes for the benefit of those in power and foreign financial or political interests.

12 Backdated to July 2005, the move would cost the country some $280m. See "Maathai Condemns Kenyan MP's Pay," BBC News, Africa, accessed on 5/12/06 at http://news.bbc.co.uk/2/hi/africa/4976046.stm.

because the ex-minister was a 'freedom fighter'.[13] In 2006, the country's per capita GDP was US$1,700.00.

The obstacles to the emergence of political leaders of exceptional vision, personal integrity and self-abnegation are clearly formidable. This kind of leaders are rare anywhere. It is even harder to nurture them in societies with weak political and social institutions and patrimonial cultural patterns. Nevertheless, Africa's post-colonial history has shown that individuals can make a difference. Idi Amin in Uganda and Macias Nguema in Equatorial Guinea sullied the African political stage in the 1970s with their bloody and grotesque regimes. However, at the same time Seretse Khama in Botswana and Julius Nyerere in Tanzania demonstrated that one could rule with integrity and even idealism.[14] In spite of his undeniable flaws, Nkrumah was an idealist who clearly tried to do the best. SO WAS Samora Machel in Mozambique.

Some of the leaders who came to power after waging heroic guerilla struggles, such as Robert Mugabe in Zimbabwe, Yoweri Museveni in Uganda, Paul Kagame in Rwanda, Isaias Afewerki in Eritrea and Meles Zenawi in Ethiopia initially appeared to promise self-less and enlightened leadership against heavy odds. However, in due course, they turned out to be less committed to tolerance and political pluralism.[15] Under the radically different circumstances of apartheid, South Africa's Nelson Mandela's exemplary human and leadership qualities have marked him out as a truly new type of leader and an African iconic figure.

---

13 The former Minister, Matthew Rukikaire, was a leading member of the National Resistance Movement during its 6-year guerrilla struggle that brought Museveni to power. The story, "Global Fund Money Diverted to Former Minister's Hospital Bill" appeared at the Simba/fm Website (http://simba.fm/index.php?option=content&task=view&id=6387&Item=2), March 22, 2006.

14 The fact that Nyerere's utopian socialism turned out to be a failure and his benign authoritarianism do not detract from his exemplary self-abnegation.

15 The governments of all five of them have been subject to regular human rights criticisms. In its report covering the previous year, Human Rights Watch (2006) stated that "The aftermath of Ethiopia's landmark May 2005 parliamentary elections has laid bare the deeply entrenched patterns of political repression, human rights abuse and impunity that characterize the day-to-day reality of governance in much of the country." On Eritrea, it reported, "(The Eritrean) government's tyranny became more ruthless in 2005. Rule by force and caprice remains the norm, as the government aggressively moves to intimidate the population and to isolate it from the outside world." The report highlighted repressive actions by the Mugabe regime in Zimbabwe: "The government continues to introduce repressive laws that suppress criticism of its political and economic policies. In August, parliament passed the Constitutional Amendment Act, which gives the government the right to expropriate land and property without the possibility of judicial appeal, and to withdraw passports from those it deems a threat to national security." The Uganda report made reference to assaults on political rights in the period before the 2006 General Elections: "Opposition politicians critical of the government faced increased threats to their safety and freedom with the stakes rising higher as the March 2006 presidential election date approached." Amnesty International's 2005 report (2006) pointed to continuing pressures on the opposition in Rwanda: "Members of the political opposition, the independent news media and civil society were harassed, arrested and unlawfully detained."

Zenawi and Aferwerki have expended thousands of lives and enormous economic resources to wage a border war between their countries and have repressed the domestic opposition. Museveni has succumbed to ethnic and regional patrimonialism, venality and political intolerance. Kagame has presided over a benign ethnic-based authoritarian regime which has restricted political contestation. By 2006, Mugabe had been in power in Zimbabwe for some 26 years and had presided over the country's steady descent into authoritarianism and economic decline. The experiences of the erstwhile revolutionaries in power suggest that the steely determination that a successful revolutionary needs to succeed is probably not suitable for post-revolutionary leadership. After the revolution, force must give way to accommodation, compromises and reconciliation. This analysis probably best explains some of the more prominent negative aspects of the erswhile revolutionary leades such as intolerance and the ready willingness to resort to force.

The Future of African Political Leadership

Objective cultural, structural and economic conditions clearly set the context within which contemporary African political leadership is best analyzed. This includes the international dimension. The fundamental changes that increasing globalization is bringing to bear on the African continent will undoubtedly play a big part in determining the future. Among other things, globalization is imposing the reign of capitalism and pushing it into all corners of global society. The individuation that accompanies this process is likely to rapidly weaken the cultural and political foundations of patrimonialism. The creation of large gaps between the political and bureaucratic class and the burgeoning population of the lumpenproletariat and workers in the cities as well as the increasingly marginalized peasantry in the rural areas will all help accentuate the issue of class and political power.

Globalization is also rapidly spreading the norms of greater democracy and individual rights. Liberal democracy in some form is increasingly the dominant basis of the internal and external legitimacy of political regimes. At the continental level, through the New Partnership for African Development (NEPAD, 2001), particularly its Peer Review Mechanism (APRM), African leaders have come to accept this reality. The Peer Review process is intended to be a voluntary exercise whereby states invite an examination of their performance in the areas of (a) democracy and political governance, (b) economic governance, (c) corporate governance, and (d) socio-economic development. It is expected to be non-adversarial (unlike many international and regional human rights mechanisms) and designed to encourage serious efforts to improve performance.

Four types of reviews are envisaged. The 'base' review is to be carried out within 18 months of accession to the process. This will be followed by the drafting of a Program of Action designed to guide progress towards achievement of the stipulated goals and standards by the state concerned. Periodic reviews are then conducted every two to four years; they are designed to ascertain progress towards achieving mutually agreed goals and compliance with agreed political, economic and corporate governance values, codes and standards as outlined in the Declaration on Democracy, Political, Economic and Corporate Governance (NEPAD, 2002). Other reviews could be arranged when a country chooses to invite the APRM system to carry it out 'for its own reasons' and when participating Heads of State decide that an impending crisis in a member country warrants a review as a form of assistance (NEPAD, 2005).

The APRM is overseen by a Committee of Participating Heads of State and Governments known as the APR Forum (APF). Below this committee is a 7-person Panel of Eminent Persons which exercises oversight over the process. It is assisted by a Secretariat that provides technical and administrative support.

Since 2003, the different elements of the APRM have been assembled and put in motion. By mid-2006, twenty-six countries had applied for the APR process (i.e. Algeria, Angola, Benin, Burkina Faso, Cameroon, Republic of Congo, Egypt, Ethiopia, Gabon, Ghana, Kenya, Lesotho, Malawi, Mali, Mauritius, Mozambique, Nigeria, Rwanda, São Tomé e Príncipe, Senegal, Sierra Leone, South Africa, Sudan, Tanzania, Uganda, and Zambia) and the process was advanced in countries such as Algeria, Benin, Ghana, Kenya, Mauritius, Nigeria, Rwanda and South Africa. One of the reasons the APRM is potentially important is the emphasis it puts on involving political and civil society organizations. It explicitly provides for the involvement of political parties, parliamentarians, and representatives of civil society organizations, including the media, academia, trade unions, business and professional bodies. It has to be assumed that, at least in the medium to long term, a state's involvement in the APRM processes legitimizes liberal and democratic discourse in ways that would be difficult to reverse.

Some observers have expressed skepticism about the 'good governance' potential of African civil society. Neo-patrimonialism has been cited as an important problem (Taylor, 2004). From a different perspective, Chabal and Daloz (1999: 21) have suggested that the state in Africa 'is so poorly institutionalized, so weakly emancipated from society, that there is very little scope for conceptualizing politics in Africa as a contest between a functionally strong state and a homogeneous coherent civil society.' These perspectives can lead to an underestimation of the political potential of African civil society organizations. Although relatively weak, they can mobilize significant segments of the population and bring about political and social change. Most analysts of the political movements that swept away authoritarian regimes in the 1980s and 1990s point to the central role of such organizations as religious bodies, labor unions, business organizations, public interest NGO's, and the media (Nugent, 2004: 368-433).

Economic and social forces are also undermining important aspects of African societies. Urbanization and the greater role of capitalist economic and social relations can be expected to erode patrimonial networks. As the process of class formation proceeds—especially as the urban based bureaucratic class and its allies accumulate wealth through access to the state—there is a desire to acquire a degree of security in one's possessions. Continuation of neo-patrimonialism makes it difficult to ensure such security. Wealth acquired through methods deemed by society to be illegitimate is always insecure. Often, the downfall of a regime leads to flight and dispossession of those who were the principal beneficiaries of the previous political order.

Neo-patriamonialism tends to promote hypocrisy and cynicism. Office seekers and those pursuing other kinds of favors sing the praises of the leader and the regime until it weakens, at which point, some of them desert it and often serve the next as fervently as they did the old. Schatzberg (2001: 130-36) has reported on the *volte face* of some former prominent members of the Mobutu regime in the Congo (Zaïre) who deserted as it crumbled in the early 1990s. If this reading of neo-patrimonialism is correct, it can be assumed that most segments of the people would welcome an alternative to the prevailing conditions.

Bracking (2005) has reported on the economic changes in Zimbabwe which are creating challenges to some of the major kinship norms that underpin traditional patrimonial networks. The poverty of the rural people leads them to put moral pressure on the urban, relatively better-off kin to share their material resources. However, increasingly, the latter are adopting the nuclear family model and are reluctant to share more than a limited amount of their resources. Globalization and the introduction of market relations can be expected to increase processes of individuation that undermine the communal bases of patrimonialism. There are already professional and interest associational groups that cut across prescriptive identities such as labor unions, journalists associations, lawyers associations, women's groups and the like. By embracing liberalization and good governance through NEPAD and the APRM, governments slowly but surely open the gates to demands for social reform and change that they will find increasingly difficult to close.

It is also significant that NEPAD highlights the promotion of women as one of the goals of the project. This commitment provides a useful ideological tool that can be effectively used in the struggles for gender equality. The improvement of the female condition will reflect the successful outcome of a cultural revolution that will most likely be seen in increased freedom and equality in other areas of private and public life. It would be one major building block for the creation of more democratic societies.

Extra-continental agents can play a positive role in the promotion of democracy. A lot of the mismanagement, authoritarianism and venality of African leaders has been abetted or ignored by powerful foreign official and unofficial interests because of narrow economic and political interests. The long-term support of Mobutu in Zaire (Congo) and the hapless Samuel Doe in Liberia by the West are only the most notorious examples. If the West is serious about the liberalization and democratization of Africa, a number of positive actions can be taken. Since most of the money that is illicitly obtained by venal leaders and others is deposited in Western banks, Western governments should assist in the recovery and return of these assets. in terms of international economic policies, Opening Western markets to African agricultural exports would not only increase the region's wealth but would also have a greater and more direct positive impact on the mass of peasant producers than traditional 'aid' flows.

More favorable socio-economic conditions would reduce the need to look for heroic leaders. Self-sustaining economic and social change would eventually mean that institutions matter more than men or women. Heroic leadership would always be appreciated but it would not be so vital for the destiny of millions.

Conclusions

Africa entered the new millennium with a certain degree of optimism about its economic and political future. The last decade of the 20th century had seen the collapse of repressive authoritarian regimes and their replacement by more liberal political systems modeled on democratic governance. Some observers doubt the authenticity of the 'democratic awakening'. They point to the evident limitations of the changes and the continuation of patrimonial and authoritarian tendencies. Many of the new regimes still fall into the category of 'illiberal democracies'. In some states, authoritarianism has managed to survive the democratizing trends. Examples include Gabon, Cameroon and the Republic of the Congo. And in others, civil war prevails. Such is the fate of Somalia, Ivory Coast, Congo, and Sudan. In the economic realm, there are signs of slow recovery in a number of countries. Real Gross Domestic Product in the region grew at a rate of 5.3 percent in 2004 and 4.9 percent in 2005. Nevertheless, poverty, the scourge of AIDS and physical and social insecurity continues to afflict millions.

The limits of liberalization and democratization should not obscure the significance of the political openings towards pluralism. Even where authoritarianism has persisted, there is usually increased political and civic space for participation and contestation. External pressures, courageous individuals in the media and segments of civil society have continued to resist political repression and push for change where the more recalcitrant autocrats continue to reign. All in all, there is room for optimism on both the political and economic fronts.

The role of political leadership is as crucial now as it was at the time of decolonization because the leaders are placed in the role of founders of new polities. How they manage power, their vision, strengths and weaknesses will have a long term impact. Some external factors can be helpful. An international trade regime that facilitates African primary and even manufactured exports would reduce the need for 'aid' infusions that are usually motivated by political rather than genuine developmental needs. To the extent that there is scope for aid, it should be directed to the people through grassroots local organizations, whenever they exist. International NGOs would be a second best alternative. However, they should spend at least as much effort helping nurture indigenous transformative civil society organizations as providing direct relief to the afflicted or poor and others in need of assistance. That would be true aid.

Internally, economic and social change, the nurture and consolidation of civil society at the grassroots, and democratization must be part of one seamless transformative process. As strong civil society institutions emerge, political parties will have to gradually move away from their dominant patrimonial concerns and become true representatives of secular and civic concerns or at least universalist class interests. Under those circumstances, the fate of the region would not be as dependent on the vagaries of political leadership as they now are.

Imperial rule began the process of transforming African societies. Globalization is continuing the process at a more rapid pace. Even as patrimonialism persists and takes on new forms, processes of class formation are proceeding apace. Africa, like other parts of the Third World, is rapidly urbanizing. This has the effect of weakening some of the traditional foundations of patrimonialism. Ethnic and regional ties tend to be eroded as material and other kinds of cross-cutting interests become more salient. As more people grow up outside their traditional ethnic locales, they adopt more general, often urban, social identitites that cut across ethnic and linguistic boundaries. This transformation makes it easier to establish personal as well as professional networks that cut across ascriptive cleavages. These processes should gradually weaken communal patrimonialism. These transformations should strengthen the evolution of secular civic forces that will induce more liberalization and democratization.

Finally, it is worth noting that observers and citizens of African countries do sometimes become too impatient and lose perspective. In many ways, the efforts of liberalization and democratization over the last decade constitute a fresh start. Political and civil society institutions—particularly the executive, legislature, electoral mechanisms, public and private interest groups—will need a very long time before they attain strength and efficacy. What we are witnessing are efforts to carry out revolutionary changes in the political culture of the region. This is the work of decades and more. Along the way, there will be inevitable twists and turns and detours.

References

Alence, Rod. (2004). "Political Institutions and Developmental Governance in Sub-Saharan Africa," *The Journal of Modern African Studies*, Vol. 42, No. 2, (June 2004).

Amnesty International. (2005). *Amnesty International Report 2005, the State of the World's Human Rights*. Chapters on Zambia and Rwanda.

Arieff, Alexis. (2005). *Freedom... with Limits, Senegal's Leaders Promise New Rights, While Its Laws Deny Them*, Committee to Protect Journalists. Accessed on 4/29/2006 at http://www.cpj.org/Briefings/2005/senegal_05/senegal_05.html

Arnold, Guy. (2005). *Africa, A Modern History*, London: Atlantic Books.

Bracking, Sarah. (2005). "Guided Miscreants: Liberalism, Myopias, and the Politics of Representation," *World Development*, Vol. 33, No. 6.

Bratton, Michael and Nicolas Van de Walle, "Neopatrimonial Regimes and Political Transitions in Africa," *World Politics*, Vol. 46, No. 4.

Brinkerhoff, Derick, W. and Arthur A. Goldsmith. (2004). "Good Governance, Clientelism, and Patrimonialism: New Perspectives on Old Problems," *International Management Journal*, Vol. 7, No. 2, 166.

Brownlee, Jason. (2002). "...And Yet They Persist: Explaining Survival and Transition in Neopatrimonial Regimes," *Studies in Comparative International Development*, Vol. 37, No. 3, Fall 2002.

Calderisi, Robert. (2006). *The Trouble with Africa*, New York: Palgrave Macmillan.

Chabal, Patrick and Jean-Pascal Daloz, (1999). *Africa Works, Disorder as Political Instrument*, Oxford, UK & Bloomington, USA: James Currey & Indiana University Press.

Clark, John F. (2005). "The Collapse of the Democratic Experiment in the Republic of Congo: A Thick Description," in Leonardo A. Villalón & Peter VonDoepp, eds., *The Fate of Africa's Democratic Experiments, Elites and Institutions*, Bloomington and Indianapolis: Indiana University Press.

Committee to Protect Journalists. (2005). "NIGERIA: Radio Station's Political Programs and Call-in Shows Suspended," *Cases, 2006.*

Easterly, William. (2006). *The White Man's Burden*, New York: the Penguin Press.

Ellis, Stephen. (2006), "The Roots of African Corruption," *Current History*, Vol. 105, Issue. 691 (May 2006).

Fonchingong, Charles, C. (2004). "The Travails of Democratization in Cameroon in the Context of Political Liberalization Since the 1990s," *African and Asian Studies*, Vol. 3, No. 1.

Global Witness. (2005). "The Riddle of the Sphynx: Where has Congo's Oil Money Gone?" (December). Accessed on 5/11/06 at http://www.globalwitness.org/

Hansen, Ketil F. (2003). "The Politics of Personal Relations: Beyond Neopatrimonial Practices in Northern Cameroon," *Africa*, Vol. 73, No. 2.

Hartlyn, Jonathan. (1994). "Crisis-Ridden Elections (Again) in the Dominican Republic: Neo-Patrimonialism, Presidentialism, and Weak Electoral Oversight," *Journal of Interamerican Studies & World Affairs*, Vol. 36, Issue 4, (Winter 1994).

Human Rights Watch. (2006). *World Report, 2006*. Chapters on Eritrea, Uganda, Zimbabwe, and Ethiopia.

Hyden, Goran. (2006). *African Politics in Comparative Perspective*, New York: Cambridge University Press.

Ihonvbere, Julius, O. "From Despotism to Democracy: the Rise of Multiparty Politics in Malawi," *Third World Quarterly*, Vol. 18, No. 2.

Jackson, Robert H. & Carl G. Rosberg. (1982). *Personal Rule in Black Africa.* Berkeley: University of California.

Kapp, Clare. (2005). "Operation 'Restore Order' Wreaks Havoc in Zimbabwe," *The Lancet*, Vol. 366, Issue 9492.

MacSherry, Brendan. (2006). "The Political Economy of Oil in Equatorial Guinea," *African Studies Quarterly*, 8, No. 3 (Online) URL: http://web.africa.ufl.edu/asq/v8/v8i3a2.htm.

Malgwi, Charles A. (2004). "Fraud as Economic Terrorism: the Efficacy of the Nigerian Economic and Financial Crimes Commission," *Journal of Financial Crime*, Vol. 12, Issue 2.

Maltz, Gideon. (2006). "Zimbabwe After Mugabe," *Current History*, Vol. 105, Issue. 691 (May 2006).

McFadden, Patricia. (2005). "Becoming Postcolonial, African Women Changing the Meaning of Citizenship," *Meridians: Feminism, Race, Transnationalism*, Vol. 6, No. 1.

McMillan, John. (2005). "Promoting Transparency in Angola," *Journal of Democracy*, Vol. 16, No. 3.

Media Institute of Southern Africa. (2006). "Malawi: Newspaper Manager And Reporter Charged With Criminal Libel for Article Critical of Health Minister," May 30, 2006.

Munslow, Barry. (1999). "Angola: the Politics of Unsustainable Development," *Third World Quarterly*, Vol. 20, No. 3.

Mutumba, Richard. (2006). "MPs to Get Shs10 billion in June," *Daily Monitor*, Kampala, (May 31, 2006).

New Partnership for African Development. (2001). *The New Partnership for African Development (NEPAD)*, Founding Document accessed on 6/3/06 at http://www.nepad.org/2005/files/documents/inbrief.pdf.

New Partnership for African Development. (2002). *Declaration on Democracy, Political, Economic and Corporate Governance*. Accessed on 11/26/05 at http://www.nepad.org/2005/files/aprm.php.

New Partnership for African Development. (2005). *African Peer Review Mechanism, (Base Document)*, Accessed on 11/26/05 at http://www.nepad.org/2005/files/apram/php.

Nugent, Paul. (2004). *Africa Since Independence*, Houndmills, Basingstoke, Hampshire, U.K. & New York: Palgrave Macmillan.

Oloka-Oyango, J. (2004). "'New Breed' Leadership, Conflict and Reconstruction in the Great Lakes Region of Africa: A Sociopolitical Biography of Uganda's Yoweri Kaguta Museveni," *Africa Today*, Vol. 50, Issue 3, (Spring).

Parpart, Jane L. (1988). "Women and the State in Africa," in Donald Rothchild and Naomi Chazan, eds., *The Precarious Balance, State & Society in Africa*, Boulder & London: Westview Press.

Shatzberg, Michael, G. (2001). *Political Legitimacy in Middle Africa*, Bloomington: Indiana University Press.

Shehu, Abdullahi, Y. (2004). "Combating Corruption in Nigeria—Bliss or Bluster?" *Journal of Financial Crime*, 12, 1.

Simon, David, J. (2005). "Democracy Unrealized: Zambia's Third Republic Under Frederick Chiluba," in *The Fate of Africa's Democratic Experiments*, Leonardo A. Villalón & Peter VonDoepp, (eds.), Bloomington and Indianapolis: Indiana University Press, 2005.

Tangri, Roger and Andrew Mwenda, "Corruption and Cronyism in Uganda's Privatization in the 1990s," *African Affairs*, Vol. 100, Vol. 117 (2001).

Taylor, Ian. (2004). "NEPAD Ignores the Fundamental Politics of Africa," *Contemporary Review*, Vol. 285, no. 1662.

Theobald, Robin. (1982). "Patrimonialism," *World Politics*, Vol. 34, No. 4, (Jul. 1982).

Tripp, M. Aili. (2004). "The Changing Face of Authoritarianism in Africa: the Case of Uganda." *Africa Today*, 50, no. 3 -2.

U.S., Department of State, Bureau of Democracy, Human Rights, and Labor. (2006). *2005 Country Reports on Human Rights Practices*. (Malawi).

Van de Walle, Nicolas. (2003). "Presidentialism and Clientelism in Africa's Emerging Party Systems," *The Journal of Modern African Studies*, Vol. 41, Issue 2.

Van Zon, Hans. (2005). "Political Culture and Neo-Patrimonialism Under Leonid Kuchma," *Problems of Post-Communism*, September/October, 2005.

Venter, Denis. (2003). "Democracy and Multiparty Politics in Africa: Recent Elections in Zambia, Zimbabwe, and Lesotho," *East African Social Science Research Review* 19, No. 1.

VonDoepp, Peter. (2005). "The Problem of Judicial Control in Africa's Neopatrimonial Democracies: Malawi and Zambia," *Political Science Quarterly* 120 No. 2 275-301.

Wrigley, Christopher. (1996). *Kingship and State, the Buganda Dynasty*, Cambridge and New York: Cambridge University Press.

Chapter 4

Africa's Industrialization: An Alternative Approach

Daniel B. Ndlela

Introduction: The Unrealized Vision

Africa is mostly characterised by small economies, with obvious disadvantages particularly as regards economies of scale that make for greater competitiveness. This would also provide access to a vaster trading and investment environment, inducing forward and backward supply linkages. It would also promote exports to regional markets, as a launching pad for venturing into global markets. And it would provide a framework for African countries to cooperate in developing common services for finance, transport, and communications. In part, this was the vision of some of the founding fathers of post-colonial Africa. According to Kwame Nkrumah, industrialisation was the only path to increasing the living standards of the African people:

> The world's economic development ... shows that it is only with advanced industrialisation that it has been possible to raise the nutritional level of the people by raising their levels of income. Agriculture is important for many reasons, and the governments of African states concerned with bringing higher standards of their people are devoting greater investment to agriculture. But even to make agriculture yield more, the aid of industrial output is needed; and the under-developed world cannot for ever be placed at the mercy of the more industrialised. (Nkrumah 1965: 7)

Nkrumah was also acutely concerned about the ever-decreasing terms of trade confronting producers of primary products, which negatively affected efforts of Africans to increase productivity. On the Nigerian and Ghanaian experiences he lamented:

> In 1954/5 when Ghana's production was 210,000 tons, her earnings from the cocoa crop were £85.5million. This year (1964/5) with an estimated crop of 590,000 tons, the estimated external earnings will be around £77 million... In 1954/5 (Nigeria) produced 89,000 tons of beans and received for her crop £39.25 million. In 1964 it is estimated that Nigeria will produce 310,000 tons and is likely to receive for it around £40 million. In other words, Ghana and Nigeria have trebled their production of this particular agricultural product but their gross earnings from it have fallen from £125 million to £117 million. (Nkrumah 1965)

At the beginning of the present millennium, the story of the African primary producers had not changed for the better. For example, whereas cotton lint was $1.56 per pound in 1995, five years later it had been reduced to 0.56 US cents. Consequently, Africa has maintained, and even deepened, the lop-sided character of its economy, in terms of structure, size and patterns of production, consumption, and trade. This constitutes a fundamental problem for the transformation of the African economies; hence their sluggish growth, poor manufacturing capabilities, and declining market share in both regional and global markets. This also partly accounts for the slow pace in the African integration. The vision of integrating African economies involves coordinated macroeconomic policies (fiscal discipline, interest rates and exchange rates) as well as growth-oriented industrial and trade policies which would be a basis for a common market for goods and services. New and upgraded physical infrastructures and improved facilitation and services would ease transport and communications across African borders. And, with a unified labour market, workers could move easily to areas affording the best opportunities.

The primary objective of virtually all African economic recovery programmes, from the inception of the Organization of African Unity (OAU) to the African Union's New Partnership for African Development (NEPAD), has been the eradication of poverty and placing African countries, both individually and collectively, on a path of accelerated growth and sustainable development. Arresting the marginalisation of Africa in every aspect, and substantially reducing its alarming level of poverty are the most urgent and challenging tasks that confront the continent. As stressed in NEPAD's Initial Action Plan, 'the issue arising out of these (challenges) is how to arrest this downward trend and put Africa back firmly on the world's development agenda, and on the path to irreversible and sustainable development, so that Africa truly claims this millennium.' (The NEPAD Initial Action Plan, July 2002. NEPAD Secretariat).

Structural Disarticulation in the African Economy

The most distinct feature of the African economies is the lop-sided nature of their patterns and size of production, consumption and trade. Yet in terms of overall performance confused messages of hope and despair have been coming out of the continent. The UN Economic Commission for Africa's (ECA) Economic Report on Africa (2002) declared:

> Africa grew faster than any other developing region in 2001, reflecting better macroeconomic management, strong agricultural production, higher than expected exports under the U.S. Africa Growth and Opportunity Act, currency depreciation in the largest economy (South Africa), and the cessation of conflicts in several African countries. (ECA, Economic Report on Africa, 2002, p. 13)

The ECA report was bullish about the relatively strong economic output of Africa in 2001 despite the global slowdown of that year and the aftermath of the 11 September 2001 attacks in the United States. Africa's overall growth had increased to 4.3 percent in 2001 up from 3.5 percent in 2000, with growth accelerating in countries such as Ethiopia (8.7 percent), Mozambique (9.2 percent), and Uganda (5.4 percent) (ECA, Economic Report on Africa, 2002 p.18).[1]

Just the previous year (2001), it was reported that Africa's agricultural sector's contribution to Gross Domestic Product (GDP), export earnings, and employment averaged 35 percent, 40 percent and 70 percent respectively. (OAU, Africa and the World Trade Organisation : Doha and Beyond, 2001), p. 1[2] The report had further lamented that, unfortunately, African agricultural trade was highly concentrated on a few primary commodities and that diversification into more dynamic products was required. It concluded that 'Africa has so far failed to achieve the necessary transformation for broad based growth'. (OAU, Africa and the World Trade organization, 2001)[3]

Why is Africa the only region of the world where numbers give hope only to disappear into oblivion as the true picture emerges? The answer is not that difficult to find, for it has always been with us for most of the past four decades of Africa's independence. By the time of political independence the disarticulated structure of Africa's economy had taken firm roots and its logic set to determine the pattern of future development. A disarticulated economy is one whose parts are not complementary, as compared to a coherent economy where there are domestic and/ or regional sectoral complementarities and reciprocities. In an articulated economic system the exchange mechanism and sectoral/regional reciprocity become pervasive following on the total commodication of the economy driven by forward and backward linkages of production.

Even if the picture of African economic performance sometimes appears to be on the mend and improving, its structure is fundamentally flawed. It is characterized by a narrow and disarticulated production base with ill-adapted technology, poor manufacturing capabilities, declining market share in international markets and sluggish growth. However, because of the lack of understanding or appreciation of the machinations of 'grafted capitalist' mode of production of a typical African economy, contradictory relations emerge in the functioning of African enterprises, in direct opposition to the pace of their integration into the global economy. Quite unlike the original capitalist mode of production, often referred to as 'endogenous' capitalism, Africa's post colonial capitalist mode of production or 'grafted capitalism' lacks the historical roots of the cradle of capitalism, i.e. feudalism which already had embodied commodification of capital, labour, consumption and market penetration into the total mode of production.

Since under endogenous capitalism, virtually all production was geared to the output of commodities, when the industrial revolution occurred it produced substantive change in society. But in the present day Africa, where commodification is only restricted to the formal sector, introduction of the productive sectors, (mining, commercial or plantation farming, manufacturing, etc.) has not produced change

---

1 Ibid, p.18.

2 Economic Commission for Africa (ECA), AERC and OAU's Report "Africa and the World Trade Organisation (WTO): Doha and Beyond" (2001), p. 1.

3 Ibid.

in the structure of these economies.[4] On the contrary, because of the high level of commodification in the capitalist economies, pressures from industrialisation and falling domestic rate of profits, the developed countries continue to want to maintain the narrow trade relations with the African formal sector. The old colonial trading relations with a minimum development of the required infrastructures and ancillary services continue to be maintained in the formal enclave sectors, bearing little relation or, at best, acquiescent relations to the other areas of the economy.

In Figure 4.1 below, it is shown that the formal sector (FS) is linked to the global economy through exports, imports, foreign direct investment (FDIs) and technology. The FS generally has lower surplus labour and higher average incomes than the informal sector (IS) and the communal sector (CS),[5] which both lag behind the formal sector income. There is high surplus labour in both the informal and communal sectors, and these sectors act as a buffer to surplus labour from FS. These sectors also provide a ready pool of labour for the formal sector if and when required. The informal and communal sectors form the non-formal sector (NFS) which is not linked beneficially to the FS, though contributing significantly to the survival of the people's economic and social well being.[6] This phenomenon is historically entrenched and enhanced by policies implemented by the African state. There are distortions in the way in which the FS and NFS of the economy relate to each other. There are also disarticulations internally, which have generally been overlooked in research compared to external disarticulations that have been studied extensively.

Three levels of disarticulations are discernible, namely, those within the different sectors of the economy (microeconomic distortions), between the sectors (structural and distributional distortions), and those caused by the external environment (macroeconomic distortions). In spite of the pervasiveness of these distortions, African governments usually focus on the FS through policies and expenditures that provide systems and infrastructures beneficial to that sector. The formal sectors of most African economies are interlinked through various forms of infrastructure (roads, rail, air, and telecommunications) mainly geared at fostering trade in exports. Yet, domestically, consumption between the different sectors is not linked,

---

4   Africa's 'grafted capitalism', thrives to integrate its modern 'formal sector' to the world economy, while over 70% of the economy is left behind in the non-formal sector, fraught with distortions: (external, structural and microeconomic) with no virtuous links with other sectors of the economy, and no capacity for capital accumulation. Thus, so long as the non-formal sector remains large, the system is self-constraining, has no dynamics for change and is continuously left outside the trading and value chain relations both internally at the individual country level and externally in terms of regional linkages and connectivity.

5   Though this terminology is typically of the Southern African economies, in the rest of the African continent it should be understood as the traditional 'rural' or peasant economy.

6   In many African economies, informal sector business may generate as much as half of GDP, handle as much as 40 per cent of all foreign exchange and over 40 per cent of exports and imports, support as much as 60-70 percent of the people. It is main provider of transport for the people and meets the basic housing requirements of poor. But the NFS remains a secondary economy reproducing disarticulated subservient relations with both the domestic FS and external economy.

and regional formal sector linkages are weaker than those between themselves and centres in developed countries.

The most dynamic sector of the African economy is the FS, which generally contributes less than 20 percent of total employment (except in a few countries like South Africa where it reaches 45 percent). As already explained, the formal sector of the African economy cannot be readily expanded because of its inherent structural rigidities. This is invariably the case, in spite of the neo-liberalism argument that the African manufacturing sector can be expanded to enhance employment, given its linkages with the global economy. This line of thinking ignores the fact that this cannot be successfully done when internally there are no virtuous relationships between the formal and non-formal sectors.

The FS is biased towards high capital intensity, even though labour intensive production processes might still be viable, while Africans cry out about the labour intensive products coming out of China. No matter how high the growth rate of the FS is, it remains a short-term phenomenon and will be unable to grow large and fast enough to eat away at the NFS. This is because of the structural distortions characterising the post colonial economy, viz, (i) the unequal access to resources (asymmetrical distribution of factors of production), (ii) productive and more efficient use of labour in the FS for capitalist gains, (iii) failure of capital to enhance value chains to allow benefits of growth to trickle down to NFS, and (iv) high unemployment and under-employment resulting in net loss to the economy in terms of lost production and net loss in aggregate demand.

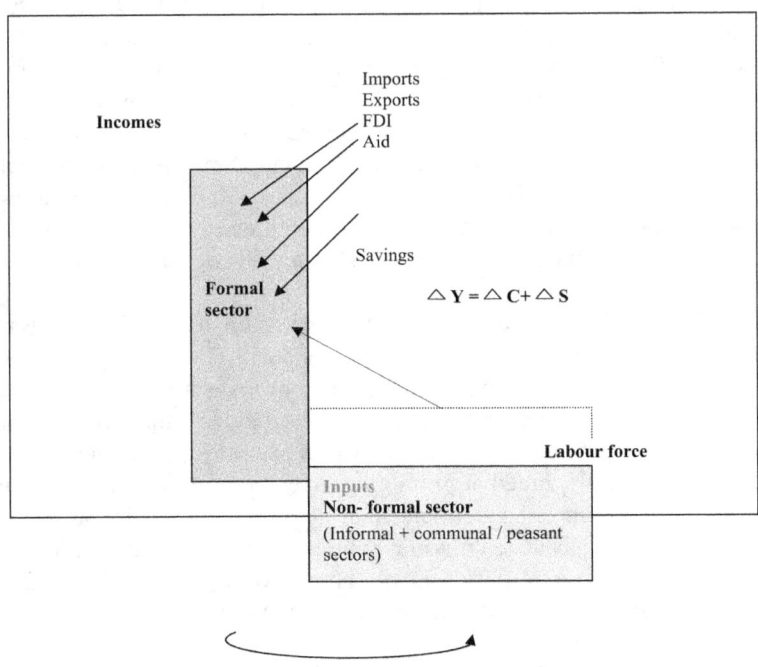

Figure 4.1 The Duality of the African Economy

Africa's Industrialization Experience

African governments and the international community have been aware of the dilemma of the continent's enclave economies, which are not driven by national or regional forces but by external forces through linkages with the global economy. Over the past three decades, steps have been taken to avert the disastrous effect of relying on external forces for dynamic growth. The first and second United Nations Industrial Development Decades for Africa programmes (IDDA-1 and IDDA-2) were initiated by the African countries with the support of ECA, endorsed and adopted by the international community, through the UN Industrial Development Organization (UNIDO).

After the adoption of the Lagos Plan of Action, IDDA-1 was launched with the assumption that Africa would industrialize in an integrated manner. Emphasis was put on the promotion of basic industries (metal, chemical and capital goods industries) as the basis for self-sustained industrial development. It was assumed that these industries would be developed in countries where comparative advantages exist and would benefit other countries in the respective African regions. The products of these basic industries would support the smaller scale manufacturing firms which would not be dependent on machinery and intermediary products from outside the continent. The strategy also included components of financing, infrastructure and human resources development, with a prominent role for the African Development Bank (AfDB) and with the establishment of regional research and technology (R&D) and technology centres.

After a critical assessment of the shortcomings of IDDA-1 a successor programme, IDDA-2, was adopted; its focus was on the private sector through the development of small and medium enterprises (SMEs). This was at a time when most African countries were implementing World Bank- supported Structural Adjustment Programmes (SAPs) which assumed that market mechanisms would lead to improvements in the investment climate and stimulate economic activities. The IDDA-2 was also based on the assumption that with regionalism taking shape within the framework of the regional economic communities (RECs) there was going to be increased trade and cross-border investments. However, these conditions did not materialise.

Both IDDA 1 and IDDA 2 did not achieve their set objectives for various reasons, the most cited being the market mechanisms under SAPs. Deregulation was not extensive enough to cause the expected big wave of investment, and dependence of the manufacturing sector on external capital and intermediary goods remained a major constraint to the growth of the private industrial sector. Macroeconomic measures that would have directly aimed at promoting investment in Africa's manufacturing sector (e.g. fiscal and monetary policies that help boost industrial development in most Asian countries) have been missing at both national and regional levels.

The failure of both IDDA-1 and IDDA-2 over two decades led UNIDO to come up with yet another programme, the Alliance for Africa's Industrialization which also failed to produce significant results.

More recently (July 2004) the African Union adopted a new programme, the African Productive Capacity Initiative (APCI), dubbed the sustainable industrial component of NEPAD.[7] The APCI was immediately adopted by the Conference of African Ministers of Industry (CAMI), who had earlier on worked on the initiative to define its concept, strategies and concrete actions to strengthen industrial production and competitiveness in Africa. It is recognition by CAMI that sustainable economic development necessarily involves the promotion of manufacturing, and that trade without production is not sustainable. CAMI also seeks to establish strategies that would simultaneously respond to the Millennium Development Goals and generate wealth and employment in sub-Saharan Africa.

The APCI aims at improving industrial performance and promoting employment using (a) the value chain concept in developing national and regional industries on a sub-sector basis, (b) direct involvement of private sector and non state actors in structuring concrete action plans to be taken jointly by all stakeholders, and (c) a proposal to have an African owned and driven fund to be called African Productive Capacity Facility.

Even with all these efforts, what remains persistent, however, are the superficial government policies and ineffective external technical assistance. As long as the international community, including UNIDO, continue to promote the SME projects paradigm, the present lop-sided structure of the African economy will remain. Change will only come when the totality of government policies (including education and science & technology, trade policies) seriously engages the private sector, its associations, as well as all the other stakeholders, including the trade unions, in tackling industrialisation in a comprehensive and sustainable bottom–up approach. Otherwise, there will be no change in the current structure of the dualistic economies, where the FS is shrinking and the NFS continues to expand. Change will also come when national and regional policies begin to target the horizontal and vertical linkages of the SMEs with formal sector enterprises. Only when the total sum of consumption (C) and savings (S) of the entire economy becomes articulated to contribute to the national income (Y) will there be a transformation of the economy. For this approach to succeed, African institutions, namely the African Union, the RECs, AfDB and ECA must go beyond rhetoric and actively support sector-level value chains where these exist and help to incubate others, where the resource base, skills and technology exist.

The Underdevelopment of Africa's Manufacturing Sector

The Continued Colonial Structure of Africa's Manufacturing Sector

Colonial administrations in Africa were never serious about industrialization. In the case of East Africa, in 1939, out of an allocation of £8 million only £151,000 was earmarked for industrialization-led projects, out of which only £23,000 was

---

7   The programme is a result of a protracted process to reorient the economic growth paths of countries in Africa by the international community – the Millennium Summit (New York, 2000), the Third UN Conference on LDCs (Brussels, 2001), the World Summit on Sustainable Development (Johannesburg, 2002) and the establishment of NEPAD as an Africa-wide framework for economic advancement.

spent. (Ake 1981).[8] Besides being discouraged by the rudimentary development of infrastructure, the type of colonial manufacturing or industrial activity was of a rudimentary type: food and beverages, tobacco, base metals, non-durable consumer goods, textiles, basic chemical products, building materials, furniture, leather and leather products. (Ake 1981)[9] As shown below, up to now Africa has not broken out of this erstwhile manufacturing product profile.

A central observation in the literature inspired by the global commodity chain approach is that the highest value added is now concentrated in the marketing and design functions and no longer in manufacturing, while increasingly the governance of value chains rests with companies controlling the former functions (Gereffi 1994). At the same time, to focus on manufacturing alone will often lead to a 'low road' activities in competition with economies characterized by low labour costs such as in the case of China (Kaplinsky 1998). The real scare is a secondary observation coming out of regional studies (COMESA 2005),[10] indicating that as regional firms continue to focus solely on the rudimentary colonial structure of manufacturing activities, this inevitably leads to a 'low road' value adding and plunges the Africa into a losing battle in competition with the rest of the world. (COMESA 2005)

Quite unlike developments in capitalist economies, which are increasingly being organized in a variety of different business systems and global commodity chains and building on distinctive institutional contexts and through co-ordination of economic activities across national boundaries, the majority of firms in African economies are still predominantly producing in isolation of each other even at the domestic level.

Even the much acclaimed strategies, such as Export Processing Zones, are far from integrating domestic and/or regional markets; they were mainly established to process exports to the European Union (EU) market and recently to the US market under the African Growth and Opportunity Act (AGOA) market access. Such are the free zones of Kenya, Madagascar, Mauritius and Swaziland. The products being produced and exported, that is, textiles and garments, are specially manufactured on orders for the Northern markets; most of them with raw materials and intermediate inputs from the Far East. As a result, regional markets are hardly affected by this development, with the exception of very limited intermediate inputs and semi-processed raw materials. The current APCI, while using the value chain approach, may as well be falling into this trap. For example, for the East and Southern Africa, under the APCI's value chain approach, the priority sectors have been split as follows: (a) East Africa – agro-food industries; leather and leather products; and cotton, textiles and garments; (b) Southern Africa – agro-food industries; metallic and non metallic products; and pharmaceuticals.

---

8   Ake "*A Political Economy of Africa*" 1981: 46.
9   Ibid.
10 See, Firm Strategies: Studies of the Manufacturing Sectors of eighteen member (18) states of COMESA (2005): COMESA Secretariat (2005).

Absence of Linkages and Connectivity of Value Chains

Only a few economies of COMESA have relatively diversified manufacturing bases to benefit from such initiatives; in cases such as Egypt, Kenya, and Zimbabwe, firms have succeeded in exploiting regional markets on a limited basis, with the active assistance of their governments. In the case of Egypt, the development of industrial exports is being achieved through the strategic geographical location of industries. This policy was a precursor to the establishment of free zones and incentives related to these zones. Major activities in the industrial parks include pharmaceuticals, garments, petrochemicals, appliances, ceramics and cement. Unlike the nearly single product approach of the other countries, e.g. garments in the case of Madagascar and Swaziland, the diversified approach of firm seeks to spread the wings of the country's market beyond the traditional northern markets and, consequently, assumes greater aggressive marketing into the regional markets.

In many African countries, part of the drive towards exports can be understood as a reaction to the shrinking of the domestic markets. For most of the companies trade liberalisation unleashes real or perceived increase in competition within the former protected domestic market. Hence, exports are seen as necessary to maintain the position of domestic industries. What is often ignored is to minimise the possible negative effects of trans-national corporations (TNCs) in Africa's industrialisation. They are increasingly focusing on exploiting their comparative advantage by making use of brand names in international markets.

As externally based retail chains or holders of 'world class' brand names, TNCs utilise a market segmentation approach to the assigned brand-name manufacturers. For example, in its international product brands, Sika Egypt, which has its TNC headquarters in Switzerland is assigned the Middle East, Near East and East African segment of COMESA (e.g. Eritrea, Ethiopia, Kenya, Somalia, Sudan and other neighbouring states), while Southern Africa (consisting of part of COMESA and SADC) are market segmented under Sika – South Africa.[11] Other TNCs apply similar market segmentation strategies in their international brand names, e.g. Levis, 'Van Heusen' and Pierre Cardin in the garments sub-sector. In the agro-industry sector, brand names include Heinz products, an international brand name, while only a few local brands are maintained by regional companies.

African states are still lagging behind other regions of the world in the upgrading of products through diversification of manufacturing activities. This is in spite of the fact that a major rational for the introduction of trade liberalisation was to enable domestic companies to streamline and focus their production, concentrating on higher value products and higher margin activities. It was under this rationale that, in response to changes in the international market for sugar, Mauritian companies were encouraged to adopt strategies to meet their export quotas. This was achieved by using less land and grouping small planters to raise productivity and effectiveness as well as introduction of high-yielding cane varieties. Innovative firms operating in the textile and garment industry adopted diversification strategies so that they could

---

11 Sika International's brand names are in construction, chemicals/industrial adhesive materials.

produce a wider range of products and services, and by relocating some parts of their manufacturing value chains to Madagascar.

Commercial networks and industrial clusters, though extremely far apart among the African economies, have in recent years thrown-up some promising examples. One such is an Ethiopian domestic firm organised to outsource from over 50 SMEs, for the supply of leather products, mainly shoes, under the supervision of a highly trained and experienced entrepreneur. The upgrading of products and diversification of activities led to production and distribution of high quality and price competitive shoes, able to withstand the cheap Chinese shoes flooding the domestic market.(COMESA 2004)[12] However, with no support from local institutions involving public, private partnerships (PPPs), the lead cluster firm will find it difficult to achieve its set objectives, including (i) sourcing of various modern designs and to produce high quality shoes, (ii) improving production techniques and productivity, (iii) provision of training to develop skills, (iv) access to financial resources, and (v) development of marketing skills.[13]

What is fundamentally lacking in all these attempts is an integrated development approach. This would require clusters to be viewed not merely as a concentration of small firms but as inter-dependent networks comprising of firms, raw material providers, machinery suppliers, transporters, buyers, sellers and support institutions. With active channels of business transaction, communication and dialogue, the networks or value chains share specialised infrastructure and labour markets. Most of the African industrial cluster development not only lack this ingredient but are hardly noticed or recognised by domestic institutions. The result is an inability on the part of domestic firms to trigger linkages and connectivity of value chains at the national and regional levels.

Lack of Dynamics to Accelerate Regional Integration

It is apparent that the regional economic integration process among African countries, in whatever form, is too slow to cope with similar developments in other parts of the world. The RECs have not evolved specific development strategies that would accelerate the pace, sequencing and diversification of products in line with their national and regional development market plans. African firms hardly exploit the proximity of regional markets where producers should naturally dominate the different parts of the region. As if time does not move, African producers have since the colonial period continued to face a monotonous and timeless segmentation in the geographical destination of their traded products.

---

12 See, COMESA Firm Strategies under Trade Liberalisation – Ethiopia Country Report, COMESA, Secretariat, 2004.

13 A similar outfit was found in Madagascar, pioneered by an entrepreneur, who organised a silk cluster through outsourcing from 100 individuals and cooperative weavers in the country side to provide raw materials, intermediate and final woven and knitted products, see COMESA Firm Strategies under Trade Liberalisation – Madagascar Country Report, COMESA, Secretariat, 2004.

The typical African country's exports are dominated by a narrow band of commodities, minerals, garments, and agro-processed products primarily directed towards European markets. The exception to this rule, though not profound enough, may be found in a few Southern African countries like South Africa and Zimbabwe which have traditionally exported industrial products to regional markets – agricultural machinery/equipment, railway rolling stock, mining machinery and equipment, motor cars and trucks in the case of South Africa. Kenya's agro-processed products, dominated by tea, are destined for neighbouring East African and the Egyptian market, taking advantage of the zero tariffs under COMESA free trade area. In the majority of African countries there is little expansion and diversification of products to take advantage of the regional markets.

The narrow base of Africa's industry and its lack of diversification are the main causes of structural disarticulation in these economies. On the more diversified economies of Sub-Saharan Africa is South Africa's industry (mining, manufacturing and construction) which contributed around 29 percent of GDP in 2000 and this share has fallen steadily from 31.1 percent in 1995. Zimbabwe's manufacturing sector was previously equally diversified but is currently on a fast-track decline, from 25 percent of GDP in the 1970s and 1980s to less than 14 percent in 2000 and is still declining. Kenya's manufacturing accounted for 13 percent of GDP in 1996-2001 compared to agriculture which accounted for 25 percent during the same period.

At the lower end of industrial development, over the past decade Ethiopia's share of industry remained around 11 percent of GDP, compared to agriculture which accounted for 53 percent of GDP in 1973/74 and for 45 percent in 2000/01. (ECA; p. 84)[14] In Guinea mining has dominated the country's economy, accounting for 20 percent of GDP, 85 percent of export income and 30 percent fiscal revenue, with manufacturing lagging far off from 3.5 percent of GDP in 1986 to 7.75 percent in 2000. (ECA; pp. 214-215)[15]

Instead of pursuing domestic policies that foster economic growth and address supply-side constraints, Sub-Saharan African countries have often wholly embraced the free market prescriptions offered by trade liberalisation that are arbitrarily dictated by external agencies. This does not mean that governments should not move on to privatize non-core activities, liberalise markets, prices, interest rates, etc. to enable the private sector to procure inputs, including raw materials, at competitive world market prices. To foster growth, this should be done with domestic and regional policies in mind. As Ha-Joon Chang has observed, it was Korea's ability to set its own domestic policy on investment – insisting on upstream and downstream benefits, or spillovers – that enabled that country to develop a world-class economy. Subsequently, Singapore and Taiwan benefited from similar policies. (Liz Stuart, 2005)[16]

---

14 ECA: p. 84.
15 Ibid. pp. 214-215.
16 See, Liz Stuart "Why the European Commission is Wrong about EPAs" in Trade Negotiations Insights: From Doha to Cotonou: Vol.4 No.2 March-April 2005.

The level of intra-African trade remains extremely low compared to that of the other regions of the world. Currently, it is 8 percent of total trade with the rest of the world, compared to 70 percent for European Union (EU) intra-regional trade and 50 percent among Asian countries. One can argue that to reverse this trend, Africa has to seriously consider adopting 'integrative regionalism', where the integrating partners (member states) are perceived to have compatible interests. Even if conflicts are anticipated, they would be 'sublimated' and subservient to the higher consideration of the common objective and common good that will come out of integrating into a single economic or political union.

To some extent, the EU is agonizingly but persistently moving in the direction of some kind of 'integrative' regionalism. The East African Community (EAC) that existed prior to independence of Kenya, Uganda and Tanzania represented this type of regionalism, possibly because of the common imperial interests of the British colonial power. However, when the three countries became independent, they resorted to calculating the distributive gains and losses, and, in the absence of an overriding integrative mechanism, the old EAC collapsed.[17]

Regionalism in the rest of Africa appears to be 'distributive regionalism' where each member state appears not to surrender anything unless it gets something in return, as if on a closely calculated basis of what the gains and losses would be from the integration arrangement. Under distributive regionalism, the states continue to pursue their individualistic interests. There is no overriding common interest except those that are negotiated on the basis of the relative strength of the negotiating partners.

Apart from the RECs, NEPAD projects and activities are fundamentally pillars for the building of a strong African economic integration. They include the socio economic programmes, matters related to peace and security, and the African Peer Review Mechanism, Advocacy and Resource Mobilisation and Shaping of the New Partnership.[18] NEPAD's socio-economic programmes consist of specific actions to be carried out at regional or country level in various fields, including: (i) agriculture and market access; (ii) energy (implementation of existing power system and gas/oil projects); (iii) water and sanitation (integrated water resources management, urgent water needs, water wisdom); (iv) transport (cost reduction, public and private investment, maintenance of transport infrastructures, facilitation and removal of formal and informal barriers, regional cooperation in the integration of markets of transport services); and (v) public and private partnership in infrastructure development (business environment and climate, investment code, legal and regulatory framework).

These projects and activities are meant to contribute to promoting regional cooperation and integration. The synchronization and harmonization process would require that, in designing their respective programmes, the AU Commission and the RECs draw from the activities promoted under NEPAD and that these activities would be based on the actual programme areas devised at national, regional and continental levels.

---

17 The new East African Community has been resurrected between the three countries.
18 See the NEPAD framework document – Initial Action Plan.

Factors Affecting Competitiveness of African Industry

Political, Macroeconomic and Meso-level Factors

The three most important factors that should influence the growth and diversification of Africa's industrialisation are the political/government, macroeconomic, and meso-level spheres. These are the source of each country's economic policy environment as well as incentives / regulatory policy instruments. They directly impact on the competitiveness, diversification and performance of each country's enterprises. The macroeconomic factors are at the centre in providing linkages with the rest of the economy. They either provide the basis for domestic industries to pursue competitiveness or prevent them from doing so. In short, consistent and sound macroeconomic economic policies, coupled with fiscal prudence, provide and nurture the availability and growth of basic factors of production which are essential for the growth of exports.

Central to policy direction is the government and political sphere, which encompasses the nature of the state, governance, and the level of participation of non-state actors. The second tier consists of macroeconomic factors which are the fiscal, social and regulatory policies, as well as trade policies, which should be supported by the meso-level policy instruments, namely, science and technology, education, infrastructure and labour policies. These influence the structure and performance of companies and firms operating at sector levels: primary, secondary and tertiary. In any modern socio-economic formation, the firm is the focal point for targeting by the totality of political, governance, macroeconomic and meso-level policy instruments.

A variety of policy distortions that often result in the lack of competition, such as soft budgets for state owned enterprises and agency problems that allow managers of enterprises to operate inefficiently, are barriers preventing enterprises from operating efficiently as competition should be a central feature of industrial restructuring strategies (AfDB 1998; 49).[19] The result is price distortions which are a disincentive to many export producers, resulting in low production. In practice, the wheels of African policy instruments have tended to come off. For example, in the case of Southern Africa, Zimbabwe has maintained an inflation rate of over 1000 percent, which is out of range compared to other countries in the region with an average inflation of less than 10 percent. It is not only registering very high inflation rates but it also has extremely overvalued exchange rates and high budget deficits[20] (Senaona and Shields, 2001).

Infrastructure

The basic conditions for infrastructural development (physical, institutional, socio-political, and human) with which firms exploit technology are lacking in most

---

19 AfDB Report, Human Capital Development, 1998, 49.
20 See Dr Moeketsi Senaona ed, John Shields presentation in "The SADC Macroeconomic Convergence Workshop". Technical Report 2001.

of African countries. This has been a major obstacle to investment, especially the pervasiveness of poor and deteriorating road infrastructures, inadequate and unreliable communication systems, high utility costs, etc. Water and electricity supplies are often cited as major problems, with fairly large factories often forced to run several boreholes at high utility charges. Poor roads and railways are also cited as constraining factors. The lack of budgetary resources and high budget deficits have accumulated into unserviceable debts, subsequently resulting in the lack of proactive policy measures to expand basic infrastructures in urban areas (commercial stands, communication facilities and electricity), and in rural areas (water, roads, communications, etc).

As infrastructure forms a crucial base for any form of development, it is important that African policy makers promote its development. For regional infrastructures to improve there must be coordinated and concerted efforts in leveraging financial resources and expertise.

Human Resources Development and Capital Formation

Skilled labour that allows for specialisation and efficiency is often in short supply in African countries and is a major problem experienced by firms and enterprises. Also militating against higher levels of capital formation is lack of skilled labour that allows for specialisation and efficiency. This has been a major drawback in improving levels of exports, bearing in mind that in the context of a globalised economic environment, which is knowledge-based, the conventional comparative advantage of raw materials and unskilled labour is increasingly becoming insignificant. High-quality services such as accounting, management, production engineering, design, packaging, processing, quality control etc. are crucial for export survival.

Many African countries have invested heavily in human capital only to lose this precious productive factor, through the brain drain, to the more advanced economies. Poor working conditions and deterioration in real wages and salaries are push factors as are civil unrest and poor political governance. Angola, Democratic Republic of the Congo, Cote d'Ivoire and Zimbabwe are cases in the latter category and all other African countries have generally been seriously affected.

The availability of and access to capital are important factors in determining production and export performance. In most of the countries in Eastern and Southern Africa banks are under-capitalised to the extent that they are barely able to issue long-term and short-term finance.

Africa's Trade in the face of Globalisation

Market Access as a Development Tool

Non-reciprocal trade preferences granted to ACP states by the EU since 1975 at the beginning of Lome I Convention, including tariff and non-tariff preferences, were rolled over until December 2007 under the Cotonou Agreement. This was to allow for negotiation of new trade arrangements. The agreement provides that as from

January 2008 there will be a new set of reciprocal trade agreements, termed Economic Partnership Agreements (EPAs). In essence the new Free Trade Areas (FTAs) will replace the current trade regimes. These new agreements should be WTO compatible by meeting provisions of Article XXIV of GATT, covering "essentially all trade." Due to the nature of its preferences, the Cotonou Agreement has been notified to the WTO and the parties have applied for a waiver.

In making reference to compliance with WTO the Cotonou Agreement notes 'the Parties agree to conclude new WTO compatible trading arrangements, removing progressively barriers to trade between themselves and enhancing co-operation in all areas relevant to trade'. It further states that:

> Negotiations of the Economic Partnership Agreements shall aim notably at establishing the timetable for the progressive removal of barriers to trade between the parties, in accordance with the relevant WTO rules. On the Community side trade liberalisation shall build on the *acquis* and shall aim at improving current market access for the ACP countries through, *inter alia*, a review of the rules of origin. (*The Courier*, 2000)[21]

While average customs duties are now at their lowest levels after eight GATT Rounds, certain tariffs continue to restrict trade, especially on the exports of developing countries — for instance "tariff peaks", which are relatively high tariffs, usually on "sensitive" products, amidst generally low tariff levels. For industrialized countries, tariffs of 15 percent and above are generally recognized as "tariff peaks". The practice of "tariff escalation", in which higher import duties are applied on semi-processed products than on raw materials, and higher still on finished products, is another example of tariff barriers used by industrialized countries. This practice protects domestic processing industries and discourages the development of processing activity in the countries where raw materials originate.

African member States of the ACP Group have a number of particular concerns, including the question of how to deal with the fragility of the economies of the LDCs as a distinct group. Under the ACP-EU Trade Arrangement, the EU has provided that this category of countries does not have to negotiate new trade arrangements in order to continue enjoying non-reciprocal preferences. It is also envisaged that some financial aid will be negotiated to compensate ACP states for the costs of trade liberalisation and economic restructuring. As from March 2001, the EU opened its market to "Everything But Arms" (EBA), extending duty and quota-free access to all imports from all LDCs except arms.[22] In this context, EBA will further complicate the configuration of negotiating groups for the proposed EPAs. Let us take the example of the East African Community (Kenya, Uganda and Tanzania) which have long been committed to closer economic collaboration and are in the process of establishing a customs union, having already established an East African Parliament. As LDCs, both Uganda and Tanzania have duty-free access to the EU market under

---

21 "ACP-EU partnership agreement signed in Cotonou on 23 June 2000". *The Courier*, September 2000, special issue – Cotonou Agreement.

22 The only variation is that liberalisation for sugar and rice will be in 2009 and for bananas in 2006, with the LDCs being given annual increases of 15 percent in the quotas for sugar and rice until full liberalisation is achieved.

EBA, a position which renders Kenya, as the negotiating group's only non-LDC, increasingly isolated.

Even with the said positive impacts of relations under the ACP/EU, AGOA and the WTO trade arrangements, most African economies continue to experience de-industrialisation. This is due to the shrinking domestic market as a result of trade liberalisation and continued marginalisation of the non-formal sector, and the flooding of domestic markets by lower-priced Chinese products. Many of these countries continue to stay out of their regional FTAs and hesitate to actively participate in regional customs unions despite being part and parcel of countries integrating into the global economy.

Africa's Trade Policy Regimes Under Globalisation

Trade policy orientations of many African countries have been characterised by shifts between protectionism and liberalisation. In the 1970/80s, there were the heavily protected import substituting industrialisation (ISI) policies, only to be replaced in the early 1990s by the SAPs under which trade liberalisation was a key component. African countries made commitments to reduce tariffs further under the multilateral umbrella of the Uruguay Round. Yet most of them have pursued more open trade policies by further liberalising trade within regional and multilateral frameworks. Trade liberalisation was seen as a vehicle to enhance domestic productivity, efficiency, improve quality and low prices, which was expected to lead to improved consumer welfare.

To some degree, various levels of trade policy objectives of the African RECs and those of their member states are generally compatible. They all follow one direction of trade liberalisation, commitment to WTO obligations, pursuance of export-led growth, seeking increased market access for their products in regional and world markets and use of tariff based protection in place of NTBs, rationalising and lowering their tariff structures.

However, questions should be raised about both the focus and variation of the level of commitment of trade policy among African states. Some have carried out trade policy liberalization, the so called "big bang approach", with overzealousness, as in the case of Zambia in the early 1990s. In a few others, such as Mauritius, these reforms are tailor-made to respond to and address internal policy frameworks intended to enhance sustained growth and investment. In the majority of cases, and for reasons such as politics and the power of commercial and/or industrial lobbyists, there was some inconsistency between the official position on trade policy and practice, including trade policy reversals. For example, after experimenting with trade liberalization in the first half of the 1990s, Zimbabwe imposed controls on some imports and exports, increased tariffs on selective products, and introduced price controls (including exchange rate controls) which adversely affected trade performance. Tanzania followed the steps taken by Lesotho and Mozambique earlier, of withdrawing from COMESA just in time for the launch of the FTA. South Africa continued to maintain some quota restrictions on imports from non-SACU/SADC member states, particularly those affecting regional exports.

Even more fundamental is the issue of whether Africa has prepared itself for facing up to the veiled and enforced regionalism where the African ACP group is subjected to the dictates of the EU, largely because of asymmetrical power relationships. In theory, one can postulate that as a weaker partner Africa can walk out of the arrangement. But, in practice, this may be impossible because of the long history of a "locked-in" situation where walking out may even be more costly than a bad bargain. As in the case of the earlier colonial relationship which was tantamount to an enforced regionalism, the current EPAs may yet be another case of enforced regionalism.

In view of these difficulties, strong political will is needed for the African ACP countries to know where the EU stands in so far as protection of their right to set policies that will support the continent's future industrial progression is concerned. The argument for rejecting EU's proposed level playing field under the guise of competition policy and equal access to government procurement is for African countries to utilise these instruments as agents for supporting industrial development. In principle, it may seem that rejection of an EPA is no more a choice, because, in so doing a country risks losing EU aid, preferential market access, and the important commodity protocols. In practice, however, by deciding on EPAs Africa would be giving priority to maintaining political links with the EU and its member states over its own sovereignty in trade policy matters.

If EPAs between African countires and the EU is to be pro-development, they would have to address the lack of diversification in ACP countries. They should also address the issue of African exports to the EU, which are dominated by commodities, textiles and garments under the Lome Agreement. This is the only way Europe can help in developing Africa's trade capacity with a view to fostering development. Further, if EPAs were to help African ACP countries to develop, they should ensure that the costs of liberalisation are met by aid. In this way, EPAs would have engendered shifts in economic and trade policy, particularly to take care of revenue losses, adjustment costs, increased competition and commitments, which these countries would have undertaken within regional and multilateral trade arrangements.

An Alternative Development Strategy

As shown above, the entire policy environment facing African producers is negatively influenced by an absence of inclusiveness in the transformation of the economy in a holistic manner. These economies are characterized by dualism between their formal sector and the large non-formal sector. African states have not adopted a development agenda that transforms a proportion of income from this narrow formal sector and invests it in the non-formal sector. Large mining concerns, the plantation sector, etc. are operated profitably for years without any systematic capital accumulation model, *a la* Mauritius where a part of the sugar profits were systematically transformed into industrial capital. Historically, the latter approach has enhanced the integration of production and marketing within the national economies while also triggering linkages and connectivity of value chains at both the national and regional level.

Even in those countries where Governments have put in place comprehensive regulations, stimulation mechanisms to facilitate firm strategies, regional trading relations and export promotion strategies, domestic firms still experience enormous challenges stemming from shrinking domestic and regional market options. Hence the need for African countries, at the regional level, to take decisive and appropriate measures to arrest the phenomenon of de-industrialisation of their manufacturing sectors, through interventions to proactively expand their existing narrow-based formal sectors.

The most pertinent gaps for intervention include the following:

Macroeconomic and trade policies: Africa has to move away from its business-as-usual high-sounding rhetoric, to mobilise the three most important factors (the political, macroeconomic, and meso-level factors) that directly influence the growth and diversification of industrialisation. Buttressing these factors with well thought-out incentives / regulatory policies will endure that the ensuing economic environment will impact positively on the competitiveness, diversification and performance of a country's enterprises.

There will be no serious and sustained development of industries without sound fiscal policies which nurture the availability and growth of basic factors of production. High interest rates, lack of strong capital base of financial institutions to finance export projects, shortages of foreign currency and misaligned exchange rates in many African countries have hindered the growth of potential as well as existing export producers. It is therefore important that the central ministries of finance and economic development play an active role in the rationalisation and alignment of fiscal, exchange rate policies, infrastructure, human resource development, in order to influence regional firms to develop value chains integrative production systems.

Infrastructure: The deterioration of railway and road infrastructures has continued to work against exporters. There is therefore urgent need for projects at the regional level to rehabilitate road and railway infrastructure, including railway-rolling stock and wagons. Particularly for land-locked countries, because of long distances from the ports high procurement costs for these countries are high and constitute a very significant share of total costs. In order to address these problems African RECs could formulate investment programmes in:

a. improving physical transport infrastructures and efficiency of operations of transit cargo to and from the seaports;
b. establishing consortia for bulk importation of 'bonded raw materials' for the land-locked states, e.g. Burundi, Rwanda and Uganda in East Africa, thereby cutting costs and improving competitiveness of exporting firms.

At the regional level, the RECs must urgently implement NEPAD programmes, projects and activities based primarily on the priorities of the region. In this connection, the most important projects are in infrastructures. The other areas include (i) information and communications technology (ICT) and energy, (ii) human resources, including education, skills development, and reversing the brain drain,

(iii) health, (iv) agriculture, and (v) access to the markets of developed countries for African exports.

Regional Capital Markets: Africa has to develop regional capital markets specifically for the support of value chain projects by firms that link production at both the national and regional levels. The AfDB, the Development Bank of South Africa (DBSA), the Preferential Trade Area (PTA) Bank, and other regional development finance institutions should be able to mobilise funds to be disbursed by national development and merchant banks at the regional level. One of the most important conditions should be the mobility of labour, at least starting with skilled and professional labour within and across the five African regions.

Rationalisation of Firms Strategies: The task of regional standardised firm strategies is not going to come about spontaneously, but through a concerted effort in implementing strategies for upgrading and diversification of products. This will be achieved by concentrating on the rationalisation of firm strategies within the member states of each African REC. Ideally, the building blocs for a firm's strategies are the policy instruments on competitiveness, innovation, up-grading and diversification of products. Incentives for inter- and intra-firm linkages will provide the breeding grounds for large domestically incorporated firms and TNCs to outsource certain products from within the country of the firm's incorporation and from other regional partner countries.

Information exchange: The dearth of information on possibilities and opportunities existing among firms in African countries is astounding. It is imperative that regional Chambers of Commerce are strengthened where they exist to form some kind of an umbrella African Chamber. This would go a long way towards making regional trading organisations aware of opportunities available in the respective regional markets. A powerful and credible African Chamber is needed to spearhead trade policy and trade facilitation measures such as: (i) exchange of data bases, market information, training and skills; (ii) exchange of information on national projects to enable African firms to joint-bid; and (iii) exchange information on Government tenders.

National Standards: There is need for Standards Bodies to work on common acceptable and corresponding regional quality standards, e.g. COMESA, ECOWAS and SADC Standards. The respective secretariats of the RECs should intervene with greater speed and urgency in the harmonisation of regional standards and certification and prepare the ground for an operational data base on standards, as a first step towards full harmonisation of national standards.

The secretariats of the RECs should actively intervene in creating, supporting and assisting in the monitoring and evaluation of the region's 'centres of excellence' such as 'productivity centres', capacity building or research & development centres, such as the Sugar R&D Institute in Mauritius, the Leather Institute in Ethiopia, or Centres for Business Development, etc.

Small and Medium Enterprises [SMEs] Support Systems: African SMEs have been treated with some degree of romance – small is beautiful. This is absolutely absurd, given the economic potential of SMEs to become the bedrock of these economies. They are treated as appendage enclaves, which act as absorbers of displaced labour from the shrinking formal sector. Meaningful policy intervention in this area by African governments could involve earmarking new resources for investment in the non-formal sectors of these countries.

Mere injection of technology, capital and entrepreneurship in the SMEs will not be effective in both the short- and the long-run as long as the government is not investing in transformation of technologies and entrepreneurship development of the larger non- formal sector of the economy. At the same time, the policy of supporting value chains linkages between large-scale firms and SMEs cannot be left to spontaneous outcomes by isolated companies, but should be part of expanding the current formal sector activities into the rest of each country's national economy.

References

Ake, Claude (1981), *A Political Economy of Africa*, Longman Group Limited, Longman Nigeria Ltd and Longman Inc. New York.

Dicken, Peter (1998), *Global Shift, Transforming the World Economy* (3rd Edition) Paul Chapman, London.

Economic Commission for Africa (2002), *Economic Report on Africa 2002 – Tracking Performance and Progress*, Economic Commission for Africa.

Economic Commission for Africa (2002), *Harnessing Technologies for Development*, ECA Policy Research Report, Economic Commission for Africa.

Economic Commission for Africa (Abuja, Nigeria 15-19 June 1987), *The International Conference on Africa: The Challenging of Economic Recovery and Accelerating Development* (The Abuja Statement), United Nations Economic Commission for Africa.

Economic Commission for Africa (ECA): *The Annual Report on Integration in Africa* (ARIA 2002).

Economic Commission for Africa (2002), *African Economic Research Consortium, Organisation of African Unity: Africa and the World Trade Organisation (WTO) – Doha and Beyond*.

Economic Community of West African States (ECOWAS), *Silver Jubilee Anniversary Achievements and Prospects 1975-2000*, CEDEAO/ECOWAS, 2000.

Gereffi, G. (1996), "Global Commodity Chains: New Forms of Coordination and Control Among Nations and Firms in International Industries" in *Competition and Change*, Vol. 4., pp. 427-439.

Gereffi, G. and Korseniewicz, M. (1994), *Commodity Chains and Global Capitalism*, Westport, Connecticut, Praeger.

Kogut, Bruce (1985), "*Designing Global Strategies: Comparative and Competitive Value-Added Chains*" in Sloan Management Review, Summer 1985, pp.15-28.

Johanson, J. and Mattsson, L.G. (1988), *Internationalisation in Industrial Systems – A Network Approach*, (In) N. Hood and J-E Vahlne, eds.: Strategies in Global Competition. New York: Croom Helm.

Ndlela Daniel B. and Torp J-E (1999), *Zimbabwe Firm Strategies under Trade Liberalisation*, Zimconsult, Harare, mimeo.

NEPAD Secretariat, *The NEPAD Initial Action Plan,* July 2002.

Nkhumah, Kwame (1965), *Neo-Colonialism – The Last Stage of Imperialism*, Panaf Books, Ltd, Panaf.

Porter, Michael (ed) (1986), *Competition in Global Industries* (Howard Business School Press, Boston, Massachusets).

Schmitz, H. and Musyck, B. (1994), *Industrial Districts in Europe: Policy Lessons for Developing Countries*, World Development, Vol. 22, No. 6.

Stuart, Liz (March-April 2005), *Why the European Commission is Wrong about EPAs*, in Trade Negotiations Insights : From Doha to Cotonou, Vol. 4 No. 2.

Szepesi, Stefan and Bilal, Sanoussi, *EPA Impact Studies – SADC and the regional coherence*, In Brief No.2A September 2003, European Centre for Development Policy Management – ecdpm.

Torp, J.E. and Ndlela, D., (1999) *Can Upgrading and Local Company Driven Commodity Chains Overcome De-Industrialization?: Some Theoretical Implications of a Study of Zimbabwean Companies*, CBS Copenhagen Business School, Occasional Paper: International Conference: Business in Development 18-19 November, 1999.

UNCTAD (1997), *Transnational Corporations and Industrial Restructuring in Developing Countries: Zimbabwe Case Study*, prepared for UNCTAD, July 1997.

Whitely, R. (1987), *Taking Firms Seriously as Economic Actors: Towards a Sociology of Economic Actors*. Organisation Studies, No. 8, 125-47.

Whitely, R. (1994a), *Societies, Firms and Markets: The Social Structuring of Business Systems*. In Whitely, R., European Business Systems, London: Sage.

Chapter 5

Revisiting the African Development Trajectory: From LPA to NEPAD

Mbaya J. Kankwenda

Introduction

Today, almost all the major powers have their initiative on Africa or, at least, a special programme for the continent: African Growth and Opportunity Act (AGOA), the Tokyo International Conference on African Development (TICAD), the Summit of Heads of State of France and Africa, the Blair Commission, the G8 Africa Plan, etc. Each has its own plethora of recommendations in terms of development policies and, sometimes, in terms of aid. Hence, a proliferation of initiatives, each initiator seeking to find a niche for intervention through a particular facility or forum. All profess as either intended to get Africa out of its multi-dimensional development crisis, in which it has been floundering for several decades, or, in a veiled manner, destined to attach the African canoe more tightly to the ship of liberal globalisation.

This results in a proliferation of solutions which would save the continent, each world power advocating its own and seeking to win over the largest number of African players through its marketing campaigns. The upshot is confusion among African policymakers, particularly in the search for and implementation of their own home-grown renaissance policies for the continent within the prevailing context of liberal globalisation.

The future of Africa should not be conceived or shaped from outside, with a semblance of African participation, individually or by a few small groups set up for the purpose. That is why Africans themselves, through their political leaders, have lately been insistent on defining for themselves the frameworks and policies through which they can position themselves in the construction of their future and, therefore, the renaissance of the continent. Within the framework of the reflection and analysis undertaken in this book, it is relevant to examine some of the initiatives of Africa's partners. However, it is even more pressing to analyse those of the African leaderships themselves. Although a thorough and comprehensive analysis of the continent's development experience would require going back in history to pre-colonial times, I have purposely chosen to restrict myself to the independence period, that is around the last forty-five years or so.

This chapter is divided into four parts. After an analysis of the international context of African development, I briefly review the development experience of the continent. This is followed by a discussion on the responses of the international community. Finally, in the fourth and last part the focus is on the response of Africans themselves, in particular from the Lagos Plan of Action (LPA) to the latest New Partnership for African Development (NEPAD). A concluding section looks at the prospects for Africa's future development.

The International Context of African Development

The World Economy as at Present

The main characteristics of the world economy may be summarised as made up of the following features:

i. The accelerated process of globalisation of the economy, in the sense of economic, trade and financial integration but also in terms of its internationalisation and its political, social and cultural dimensions, and of established transnational companies with their immense networks which dictate the process in its different dimensions. The notion of national space, be it economic or other, and the powers linked to it are increasingly eroded and without effect in designing development policies.

ii. Strengthening of "economic *tarzanism* and the collective dictatorship of the North", on the world scene. The balance of power is certainly uneven, but this inequality is increasing. Indeed the present system recognises neither "the economic democracy" at the international level nor the peoples' economic right, that is to say the right to produce and trade in the world on a fair basis. Quite the contrary. Not only are the great powers not ready to accept fundamental changes in the established order in economic relations and structures which they dominate for their benefit, but they strive to entrench their positions and to integrate the rest of the world into their basic economic equation. The powers of the North will continue to forcefully fight against the project of a New International Economic Order, equitable and balanced.

This development has been accompanied by the projects of forming large regional entities, notably in the most economically dynamic zones in North America, Europe, and the Asia-Pacific Economic Cooperation Forum. These large entities are also instruments for settling internal conflicts in sharing the advantages of economic globalisation between the member countries of the economic grouping. At the same time, they are instruments for strengthening collective competitiveness vis-à-vis non members.

iii. The rise of conservative neo-liberalism results in development itself disappearing as a preoccupation in economic and social policies. In fact, and no doubt thanks to the collapse of the Soviet empire, the dominant tendency in the countries of the North favours a noticeable disengagement of the government in the management of economic and social affairs especially through privatisation, deregulation, and the dismantling of the welfare state.

The fundamentalism of this credo has, unfortunately, become the bible of the forces directing the globalisation process.

This has been evident in the structural adjustment policies in Africa, which tended to obscure the fundamental question of development as human and social security for all in the economic, social, and political fields. These policies tended to significantly reduce or weaken the role of the African state and to preach the efficiency of the market, to the detriment of real development; this is the situation in the Africa of today and the driving forces of globalisation want it to remain so in the Africa of tomorrow.

iv. The principle of competitiveness at the level of the world market is increasingly becoming the guiding principle, and perhaps the only point of reference and the only criterion for production at the national level. Yet, to confront competition, not only do companies become international but through the game of alliances and mergers they transform themselves into gigantic oligopolistic structures; they thereby bypass national standards and make light of the roles of national parliaments and governments. As in games theory it is more or less known who is going to win. Consequently, the only ring in which the Northern heavyweight and the African feather weight have the same chance, and are subject to the same rules, is in the discourse on how to cover up the economic *tarzanism* of the North.

v. Then there is the struggle between globalisation powers for scientific and technological control of (i) information highways, (ii) natural and environmental resources, (ii) space resources, (iv) commercial and financial markets, and (v) advanced techniques to replace basic raw materials. Sciences and technologies are generally cumulative. Twenty-first century sciences and technologies are therefore going to be built on the existing structures in different countries and regions. Also, considering the rapid speed at which scientific and technological progress is taking place the context of Africa's development is agonizingly limited.

vi. The increasing marginalisation of Africa as regards trends in world trade is due, firstly, to the structural decline in demand for African goods in the countries of the North and to the fall in Africa's capacity to import. As regards capital movements in general many factors contribute to the marginalization of the continent; these include the narrowness of the African market, the relatively high level of risks and of production costs notably due to poor infrastructure. Much the same applies to investments in particular.

Globalisation and Challenges for Africa

Under this theme I will restrict myself to a few major challenges which globalisation presents for the African continent. Of particular interest the nature of the process, competitiveness and the African private sector, economic growth and poverty reduction, the State player as the guarantor of the nation's wellbeing, and development and integration policies in their global and regional dynamics.

An intrinsically unbalanced dynamic for Africa

While the advantages of economic globalisation seem generally greater than the costs they mask disparities among countries especially developing countries. The losses from globalisation affect the least advanced countries the most, that is, the majority of the sub-Saharan countries. These losses in incomes in hard currency, to the tune of US$ 1.2 billion for African countries, have important implications for economic growth and poverty in Africa. They are manifested in, for instance, a compression of income, a reduced ability to import, and greater dependence on outside aid; they also have repercussions on a state's ability to invest, whether in social or economic infrastructures.

For the poor African countries, there is no question of benefits of the international trade expansion. Between 1971 and 1990 the Least Developed Countries (LDCs), of which more than two thirds are in Africa and which account for 10 percent of the world's population saw their share of world trade decline by half, dropping to 0.3 percent. Similarly for foreign direct investment, of which only 10 percent is destined for 70 percent of the world's population in developing countries. There are multiple reasons for such distortions, including the weakness of national policies, pressures of outside forces, inequality and discrimination of international legislation, and to the intrinsic imbalance in the globalisation process.

An analysis of the flows in economic gains shows that the distribution of trade globalisation remains inequitable. At a maximum, developing countries will reap 25 percent to 30 percent of the advantages of trade liberalisation; from this the greater part will go to a minority of Asian and South American exporting countries. The Uruguay Round negotiations did not affect the situation much as it failed to address squarely the issues of the industrial and agricultural protection systems of the industrialised countries, questions on debt or markets for raw materials, all of which are strategic questions for developing countries.

As seen in the latest negotiations of the WTO Conference of Ministers in Cancun (10-14 September 2003) the Northern Coalition (EU and United States) caused these negotiations to fail mainly because they did not want to make any concessions which would have benefited the developing countries; the problem of tariffs on agricultural products which they subsidise heavily remained unresolved. In fact, subsidies were non-negotiable. Contrary to the rule of the majority the numerical majority of developing countries proposed another text which was not accepted by the few rich countries united for the cause. The popular vote of the poor did not weigh much against the economic and political weight of the rich countries, even if they are in a minority, another proof of the absence of democracy in world economic governance.

The other point of divergence between the united North and the poor South was the set of questions on the so-called Singapore problems relating especially to the transparency of state procurement, the liberalisation of trade and free competition. The developing countries, disappointed by the attitude of the countries of the North on the agricultural questions, did not even wish to hold any negotiations. Though at the recently concluded WTO Bangkok meeting the industrialised countries accepted to change their policies on agriculture subsides it will take more than a decade for concrete action to be taken.

So, while the globalisation process advances with giant strides it does not benefit everyone on the globe equitably, but it gives the industrialised and powerful countries more than their due. The 1992 UNDP Human Development Report estimated the losses suffered by the developing countries, due to their marginalisation in international trade and on the labour and capital markets, at US$ 500 billion annually or ten times the volume of foreign aid received by these same countries. Annual Third World repayments of US$ 340 billion flow northwards to service a US$ 2.2 trillion debt, more than five times the G8's development aid budget (Patrick Bond, 2005). Along the same lines Christian Aid estimates that since 1980 the damage done to African economies by trade liberalization amounts to US$ 272 billion, meaning an average of more than US$ 12 billion per year over the last twenty five years. This new economic and financial order contains the seeds of economic contraction, destruction of the environment, social destruction and nationalist or ethnic conflicts which could lead inevitably to what Michel Chossudovsky called the 'globalisation of poverty' (Chossudovsky, 1998).

The challenge of competitiveness or of economic governance and of adjustment to the global market

For more than two decades, economic reform policies have been imposed on African countries under different versions, and always with a variety of conditionalities. In reality these economic reforms are intended to ensure 'good management of African economies' as donor countries want. More so, they ensure debt repayment and further integration of African economies into the globalisation process, and their continued control and manipulation. But, as already indicated the benefits are not evident; on the contrary there are huge risks and threats to the prosperity of African countries.

Universal convergence and the paradise of shared world welfare do not seem to be just over the horizon. nor fit into the dynamics of the logic in progress. The economic reforms would be working against their fundamental objective if they were to row against the current, and lift the African countries out of the dynamics of polarisation and marginalisation. The revision of the Washington Consensus to recognise some role for the state merely seeks to bring on board an important player to accompany and facilitate the dynamics advocated in the Consensus's basic doctrine.

In reality, Africa is the continent which is the most integrated into the world economy and depends most on it. And this dependence has grown further during the last two decades, that is to say the decades of the reform policies. Between 1986 and 1996 this integration and dependence has gone from 15.8 percent to 18.9 percent against 10.4 percent and 15.2 percent for all the low and intermediate income countries. But as African exports are essentially primary products, the prices of which are constantly falling, this manner of inserting Africa into the globalisation process is clearly understood.

It is useful to note how the African economies under adjustment have reacted to this process in other to show that getting into line by the said reform policies and strategies has not served the continent. Indeed, World Bank data show that GDP growth in Africa south of the Sahara (in which countries are the most subject to the reform policies), went from 1.8 percent in the period 1980–1990 to some 2.2 percent in the period 1990–1998; it improved slightly recently at 3.9 percent for the period 2000-2004 because of oil prices (see Table 5.1) As a rate of global economic growth this is miserable. In addition, it is not demonstrated that the growth can be attributed to the reform policies, when the weight of agriculture in the economic growth of SSA is considered for example and the non-negligible positive effects of good rainfall in this sector. Furthermore, excepting for the last four years this growth does not even match that of population growth on the continent during the same period. Arguably, wealth per head of population is evolving on a downward slope and poverty increases all the more during periods of economic reform peddled by the Development Merchant System (DMS) (Kankwenda, 2000).

Table 5.1 Economic Growth in Africa and in the World 1980-2004

Country	GDP Growth Rates			Value of GDP (millions of dollars)		
	1980–90	1990–98	2000–04	1980	1998	2004
Argentina	-0.4	3.2	-0.1	76,962	344,360	151,501
Australia	3.4	3.6	3.3	160,110	364,247	631,256
Brazil	2.7	3.3	2.0	234,873	778,292	604,855
Canada	3.3	2.2	2.5	266,002	598,847	979,764
France	2.3	1.5	1.4	664,596	1,432,902	2,002,582
India	5.8	6.1	6.2	186,439	383,429	691,876
Italy	2.4	1.2	0.8	449,913	1,171,044	1,672,302
Japan	4.0	1.3	1.3	1,059,254	3,783,140	4,623,398
South Korea	9.4	6.2	4.7	62,803	297,900	679,674
Mexico	0.7	2.5	1.5	223,505	393,224	676,497
Netherlands	2.3	2.6	0.3	171,861	382,487	577,260
Nigeria	1.6	2.6	4.9	64,202	41,353	72,106
Norway	2.8	3.9	1.7	63,419	145,896	250,168
Singapore	6.6	8.0	2.8	11,718	85,425	106,818
South Africa	1.2	1.6	3.2	78,744	116,730	212,777
Spain	3.0	1.9	2.5	213,308	551,923	991,442
Thailand	7.6	7.4	5.3	32,304	153,909	163,491
United Kingdom	3.2	2.2	2.2	537,389	1,357,429	2,140,898
United States	3.0	2.9	2.6	2,709,000	8,210,600	11,667,515
SS Africa	1.8	2.2	3.9	270,391	316,517	543,990
World	3.2	2.4	2.5	10,939,459	28,854,043	40,887,837

Source: Drawn up by the author from World Bank data, World Development Report, 1999/2000 and 2005/2006.

The table shows also that while non-African countries have seen their GDP multiplied by two, four, six and even seven times those of African countries, and African countries under stabilisation and adjustment programmes, have practically vegetated. In twenty years of economic reform policies (1980-1998), the GDP of SSA has gone from US$270 billion to US$316 billion, or an increase of 17 percent! Individual countries such as Argentina, Brazil, India, Mexico, the Netherlands or Spain whose GDP was less than or even far behind that of SSA in 1980 before the implementation of the adjustment programmes, have today a level of GDP far superior to that of black Africa as a whole. Some have even become providers of aid to Africa! The case of Norway compared to Nigeria or Africa as a whole is more than instructive.

The challenge of sustainable growth and growing poverty

The propagandists and theoreticians of globalization present this process as the path to salvation for sustained growth and the reduction if not the eradication of poverty. The opportunities it is supposed to offer and the governance and economic reform programmes which serve as its base, as well as the theories of growth through foreign trade and integration into the world market are the major elements of their doctrines.

However, sustained growth has not been realizable in Africa (Tables 5.1 and 5.2). Quite the contrary, the situation has got worse during the last two decades of the 20th century. As afore-noted, the number of countries in the category of the LDC's has increased in Africa, constituting more than 75 percent of Sub-Saharan African countries. The populations in absolute poverty have increased both absolutely and relatively (World Bank, 2001 and 2002; Annan, K., 1997). Africa is well integrated into the global market but in a dependent manner.

The World Bank estimates that the millennium development goal of reducing absolute poverty by half by 2015 can only be attained if developing countries double their growth rate per head on a continuous basis over the period, that is going from 1.8 percent at present to 3.6 percent. But even if that could be achieved at the level of developing countries as a world, in Africa it would only reduce the rate of absolute poverty (US$ 1 or less a day) by 39 percent. Simultaneously, the population of the poor would increase in absolute terms, going from 240 million in 1990 and 300 million in 1999 to 345 millions in 2015. In such a gamble Africa would succeed with difficulty. It is starting from a position of poor economic performance, lower than the rate of population growth of 1.7 percent for the 1980s and 2.4 percent for the 1990s (see Table 5.2). The decline in average living standards is thus a direct consequence (see Table 5.3). To succeed in reducing poverty by half in 2015, an average rate of economic growth greater than double the rate of population increase, that is to say, close to 7 percent would be necessary; and this would be continuous over the period.

Table 5.2 Real Economic Growth Between Africa and Asia

Countries or Regions	(Average annual growth in %)			
	1965-1969	1970-1979	1980-1989	1990-2003
Sub-Saharan Africa	4.2	3.6	1.7	2.6
North Africa	5.2	6.5	4.2	3.6
All Africa	4.5	4.4	2.4	3.0
China	2.0	4.8	10.6	9.6
India	4.6	3.4	5.7	5.8
Indonesia	5.9	7.8	5.8	3.5
South Asia	4.6	3.4	5.6	5.4
East Asia	4.2	6.1	7.5	7.6

Source: Global Coalition for Africa, Annual Report 2004/2005.

Table 5.3 Real Economic Growth Per Head Between Africa and Asia

Countries or Regions	(Average annual growth in %)			
	1965-1969	1970-1979	1980-1989	1990-2003
Sub-Saharan Africa	1.5	0.8	-1.2	0.1
North Africa	2.5	3.9	1.5	1.7
All Africa	1.8	1.6	-0.4	-0.5
China	-0.7	2.9	9.0	8.5
India	2.2	1.0	3.4	4.0
Indonesia	3.5	5.2	3.9	2.0
South Asia	2.1	1.0	3.3	3.5
East Asia	1.5	4.0	5.8	6.4

Source: Global Coalition for Africa, Annual Report 2004/2005.

Trend forecasts indicate that Africa will not achieve continuous growth and a reduction in poverty over the said period. Poverty will increase for the following reasons:

i.   With a few exceptions, the poor economic performance in the continent as a whole, on the basis of growth projections for main sectors such as agriculture, industry and mining;
ii. The weakness of internal capital accumulation and therefore of investments, both domestic and foreign direct investments, in the foreseeable future;
iii. (The absence of a growth model oriented towards the fight against poverty (pro-poor economic growth), itself tied to the absence of policies for eliminating poverty;
iv. The fall in social indicators or their very slow progress, notably in terms of education (rates of school attendance and access to basic health services). This fall is linked to the HIV/AIDS pandemic which affects more than 30 million Africans, and its negative economic and social consequences. The overall result is that life expectation at birth has fallen from 53 years in 1990 to 50 years today for the whole continent, while it has fallen from 50 years to 47 years for sub-Saharan Africa during the same period;
v.   The impact of political crises and conflicts which continue to have negative consequences for economic growth and poverty;
vi. The fragility of the capacity base due to the regression of social indicators, the effects of crises and conflicts, and neo-colonial state structures which are not development-oriented;
vii. The pattern of income distribution and therefore of the dividends of any growth which is very unequal and discriminatory in Africa, so that all growth is not necessarily reflected in the improvement of the living standards and the reduction of poverty of the populations. Rather, it is cornered by the upper layers of the "predatocracy" and their internal and external allies;
viii. The vicious circle of poverty whereby poor countries and populations tend to remain poor because of the lack of physical, economic and human assets to propel them out of the circle;
ix. The absence of a consistent cooperation policy on the part of the development partners who do not respect their undertakings repeated in different UN and international fora. In reality, the downward trend in development aid to Africa means it is barely benefiting from a third of the commitments of donors. Gross concessionary aid to Africa fell from close to 3 percent of African GDP at the end of the 80s to 1.2 percent today while for sub-Saharan Africa it fell from 3.6 percent in 1985 to 1.7 percent of GDP today (Global Coalition for Africa, Annual Report 2002/2003).

That is why the World Bank has concluded that the trend of growing poverty in SSA will persist during the coming years.

The Challenge of Values Inversion and Role of the State in Africa

In the Washington Consensus, whether in its original or in the so-called revised version, and just as in the discourse between defenders and adversaries on the paradigm on which it is based, the fundamental question of the relationship between the economy and the society remains. For the defenders of the paradigm, the economy

– understood in the sense of the liberal economy and its market values, private profit, and free trade – is indisputable and cannot be called into question. The full functioning of this paradigm is society's objective while the public interest or human and social wellbeing are a result. It is therefore in society's interest that this paradigm does not suffer any constraint to its full realisation. The state in this conception becomes a tool to service the paradigm, and its *raison d'être* is to facilitate the full play of the paradigm's ideal functioning, and to ensure the safety of these values and the players in the service of the paradigm. In this sense, globalisation, which is a stage in the development of the liberal economy, is presented as inevitable. It is presented as a benefactor or in any case as bringing welfare to all and one must just resign oneself to actively joining in. The economic reform strategies applied to Africa arise from this credo.

As for the adversaries of the Consensus, they think that there is an inversion of values in the relationship between the economy and society. Society, which means the public interest and human and social wellbeing, is the primary value and the objective in the service of which the economy, even if liberal, must function and develop. The economy and its development are means and not ends in themselves. In this sense, the state as the guarantor of, and with primary responsibility for, the public interest must not be a 'soft' agent but rather an active and dynamic player responsible for regulating the economic, social and political distortions inherent to the market. The market cannot be left to self-regulate its own inherent distortions. It is incapable of doing so, and history has proven it.

The ideologists of the market fundamentalism paradigm are economically, financially, politically and militarily powerful. They mobilise all the means at their disposal not only to convince those amongst them who might be hesitant, but more so those who have not adopted the paradigm. Financial and economic organisations just as media and universities have become active agents in the service of the paradigm. Its success sometimes requires that those who resist are economically or even militarily brought into line. Bringing one into line economically has, quite obviously, a military connotation through its conditionality mechanisms, instruments to control policies aimed at implementing the paradigm and monitoring progress.

Thus, the globalisation being talked about is that of the market paradigm. It is used to strengthen the power of the masters of the process so that they can bring the majority of those who oppose or resist in line, or so that they can distribute 'free of charge' a few crumbs in an outburst of humanism. For this reason it needs 'soft' states elsewhere other than in the countries of its main masters – soft in relation to the market paradigm but also soft in relation to the direction and the driving forces of the globalisation process. The rest flows from this conception and its 'natural' implications.

The question of the role of the state in society becomes a central strategic question for the African state in particular. Should it just be made an instrument of this inversion of values and therefore subject to, and functioning in, the service of the market? That is what the Washington Consensus doctrine and ideology advocate. However, the reality in the major industrialised countries is that the state, although relatively diminished compared to the past, still plays a key role at both the national and international levels. Indeed, states have a primary role to play in guaranteeing a certain level of human security to their populations, especially those that are marginalised or excluded by the globalisation process. That is what all states in the industrialised countries do using appropriate means. That is to say that what is refused to African states under the economic reforms conditionality regimes, is common practice in the industrialised countries. A dynamic and strong private sector needs a strong state as a partner able to protect it but also to oversee its inevitable excesses. But that is accepted primarily for the developed world.

The revised Consensus only partially recognises this reality. Today, the most important players in the globalisation game are transnational companies. Certainly, sometimes they have conflicting relations with their states but, fundamentally, they are in complicity or in league with their states. The strategic considerations taken into account in their expansion and the global strategic interests of their states are complementary. Globalisation benefits from the decisions of states in favour of transnational companies and the powerful oligopolies they constitute. These firms and oligopolies expect political support from these states in their expansion, support for buying foreign companies being privatised, security of their business abroad, capacity to generate and manage the use of new technologies, to organise the monetary and financial system, to control access to the planet's natural resources, and to manufacture or retain weapons of mass destruction.

But transnationals also expect from their states the capability to impose management policies which transfer the burden on to the third world countries particularly those of Africa. The conditionalities in economic reforms arise from this perception of the role of the capitalist industrialised state as the saviour of national enterprises in difficulty or running the risk of difficulties. It seems that the Asian crisis should also be analysed from this perspective of destabilising emerging economies for the sake of boosting some activities for transnational companies and the economies of industrialised countries. Even the so-called growth driven by exports or greater insertion in external markets is practically and historically a result of the Northern state intervention in the economic field.

The challenge of the future

In a recent report the Organization for Economic Cooperation and Development (OECD) claims that if things continue in Africa south of the Sahara as they now are, the situation will be catastrophic by 2020. The reasons are simple: Africa will have a population of 1.1 billion of which close to half will be under the age of twenty. Inappropriate policies will result in intolerable human costs in terms of growing poverty, the generalisation of crime, migrations, health and food insecurity, financial crises, the expansion of AIDS, etc. This will threaten the security and wellbeing of the rest of the world and in particular the OECD member countries. The report thinks nevertheless that if Africa adopts appropriate policies it will experience significant development in trade and be a partner in the 21st century.

From this vision of making the Africa of the 21st century a partner for OECD countries in trade, policies are proposed for it to share in the 'New Global Age' paradise envisaged for 2020. This is considered a high performance scenario compared to the classic scenario. The implementation strategy for this vision includes of course economic reforms in developing countries and, for OECD countries, the liberalisation of trade and financial markets as well as the search for social cohesion. The strategy also involves strengthening of the multilateral system, the consolidation of the integration of the economies of non-OECD member countries in the global economy, and greater attention to environmental issues (OECD, 1997).

But the 'New Global Age' is nothing more than the shared welfare in globalisation as advocated by the Washington Consensus doctrinaires. It is a call to the developing countries, particularly those of Africa, not only to understand the advantages and opportunities that the market globalisation paradigm offers, but also a somewhat muscular invitation to join in. In this perception, the only possible policy for the future well-being of Africa is that which enjoys the approval of the rich countries and which is in line with the interests, priorities and ideology of those who control global capital.

The reality of the neo-liberal globalisation and market paradigm is nevertheless, as indicated above, that of the cumulative asymmetry of wealth between the globalisation 'barons' and other peoples and countries. The shared wellbeing projections in the 'New Global Age' do not change this asymmetry even if they show some hope of improvements for the developing countries. Being integrated in the globalisation process must be justified by holding out hope of some benefit.

As the United Nations Secretary General recalled at the annual meeting of the World Economic Forum in 1997 (Annan, K. 1997), today more than 60 percent of the world's population lives on less than US$2 dollars a day; around 100 countries are in a worse situation than fifteen years ago! Nevertheless, the flow of private capital towards the developing countries has been multiplied thirty-five times, going from US$ 5 billion at the beginning of the seventies to US$ 176 billion today; the flow of public aid for development has not stopped declining. The present situation of cumulative asymmetry of wealth is thus the product of this massive flow of private capital towards the developing countries and the policies it supports. In other words, the market has not been capable of distributing the welfare of globalisation equitably. Rather, it has been an active negative agent. The question can legitimately be asked as to who benefits from globalisation and why some staunchly defend it and even impose it on others. The question can also be legitimately asked as to how much or what percentage of the wealth accumulated by the globalisation 'barons' comes from developing countries in general, and Africa in particular.

But neo-liberal globalisation is there and it cannot be ignored nor escaped from in the context of the global market and of weak African economies. That would be suicidal for an isolated African country or a group of countries. Confronted with this situation, some opt for the pure and simple participation in the process with its arsenal of economic reforms and conditionalities, but also in the hope of guaranteed aid and other components of the promised welfare. It is thus accepted, whether or not in full knowledge of its limits, while hoping to continue the dialogue and discussion so as to gradually obtain a non-polarising humanisation of the system.

Others opt for a collective regional or individual approach of controlled and strategic insertion into globalisation. This has the possibility of benefiting from opportunities which are not in conformity with the illusion of progress through the global market but, rather, are in conformity with the transformation of economic and social structures as strategic components for true continental development. It is what Walden Bello (Bello,1999) calls a limited de-globalisation model. It is in this sense that a possible multi-polarisation of the system must be envisaged.

It is at this level that the role of the state, and the African state in particular, is crucial. Indeed, the state is a player which has a strategic position in the globalisation dynamics. Its role and even its nature will depend on the option chosen. In this second option, which consists of what I call development democratisation or development socialisation, its role will be far more active in the whole development dynamics and in the partnership with both civil society and the private sector. This compares favourably with the first option in which the dynamics of total profit through the market marginalises the State and reduces it to the specific functions of preparing the ground for those making profit and then supervising profit security. Nevertheless, when the market enters into crisis it is up to the state to save it. Therefore, it cannot be imagined that a problem as important as the development socialisation, which goes beyond the framework of the market rules, can be reduced to an outcome of its operation. It is, on the contrary, the primary responsibility of the African State.

There is not and should not be a doctrinaire approach, either in the matter of competitiveness and its instruments or in the matter of economic reform policies, and less so in the matter of development paths and strategies. African countries have the right and the duty to explore other paths, to imagine and to innovate, in the perspective opened by the paradigm of sustainable human development. The challenge for African countries is to conduct autonomous policies for national and regional development to which insertion in the globalisation process is subject, and not the converse as at present where globalisation dictates growth and development policies in Africa.

The continent should, above all, take the liberty of seeking innovative and alternative paths for another globalisation which is in their interest, and with diverse implementation strategies and players, of which the state is the body responsible for social wellbeing and the public interest including the market. Finally, the continent should position itself as an effective player for a controlled insertion into globalisation and not just as an agent seeking formulas for adaptation and self-adjustment to the pressures from globalisation and its 'barons'.

The African Development Experience: The Illusory Decades

In spite of national or regional development programmes and decades of general or sector development the indicators show that despite the progress made in the social field in the first two development decades, African countries have experienced serious economic and social crisis and increased levels of poverty. Confronted with an unfavourable global context and wide-ranging challenges arising therefrom the continent is characterised by (i) a development crisis, (ii) a dual process of economic and political liberalisation, and (iii) an absence of a peaceful and stable framework which provides an appropriate environment for development.

The continent's crisis has contributed not only to slowing down the 'development trade' and to reducing business for the Development Merchant System (DMS) but it has also tended to discredit the development mastermind in Africa (the development priest) and unveil its real face. The DMS then multiplies studies and reports, seminars and workshops, miscellaneous conferences and forums to the point where Africans find themselves drowned in the DMS productions, be it on the general and/or sector paths for escaping. Their output was vast and voluminous but not always coherent so they ended up confusing African leaders.

The system strengthened itself on the ideological level by inspiring development doctrines and policies which are the basis for selling development merchandise to Africa. The first two decades of independence were thus mainly decades of development appearances which, despite the economic miracles and take-offs which have been made much of, have not prevented the continent from profound economic and social crises.

The third decade thus became that of stabilisation and structural adjustment policies, more to manage the African crises as far as it disturbed the West (debt repayment, integration into the global market through exports growth and opening of borders) rather than to get African economies out of the crisis. With the end of the cold war and the crisis of the liberal economy the economic reforms were to be prize exhibits of correct development policies, and they became conditions imposed on the African countries to be able to benefit from development aid and loans. The development trade took on another dimension because it is rationalized as development policies and, like merchandise, has its producers, salesmen, buyers and financiers.

The fourth decade has seen the strengthening of the globalisation of the economy (ultimate reason for the economic reform policies) by globalising politics, with demands for political reform and 'good governance' as a new condition.

But the result is there, obstinate and deriding both to Africa and its partners: neither sustainable economic growth nor less human development are at the rendezvous with Africa. Africa has however continued to remain under the sway of its partners within the DMS, partners who have sold her 'development' projects, programmes, and economic and social policies and have financed them throughout the last 45 years.

In summary, the result of four and a half decades of African development is, at the very best, rather mixed (see Kankwenda, et al, 1999) Over the last ten years, more than 80 percent of the 36 countries considered as having the lowest level of human development index in the Human Development Reports are in Africa. In its report on Global Development 1998-1999, the World Bank estimated that the number of low income African countries rose from 34 to 38 proof of the deterioration in living conditions on the continent. Moreover, it should be noted that the 34 or 38 countries represent 75 percent to almost 84 percent of all 45 sub-Saharan African countries which are in the category of the destitute.

According to other estimates, Africa south of the Sahara counts about 250 million poor people, or about 45 percent of the population. Real GDP growth has noticeably dropped in the continent as a whole, falling from 4.5 percent during the period 1965-1969 to 4.2 percent in 1970-1979, 2.5 percent in 1980-1989, 2.3 percent in 1990-1999 or respectively 0.9 percent and 3.5 percent for the sub-periods 1990-1994 and 1995-1999. The recent period (2000-2004) shows good economic recovery with a growth rate reaching 3.9 percent; but this is an artificial growth due to huge increases in oil prices and, as such, it does not reflect actual improvement in the wellbeing of the population.

Still more alarming, poverty is growing because of a negative trend in income growth per inhabitant, which fell from 0.4 percent annually on average in 1970-1987 to 4 percent during the period 1988-1997. Prospects for economic growth for the African continent as a whole are modest: 4 percent on average against 5.4 percent for developing countries during the 1997-2006 decade, and 6 percent to 7 percent for the period 2010-2020 (World Bank, 1997). One notices, however, that SSA failed to reach such a growth rate during the 2000-2004 period (see Table 5.1). As a result, Africa's share in global trade fell significantly, from 4.6 percent in 1980 to 1.6 percent in 1999 for exports and from 3.6 percent to 1.9 percent for imports during the same period. This negative trend also affects foreign direct investments in Africa, with the exception of investments in the oil sector. Taking account of the fact that the rates of domestic saving and of investments are the lowest for all developing regions, and that the external debt is on average two times greater than gross national income and four times export receipts, Africa south of the Sahara risks having to wait for a period equivalent to two generations to be able to recover its average standard of living of 1975. Indeed, the 1998 Human Development Report confirms a regression of 20 percent during the 1975-1995 period.

As regards human development, the challenges for Africa south of the Sahara are considerable despite some manifest progress. The health and education indicators show important deficits. Morbidity and mortality rates are at present higher in Africa than in the rest of the world. Health and nutrition standards have deteriorated, and Africa is the continent that is most hardly hit by AIDS. In addition, armed conflicts have caused terrible ravages. Some years back, the 8 million refugees on the continent represented close to half of the total number of refugees world-wide, while there were about 20 million internally displaced persons within national boundaries.

Dazzling successes have nevertheless been recorded in SSA. Between 1960 and 1995 life expectancy at birth went from 40 to 51 years. Between 1970 and 1995, the adult literacy rate more than doubled. From 1960 to 1995, the net rate of school enrolment went from 25 percent to 50 percent at the primary level and from 13 percent to 38 percent at the secondary level. The proportion of the population having access to clean water which was 25 percent in 1980 reached 43 percent in 1995. Important achievements have also been recorded in the advancement of women: for example, the proportion of women able to read and write compared to literate men is greater than 60 percent, a higher proportion than in the Arab states and in south Asia (Kankwenda et al, 1999). Moreover, and despite violent political crises, Africa is making some progress in the matter of political democratisation. Unfortunately, over the last ten years there have been declines in some of the social achievements.

Responses of the International Community

The experience of African countries in promoting development has led some to characterize it as development breakdown or as a development crisis. This has become obvious to everyone particularly during the last thirty years. Various solutions have been designed and implemented, including one or other of the following: (i) economic reforms (including aid and debt problems), (ii) political reforms, (ii) environment protection, and (iv) humanitarian assistance. The results have not been convincing.

The United Nations and Africa

The international community has played an important role in assisting development efforts in Africa or in just getting them out of crisis. The UN concerns itself with the construction of a 'globalised' world, inclusive and beneficent for all peoples of the world. With its dismal record of economic performance in most African countries and the risks it represents for the rest of the world the continent has become a major preoccupation for the international community. It is in this context that the UN has been continually involved in the search for solutions to the crises in Africa. On the political level, working with the OAU, and AU, it has been active in conflict management and in sustaining peace, security and political stability. On the economic front, special meetings or sessions on Africa have been organised. Special programmes have been drawn up to find lasting solutions to the development crisis, to put the continent back on the right path of accelerated growth, solve the problems of external debt, build national capacities, support the integration of the African economies at the regional and global level, etc.

The UN specialised agencies and the different funds and programmes have been instructed by their policymaking bodies to give priority to Africa in their development cooperation programmes. Many have done so and the example of the UNDP can bear witness to this. It has devoted more than 40 percent of its resources and its activities to development in Africa in addition to a series of specific programmes which began with the crisis of the end of the seventies and beginning of the eighties and the problems provoked by the adjustment programmes.

The successive three development decades in the sixties, seventies and eighties did not have significant effects on development in Africa. The organisation then changed its approach during the third development decade with the UN Programme of Action for African Economic Recovery and Development, 1986-1990 (UNPAAERD), adopted by the General Assembly in 1986 at an extraordinary session devoted to the critical situation on the continent. The programme was based on two priority sectors, namely, the development of agriculture and of human resources. The basic UNPAAERD objective was to mobilise political and financial support for these sectors but especially for the SAPs which were expected to lead to economic revival and development. However, the economic reforms have turned out to be essentially debt repayment programmes and for integrating these economies into the global market by means of developing export sectors and activities. The UN therefore became a party to these outcomes.

Half way through the implementation of UNPAAERD it was realised that the situation in Africa had got worse, the causes of the crisis was were still there, the financial commitments of the international community had not been honoured, losses in export incomes had increased, and Africa had become a net exporter of capital to the industrialised countries and the international financial institutions. African countries did not hide their feelings of disappointment or even betrayal.

The failure of UNPAAERD, confirmed at the General Assembly session in 1991, provided the impetus to launch another initiative, the New Agenda for the Development of Africa in the 90s or NADAF. Its declared objective was to ensure the continued support of the international community to enable the continent achieve a GDP growth rate of at least 6 percent annually throughout the 1990's. NADAF paid particular attention to human development and the employment situation, and therefore favoured programmes in the areas of basic social services (health, education, drinking water and sanitation, nutrition, housing) and the integration of women in the development process. NADAF had taken its basic ideas from the ECA document, the African Alternative Framework for Structural Adjustment Programmes for socio-economic recovery and transformation (AAF-SAP). It insisted on real partnership and shared responsibility between the African countries and the international community, each having explicit commitments to honour.

The NADAF seemed better prepared than UNPAAERD due to its approach as there was more active participation of African countries in its design; the basic principles were borrowed from AAF-SAP emphasising the need to transform structures, the diversification and integration of African economies, ownership of the development process by the African countries, and the promotion of autonomous development in a real partnership with aid providers. But more than that, NADAF had fixed quantified and therefore measurable objectives: GDP growth rate at an annual average of 6 percent over the decade, a minimum of public development aid of US$30 billion by 1992, with an average annual growth of 4 percent over the rest of the decade.

The same problems at the root of the failure of the UNPAAERD and the unrealism of NADAF's objectives resulted in the economic situation in Africa further deteriorating. Even AAF-SAP which was adopted by African leaders was not able to gain the necessary support from donors. It was even ridiculed and resisted by some of them. The NADAF spirit no doubt influenced or inspired the work and the programmes of some UN-system organisations, but there were not significant positive results on the ground. Some saw in the fuss which was made about it and the hopes it raised a diplomatic gesticulation from the international community using the slogan: 'Africa, master of its economic destiny in a more cooperative global environment'. This contributed to keeping the hopes and faith in the system and in international cooperation alive. But the deceptions were at the level of the hopes and affected the organisation's credibility on the continent.

Less than three years after the adoption of NADAF and even before its mid-term assessment, the UN Secretary General launched two other initiatives in 1993 : the creation of the Office of the Special Coordinator for Africa and the Least Developed Countries (OSCAL) and the setting up of the group of high level experts and eminent personalities. The first was to some extent a duplication of the ECA because the office's major work was to prepare studies and disseminate them in Africa or to participate in the organisation of some conferences which were of interest to the continent. It was also supposed to deal with the follow up to the implementation of NADAF. But at the same time the Secretary General wanted to goad the ECA into becoming a real development instrument on the continent. Unlike its sister Economic Commission in Latin America and the Caribbean, for example, which has historically played a prominent role in the development of the region by counselling governments on their strategies and helping them in developing regional policies and collective negotiations, the ECA has hardly played such a role in Africa. No doubt it prepares interesting studies and organises useful meetings, and it has been effective in raising the awareness of governments about certain development problems. But its mark on the continent's development has not been very obvious, even in the field of development thinking in Africa which has been usurped by the World Bank.

As for the group of high level experts and eminent personalities, its mission consisted in studying the critical situation in the continent, proposing innovative solutions and reflecting on the best means of implementing the NADAF recommendations, all that as advice and proposals for the Secretary General. But apart from a few meetings and recommendations to the Secretary General, the group was not very effective. It disappeared with the departure of its initiator who, moreover, hardly convoked it during the last part of his term.

After the mid-term evaluation of NADAF and taking into account its not very convincing results, the Secretary General launched another initiative in 1996, the United Nations System-wide Special Initiative on Africa (UNSIA). Here the fundamental objective was to rationalise and coordinate the intervention programmes of the UN system agencies, the Bretton Woods institutions and other providers of development assistance. UNSIA's strategy was to forge a coherent partnership in the aid efforts and programmes to concentrate on priority development issues identified by the African countries such as governance, peace and security, basic education, primary health care and environment. The time horizon of the initiative was 1996-2005 and the resources needed and sought amounted to 30 billion dollars.

UNSIA was doomed from the outset. The resources mobilized for this ambitious programme was inadequate and its value-added to other initiatives in progress was not obvious. The initiative was launched during the last year of the term of its author which augured an uncertain future and some saw it simply as an electoral manœuvre intended to win support for the Secretary-General in his quest for a second term in office.

All these initiatives are practically dead and in their places the Office of Special Adviser on Africa has been set up; it also deals with questions of conflicts and especially with support to NEPAD.

A few remarks can be made at this point. First, institutional proliferation. The multiplication of initiatives often goes hand in hand with the creation of new structures and bureaucracies even if initially they are intended to be light. This does not always make for effectiveness. What Africa needs for its development is less new institutions or a more strengthened United Nations but rather new ideas, approaches and concepts solidly and effectively supported by the UN system, and backed by the other development partners.

The weakness of the capacities and authority of the UN in these areas is glaring; a programme officially adopted unanimously by the General Assembly is hardly more than an incantatory and indicative document. All the more so because the mandate of the Assembly, though central, is limited to making recommendations to the member

States. This weakness affects the financial means for development in particular. In this regard., it is significant to note that the totality of the annual financial resources of the agencies in the UN development system is more or less equivalent to that of the World Bank alone. Since the UN system is a collective of more than thirty agencies, funds and programmes working in several fields without effective coordination it is easy to understand why they have limited impact in implementing new conceptual approaches or in advocating development paradigms different from those supported by bilateral and multilateral donors whose financial resources are much greater.

Thirdly, expanding on the above, the UN may question the conventional concepts and approaches and advocate new and innovative strategies and paradigms but the shakers and movers in the organization must accept and adopt them in their own policies. Otherwise, not only will they not support them but may undermine them and even deprive the UN of their contributions and other funding support.

Finally, the emerging tendency within the UN system of providing increased support to the humanitarian agencies. The fact is that in addition to their 'missionary' outlook they salve the consciences of the donor countries whilst also promoting the pharmaceutical, textile and agricultural industries in the donor countries. This goes hand in hand with the marginalisation of the agencies that advocate different perspectives on development which happens where the policymaking organs of these agencies are democratic in their decision making processes and do not differentiate according to their financial contributions. That also explains why the major industrialised countries often prefer to rely on the Bretton Woods institutions which manage their interests well and over which they have more assured control.

The case of AAF-SAP and what happened to the ECA is an example which is eloquent and very illustrative of the above argument. AAF-SAP was presented by the ECA as an alternative approach to the stabilisation and structural adjustment programmes formulated by and under the leadership of the Bretton Woods institutions and supported politically and financially by the donors countries of the development merchant system (DMS). The SAPs were in the interests of the donors because they ensured (i) the repayment of the debt despite the economic crisis situation in Africa, (ii) the promotion of exports and thus Africa's integration into the global market and the globalisation process which is beneficial to them, and (iii) maintaining the functions assigned by the system to the present economic structures in Africa. The AAF-SAP reference framework proposed transformation of economic structures going beyond crisis management to repay the debt; it strongly favoured reducing external dependence and promoting autonomous development based on growth in response to internal and regional needs. That was enough to deprive the programme of support on the part of the international community. ECA and its AAF-SAP were a challenge to the Bretton Woods institutions and their SAPs. They were resisted at every opportunity.

This can happen to any other agency of the UN system if in its sector approach it adopts development strategies which may disturb the interests of major donors, generally or in a given country. The representatives of donors in African countries have a 'mandate' to monitor what the UN agencies are doing and to report to their headquarters. How many times have agency representatives not been convoked to their head offices or to appear before their policy organs to explain themselves on matters reported by donors' representatives in their countries of assignment?

All this is indicative of the limits of the UN in promoting a globalisation different from that of the present neo-liberal order, that is to say a more human and more equitable globalization. More fundamentally, the UN will always be a reflection of the balance of power and thus of the dominating forces in the world. The UN cannot seriously oppose the forces of market fundamentalism and neo-liberal globalization without threatening its very existence. In order to establish its legitimacy the organisation can only try to position itself as the advocate of the interests of the poor and weak, that is to say of countries which are desperately seeking alternative approaches and paths for the dominant order. It will only be able to fully play the role of an active force for promoting the alternative to the neo-liberal order if the balance of power in the world of which it is a reflection changes drastically in favour of countries and societies which support an alternative.

Bilateral and other Multilateral Donors

The principal development partners for Africa are the donor countries and the international financial institutions. For them, development aid has assumed another nature and development has taken on the character of trade. It is a market which has its supply and demand. The buyers are the developing countries (especially in Africa) and the supply comes from the developed countries and their institutions which are producers and suppliers of development products. These are products, equipment, project ideas and projects, development policies and programmes, conceptual and practical know-how, human expertise and material technologies.

During the first development decade in Africa, the suppliers seemed to go it individually, in a more or less disorganised manner. But in more recent decades the development trade has become more and more organised into a veritable development merchant system – DMS – which comprises institutions, structures, operational market openings, client loyalty and business expansion mechanisms. The development business through the DMS has three specificities:

i. The suppliers at the level of the trans-national companies and the big development business institutions sell their products and services by financing the buyer or advancing him/her money. Whether this is a grant or a loan, the seller always does good business, directly or indirectly, individually or as a system.

ii. The development merchants do not wear the suit of trader, but rather that of the guru, development prophet, priest or *marabout*: benefactors and humanists preaching the salvation path, they finance those who follow their predictions and prescriptions.

iii. A new category of development merchandise has assumed greater importance, that is, economic reform policies. The merchandise is special because it is not only consumed like the others but it orients the development path and the future and the destiny of African countries; it also defines the nature of development and the mode of insertion into the global economy. It opens up and accelerates trade in other development products and services and is therefore broadly and rapidly financed by the DMS.

The right for Africans to define their own development path without any paternal, merchant or priestly interference is not recognised; it is not yet democratised even in a historic period of democratisation in Africa. However, development policies are not bought from a few merchants and cannot be wholly subjected to the prescriptions of priests, whatever their financial, conceptual or other powers. Forty five years of development directed or inspired by the merchants and supposed development priests show that Africa is still not properly engaged in the path of sustainable human development. Development is constructed from within (the interior) and this from its conception to its implementation. It is owned and controlled as a process by its players and beneficiaries, particularly in this period of accelerated globalisation. The DMS concept reflects this reality as both an error of approach – making development a merchant system for the benefit of the North – and a voluntary ideological tool for harnessing the African canoe to the North's neo-liberal boat on the waters of globalisation.

The DMS is thus a set of institutions (public and private agencies, organisations, programmes and funds) but also their procedures and working methods for passing or selling ideas, advice, services, projects, programmes and development policies to developing countries, financing them and implementing them, assessing them and knowing how to draw profit from them, regardless of their real results in terms of human development.

Development has an ideological dimension. Since independence Africa has also had its ideologists and its doctrinarians who in their quest for improved welfare of the continent have also traded in development products, particularly economic and financial infrastructures and other material equipment. And as in all trade the sellers and the buyers (the African political regimes) have done good business on the altar of the continent's development. That is why the DMS does not present itself as a merchant system but rather as a system of disinterested donors, depositories of know-how in development, benefactors willing to finance the efforts of the Africans in implementing the knowledge which they lavish on them even if with a number of conditions.

They present themselves as development prophets, priests or marabous in Africa. In traditional Africa, the priest is the person who holds the secrets of the existence; he has vast knowledge and is recognised or has succeeded in having himself recognised as such. Recourse to him goes hand in hand with the hope of a cure and a belief in his technical force and almost magical powers. Being in dialogue and friendship with him reassures and relieves part of existential anxieties. This is the frame of mind of those who take themselves for or pretend to be development priests in Africa.

The development disease in Africa has been the concern of large numbers of development priests and even the developmental priestly system as a whole. The recipes and other prescriptions intended to bring the continent out of its underdevelopment is always being updated and reviewed by the development priests and prophets who do not stop proliferating and confusing minds further every day. The prophet who comes to solve the existential development anxieties in Africa is well known by the continent. He has been prescribing recipes and solutions to Africa development invalids since independence. While his prescriptions have evolved in the course of these four and a half decades the prophet himself has remained the same, with the same basic canons and paradigms which are the basis of his development doctrine.

The first two were decades of development by projects, with the emphasis mainly on industrial projects (import substitution strategies) and sometimes on agriculture and infrastructure projects, etc, very much marked by the cold war climate. The end of the 1970s already showed that the system was in crisis: the projects no longer sold well, Africa became more and more incapable of paying its debts, and exports did not earn enough to meet the system's internal and external debts. It is in this context that the DMS launched other recipes on the development market. The third and fourth decades thus became the decades of economic reform policies and of political reform policies.

The development trade has evolved and entrenched itself. Now it constitutes a veritable organised system – the DMS as defined above – which comprises several levels of action with a senior high prophet/priest, regional *imams*, district and village priests, *muezzins* and other players or activists of the priestly development merchant system. The senior high priest (basically the Bretton Woods duo), who operates at all levels, has the power of (i) information, consequently becoming the reference and giving himself the authority he can draw from it, (ii) doctrinal learning and inspiration by the production of knowledge, (iii) inspiration of ideas and policies for both macro-economic and sector development, (iv) coordinating the development aid and loans system, and (v) the power of financial pressure to ensure implementation of DMS prescriptions.

As such, the senior high priest takes the initiative for development programmes, determines the type of development merchandise to sell and the approach to follow. He coordinates and controls the intervention of the other players in the system. That prevents the interventions from being disorderly and enables the DMS to control development policies in Africa, to choose those that best meet the interests of the DMS and which can therefore be supported. This function is so important that African countries themselves feel obliged to keep good business relations with the senior high prophet/priest and to obtain his certificate of good conduct in order to be sure of being in the good books of the other members of the DMS.

At another level, the DMS comprises the other priests and *imams*, large and medium-sized, who are the other bilateral and multilateral donors. Beyond the joint common roles they play in the system they also have specific function according to sectors or geographic zones.

The DMS operates, above all, thanks to its army of little neighbourhood and village priests, *muezzins* and other players in the development market: (i) the institutions and the more or less institutionalised forums under the patronage of the high priest and/or several *imams*, (ii) the consultancy companies to which must be added the multitude of technical development merchants' workers, (iii) the private so-called development companies and organisations, whether voluntary or non governmental. A special place in the DMS is accorded to so-called consulting companies, research bureaux and to NGO's who act much as boy scouts and brokers of the DMS.

The DMS thus occupies the development ground in Africa not only in the capital markets and for other traditional goods and services but also in that more crucial area of development policies which have become both merchandise and frameworks for selling other development merchandises. Unfortunately for African countries, these are mainly what one can call development appearances.

All this to say that in reality there is no development prophet, priest or *marabou* for Africa outside Africa, but rather the DMS. Development is not supplied by or bought from others, however missionary they may be. That is why the continent's development path in the 21st century must be critically reviewed and its nature and operational modalities be redefined, in relation to the DMS.

African Responses

Given the promises made during the struggles for political independence and faced with the problems of development, the African states have not failed to react. Beyond national efforts, whether or not in the form of development plans, African countries have advocated collective responses to the continent's development problem.

The Lagos Plan of Action (LPA) 1980-2000

On the basis of preparatory work organised by the OAU with the technical support of committed African experts, the 26th ordinary session of the OAU Conference of Heads of State and Government held in Monrovia, Liberia, in July 1979, solemnly adopted the Monrovia Declaration, also known as the Monrovia Strategy. After assessing the developmental problems, challenges and constraints the African leaders proclaimed that the document provided 'the guiding principles to respect and the measures to take to achieve national and collective self-sufficiency in the economic and social field, with a view to establishing a new international economic order'. On the basis of the strategy of national and collective self-sufficiency and establishment of a new international order they affirmed:

> we commit ourselves, on behalf of our governments and peoples, to promote the social and economic development and integration of our economies with a view to achieving an increasing measure of self-reliance and self-sustainment, and encourage an endogenous and self-sustaining development to facilitate and strengthen our social and economic relations, to erect on the national, sub-regional and regional level a dynamic and interdependent African economy, and to establish each year specific programmes to materialise this sub-regional, regional and continental economic cooperation.

In April 1980, the Monrovia strategy was translated into the Lagos Plan of Action (LPA), adopted at the special session of the OAU Conference of the Heads of State and Government held in Lagos, Nigeria. The LPA was to span a period of twenty years, 1980-2000, thus a long term vision. It was nourished and inspired by the dominant pan-African ideal, the patriotism of the years of the struggle for independence, the dedication of the technical experts who drafted the document, and the lessons from the development crisis of the end of the sixties. The LPA set the bar sufficiently high given the strong consciousness of Africa's development problems on the part of its authors and initiators.

As a result, it covered the following priority sectors: (i) agriculture and food security, (ii) industrialisation, (iii) control and sovereignty over natural resources, (iv) development and use of human resources, (v) promotion of science and technology to service Africa's accelerated development, (vi) transport and communications and economic infrastructures, (vii) energy, (viii) the promotion of commercial and financial exchanges, (ix) environment for development, and (x) the promotion of cooperation and integration. In all these sectors, the LPA defined priority activities or strategic directions of action, the expected role for each category of actors, that is, governments, the private sector, regional cooperation and integration communities, and development partners. As decided by the leaders, the LPA was to be implemented mainly through short term programmes which would be regularly evaluated.

But in reality the LPA was not implemented. It remained a sort of regional economic constitution, approved by a referendum of the heads of State and Government. They subsequently hung it on the wall or put it in a drawer, continuing to evoke it whenever it suited them. It was to be of little value as far as concerned policy-development in African countries or in their regional organisations.

The reasons for of the failure of the LPA was not that it was ambitions but, first, the weakness of the political leadership that adopted and was entrusted with its implementation. The African state which adopted the LPA was not such as would implement it. It can be said that there was a gap between the pan-African desire to construct an Africa economically autonomous and responding to the aspirations of the African peoples and the real nature of the ruling regimes and their capacities to be politically committed to a cause.

Second, the LPA remained stillborn because the powerful external partners fought against it or simply ignored it; they were not and are still not disposed to help an Africa comply with the Monrovia strategy which advocated self-centred development and a new more equitable international economic order. The powerful external partners combated the LPA through the 'sale' of stabilisation and adjustment programmes whilst also applying political, economic and financial pressures. The LPA had very limited donor support either at the regional level or even less at the international level. But the SAPs were never short of such support. From crisis programmes they became development policies and programmes. The resources of African states were thus mobilised to design and implement the SAPs rather than other development programmes; there were even less for an LPA which proclaimed socio-economic self-determination.

Moreover, shortly after the official launch of the LPA and the large and enthusiastic welcome it received in Africa, in 1981 the World Bank published a counter-LPA entitled 'Accelerated Development in Africa South of the Sahara : Indicative Action Programme', prepared by a World Bank team under the direction of Professor Eliot Berg. The Bank organised conferences and seminars all over Africa to market its indicative programme, silencing that of the Africans, the LPA.

Other African initiatives

Other African initiatives comprise (i) the Priority Programme for Economic Recovery in Africa (1985) for the period 1986-1990, (ii) the African Alternative Framework for Structural Adjustment Programmes (AAF-SAP) (1989), (iii) the Abuja Treaty (1990) ,and the Cairo Agenda for Action (1995), before NEPAD which I will discuss in the next section. It appears that there was a cyclical reawakening of the African leadership about every five years.

With the exception of NEPAD all the other initiatives refer to the LPA in one way or the other and claimed to be in line with its vision and strategy. Their contents up-date the primary document and declare the need to accelerate the implementation of the LPA or some of its components in the changing regional and international context. They continued to reaffirm the strategy of self-centred development and the demand for a new more equitable world economic order in which Africa would have a bigger say. The Priority Programme got less media coverage as if it wanted to be a sort of stage in the implementation of the LPA, and especially as it coincided with the UNPAAERD. It was not much spoken of and, for this reason, was easily drowned in the marketing of the preferences of the Bretton Woods institutions.

The Abuja Treaty, while placing itself in the LPA perspective, focused on the implementation of the integration component with a clear delineation of the stages for implementing the African Economic Community. It could be argued that external resistance or the lack of outside support put a brake on the implementation of the Abuja treaty. Whatever support was forthcoming was in the framework of the individual strategies of the external powers who saw implementation of the treaty as an opportunity to broaden or preserve their markets.

The Cairo Agenda was also one of these little known initiatives because it was not marketed as well as it deserved. Besides, it recognised the primacy of the Lagos Plan of Action which it aimed to revive by indicating some new priority action-areas that had emerged since 1980 when the LPA was adopted. Like the LPA the Cairo Agenda has remained stillborn.

The only initiative which really caused a stir in its time was the AAF-SAP. Still positioned in the LPA perspective, the initiative reaffirmed the right of Africans to own their development and to think of it in as a strategy for structural transformation and self-centred development. It reaffirmed that Africans have not only this right but also the capacity to exercise this right, not to leave the monopoly of development ideas and thinking to their partners. Moreover, the AAF-SAP pointed a critical finger at the stabilisation and structural adjustment policies of the World Bank and the IMF which were lording it in Africa. By launching a challenge to these powerful institutions the ECA made itself important and known, but that provoked an angry response. The World Bank once again brought out a counter-AAF-SAP some four months later (November 1989). In it the Bank proposed a new accelerated growth programme in Africa, benefiting here and there from the criticisms of the SAPs from some of the proposals of the AAF-SAP. But its fundamental thrust was that of bringing Africa into line in the process of insertion into the global market. The AAF-SAP was ignored and was not implemented. It lacked both serious political leadership and the required minimum financing. The ECA lost some feathers. The philosophy of one-track thinking in the field of development triumphed once again in the face of the 'utopian' dreams of Africans. It was in this context that NEPAD was born.

The New Partnership for Africa's Development, NEPAD

NEPAD's origins

At the level of development thinking in general, there was a certain gap in the implementation of development instruments. For the African countries things were even clearer. Their various regional initiatives remained empty declarations without any chance of being realised, and many of them died natural deaths. Only a few retarded people or researchers in libraries still talked about them. They had become pieces in the museum of African dreams. On the contrary, SAPs, in their different versions, laid down the law on the continent and enjoyed massive political and financial support.

On the side of the donors and DMS powers, uneasiness took hold progressively. The SAPs had been reformulated, sometimes with changes of name while keeping their basic credo. The implementation instruments of this credo were successively labelled SAPs, economic reforms, comprehensive development frameworks (CDF), poverty reduction strategy papers (PRSP), etc. But in the face of the continued crises in Africa there was general fatigue with the different generations of SAP on the sides of both the DMS initiators and their Africans executants. The suggestion box no longer seemed to hold. The door was open for further reflection on new concepts and approaches even if they did not fundamentally solve anything.

The President of the World Bank took the initiative of bringing together a few African Heads of State selected through one of their peers' intervention first in Kampala and then in Dakar. He succeeded in selling the idea of the comprehensive development framework and a capacity building initiative. As long as this was to be accompanied by financial resources, African leaders did not quarrel about it but accepted it. Again, however, the impact was very restricted. Moreover, there were widespread criticisms of the approach of the Bretton Woods institutions and the DMS in general to impose their new development merchandise to African countries. Reservations started to appear even within the DMS.

In the course of the year following the Bank President again proposed to a few African Heads of State – among whom president Mbeki then Vice-President of South Africa – the idea of an initiative coming from African political leaders themselves which they could propose to their development partners and for the implementation of which they would be responsible. The Bank was disposed to and offered to assist. The African initiative would fill a gap in terms of development policy and at the same time the DMS was no longer going to be accused of imposing it on the African countries.

NEPAD's birth process

In response, three initiatives were launched on the continent. First, that of President Mbeki who in consultation with his peers in some SADC countries advanced the idea of an African renaissance with which President Obasanjo of Nigeria and later President Bouteflika of Algeria were associated. The idea became their joint project. In its first structured presentation the renaissance plan was entitled the Millennium Africa Programme or MAP. Drawing on the United Nations Millennium Development Declaration and Objectives, MAP emphasised the negative effects of the historical North-South relationship and suggested a partnership based on shared responsibilities between Africa and development partners.

But MAP also had a hidden connotation of promoting the repositioning of the South African economy in the region and of attracting foreign investments into South Africa. In this sense, its priority directions responded to the preoccupations of the World Bank and the DMS but also to the preoccupations of South Africa in Africa and in the global economy. MAP announced the creation of an Algiers-Abuja-Pretoria axis around which the DMS could intensify its stranglehold on Africa. This was unacceptable to other forces in the continent.

The second initiative was that of President Wade of Senegal, titled the Omega Plan, first presented at the France-Africa summit in Yaoundé, Cameroon. The summit gave him an official mandate to finalise it. The ultimate objective of the plan is to enable Africa to catch up with the developed world by achieving a high rate of economic growth with big doses of foreign investments. It identified critical factors which explain the disparities between the North (developed world) and Africa in areas such as infrastructures, education, health, agriculture and the ICTs.

For the third initiative, the ECA's Conference of African Finance and Planning Ministers had adopted a Compact for Economic Recovery in Africa. Essentially, it had nothing special excepting that it up-dated the reform policies in progress from a perspective that claimed to be African.

As if to inspire these initiatives which it applauded as African, the World Bank published a document entitled 'Can Africa claim its place in the 21st century?' Its answer was in the positive – but on condition that the continent fulfilled some critical conditions as advocated in the Washington Consensus and SAPs.

The next stage in the birth process of NEPAD was the marketing of the two main initiatives, the MAP and the Omega Plan. It appeared obvious both to the partners and to Africans themselves that the continent should not go to donors in a disunited way. It was therefore considered necessary to integrate if not to merge the two initiatives. The ECA was associated with the exercise and its document played the role of the merger facilitator. Each initiator had his technicians and experts to ensure that the key elements of his vision were properly taken into account. Of course, the Bretton Woods institutions made sure that they also were in contact with the process.

The integration exercise resulted in the production of a document which was adopted in July 2001 by the 39th OAU Summit of the Heads of State and Government in Lusaka. It was entitled the New African Initiative (NAI). Three months later, at a meeting on 21 October in Abuja, Nigeria, the Heads of State and Government committee in charge of implementing the New African Initiative changed its name to the New Partnership for Africa's Development or NEPAD. From it being an African initiative the document now stressed partnership with external actors. It was quite a significant nuance.

A week after being adopted in July 2001, the document was presented at the G8 Summit in Genoa, Italy, seeking, as it were, their approval and blessing. Since then it has been discussed periodically at G8 meetings, meetings of the international financial institutions, the World Economic Forum, and sometimes among Heads of State of the industrialized countries and the donors. African leaders who are the initiators, or considered as such, are often invited to these forums to make presentations, or since 2003, to give an update on implementation of the NEPAD. Regrettably, the document was never submitted to African people or people's representatives (parliaments or civil society) for discussion before the external marketing was launched. The African base was kept aside in the process until there was an outcry a few years later. In a way it was just to say to the DMS as NEPAD sponsor 'we have done the homework you gave us'.

NEPAD and African Development Problematique

NEPAD thus includes MAP's major ideas, notably in its overall historical analysis, the Omega Plan's operational proposals and a certain broadening of the priority sectors for action. After reviewing the current situation in the continent the document presents an action programme, describes its prior conditions and the priority sectors. It then calls for partnership with the industrialised countries before ending with the presentation of a few sector projects and the operational mechanisms of the new partnership.

NEPAD has sought to fill a gap at the regional level given that the other initiatives were in the museum. For this the initiative must be saluted. Africa needs sound and confirmed leadership. Through this initiative African leaders wished to affirm a new leadership dimension. Moreover, the overall objectives and the choice of priority sectors, even if nothing especially new, testifies to a consistency in Africans as to how they perceive their continent's development.

Above and beyond these positive aspects, NEPAD must be read from different perspectives one of which is in relation to Africa's current challenges in the context of globalisation and the hopes which it represents for the continent. The whole document is an appeal from African leaders to the donor countries telling them: 'Our countries are poor and under-developed because they are too far behind in certain sectors which we consider as priorities, our natural and human resources can constitute the basis for change, we are ready to fulfil the required conditions which will also ensure our countries' insertion into the dynamics of globalisation.' Such is NEPAD's principal message. And as one of drafters involved in the merging exercise notes:

> On analysis, there are possibilities of resolving this situation of the African economies. Today the global system has enormous technical and financial means while Africa possesses important assets among which her gigantic potential of unexploited natural resources, as well as demographic and cultural reserves with promise for growth. What

is then needed is coherent and regionalised economic policies in favour of sustainable development through integration, and the foundations of which could be:
- the improvement of governance which stabilises the institutions and the fundamentals of the macroeconomic framework; the management of conflicts which stabilises the African space;
- the setting up of an environment inciting investment in sectors that drive growth and increase both the competitiveness and the diversification of the economies;
- a big reduction in dependence on aid and indebtedness duo (Kassé, M. 2002 p. 57).

Another question about this initiative concerns its vision of African development which remains fundamentally neo-liberal. NEPAD does not define another development strategy or another development paradigm for Africa. It fits into the current development model that the globalisation process and its barons have put in place for the continent. That in itself constitutes an important limitation on any development based on NEPAD. At a time when resistance to the current globalisation is becoming 'globalised' with sound political, economic and social arguments, it would have been expected that African leaders would be more innovative and creative in redefining the development paradigm which they wish to advocate for the continent. Although NEPAD reaffirms that globalisation is to the detriment of Africa it does not respond to this important challenge by coming up with a proposal for changing either the operational mechanisms of globalisation or the way in which Africa is integrated into it.

What the Africa leaders have done in NEPAD is to affirm that their objective is to bridge the gap with the industrialised world in a number of areas. On the other hand, as reports on the current dynamics of globalisation show that the gaps between the North and the South – and particularly Africa – are continuously widening, it is difficult to understand why African leaders would want to pursue the Western world following its model and even with the hope of its aid! What is worse is to make it the ultimate objective of this new partnership and of their vision of the development of the continent.

That is why from the point of view of its strategy NEPAD is clearly and directly in line with the DMS instruments: integration into the global market according to the directions of the World Trade Organisation (WTO), recourse to the PRSPs of the Bretton Woods institutions, demand for an increase in aid from the OECD/DAC countries, aid policy in the line of the HIPCs, economic reforms and privatisation policies according to the Bretton Woods credo, etc.

Because of this NEPAD does not advocate a fundamental transformation of the African economies. That is why industry is absent as a priority sector. Its strategic objectives consist of two elements: the mobilisation of foreign capital to increase capital flows to the continent and access to external markets. The new partnership is thus a process of true integration into the global economy without contesting the current global market dynamics and its driving forces. It is as if Africans themselves have traced the path of their harnessing to this global economy and have simply reaffirmed their commitment in this direction.

It is for all these reasons that NEPAD has been continuously and is still the subject of intense marketing on the part of the African leaders to the leaders of the industrialised countries and their different decision making and action groups. All the Northern donors and their organisations have thus approved if not applauded NEPAD without too many questions, offered their support and put dialogue and sometimes financing mechanisms in place. The G8 has adopted an action plan for Africa to support NEPAD, the partnership with Africa Forum has been set up and meets twice a year to do the follow up, individual countries have established support and financing mechanisms: the Blair commission in Great Britain, Japan through TICAD, etc. Initiatives to facilitate access to the American, Canadian and European Union markets have been introduced or strengthened. The World Bank and the IMF have affirmed their support particularly through their classical intervention instruments such as the PRSPs (World Bank) and the PRGFs (IMF). The United Nations both at the level of the General Secretariat and of the agencies, funds and programmes have pledged their active support either for NEPAD sector initiatives or for the NEPAD operational structures.

Unlike previous African initiatives, particularly the LPA and AAF-SAP, were condemned and ignored by the donors NEPAD enjoys their full support and its flag is carried high both by its African initiators and by their external partners. A gigantic machine has been put in place to guarantee NEPAD's onward march. The reason is simple: unlike previous African initiatives, NEPAD does not challenge the current order of things in the global economy neither does it seek to position Africa otherwise than she is today. The external orientation of NEPAD is confirmed not only in its content and its aggressive marketing in the industrialised world but also in that it has been essentially a top-down process, cooked/confectioned from above without meaningful participation of the African populations. As afore-noted, it was well afterwards, when faced with internal protests notably from African civil society organisations, that a minimum of information and internal marketing began in the form of consciousness-raising seminars funded by he donor community. It is difficult to understand how political leaders who claim to be representatives of democratic regimes did not democratise the process of definition and crafting the future of the continent. Further, the place of women in Africa development and the partnering process do not arise in NEPAD as a crucial question. Similarly, science and technology and culture, which are strategic areas for development, have only two paragraphs each.

The lack of democratisation in the process of formulating and adopting NEPAD is explained no doubt by the fact that it has adopted a mode of integration into the global economy directly in line with DMS reform policies, very much contested in Africa especially by civil society. Thus, NEPAD appears as the new DMS hobby-horse in Africa. Democratising the process of working it out at this time would have resulted in its rejection and in the design of an alternative more in line with the LPA or a model not including the ingredients of the DMS credo. As a result, NEPAD has a major weakness linked to that of ownership of the process and its implementation by important segments of African society. This explains why NEPAD ignores the LPA and does not refer or allude to it at all. But it is structurally less sound than the LPA having bypassed not only industrialization and gender but also issues of population, statistics, development planning and the specific problems of the African LDCs.

Another important question is the financing of NEPAD operational structures, sector initiatives and projects. The needs are estimated at some US$64 billion annually. This is 160 percent of Nigeria's GDP! NEPAD hopes to mobilise these resources both internally (within Africa) and especially externally (it is hoped to attract massive foreign direct investment) through the two means mentioned above, namely, the flow of capital and access to external markets. It is obvious that this is not realistic in view of the continent's present economic conditions, and globalisation driving forces which have resulted in a decline in ODA, collapse of FDI except for oil resources, and African indebtedness. This puts another limit on the hopes which NEPAD nourishes among the African populations.

NEPAD's implementation depends on its translation into sector initiatives and programmes. But as it is not easy to manage the development of a continent at the regional level, each country's national development plan must be integrated into NEPAD, or more exactly, must be a national segment of NEPAD. That is not yet established, even if the DMS is pressing strongly for it.

From the point of view of implementation structures, NEPAD, while recognized as the African Union's economic programme is not under the direct supervision of the AU and its Commission. It has been set up – it is said that this is a temporary situation – as an autonomous structure and is examining the modalities of its integration into the AU. The DMS does not wish NEPAD to be put in the centre of the AU's political discussions until it is strong enough. But it is well known that the provisional often tends to be institutionalised and become permanent.

NEPAD's operational structures comprise the Implementation Committee composed of fifteen Heads of State and Government. It is chaired by President Obasanjo with three Vice-Presidents who are in fact the other three initiators of the MAP and the Omega plan, that is, Presidents Mbeki, Wade and Bouteflika. At the second level is the Steering Committee composed of representatives of the four so-called founder countries: South Africa, Algeria, Nigeria and Senegal, under South Africa's leadership. The third level is that of the NEPAD Secretariat, based in South Africa, and directed by the president of the Steering Committee. From a technical point of view the Steering Committee is the operational organ at the disposal of the Heads of State and Government Implementation Committee. There are also five sector implementation committee attached to the Steering Committee and presided over by each of the four founding presidents of NEPAD, to whom has been added the President of Egypt. These are: Algeria for human resources; Nigeria for 'good' economic governance and the flow of capital; Senegal for infrastructures, environment, energy and ICTs; South Africa for 'good' political governance, peace, security and democracy; and Egypt for market access, diversification and agriculture.

NEPAD's operational machinery comprises, in particular, an African Peer Review Mechanism (APRM) for assessing and monitoring a country's application of the principles of 'good political governance' in the sense of the 'liberal' democracy advocated by the DMS and the globalisation forces, 'good' economic governance with its principles as defined in the different versions of the reform policies, etc. Although adhesion to this mechanism is voluntary, there is a good chance that it will be another conditionality for countries wishing to receive aid from the North.

The difference now is that the conditionality is self imposed by Africans leaders themselves.

This mechanism raises another set of questions. First, it is difficult to imagine Asian or Latin American political leaders self-monitoring themselves just to prove to their partners in the North that they are progressing in the implementation of agreed policies and, for that reason, deserve their confidence and support. The African leaders have gone this far. Then second, this mechanism, like NEPAD as a whole, assumes the right to 'correct the exercise book' of the Heads of State and Government and therefore to grade them; this is a direct undermining of the prerogative of African parliaments in relation to their governments. Third, questions of political governance and democracy, peace and security are within the competence of the African Union and not of an Africa/foreign partnership mechanism.

The idea of this mechanism comes from the partners themselves. Indeed, well before NEPAD's birth, I had written that the DMS already proposed to set up other mechanisms for monitoring good governance in Africa in addition to those already existing. Among others, USAID had launched the idea of creating the African Commission on Democratisation as an international mechanism to assess progress of African countries in this area so that the successful countries would benefit from western aid. That was an indirect means of pressuring Africa into line with globalisation (USAID, 1992). In the same document, USAID reported that even the Global Coalition for Africa, another DMS instrumental creation, had proposed setting up a special forum bringing together bilateral and multilateral donors and Africans to discuss progress in implementing good governance strategies, and to coordinate the response from among donors in terms of aid.

Fourth, it is obvious that the APRM while not inspired by globalisation forces responds to a DMS preoccupation. It is a tool for political control. Like NEPAD itself, it illustrates the neo-liberal commitment of the African leaders confronted with their external partners. The document is silent on a time horizon, unlike other previous African initiatives. This is because it is intended to make it a permanent African programme for the neo-liberal way of integrating the continent into the global economic system.

The implementation of NEPAD is going to come up against numerous deficits of democratisation in Africa, including political democracy. The state is not the government. The private appropriation of the political sphere and the state machine by some political operators through non-democratic political parties and militarised mechanisms for controlling power still reigns in most African countries including the NEPAD founders. That constitutes another limitation to NEPAD.

It is obvious from the above critical assessment that there is fundamentally nothing new in NEPAD compared to the current prescriptions of the DMS and globalisation driving forces, excepting for the fact that it is the collective commitment of the African leaders to join in neo-liberal globalisation. It is even a step backwards compared to the Monrovia strategy and its implementation plan, the LPA. Doubts about NEPAD's chances of achieving its avowed results are valid. The fundamentally unequal relations and the polarising nature of globalisation cannot be changed in favour of Africa by means of NEPAD, all the more so since NEPAD does not even envisage questioning them. Quite the contrary, it is the implement for consolidating them. The situation of poverty, meagre growth or lack of sustainable growth, unemployment and crisis will still continue if Africa restricts herself simply to doing what is proposed in the NEPAD framework.

Conclusion

At the conclusion of this analysis we ask: what is to be done and where do we go from here? Numerous are Africans from civil society organisations and some strata of the intelligentsia who have advocated the NEPAD be rejected pure and simple. Some of the programme's initiators have recognised weaknesses both in the process and in its contents, without any questions asked. But, the reality is that it would be illusory to hope that it will be rejected or abandoned by the continent in the near future. NEPAD is herepresent, strongly benefiting from the political, economic and financial support of the current neo-liberal globalisation driving forces and from African leaders with a political commitment favouring so-called partnership. The brotherhood of African leaders know so and benefits from it in that it gives external forces 'legitimation' of their economic policies. They need external 'legitimation' as they are fully conscious of what external forces are capable of, including militarily, in imposing their positions.

It remains obvious that Africa will not see the development lights by inserting herself in the accelerated globalisation process in this manner. And it seems to me predictable that other NEPAD versions, variants, and offspring will be reformulated after the first serious failures in implementing the current version. The African populations must not wait for the failures of this new series of programmes as was the case for the SAPs. The continent must define another development paradigm for itself, translate it into a sound strategy and national programmes, after clearly identifying the current and future challenges. It must above all mobilise its populations at every stage of the process.

The failure of previous initiatives, notably the LPA and AAF-SAP, the challenges of the current global context, the effort by NEPAD to fill the gap in terms of vision and regional development strategy, all these constitute a pressing appeal on the part of the African populations and their mass organisations. This also constitutes a strong appeal, particularly to leaders of mass democratic movement and the African intelligentsia and African think tanks, to craft another strategy inspired by a new development paradigm which will borrow from past initiatives and enriched by the experience in responding to the challenges of the moment. The objective of such a process should not be to reproduce the Washington Consensus at the Africa level as NEPAD does but, rather, a genuine consensus of Africans on the development of the continent, or the 'African Consensus'. As an inclusive process it will be a Whole African Consensus. It will serve as a reference framework for regional and national development programmes as well as for partnership and alliances with external players. Then the problem of the nature of the state and the development leadership called on to steer the Whole Africa Consensus will arise. That represents an important challenge for the continent.

References

ADB, *African Development Report*, 1999.
Annan, K., *Building partnerships to address the challenges of globalization*, Feb 1997.
Bello, W., 'It's the development model, stupid', in *The Nation*, Bangkok, 24 March, 1999.
Bond, Patrick, 'Dispossessing Africa's wealth', in *Pambazuka News*, No. 227, October 27, 2005.
Chimphango, Annie, 'The African Voice on the New Partnership for Africa's Development (NEPAD): A compilation of declarations, statements and critiques from the African Civil Society on NEPAD', prior to World Summit on Sustainable development (WSSD), in *Towards People's Appropriation of NEPAD*, op. cit.
Chossudovsky, M., *La Mondialisation de la pauvreté*, Montréal, 1998.
de Brie, Ch., De l'art de faire parler les statistiques: l'Afrique à l'aune du développement virtuel, in *Le Monde Diplomatique*, Oct 1997.
ECA, *African alternative frame of reference for structural adjustment programmes for socio-economic recovery and transformation*, Addis Ababa, 1989.
Global Coalition for Africa, *Annual Report 2002/2003 and 2004/2005.*
Global Coalition for Africa, *Economic and Social Trends in Africa*, Annual Reports, various issues, 1995–2005.
Hammouda, Ben., Hakim et Kassé, Moustapha (eds), *Le NEPAD et les enjeux du développement en Afrique*, Maisonneuve et Larose, Paris 2002.
Husain, Ishrat, *The evolving role of the World Bank: The challenge of Africa*, Washington DC, 1995.
Justice, Development and Peace Commission, *Towards People's Appropriation of NEPAD*, Ijebu-Ode, 2002.
Kankwenda, M., Crise économique, ajustement et démocratie en Afrique, in Chole, E., et Ibrahim, J., (sous la direction de), Processus de démocratisation en Afrique, CODESRIA Dakar, 1995.
Kankwenda, M., Mondialisation, défis économiques et régionalisation en Afrique, in *Alternatives Sud, Vol VIII (2001) 3.*
Kankwenda, M., Crise économique, ajustement et démocratie en Afrique, in Chole, E., et Ibrahim, J., (sous la direction de), Processus de démocratisation en Afrique, CODESRIA Dakar, 1995.
Kankwenda M. et al., *Poverty Eradication, Where Africa Stands?*, Indiana University Press, Bloomington, Indiana.
Kankwenda, Mbaya, 'Globalization and the need for development leadership in Africa', in *Towards People's Appropriation of NEPAD*, op. cit.
Kankwenda, Mbaya, Place et Rôle possibles du Système des Nations Unies dans la recherche d'une alternative à l'ordre mondial libéral, Ronéo, Lagos, February 2001.
Kankwenda, Mbaya, 'Revisiting the AAF-SAP, first step on the African path to Sustainable Human development', in Onimode, Bade et al (eds), *African Development and Governance Strategies in the 21st Century*, ZED Books, London & New York, 2003.

Kankwenda, M., Grégoire, L.J., Legros, H., and Ouedraogo, H., 'Poverty Eradication: Where stands Africa?' *Economica*, Paris 2001.
Kankwenda, Mbaya, *Marabouts ou Marchands du Développement en Afrique*, L'Harmattan, Paris 2000.
Khor, M., L'ONU, plus nécessaire que jamais dans un monde plus interdépendant que jamais, in PNUD/CPTD, *Coopération Sud*, New York, 1996.
Khor, Martin, *Globalization and the South: some critical issues*, Third World Network, Penang 2000.
Laki, Zaïdi, *Enquête sur la Banque Mondiale*, Fayard, Paris 1989.
L'Hériteau, M.F., *Le Fonds Monétaire International et les pays du Tiers- Monde*, IEDES-PUF, Paris 1986.
Melber, Henning, 'NEPAD: South Africa, African economies and globalization', in *Pambazuka News* no 141, Weekly Electronic Newsletter, January 29 2004.
Mcintosh, T. and Woods, J., *Globalization and Africa's Future: Policy issues for managing the development process*, New York, 1999.
Mistry, P., *The present role of the World Bank in Africa*, Institute for African Alternatives, Oct 1989.
OECD/DAC, *Globalization and linkages to 2020: Can poor countries and poor people prosper in the new global age?*, Paris, 1997.
Organization of African Unity, *Lagos Plan of Action for the economic development of Africa 1980-2000*, International Institute for Labor Studies, Geneva 1981.
Organization of African Unity, *Relaunching Africa's Economic And Social Development: The Cairo Agenda for Action*, Ronéo, Cairo, 1995.
Petrella, R., 'Une machine infernale', Communication to a debate organised by the *Financial Times*, le Monde Diplomatique and the LSE, May 1997.
Speth, J.G., *Call for Africa*, UNDP, New York, 1994.
The New partnership for Africa's development (NEPAD), October 2001.
The LRS Report, 'Policy Review: The New Partnership for Africa Development', *NEPAD : A critical review*, Ronéo, 2003.
UNDP, Economic growth and human development: Africa, New York, 1996 p. 3 and Human Development Report, 1996, Economica, Paris, 1996.
UNDP, *Human Development Report*, various issues 1992-2003.
UNCTAD, *Economic development in Africa: performance, prospects and policy issues*, New York and Geneva, 2001.
UNECA, *Africa's condition on the eve of the twenty-first century*, Addis Ababa, 1989.
UNESCO, *Les assises de l'Afrique*, Paris 1994.
USAID, *Governance and political reforms in Africa*, Ronéo, Washington 1992.
UN-ECA Southern Africa Office, NEPAD, 'A framework for Africa's development in the 21st Century', in *Southern Africa Development Bulletin*, issue no 11, December 2002.
World Bank, *Accelerated development in Africa south of the Sahara: Indicative action programme*, Washington 1981.
World Bank, *Sub-Saharan Africa: from crisis to sustainable growth*, Washington, 1989.
World Bank, *African poverty at the Millennium*, Washington, March 2001.

World Bank, *Annual report 2002.*
World Bank, *World Development Report, 1999/2000* and *2005/2006.*
World Bank, *African development indicators*, various numbers.

Chapter 6

Institutional Architecture for Managing Integration in the ECOWAS Region: An Empirical Investigation

Jeggan C. Senghor

Regional cooperation and integration have been major preoccupations in Africa, perceived, *inter alia*, as instruments for accelerated growth and sustained growth. Through collective exploitation of an enlarged economic space productive capacities in industry and agriculture would be rationally utilized. Transport, communications and other infrastructures, which are well beyond the means of individual countries, would be embarked on jointly. Trade promotion through extensive liberalization schemes and unfettered factor mobility would lead eventually to an economic union. Particularly since the end of the Cold War efforts have been directed at deepening the integration process in the continent as in other parts of the world.

This chapter focuses on the much-ignored and unglamorous subject of the institutional infrastructure for regional integration in West Africa. An effective institutional system can only have a positive impact on the outcomes of any integration scheme, if only through invigorating the regionalization process by providing leadership, direction, technical and political support. The chapter critically assesses existing institutional arrangements for achieving the cooperation and integration objectives of the Economic Community of West African States (ECOWAS). The contention is that the institutional architecture at the level of member states, the central secretariat, and at the interface between the two is inadequate and inappropriate, particularly in terms of structures, resources, and other capacities. Against the background of a general discussion on contextual issues, the prevailing situation at the three levels is examined. This is followed by a detailed presentation on five country cases, concluding with some thoughts on the way forward.

Introduction: Lofty Ideals – Performance Gaps

The aims of ECOWAS, as enshrined in its establishing treaty, were essentially economic. Article 2 of the 1975 Treaty explicitly states the aims to be:

> to promote cooperation and development in all fields of economic activity…and in social and cultural matters for the purpose of raising the standard of living of its 200 million peoples, of increasing and maintaining economic stability, of fostering closer relations

among its members and of contributing to the progress and development of the African continent.

The treaty defines nine stages leading to the realization of the above aims in the classical tradition of free trade area (stages (a) and (b)), customs union (stage (c)), common market (stage (d)), and economic union (stages (e) to (i)). The key sectors for cooperation and policy harmonization include: trade liberalization; free movement of persons, services and capital; development of transport, communications, energy, and other infrastructural facilities; industrial and agricultural growth; and monetary policies.

The Revised ECOWAS Treaty (1993) reconfirmed and comprehensively elaborated on the economic *raison d'etre* of the organization. The third paragraph in the Preamble posits that 'the promotion of harmonious economic development of our States calls for effective economic cooperation and integration largely through a determined and concerted policy of self-reliance.' The treaty is unequivocal as to the fundamental objective of such economic cooperation and integration, i.e., 'to encourage, foster and accelerate the economic and social development of our States in order to improve the living standards of our peoples.' (Preamble, paragraph 2) This is buttressed by an even more categorical affirmation, that 'our final goal is the accelerated and sustained economic development of Member States, culminating in the economic union of West Africa.' (Preamble, paragraph 11).

These dispersed pronouncements are brought together in the statement of the aims of the Community, the first of which is:

> To promote cooperation and integration, leading to the establishment of an economic union in West Africa in order to raise the living standards of its peoples, and to maintain and enhance economic stability, foster relations among Member States, and contribute to the progress and development of the African Continent. (Article 3, para.1)

The Revised Treaty also specifies the various stages in which the process is to evolve; further, it identifies the measures to be taken to realize the prescribed goals. Particularly noteworthy are: harmonization and coordination of national policies and the promotion of integration programmes, projects and activities in all development sectors; establishment of joint production enterprises; establishment of a common market; establishment of an economic union; promotion of joint ventures by private enterprises and other economic operators; establishment of an enabling legal environment; and harmonization of national investment codes and of standards and measures. The treaty deals in greater detail than its predecessor with each economic sector and sub-sector and with actions to be taken for the realization of the overall Community cooperation and integration aims. In cases, the document is very detailed as to its assessment of the existing situation, the objectives to be pursued, and the precise means for achieving these objectives.

After 30 years of existence ECOWAS is far from achieving its fundamental aims and objectives, as quoted above.[1] Granted, initiatives have been mooted in core

---

1 Davies, Arthur, 'Cost-Benefit Analysis with ECOWAS', *The World Today*, vol.39 no.5, May 1983, pp. 170-176.

areas for regional economic union such as market and production integration, factor mobility, infrastructural development, monetary integration, and regional peace and security. But the overall consensus in the literature remains that 'The ECOWAS march towards West African economic cooperation and integration has been painfully slow' and 'no effective integration has taken place in ECOWAS – either in trade nor production nor in laying foundations for economic transformation.'(Asante, 2002) Successive chief executives of the organization have bemoaned the non-implementation of ECOWAS programmes, most vocally in their annual reports to the Heads of State. Nigeria's President Babangida declared in 1986, 'The hallmark of integration has been inaction and cosmetic commitment.'[2] (Africa Research Bulletin, 1986).

Numerous and diverse are the domestic and external variables explaining why ECOWAS has not produced more concrete economic integration results.[3] Among these is the shift of 'attention' from economic cooperation and integration to conflict prevention, management and resolution and to sustaining political and regional security in its catchment area. Over the last 15 years, the scope and magnitude of the conflicts and civil wars experienced in the region warranted direct involvement of the regional organization. Their frequency and complexity meant that vast quantum of human and material resources were expended for the immediate resolution of these conflicts. The primary economic integration aims and objectives of ECOWAS took a back seat to conflict management and resolution.

Thus, the early 1990s, which saw the regional organization take on the challenge of peacekeeping in Liberia and Sierra Leone, evidenced the shift. The venture into regional peace and security had an impact on the approach to and methodology of integration in the region. For one thing, the successes of the organization in the political and security sector rescued the organization from near-abject dormancy. Quite consequential, it ushered in a more open and inclusive approach to integration which recognized the importance of non-economic variables. This *glasnost* in conception of integration is reflected in the adoption of the Declaration of Political Principles, the first meeting of ministers of foreign affairs to consider the political dimension of Community programmes in May 1990, and of ministers of information in March 1991, as well as the decision to revise the establishing (1975) treaty, and the rationalization of inter-governmental organizations (IGOs). The Revised Treaty itself devoted several of its 93 articles to previously downplayed sectors such as political and security, social and culture, and women in development. These, though, are not ends in themselves but means in the pursuit of the economic integration objectives of the Community.

---

2 The UN Economic Commission for Africa identifies some of the problems experienced in its seminal publication *Assessing Regional Integration in Africa*, Addis Ababa, 2004, pp. 57-63. A succinct discussion on the achievements of ECOWAS is given in Asante, S.K.B., 'A Comparative Analysis of ECOWAS and UEMOA Integration Schemes,' *West Africa Journal of Monetary and Economic Integration*, vol. 1, no.1, 201, pp. 31-32.

3 See discussion in: Asante, 'ECOWAS and West Africa,' pp. 8-12; Adedeji, A., 'History and Prospects for Regional Integration in Africa' UN Economic Commission for Africa, African Development Forum III, Addis Ababa, March 2002, p.10; UN Economic Commission for Africa, *Assessing Regional Integration in Africa*, pp. 32-33.

In the same direction, in later years, were the Protocol on Democracy and Good Governance and establishment of the elaborate Mechanism for Conflict Prevention, Management, Resolution, Peace and Security whose implementing institutions are the Authority, the Mediation and Security Council, and the Secretariat with its Early Warning System; the organs of the mechanism include the Defence and Security Commission, the Council of Elders, and the ECOWAS Cease-fire Monitoring Group (ECOMOG).

The argument has been that without peace there can be no development. Conflict resolution, good governance and security are necessary preconditions for poverty reduction and economic welfare. The UNECA captures several aspects of this argument, as follows:

> The persistent absence of peace, security and stability has serious consequences for Africa's development and integration. Conflicts and wars have slowed integration in some regional economic communities – and brought it to a standstill in others. Conflicts have also diverted resources from development efforts and prevented countries from participating fully in regional economic community activities. Moreover, unrest in one country can reduce foreign investment in neighbouring countries and throughout a sub-region-particularly damaging since such investment is linked to much of the development of infrastructure and productive capacity in regional economic communities. (UNECA, 2002)

Without peace there can be no economic integration either. On this, Okolo and Wright have rightly argued that 'Planning [within regional organizations] in particular becomes problematic because political fluidity detracts from long-term stability desired for the success of these development schemes'. (Okolo, Julius E. and Stephen Wright, 1990) Tunji Lardner notes what he calls a 'Nigerian consensus' that 'ECOWAS cannot achieve its ultimate objective of economic integration and cooperation unless the sub- region was considerably free of political tension and conflict'. (Lardner, Tunji, Jnr. 1990) Abass Bundu, the ECOWAS Executive Secretary in the early 1990s puts it more pointedly:

> You cannot talk meaningfully about economic integration by itself without also relating (it) to the underpinning political instability within the sub-region. The two are inseparable and have to be discussed *inter alia*... Regional solidarity and commitment to integration will be considerably enhanced where political stability becomes a common identity and is also perceived as a shared responsibility. (Aning, Emanuel K, 1999)

Studies abound on various aspects of this drastic shift in focus and resources and on the argument that a peaceful environment is a precondition for the realization of higher levels and scope of integration in the region.[4] Invariably, however,

---

4 Examples are: Francis, David, *The Politics of Economic Regionalism: Sierra Leone in ECOWAS*, London: Ashgate, 2001; Adeleke, Ademola, 'The Politics and Diplomacy of Peacekeeping in West Africa: The ECOWAS. Operation in Liberia,' *The Journal of Modern Africa Studies*, vol. 33, no.4, 1995, pp 569-593; Howe, Herbert, 'Lessons of Liberia: ECOMOG and Regional Peacekeeping', *International Security*, vol. 21, no.3, 1996, pp.145-176; Adibe, Clement E. 'ECOWAS in a Comparative Perspective,' in Emeka Okolo and

academic and non-academic research tend to be concentrated on the region as actor and on region-level actions. Regrettably, scanty empirical research has been done on ECOWAS member states as the primary unit of analysis, in their relationship with regional economic integration processes. This, even though a focus on the member state offers insights into the two issues raised above. On the slow pace in the achievement of the economic integration aims and objectives of the regional organization, it cannot be gainsaid that national governments are reluctant to relinquish control over their economies to any regional organization; the fact that the linkage between regional economic integration and national development has not been sufficiently demonstrated is a related factor. On the shift in preoccupation to regional peace and security, national governments are likely to be actively supportive in that peace and security are public goods and, as such, are not likely to compromise national sovereignty and independence.

Increasing Loads and Unit-level Institutional Capacities

A primordial question that must first be broached is that of the commitment of national governments in their obligations to regional integration in West Africa. One source of evidence on the extent of commitment is the status of ratification of the Revised Treaty, protocols, the conventions and decisions of the ECOWAS legislative organs.[5] Here the chasm between rhetoric and realities of ECOWAS regionalism is palpably discernable. After signature, ratification is the initial action-point in the implementation, monitoring, and evaluation continuum. It was calculated in 2003 that only the protocol on free movement of persons had been implemented by all member states; all other key protocols had been ratified by only 50% of member states. (Amoako, 2003) The treaty itself was signed by the Heads of State and Government on 24 July 1993 but it was two years after, on 23 August 1995, that it entered into force after ratification by the required two-thirds of the membership. Two (Benin, Togo) ratified later in 1995, two (Cap Vert, Cote d'Ivoire) in 1996, and one (Gambia) in 1997. As at May 2005 the instruments of ratification had still not been received from Guinea Bissau.[6]

Of the 34 protocols and conventions that have been ratified and entered into force as at 30 May 2005 there is an average of three-and-a-half years between signing

---

Timothy Shaw (ed.). *The Political Economy of Foreign Policy in ECOWAS,* St. Martin's Press, New York, NY, 1994, pp. 187-217) Dennis, Peter and Brown, M. Leann Brown, 'The ECOWAS: From Regional Economic Organization to Regional Peacekeeper', in Laursen, Finn,(ed), *Comparative Regional Integration Theoretical Perspectives,* Ashgate, Publishers, London, 2003, pp. 229-249).

5   Low rate of replies to correspondence addressed by the secretariat to member States and low level of member States' participation in ministerial and technical meetings are other indicators that have been of concern to the organization. See, for example, ECOWAS Secretariat, *Final Report-Meeting of Heads of ECOWAS National Units,* Lagos, 29-31 May 1996, pp. 3-4.

6   It compares unfavorably with the UEMOA Treaty which was signed in January 1994 and ratified by all member states by August the same year.

and ratification. Nine protocols have taken five years or more to come into force. Of these four relate to economic matters (the trade liberalization schemes), two with legal matters (mutual assistance in criminal matters, Treaty amendment), two deal with Community institutions (Court of Justice, Parliament), and one deals with political matters (mutual assistance on defense).

Nine protocols have not yet been ratified by the required number of states in order to come into effect. Of these one was signed in 1994 (on extradition), one in 1996 (establishing Value Added Tax in member states), three in 2001 (fight against corruption, democracy and good governance, brown card scheme relating to motor vehicle insurance), three in 2003 (recognition of equivalence of degrees etc., education and training, and energy), and one as recently as January 2005 relating to the Court of Justice. (ECOWAS, 2005)

This record leads to the conclusion that ECOWAS member states do not accord to the organization and its aims and objectives the importance they are supposed to have. Much lip service is paid to the imperative of sub-regional cooperation and integration but there are significant shortfalls in terms of action. At the point of signature of the protocols and conventions there is usually unanimity. The problem arises in the subsequent incorporation of these acts in national legislation through the ratification process. Even for the pivotal and much-vaunted trade liberalization scheme implementation was delayed for over a decade because some of the protocols were not ratified by the required number of states. (Jebuni, Charles, 1998)

Where there is a high level of ratification of protocols an equally fundamental question that arises is how high are the levels of actual implementation, coordination, and monitoring of the integration programmes. A key variable is whether or not effective and efficient national institutional capacities exist. In an earlier reflection on unit-level institutional dimensions of regional integration I had argued:

> The focus of policy and research on the subject [of regional cooperation and integration in Africa] is still overwhelmingly on issues and problems associated with the "top-down" regional institutions and processes. Yet policy and programme decision-making and implementation must also inevitably involve a "bottom-up" process of actions by "unit-level actors". It is what national governments do that effectively determines become more interlinked in an integration framework. (Senghor, 1994)

More recently, David Francis has commented:

> Putting into place an effective national institutional structure to supervise and monitor the implementation of the ECOWAS protocols, decisions and programmes is a necessary prerequisite for member states if they want to share in the benefits of regionalism. There is the expectation of rewards and gains from regionalism...But such rewards can only be reaped if the appropriate policies are adopted and structures are put in place. (Francis, 2001)

Ultimate responsibility for executing the gamut of protocols and conventions adopted in various ECOWAS fora and the substantive integration programmes derived from them rests squarely with national governments which, in turn, benefit from them in terms of the outcomes of the integration process. Noticeably, over the decades

Community priority programmes for national-level implementation and requiring involvement of national institutions have multiplied astronomically, expanding to all development sectors as provided in the Revised Treaty.[7] Of those emanating from continental initiatives, the New Partnership for Africa's Development (NEPAD) is the most recent. The extraordinary summit of the Authority, in Yamoussoukro, Cote d'Ivoire, in May 2002, decided to adopt a regional approach to the implementation of NEPAD in West Africa; it designated ECOWAS 'as the regional organization responsible for the coordination and monitoring of the implementation of NEPAD programmes' and directed that a NEPAD focal point should be created in the secretariat. It adopted a Plan of Action specifying the methodology and guidelines for NEPAD implementation. (ECOWAS, 2002) As there is a high degree of congruency between the already-heavy ECOWAS programmes and the ambitious NEPAD agenda a synergization process was launched in 2003. The regional secretariat has developed its own short-term action plan for capacity building to better position itself to respond to the new challenges in the implementation of the Authority's Plan of Action.

As for the earlier ECOWAS programmes, whilst there has been this flurry of activity at the regional level as regards NEPAD programmes, requirements at the national level, where the programmes will actually be implemented, have been of limited concern.[8] The ECOWAS Executive Secretary is clear on the inter-relationships when he warned:

> The guidelines for the revitalization of the integration process contained in the NEPAD Plan of Action adopted by the Authority in Yamoussoukro will become operational only if the Member States take concrete measures to overcome the problems of implementation of ECOWAS decisions and integration programmes, which we cannot afford to delay any longer. (ECOWAS, 2002)

In sum, the exponential increase in loads is mainly derived from four sources, namely, the original economic agenda, political/security engagements, the expanded mandates of the Revised Treaty, and continental demands especially as regards the African Economic Community treaty of 1991 and the NEPAD of 2002. The logical question that follows is: Are institutional capabilities of the type and quality required for programme delivery? Integration objectives, plans and programmes must be integrated into national development strategies. National level institutions must be streamlined and equipped to deal with the complexities of integration by strengthening their skills and resource base and their authority to drive the process. Similar measures are required at the regional level to improve on interaction with national-level operations. Quite commonly, the disconnect between regional and

---

7 These include: the trade liberalization scheme; monetary integration; free movement of persons; trans West African highway network; inter-state telecommunication network; energy; tourism; seed and cattle centers; the industrial master plan; and rural water programme.

8 The multiple institutional and programmatic implications of this responsibility for the regional NEPAD programme was discussed at length in the ECOWAS Secretariat, Status Report on the ECOWAS Short-term Capacity Building Programme of the NEPAD, Abuja, November 2003.

national levels is more pronounced at the programme implementation phase than in political decision-making.

Comparative Analysis of Institutional Architecture

Before proceeding to a review of the institutional architecture it is relevant to point out that the empirical material was collected as part of a larger project commissioned by the ECOWAS secretariat on national focal points for ECOWAS and NEPAD programmes.[9] In terms of data collection instruments the research team depended on desk study of a wide range of documents, on completed focused questionnaires, and on extensive interviews during field missions to all 15 member states in April 2004. The material discussed in this chapter is limited to the five countries for which the author was responsible, namely, Benin, The Gambia, Nigeria, Senegal and Togo. However, for emphasis and comparison, references are made to experiences in the other countries in several places.

The thrust of the case studies is on five aspects of the national institutional arrangements: the nomenclature, location and reporting arrangements; organizational structures; functions; the resource base; and the relations with sector ministries. Other elements, such as the strategic objectives, are important in any institutional assessment but they are not germane to this study. The matrix presentation makes for easy comparisons between countries which is useful in itself. But, beyond that, it helps in identifying best practices in one country which can serve as models for other countries to emulate.

Nomenclature, Location and Reporting Arrangements

Five years after ECOWAS became operational, in May 1982, the Council of Ministers set up an Ad-Hoc Ministerial Committee to look into the slow implementation of programmes and to formulate a short-term revival action programme. Based on its report the Council recommended, in November, that each member state 'establishes a national structure responsible for the coordination and follow up of Community activities in the member state.' The Authority, in May 1983, concerned that despite the above recommendation some states had not established national structures, decided that information on actions taken by each state should be communicated to the secretariat; defaulting nations would then be more easily identifiable.

All the countries in the region have now established national structures for ECOWAS matters. However, the nomenclatures and hierarchical ranking differ from country to country: Benin, Nigeria, and Senegal have the national unit as a department within a ministry; Togo has a section within a division and Gambia has a unit/desk officer within a section. Of the other countries Burkina Faso, Cote d'Ivoire, Cap Vert and Guinea Bissau fall in the first category whilst Ghana, Guinea Conakry, Liberia, Mali, Niger, and Sierra Leone have the unit as a division within a

---

9   See *Study on National Focal Points for ECOWAS and NEPAD Programmes*, ECOWAS Secretariat: Abuja, Nigeria, May 2004. It was funded by the World Bank and conducted by a three-man team.

department. The organizational ranking is indicative of the status accorded the roles, functions and outputs, and with which goes resources. Thus, a department compares very favorably with a section or a unit. In this regard, is it of any significance that most of the French-speaking countries have departments in charge of ECOWAS affairs as compared to the English-specking countries which have mainly assigned the responsibility to divisions and sections?

In three of the five cases (Benin, Gambia, Togo) the national units are located in one or other of the economic ministries (finance, economic affairs, trade and industry); this is also the arrangement in six other countries. Whereas in Nigeria, as in four other countries, it is in the ministry for African integration, in Senegal it is located in foreign affairs after the incorporation of the former ministry of African integration into this ministry in May 2001. In that these ministries are high-status core ministries the national unit enjoys residual visibility. In comparison, all UEMOA focal points are located in ministries of finance; this is primarily because responsibility for overseeing the Central Bank for West Africa (BCEAO), the midwife to UEMOA, has always been with this ministry. The African Union, on the other and, is placed in ministries of foreign affairs or African integration.

As regards reporting arrangements, the number of layers is in direct relation to the hierarchical ranking of the ECOWAS unit. Where a department or division, reporting by the head, usually a director, is of shorter span, i.e., to the director-general or secretary-general in the ministry (Benin,) or directly to the minister. Where a section or unit, the span tends to be much longer, i.e., to the Director, Deputy Permanent Secretary, Permanent Secretary (Gambia). In Nigeria and Senegal where there are departments, reporting is to the Permanent Secretary. In Togo, where the unit is, in effect a section, it also reports directly to the Permanent Secretary. In principle, the longer the span of the reporting arrangements the longer the time-frame for taking action. This is another dimension to the argument that it is preferable for the ECOWAS unit to be of high hierarchical ranking.

Institutional Structures

The institutional structures are at two levels, namely, the larger organizational system and the ECOWAS national unit itself. Concerning the larger organizational system, in cases where the unit is a department or a directorate it is usually one of several in the ministry; examples are Benin and Nigeria. Sometimes, as with Nigeria where the other departments are numerous, the national unit risks being at the periphery, especially if it lacks other attributes to counter such possibilities. For several countries, however, even where the national unit is a division the number of other divisions is few; Senegal is a case in point.

Table 6.1 Location and Reporting Arrangements

	Benin	The Gambia	Nigeria	Senegal	Togo
Location	The Department of Regional Integration (DRI) is the national unit located in the Economic Affairs branch of the Ministry of Finance and Economic Affairs (MFA)	The Desk Office is in the Trade Division of the Dept. of State for Trade, Industry and Employment	The ECOWAS Unit is also the Department of Cooperation and Develop, which has 3 additional technical depts. (Pol. Aff, Collective Defense and Security, and Regional Econ. Integ).	Department for Inter-African Organizations and Communities of the Ministry of Foreign Affairs, the African Union and Senegalese Abroad	The ECOWAS NatCom & Permanent Secretariat comprises the national structure for ECOWAS matters. The former's location is not clear cut whereas the latter is under the Ministry of Economic Affairs, Finance and Privatization. About 7 other offices are in the ministry, reporting to the Minister.
Reporting arrangements	Director of DRI through Director General of branch of MFA to Minister of MFA	Economist through Deputy Permanent Secretary, Permanent Secretary, to Minister; and to IMC and IMC-Technical Committee	Director of DCD through Permanent Secretary to Minister of Cooperation and Integration in Africa	Director through Permanent Secretary to Minister	Chief of Unit to Minister

In principle, the higher the position of the national unit in the organizational hierarchy the more complex the internal organizational structure. This hypothesis is only partially confirmed by the empirical data. On the one hand, in Benin, the national unit, the Department for Regional Integration, has only two substantive divisions each with only two sections. In Senegal, the unit, the Department for Inter-African Organizations and Communities, also has two divisions, which are non-functional anyway. On the other hand, the Director General for Integration Policy in Cote d'Ivoire has seven divisions, including UEMOA, NEPAD, AU, and other regional organizations. Further, the ECOWAS Division in the Ministry for Regional Integration and NEPAD in Ghana comprise six sections. In Guinea Bissau, the Directorate for Regional Integration cum ECOWAS national unit is serviced by seven divisions.

In contrast to these two types, in the smaller countries the organizational structure is very flat. In Gambia, the ECOWAS desk office has no structure; it is one of four desk offices in the trade division in the ministry of trade, industry and employment. In Togo, the ECOWAS national unit, the Permanent Secretariat, is composed of a small team of technical polyvalent experts.

On what basis are the subordinate structures organized? There are three possibilities, that is, sectors, organization, or theme. In the case of the ECOWAS units there is again a mixture. In Benin, the divisions are organized on sectoral lines. Senegal is an instance where the arrangement is on the basis of organizations. There is no case of the third type.

Institutional Functions

The functions to be performed by the national unit determine, to a great extent, the level of performance and the impact of regional integration programmes on-the-ground. The first positive observation is that in all countries in the region the functions of the national units are clearly articulated. The functions common to most of the units, if not all, fall in the following six categories:

- Advisory services: To governments on matters relating to the design, implementation, and evaluation of policies, and on government positions on issues before ECOWAS policy organs.
- Liaison: Serve as links between member governments and ECOWAS institutions and between government ministries.
- Think tank: Undertake research and reflect on the impact of integration on national development and on how to increase national benefits from integration schemes.
- Coordination, monitor and follow-up: Lead role in ensuring that actions are taken for the implementation of ECOWAS policies and programmes.
- Outreach: Mobilize participation of civil society, private sector and other actors in the integration process.
- Representational: In meetings and other activities of ECOWAS the unit represents or arranges representation of the government or other concerned parties.

Table 6.2 Structures

Benin	Gambia	Nigeria	Senegal	Togo
Department for Regional Integration serves as national unit (headed by a Director) has: i. Sectoral policy Division (with 2 sections); ii. Trade Division (with 2 sections); iii. Admin, Fin, Legal and Political Division (with 3 sections). Accts. and Secretariat are under Director's office.	A national Desk Office / Focal Point in the Trade Division (headed by a Principal Economist) in the Dept. of State for Trade, Industry and Employment (DoSTIE) which has a Statistical Unit, WTO Desk Office, UNCTAD Desk Office, and an ITC Desk Officer. Desk Office is part of a structural system including an IMC, IMC-Tech. Comm., etc.	Dept. of Cooperation and Development (DCD) serves as national unit under the Min. of Cooperation and Integration in Africa which has additional 3 tech. depts. (Political Affairs, Collective Defense and Security, and Regional Econ. Integration); 2 Service Depts. (Fin., Admin. & Planning); 3 statutory units (Int. Audit, Legal Affairs. & Press & Public Relations); & 2 parastatals.	A national unit at the Dept for Inter-African Org. and Communities of the Min. for Foreign Affairs, the AU and Senegalese abroad - headed by a Director - has 2 non functional sections ('Regional Org.,' & Communities, and Continental Org. Communities & Cooperation.	Comprising ECOWAS National Committee and ECOWAS Permanent Secretariat. Former is a non-exclusive mixed body and latter is a slim structure headed by a Chief, under the Min. of Econ. Affairs Fin. & Privatization.

Table 6.3 Functions

Benin	The Gambia	Nigeria	Senegal	Togo
Dept. for Regional Integration	Desk Office/Focal Point	National Unit / Dept. of Cooperation & Dev. (DCD)	National Unit	National Committee is responsible for all matters relating to ECOWAS; and Permanent Secretariat
i. Serves as an antennae for regional economic integration organizations, on the one hand, and as a transmission channel between them and the Republic, on the other	i. Coordinating the activities of the IMC and TCs	i. Fashion effective and results-oriented strategies for establishing, harmonizing, strengthening and sustaining bilateral, regional and multilateral cooperation among African countries	i. Acts on and follows up on matters related to inter-African organizations and commitments, as well as those relating to cooperation between these organizations and communities and non-African countries	i. Prepares the work of the National Committee
ii. Reflects on ways and means for accelerating the process of economic integration	ii. Making recommendations and advising the Government on ECOWAS matters, relating to policies and programs	ii. Ensure peace and stability thro' collective defense and security systems which facilitate the prevention, management and resolution of conflict in Africa	ii. Ensures the participation of Senegal in communities and organizations in which she is a member at the sub-regional, regional and continental levels	ii. Coordinates the activities of the NATCOM. and its sub-committees
iii. Defines and implements actions required to derive advantages from its membership of regional economic integration organizations	iii. Follow-up and facilitate the implementation of decisions relating to agreements, protocols, conventions, programs, etc.	iii. Maintain and strengthen relations with regional and international organizations such as ECOWAS, SADC, COMESA, AU, UN-ECA, UNDP, FAO, GEF, etc.	iii. Collaborates with relevant departments in the Ministry of Foreign Affairs and organize and follows up on the work of joint commission of Senegal and African countries	iii. Disseminates Community decisions and follows up on their implementation
iv. Analyzes the implications of activities of different sectors of the economy for Community actions, projects and programs, and vice versa	iv. Serve as liaison and principal conduit between the ECOWAS Secretariat and national institutions and other bodies.	iv. Promote and facilitate regional economic integration in West Africa, thro' ECOWAS, and encourage massive expansion of Nigerian exports to Africa and the rest of the world.	iv. Disseminates decisions of ECOWAS policy organs to sector ministries for action and monitors performance	iv. Centralize ECOWAS documentation
v. Services the National Commission for Economic Integration for which it is the secretariat			v. Participates in the formulation of Government's position on ECOWAS matters and ensures coordination and coherence in such positions.	v. Maintain the archives.

Having noted the commonalities, a comparative analysis reveals some variations between the countries. In the first place, whereas the units in most of the countries have self-defined functions, in others the functions are directly sourced from those of the parent organization. Nigeria is a good example of the latter; from the mandate of the Ministry for (African) Integration the department/ECOWAS national unit applies relevant elements to its own field of operations. This can be a source of problems as it is open-ended. Furthermore, the derived functions are stated in broad and general terms. Good organization design principles require that an organization be ascribed its own set of clearly-defined functions to guide performance; a comprehensive and precise definition of functions is a clear basis for goal-setting, activity-planning and execution, and performance monitoring and evaluation.

It is also vital that the functions of an organization are reviewed and updated from time to time, in line with changing circumstances and situations. This is important in that in every respect, the environment of integration in the region and continent has changed vastly from three decades ago when most of the national units were set up. Similarly for the domestic environment. In no case was evidence provided to show that this has been done in any of the countries.

There are instances where the functions actually being performed by the national unit do not correspond with the official legal functions. Togo is an excellent example. The all-important Decree 83-37 which laid down the national structures for ECOWAS matters and their functions has not been fully implemented. Indeed, the greater part of its provisions has not seen the light of day. Most important among these are those pertaining to the high-level inter-ministerial National Committee. Neither the Committee nor its sub-committees have been operational. Thus, in effect, the ECOWAS Permanent Secretariat has been without the high-powered body it was supposed to service. Given the vacuum, the Permanent Secretariat which, according to law, was merely to service the *de jure* National ECOWAS Committee, is now the de facto ECOWAS national unit. Its stated functions are highly divergent from it actually does at present.

Resources

As for most public organizations in African countries, in the ECOWAS national units resources are a bottleneck and a major constraint affecting productivity. For all countries in the region the total number of personnel of all categories in the ECOWAS national units number 110, broken down into 52 professional and 58 support staff. Among the professional personnel the range is from 1 to 12. Excluding Liberia, the distribution is as follows.

1 staff = 2 countries (Cape Verde, Senegal)
2 staff = 5 countries (Burkina, Gambia G.Bissau, Liberia, S.Leone)
3 staff = 2 countries (Niger, Togo)
5 staff = 2 countries (Ghana, Guinea Conakry)
6 staff = 2 countries (Mali, Nigeria)
12 staff = 1 country (Benin)

Table 6.4 Resources

	Benin	The Gambia	Nigeria	Senegal	Togo
Human	12 professionals (min. 10 yrs experience) 8 support staff	2 professionals (junior level with 1 to 3 yrs exp) 2 support staff	6 professionals en post (min. 10 yrs exp) against 11 indicated in establishment 10 support staff	1 professional, i.e. Director 2 support staff	3 professionals 5 support staff
Material	12 computers 1 electric typewriter 3 photocopiers 2 international tel. lines 2 local tel. lines	1 computer 1 local tel. line internet facility	Nil/Not indicated. No internet facility	3 computers 1 electric. typewriter 1 photocopier 2 intl. tel. line 2 local telephone line Internet not working	1 computer 1 photocopier 1 local tel. line Internet facility partly operational
Financial	2003- CFA 980 mn 2004- CFA 950 mn mainly from ECOWAS subvention but exceeds 5% levy grant	Highly inadequate. Unit's estimated budget is about $102,000 for allowances, O&M, capital (vehicles, equipment, etc.)	Government budget indicating 2003- N60 mn. for capital programme. And N70 mn. for recurrent. Less than 5% of proposed budgets had been released in the last 2 preceding years	2004- CFA 5.7mn i.e. 20% of budget provided by Govt. Balance comes from ECOWAS subvention	

Among our five selected countries Benin has the highest professional staff complement of 12, whereas Senegal has the lowest at 1 professional staff. Is there a correlation between technical staff size and organizational performance, in terms of levels of implementation of ECOWAS programs? The evidence is mixed. Benin and Nigeria, with large staff, rank among the high performers. But so also does Senegal, with only 1 professional.

It is noted that Nigeria has a total establishment of 12 but there are actually only 6 persons on board, due to the fact that staffing of the unit falls within the framework of national policies on movement of personnel within the civil service as a whole. This is one of the inherent consequences of staffing the unit with regular civil servants whose conditions of service are governed by the general civil service orders. The same situation may prevail in other countries, particularly the English-speaking countries.

The average level of education and the experience of the personnel are impressive. In the majority of countries the professional staff is university educated, some at the Masters degree level. Quite commonly, personnel have a minimum of 10 years experience; of course this experience may not necessarily be in the ECOWAS unit. The facts lead to the observation that professional staff in the units have a longer tenure in the French-speaking bureaucracies.

The ECOWAS national units are most deprived in terms of material resources. The spectrum ranges from Benin, which is well endowed with computers, printers, photocopiers, international and local telephone lines, to The Gambia with one computer/Internet and one local telephone line. Interesting also is the proportional distribution of equipment among the staff. From the information available on the ratio of computers to professional staff the best performers are: Senegal (1: 3) and Benin (12:12). In the middle range is The Gambia (1:2). Togo comes off poorly at 1 computer to 3 professionals.

Communications facilities are most essential, particularly Internet services. For one out of the 5 countries for which information is available Internet facilities are available and functional (Gambia). Senegal, and Togo have non-functional Internet and the national unit in Nigeria does not have any such facility. For other means of communications each country has at least one local telephone line and most have international lines even though their use may be restricted.

Financial resources are inadequate for all national units. Governments provide the budgets in most countries but not at the level of actually requirements. Not only are there shortfalls but funds may not be released as and when required.

Relations with Sector Ministries

As the greater proportion of ECOWAS programmes are sectoral in character the level of overall programme implementation depends on the sectoral institutional arrangements and on interrelationships between the central units and the sector ministries. Ideally, there should be five types of structures, namely, focal points in the sector ministries and agencies, inter-ministerial coordination committees as established by Council in decision C/DEC.3/12/90, intra-sectoral implementation bodies, national monitoring committees (e.g. for multilateral surveillance mechanism, free movement of persons and goods, tourism facilitation, trade liberalization), and multi-sectoral coordinating bodies bringing together relevant government ministries, the private sector, civil society and other stakeholders.

In no country throughout the region do all of these structures exist. As concerns the sector focal points, the most common arrangement is to have focal points/ desk officers/individuals that have been dealing with handling ECOWAS matters historically but on an ad hoc basis and as a part of a range of other tasks. In Nigeria they have been formally and officially designated in each ministry.

From the information available, an inter-ministerial coordination committee has been formally established in Gambia and in other countries such as Burkina Faso, Cote d'Ivoire, Ghana, Guinea Conakry, and Sierra Leone. However, most are actually moribund. They meet only occasionally, usually to prepare for major summit meetings of ECOWAS. Much the same can be said of the intra-sectoral committees directly responsible for monitoring implementation of specific sectoral programs.

As seen in the matrix, the national units work with whatever arrangements are in place in sector ministries. Commonly, the activities undertaken are:

- Coordination of the work referred to the sector ministries.
- Organization of meetings to determine sector representation in ECOWAS statutory and other meetings, to review outcomes of these meetings.
- Follow up on program implementation and on related actions.
- Dissemination of incoming communications from ECOWAS secretariat.
- Provide inputs to integration activities of sector ministries.

Given the difficulties currently being experienced by the national units most are not in a position to carry out these functions with any appreciable degree of effectiveness. They are themselves confronted with various problems. Typically, these include:

- Non-existence or ineffectiveness of the inter-ministerial or intra-sectoral committees, e.g., Benin, Gambia, Senegal, and Togo.
- Absence or inadequacy of focal points in sector ministries, e.g., Gambia.
- Rapid turnover of focal points, e.g. Gambia, Nigeria, and Senegal.
- Inadequate resources for relating to sector ministries, e.g., Gambia, and Nigeria.

Table 6.5 Relations with Sector Ministries

Benin	The Gambia	Nigeria	Senegal	Togo
Directorate of Regional Integration *coordinates the work of all sector ministries relating to integration, ECOWAS UEMOA *meetings are organized with sector experts in ministries for a) deciding on sector representation in ECOWAS UEMOA meetings, b) reviewing outcomes of meetings, c) monitoring follow-up actions on decisions reached. *ad hoc inter ministerial meetings at experts levels are convened. Problems include i) dormant inter ministerial committee, ii) unestablished intra-sectoral committee, iii) un-established national committee on integration.	The Desk Office collaborates through the established IMC, the technical IMC, various sub-committees (e.g. Common External Tariff, Community Levy) and with individual sector ministries - disseminating information and follow-up on necessary action. Problems include non-functioning of the committees, absence of Focal Points in sector ministries, rapid turn-over of Desk Officers, and inadequate resources at the Desk Office.	The DCD/National Unit *collaborates with sector ministries through several channels, including: designated sector Desk Officers/ Focal Points, ECOWAS Permanent Committee of experts & sub-committees. *DCD coordinates at two levels (i) internally, within the Ministry of Cooperation and Integration in Africa, and (ii) externally, all sector ministries concerning ECOWAS. * sectors also have ad hoc intra-sectoral committees (Common External Tariff, Macroeconomic Surveillance, WAMZ Sensitization, Transport Coordination) to deal with specific issues in the course of policy and programmed implementation. Frequent meetings are held where brief reports are presented on the status of implementation of the ECOWAS programs under each ministry, etc.	The National Unit collaborates through its parent Dept. of Inter-African Organization and Communities, informally with individual experts in sector ministries, and few intra-sectoral technical committees. Problems include the frequent changes / movements of sector experts causing inconsistency and delays, absence of an IMC and the inaction in creating the National Committee on Integration to deal with ECOWAS matters.	The National Committee/ Permanent Secretariat collaborates through sectoral and departmental contact points by disseminating ECOWAS decisions and regulations, following-up on actions, organizing ad hoc inter-sectoral meetings, and contributing to integration activities of sectoral ministries. Problems include the inaction of the National Committee to create the four sectoral sub-committees and other ad hoc sub-committees mandated by the decree, the non-functioning of the National Committee, and the non-establishment of intra-sectoral sub-committees.

Country Assessments of Institutional Arrangements

Benin

Having a full-fledged department in charge of ECOWAS affairs, in a very key ministry, as in the case of Benin, gives it visibility and recognition. Its status is further enhanced by it being a department rather than a division, section or unit; it therefore is of high ranking within the hierarchy of governmental structures. This is indicative of the importance attached to regional integration by the government. There are decided gains in having primary responsibility for both ECOWAS and UEMOA programs vested in the same body. Among these, the two experiences can be compared and one can benefit from the experiences of the other and areas of convergence and collaboration can be easily identified. It is also a more economical use of resources and expertise, which are limited in any one country.

The national unit is also well structured with clear inter-organizational relationships. The structure covers all aspects of integration in a single organizational entity. This encourages the development of high levels of expertise, familiarity with issues, procedures, the substantive work itself, etc. At the same time, the structure links together allied sectors, which makes it easier to appreciate the inter-dependence of sectors. Lines of authority are clearly delineated which means that confusion in reporting is reduced. In addition, it makes it easier both to determine who should take action on any matter and to monitor follow-up actions, thus promoting accountability.

The functions are spelt out in broad terms in Decree No.99-514 of 02 November 1999. This has the advantage of giving the department some leeway in working out the precise scope of its responsibilities in practice; it also gives it room to adapt to changing situations and circumstances. In this regard, it is noteworthy that, unlike some other country cases, the work of the national unit is not specifically limited to ECOWAS; it is open to all integration schemes, at whatever level.

The functions of the ministry as a whole, those of each of the six technical branches and of the large number of departments within them, are defined in the same Decree. Those of each of the component divisions are also elaborately laid out in ministerial directive No. 432 of 28 April 2000 bearing on the functions, organization, and operation of the Economic Affairs Branch.

This clear articulation of the functions at each level of the organization minimizes possibilities of jurisdictional conflicts, which would negatively affect performance, productivity, and effectiveness of each unit and of the department as a whole. It facilitates prompt action and evaluation of performance.

The national unit is comparatively well resourced in Benin. All of the leadership positions in the elaborate structure are currently encumbered and by professionals who are seasoned; some of whom have been with the DPI for over 15 years. There is a strong emphasis on specialization and high-level technical competence in various sectoral fields within the DPI. Thus, both in terms of quantity and quality the ECOWAS national unit is in a good position to execute its mandate.

In like manner, in terms of material and financial resources, the situation is relatively healthy.

The arrangements for consultations and coordination between the DRI, as ECOWAS national unit, and the sector ministries, appear to work satisfactorily, even in the absence of a permanent inter-ministerial committee. This is due, in no small measure, to the fact that the DRO is itself well established in terms of sectoral technical expertise; it has a solid institutional memory, and over time has institutionalized communications channels and procedures. The existence of designated focal points in the sector ministries, rather than personalized contact points has been a most significant contributory factor.

Even with this, however, there is still a place for the inter-ministerial committee. The National Committee on Integration should be established and provided with the resources required for its proper functioning.

The Gambia

The Gambia's approach to ECOWAS has been minimalist; that is, it acts 'just enough' to meet its obligations to the organization. This is reflected in the fact that it has no substantive structure for managing relationships with the regional body. It is yet to establish a full-fledged national ECOWAS unit as directed by the Authority in 1983. In theory, it has maintained a desk office. In practice, ECOWAS is more of a *dossier.*

The Gambia is the only country in the region that has a desk office, about the lowest, most loose, and least formal type of arrangement. Significantly, the office has had an itinerant location. When first created in response to the recommendation of the ECOWAS Authority in1978 it was located in the ministry of economic planning and industrial development. With the dissolution of that ministry in 1985 the office moved to the newly created ministry of finance and trade. In 1990, this ministry was divided into two separate ministries and the desk office was transferred to its current abode in the renamed ministry of trade, industry and employment. In itself, this constant shift can be interpreted as indicative of uncertainties as to what really ECOWAS is all about or lack of interest in its mission and purpose. Interestingly, also, The Gambia is the only country in which the national unit is not located in the ministry of finance, economic affairs, or a close variant, excepting Senegal but where the location in foreign affairs is relatively recent.

Within the ministry, the office is directly under the Trade Division which is one of five divisions. ECOWAS deals with more than trade but this is the most convenient fit for it in that particular ministry. Reporting is through the Permanent Secretary to the minister. The ministry also reports to the Technical and Inter-ministerial Committees which have been reportedly established in February 2004. This short reporting span is advantageous in terms of speed in decision-taking and action.

The desk office is one of five other offices in the Trade Division, the others being the Statistical Unit, World Trade Organization, UNCTAD, and the International Trade Centre. Its functions are limited to the barest minimum, with an emphasis more on routine task-administration.

As in other areas the resource provision is at a minimum. The narrowness of its human resource base is seen in the fact that it is headed by a Principal Economist assisted by a Senior Economist, an Economist who serves as the current Desk

Officer and another economist as back-up Desk Officer. This low-level (quality and quality) staffing is aggravated by the fact that ECOWAS matters is not the exclusive assignment of these officials; rather, they are engage more with other departmental schedules and ECOWAS matters are mere incidental responsibilities. In a similar vein, the material resources available to the desk office are not for sole use in dealing with ECOWAS matters. In fact, they are mostly used for other diverse activities in the ministry. The Desk Office does not have a budget of its own and depends on allocations from the very skimpy budget of the Trade Division.

The relationship between the Desk Office and other sector ministries is a formal one and is through an Inter-ministerial Committee (IMC) working in conjunction with a Technical Committee (TC). Besides the home ministry, representation on the IMC is from the ministries of finance, foreign affairs, agriculture, works, justice health and social welfare. It is at ministerial level with experts from these ministries constituting the TC. The IMC can co-opt members from the private sector, NGOs, and civil society organizations. It has authority to establish committees and sub-committee; this it has exercised in the creation of national monitoring committees (e.g. the Community Levy Committee, the Common External Tariff Committee). Quarterly meetings are supposed to be held by both the IMC and the various committees to facilitate review, consultation and monitoring. However, as noted in the relevant matrix, there is a gap between theory and reality: where they exist the committees are non-functioning, sector ministries lack focal points, and the turnover of the ECPOWAS Desk Officers is somewhat rapid. Meetings are infrequent and do not take place for lack of quorum, lack of collaboration or lack of funds.

Nigeria

The Ministry of African Cooperation and Integration is a full-fledged ministry of Cabinet rank independent of the Office of the President where it was originally located. This is advantageous. It gives the ministry high status, at par with other ministries. Access to the Presidency and its resources is not negatively affected; rather, direct participation in the Cabinet compensates for what is lost by moving out of the ambit of the Presidency. As an established ministry, there is the added advantage of its very existence not being at the mercy of the President.

To further consolidate and bolster the status of the ministry, both the Senate and House of Representatives of the National Assembly have established Committees on Cooperation and Integration which review the ministry's budgets and monitor its program implementation.

Having a separate and full-fledged ministry has put the focus pointedly on the very critical subject of regional integration in Africa, for which Nigeria has been a vocal and devoted advocate. It has contributed significantly to the positive activism of Nigeria on the ECOWAS scene and to the noticeable progress achieved in advancing cooperation and integration in the region.

On the structure of the ministry as a whole, the main observation is that there is a possibility of overlap among the four departments, going strictly by their nomenclatures. This is more likely in the instances of the Department of Cooperation and Development, which deals with ECOWAS, and that on Regional Economic

Integration, which is supposed to be continental in coverage. Much depends, however, on how precisely the functions are defined and what practical arrangements are in place to avoid duplication. This point becomes more relevant in that there are sector ministries also responsible for integration activities which may, at the same time, be handled by these departments.

The structure of the national unit is quite lean. Generally, this is a realistic approach, especially where resources are not in abundance. However, in this case, it is apparent that not all technical fields covered in ECOWAS programmes are reflected in the domains covered in the structure. To deal with this problem resort is made to the expertise available in the other departments in the same ministry or to the sector ministries. This then implies that coordination capabilities should be strong.

On the resources situation, first, it is noted that the DCD is poorly staffed. Less than 50% of the professional establishment is currently filled. For the first three years only one division was staffed and operational. Since then, staff has been posted to both. However, neither of the two divisions has a head (Assistant Director). One division has a second level officer (Chief Administrative Officer) at the branch level and none at the section level, whereas the other division has no staff at the branch level and one fourth level officer (Principal Administrative Officer) and one fifth level officer (Senior Administrative Officer) at the section level. The result is that in terms of staffing the organization is bottom heavy, particularly when one includes the ten (10) support personnel. Apparently, the situation in the other departments is no better. The fact that the ministry is relatively new partly accounts for this: established ministries resist reductions in their personnel complement for the benefit of a new ministry.

In terms of work schedules it is significant to note that the staff of the DCD works exclusively on ECOWAS matters. This permits them to accumulate experience and familiarity with all aspects of the work of the organization; it also prevents them from being distracted with other tasks which may be completely unrelated.

The staff are generalists who are posted to the ministry as part of their service career progression. Many are new, having been recently transferred from other ministries in the normal course of staff deployment in the public service as a whole. In principle, there is no guarantee of long tenure in the department and the personnel can be moved at any time. This accounts for the generic character of the post titles, i.e., they are of the Administrative cadre.

The turnover has been relatively stable with the senior-level professionals; those appointed to the ministry and to DCD in July 1999 were transferred elsewhere only in August 2003. The lack of stability has been more pronounced at the level of the political leadership where there have been four ministers in the five years of the existence of the ministry. At the lower end, it seems that staff performance is significantly hampered by such factors as inadequate funding, lack of material resources, poor motivation, inadequate training on integration, and frequent personnel movements.

As a consequence, there is likely to be less inclination to develop expertise in integration, in general, and ECOWAS in particular whereas, quite clearly, the fields covered in the various organizational units in the DCD are highly technical, e.g., physical infrastructures, trade and investment, monetary issues. Here again, the potential negative consequences can be reduced if there are solid systems and processes for interaction with the sector ministries.

For material and financial resources, there are significant shortfalls, in relation to staff size and organizational tasks.

The arrangements for the DCD to relate to the sector ministries and for the sector ministries to relate to each other appear satisfactory, in theory. In practice, however, it was observed that in recent times they have not been effective, again because of such problems as lack of funding, poor motivation, limited resource support, constant changes of staff, etc.

Senegal

Senegal was one of the first countries to establish a full-fledged Ministry for African Integration in 1991. Having a full-fledged ministry upgraded the importance of African integration in the governmental machinery. As in the instance of Nigeria, it gave the ministry a distinct identity, in line with Senegal's long-standing commitment to and its leadership role in integration schemes in the continent. In 2000 the national unit was integrated into the Ministry of Foreign Affairs where it has lesser prominence and status. Not only is the focus blunted but the DIOC now has to operate in a more complex hierarchical structure which included the Cabinet Office, the Office of the Secretary General, the Technical Advisers, the Regional Directorates, etc. In this respect, it is relevant to note that the Cabinet Office of the Minister and the Africa-Asia Department also deal with integration matters and the African Union, thereby giving rise to overlaps and jurisdictional problems.

Interestingly, the DIOC has still not been accommodated in the main building of the Ministry of Foreign Affairs and operates out of the old Ministry for African Integration, this apparently because of space limitations. This physical separation also has a symbolic dimension.

As in other member countries, UEMOA, on the other hand, is located in the Ministry of Finance. Though launched three years after the Ministry for African Integration was created it has always been in Finance where it enjoys visibility and more access to resources. Would it have suffered the same fate as the ECOWAS national unit if at the outset it been located in the Ministry for African Integration? The UEMOA National Committee, its official designation, is headed by a senior Technical Adviser to the Minister.

The functions of the national unit, the DIOC, are stated in generic terms; they are not precise enough. It really does not have a legal basis to manage the regional integration process. In effect, its functions are limited to coordinating and facilitating implementation and monitoring of ECOWAS decisions and programs and not policy initiation.

There are inherent possibilities of confusion in executing the functions of the DIOC. This is particularly so in respect of the sister Department of Studies and Project which has among its responsibilities those of initiating sectoral integration programs, and of undertaking general or proactive studies on African economic integration. Both departments have to deal with ECOWAS in one form or another.

But both also go beyond ECOWAS to deal with African integration issues more broadly.

The unit's resources are obviously scanty. It is noted, though, that the incumbent Director is technically highly qualified and is well experienced in integration matters. For good measure, the UEMOA focal point is staffed with a chief and two assistants but it receives more in-kind assistance from the UEMOA Commission. It has its own budget from the ministry and a subvention of 25 million CFA francs from the UEMOA Commission.

As regards relations with sector ministries the prevailing situation is second-best. By way of contrast, the National UEMOA Committee brings together experts from all sector ministries dealing with regional integration, particularly within the UEMOA framework. It meets monthly and has representation from the private sector, civil society and BCEAO. It reviews the status of implementation of UEMOA programmes and needed reforms, and advices on policy matters and on Senegal's position on issues before UEMOA policy organs. It appears, though, that there are good channels of communications between the ECOWAS national unit and the UEMOA focal point, especially as many of the programmes of the former deal with financial issues.

Togo

There are two initial observations on the all-important Decree 83-37 which lays down the national structures for ECOWAS matters. First, it has not been fully implemented. Indeed, the greater part of its provisions has not seen the light of day. Most important are those pertaining to the creation and functioning of the National Committee which has not been operational since the early days. Neither have its sub-committees been in existence. Thus, in effect, the ECOWAS Permanent Secretariat has been without the high-powered body it was supposed to service.

Second, the Decree needs updating. There has been a sea change in the situation existing in ECOWAS and in regionalism in the region in general since 1983 when the Decree was adopted. Though the Permanent Secretariat has adjusted to these new realities and satisfactorily executed its mandate, particularly as regards follow-up of implementation of ECOWAS programmes, this has been without legislative basis. In any case, having two separate bodies responsible for ECOWAS affairs, that is, the Committee and the Secretariat, gives rise to a range of problems, including problems of accountability.

Turning next to the contents of the Decree, the location of the ECOWAS Permanent Secretariat gives it prominence and clout as the Ministry of Finance is one of the most powerful in the Government of Togo and enjoys very high status. This strategic location should also facilitate access to resources, especially finance, and co-operation from other governmental structures. But, one disadvantage is that it is one of numerous entities within the office of the Minister; this implies that it would have to compete with a number of key organs for "attention," with potential crowding-out consequences.

Another observation is that while located in a high status ministry, as a secretariat the ECOWAS national unit is lower down the organizational hierarchy than if it were a department or division, of which there are 15 in the ministry. This means that its autonomy in formulating policies and programmes, in relating to other entities, and in the mobilization and use of resources, is restricted.

The Decree provides for the Minister of Economic Affairs and Finance to structure the Permanent Secretariat. The reality is that no formal structure exists. Rather, the Secretariat has remained small and, as a result, operates on the principle of generalist not specialist allocation of responsibilities.

Concerning membership, it is understandable that the National Committee is broad based as ECOWAS programmes and activities are themselves multi-sectoral. However, the Committee is unwieldy and unmanageable. Membership spreads over different levels of authority and is too expansive and catholic. It comprises ministers, technical directors in some of the same ministries and parastatals, legislators, and external banks that in other matters report to the same ministers. Finally, the multiple leaderships at the level of the Vice-Presidents have inherent possibilities of abnegation of leadership responsibilities and for conflicts.

On functions, those of the National Committee are very general and broadly defined. Usually, a diffused definition of functions makes an organization unfocused and dispersed. Furthermore, in this case, there is a strong likelihood of jurisdictional overlaps with other governmental bodies such as the Cabinet, the host ministry itself, and the legislature, especially in policy making and oversight. These possibilities would have been reduced if the conception of the Committee was that of an inter-ministerial coordinating body which it was supposed to have been, in effect, if it had been in operation.

On the other hand, the functions of the Permanent Secretariat are very restrictive. It is intended to operate purely as an administrative secretariat in that it services the National Committee, it co-ordinates the work of the Committee and that of its subsidiary bodies, it prepares reports on its work, it disseminates information, and it maintains a resource centre. If even the National Committee and Permanent Secretariat had functioned as prescribed in the Decree there are a number of key functions which would have remained in limbo. Among these six are particularly important. First, formulation of government policy on sub-regional integration. Second, direct monitoring and follow up on the implementation of ECOWAS programmes. Third, co-ordination of actions on ECOWAS matters cutting across all government ministries, the private sector, civil society, etc. As the Decree stands, the Secretariat does some coordination but only as regards the work of the National Committee, as noted above. Fourth, serve as a link between the ECOWAS Secretariat and the Government. Fifth, actual implementation of some ECOWAS programmes or elements of such programmes. Sixth, organize participation in ECOWAS meetings and backstop any subsequent actions.

In actuality, the Permanent Secretariat has evolved to assume responsibility for performing these and related functions. In that the National Committee is stillborn, and given the limitations in other areas of the Decree, as discussed above, the Permanent Committee has deviated from the role originally conceived for it and expanded its functions to fill the vacuum.

The non-formal arrangements for interaction with the sectoral ministries seem to work smoothly. For example, in the Ministry of Foreign Affairs officials from the division for multilateral co-operation meet from time to time with those from the secretariat to prepare for ECOWAS, NEPAD or UEMOA meetings. However, the inter-sectoral committee and the inter-ministerial committee have not been set up; very few intra-sectoral bodies are in existence. This is unfortunate as the government played a lead role in the deliberations of the ECOWAS policy organs which took the decisions for their creation. The success of informal arrangements depends on personal relationships. The departure of the personae in the secretariat would adversely affect these arrangements. Given the importance of inter- and intra-sectoral links for meaningful monitoring and follow-up on program implementation it is imperative that these structures be formally instituted.

The resources at the disposal of the secretariat are woefully inadequate. If even the body was responsible only for ECOWAS matters they would be considered so. When to this are added responsibilities for UEMOA and NEPAD programmes effectiveness is likely to suffer. It is noted that only one of the three professional staff has had long experience in integration matters and that only in 2003 was the human resource base beefed up with the addition of two new experts. The fact that the ECOWAS subvention is the lifeline of the national unit does not favorably reflect commitment to sub-regional integration on the part of the government.

Interface between National Units and ECOWAS Secretariat

The preceding section has focused on the situation at the national level. It is equally important to review the points of interface between the ECOWAS national units and the regional secretariat as far as capacities for coordinating and monitoring implementation of integration programmes are concerned. First, however, as a backdrop, it is instructive to examine the views of officials in the national units as regards performance of the ECOWAS secretariat, as revealed during the field research.

Secretariat Performance

There was general dissatisfaction with the performance of the secretariat. Criticisms were mainly in the following areas:

a. Organization of meetings: Invitations to meetings arrive late, sometimes only 48 hours before the meeting date. In such cases, there is limited time to decide on the government's official position on agenda items, to prepare substantively, and to consult and organize representation especially of sector ministries. Occasionally, meetings are postponed without informing the member states or they are informed only on arrival at meeting venue.
b. Documents: It is not unusual for documents to be received on arrival at meetings; agenda items may not be supported with background papers. Sometimes, technical documents are of dubious quality. Usually, reports of meetings are good compared to substantive technical studies prepared

by the secretariat. Often, there are translation problems, especially of legal documents.
c. Annual Meetings of Heads of National Units: See below.
d. Contacts with national units: Apart from the Annual Meetings, officials from the secretariat hardly ever visit the national units for the purpose of looking into their situations on-the-spot and, in particular, their specific problems and how to deal with them. Physical contacts and regular direct consultations should enable the units to better execute their coordination function. At a minimum, there should be increased communications by telephone and Internet.
e. Transmission problems: Departments in the secretariat often communicate directly with the sector ministries. If not copied to the national unit then monitoring of follow-up actions is difficult. If a meeting is involved the report may not reach the unit and this can have undesirable consequences for coordination.
f. Funding of missions: Participation in most ECOWAS meetings is funded by the countries. Where ECOWAS is responsible usually pre-financing is required; it then becomes problematic to obtain refunds.
g. Publications of ECOWAS, including the Official Journal, are received late, if at all. It is not uncommon for them to be collected during missions to the secretariat.
h. Lack of response to requests for information, particularly on legal matters.
i. In several national units it was stressed that these and related concerns have been aired at meetings of the Heads of National Units, the Administration and Finance Committee and other bodies. It becomes relevant then to examine the main institutional and other arrangements within the Secretariat for relating to the national units.

Organizational Arrangements in ECOWAS Secretariat

In May 1983, the Authority of Heads of State and Government adopted decision A/DEC.2/5/83 which authorized that a specific unit should be set up at the ECOWAS Secretariat to monitor implementation of Community Acts and Decisions. This was closely linked to two concerns on the part of the Heads of State. First, decisions and acts of the Community decision-making bodies were not being implemented at the national level. Second, despite an earlier recommendation made to member States by the Council of Ministers some countries had still not set up national structures to follow up on implementation. The purpose of the unit to be set up within the secretariat was to serve as the main point of interface with the national units.

As at the time of the research the May 1983 decision of the Authority had not been implemented at the ECOWAS secretariat. Member States should therefore not be criticized if they similarly ignore decisions taken at this or any other level. Or if, as is noted in several places in this study, they have weak structures in place for monitoring programme implementation and whose effectiveness is questionable.

The Department of Economic Policy, under the Deputy Executive Secretary for Policy Harmonization, manages relations with the national units. It has five divisions, i.e., Private Sector Development, External Resource Mobilization, Statistics,

Monetary Cooperation, and Economic Research. The department is the nerve centre and backbone of the ECOWAS secretariat, both in terms of its catch-all functions and of the overall strategic goals of the organization. Officially, its responsibilities include the coordination and harmonization of common policies in monetary cooperation, economic analysis, multilateral surveillance of convergence and performance of macroeconomic policies, statistical standards and database, coordination of external assistance and relations with inter-governmental organizations (IGOs) including the African Union, and investment and private sector direct involvement in the regional integration process. Its products are the principal outputs of the secretariat, particularly its technical studies and reports. Besides its formal wide-ranging attributions to this department is assigned primary responsibility for new initiatives such as the coordination and implementation of NEPAD programmes in West Africa and the second monetary zone.

With such critical responsibilities, it is likely that the additional one of managing relations with the national units will not be of the highest priority. The Economic Research Division within the department undertakes the tasks involved. But, the division itself carries out most of the roles and functions of the department, with the other divisions having more narrowly defined attributions.

The resources at the disposal of both the Department and the Division for carrying out these extensive and critical tasks are scandalous. As provided in the new 1999 staffing tables, the professional posts number eight, of which only four were encumbered in 2004, i.e., one each in Statistics and External Resource Mobilization Divisions, the Director and a middle level staff in the Economic Policy Division. The upshot is that in addition to his multifarious functions the Director of that Division has responsibility for the national units. Consequently, only sporadic attention is devoted to the units, limited, essentially, to organizing the meetings of the Heads of National Units. To deal with this problem, focal points in the other departments monitor country-level implementation of programmes in their respective sectors and provide inputs to the work of the Economic Policy Department. The Legal Affairs Department in the secretariat, in that it follows up on ratification and execution of Community protocols, conventions, decisions, and regulations, also relates to the national units. Its own parlous resource situation does not permit it to do more than collect and collate information on the status of ratification, for reporting purposes.

The Annual Meetings of Heads of National Units

The first meeting of Heads of ECOWAS National Units in June 1988 recommended that it should be institutionalized and held once a year. Action was taken two years later, in December 1990, when Decision C/DEC.6/12/90 was adopted by the Council of Ministers. As stated in the preamble, the main justification was "the need to consolidate the integration process within the Community through regular meetings of Heads of National Units to exchange ideas and seek appropriate solutions to problems encountered at national level in the follow-up of ECOWAS activities."

This then was to be the principal forum for interaction and dialogue between the secretariat and the national units. The fact that participation is more often than not at the level of the Heads of Units themselves is indicative of the significance attached to it. The meeting is the sole occasion for sharing experiences on the critical subject of the implementation of ECOWAS policies and programmes. On the negative side, they have been held only in eight (8) out of fourteen (14) years which raises questions as to the value attached to this body. In fact, its effectiveness would be increased if instead of one meeting at least two meetings were to be held annually, as proposed in a number of its sessions.

The Annual Meetings are becoming ritualistic. Given the narrow conception of their purpose, the agendas are dull and unimaginative; some agenda items have been recurring since 1988. The national reports on programme implementation, which should generate enthusiasm and cross-fertilization of experiences, have become formalistic; this is partly because the data collection questionnaire itself lacks scientific rigor. It is not surprising therefore that in 2003, in spite of reminder letters, only six countries completed the data-collection questionnaire; the available information was not comprehensive enough for the secretariat to prepare its memorandum of the subject. The deliberations are ceremonial; rarely are ideas proffered for performance improvement from one year to another.

A number of the areas of dissatisfaction noted in an earlier section regarding planning and organization of meetings apply to the annual meetings of the Heads of National Units. A review of the reports of these meetings confirms that these preoccupations have been frequently brought to the attention of the secretariat. Altogether, this has had the effect of projecting a poor image of the secretariat among the heads of units who are its frontline agents in the member States.

The recommendation of the April 2005 annual meeting of the Heads of National Units that the secretariat should present a memorandum to the 2006 session of the Administration and Finance Commission clearly defining 'the mission, role, duties and obligations of the ECOWAS National Units' points to some degree of skepticism about the usefulness of the meetings among the leadership of the units.

Community Subvention to National Units

The payment of a subvention to the national units by the ECOWAS secretariat has gone through various stages. First, upon the proposal of the Administration and Finance Committee, the Council of Ministers, at its November 1989 session, decided that a subvention of Units of Account (UA) 10, 000 should be paid out, on an annual basis, to the national unit of a member State which is up to date in the payment of its contributions to the operational budget of the organization.

Second, soon thereafter, there arose the question of whether the subsidy should not also be paid when previous arrears were cleared. This was agreed to and, in 1997, Council decided that the same amount should be paid for each year of contribution settled by a member State regardless of the date of settlement. Third, a flat subsidy was to be paid to all states whether or not they had paid the contributions; an additional amount would be paid for each year for which the contribution was paid. Fourth, Council, in Regulation C/REG.1/9/03, adopted in September 2003, again decided that 5% of the amount collected from the Community Levy should be transferred to the units.

This unprecedented gesture has been justified on the grounds that the paramount problem confronted by the units is that of funding. Initially, the subsidy was viewed as an incentive to the units to pursue more vigorously the payment of annual contributions. Those who succeeded were rewarded. And the more a unit succeeded the more it was rewarded. The rationale subsequently shifted to the more reasonable argument that limited capacities in the national units were frustrating them in carrying out their task of ensuring implementation of ECOWAS programmes. As revealed in the comparative and national assessments above, the units lack basic material resources, especially equipment such as computers and printers, accessories, laptops, electric typewriters, fax machines, vehicles, and Internet and local and international telephone services. The Preamble to the Council of Ministers 1997 regulation on the subsidy explicitly recognized that 'the granting of subsidy to the national unit would enable them to acquire a minimum of equipment and material to make them optimally functional in carrying out their task of ensuring implementation of ECOWAS Programs and Decisions.' Accordingly, the subsidy was to be 'channeled into the acquisition of machinery, equipment and materials required for the functioning of the ECOWAS national units.'

All of the units are dependent, in varying degrees, on this subvention. Indeed, for more than one it is the means of survival as governments are not providing resources in the quantum required. This raises two problems. In the first place, the dependence on a regional organization to fund the budget of a national organ over which it has no control is problematical. It is noted, in this regard, that the dependence has been increasing over the decades; the most recent decision of Council quoted above will deprive the organization of voluminous resources. The secretariat has no influence in how the subvention is utilized. In other words, the recipients are not accountable to the secretariat for the funds disbursed to them.

Then also, is not the fact that the governments have not been providing adequate resources for the units indicative of their lack of interest? Where governments have an interest in anything they always produce the resources for its realization. Besides, there is the danger that, particularly as the financial situation in the secretariat improves with the coming into full effect of the Community Levy, the member governments will transfer to the secretariat more of their obligations that involve funds.

ECOWAS Representation in Member States

In 2002, the Administration and Finance Commission (AFC) recommended that ECOWAS should create Representation in the member States; this because of the many problems that bedevil the national units and constrain their impact. Both the meetings of the AFC and the Heads of National Units, in 2003, raised the issue.

In favor of the proposal it can be argued that the office would basically be representational; it would serve as a bridge between the Executive Secretariat and the member States, a role that the national units are not meant to play. Another benefit is that the incumbent can better monitor the operations of the units, and be more sensitive to their problems whether within their governmental structures or in their interface with the regional secretariat. It is likely that with such close monitoring programme implementation levels will increase. Similarly, an ECOWAS representative, answerable to the Executive Secretary, will be expected to deliver more thorough and objective reporting on the status of policy and programme implementation.

It cannot be denied that the presence of ECOWAS in the countries, in the person of the Representative, would give a stronger presence to the organization and its work. However, one caveat is that the roles and functions of the Units and the Representatives must be clearly distinguished. It is preferred if the Representative is appointed by the ECOWAS Executive Secretary to whom he will report. Also, there is some merit if initially the Representatives are selected from the staff of the existing national units, given their knowledge and experience, and their contacts within and outside governments. Alternatively, they can come from within the secretariat. In any case, at a later stage, all positions can be advertised and recruitment done on a competitive basis. Ultimately, the paramount consideration is that competent and capable persons are selected and that through their work the Executive Secretary would be able to influence developments in the countries. Of course, it is assumed that the Representative would not be a national of the country to which he is accredited and that his staff would be answerable to the secretariat and not to the member governments.

Finally, taking into account the costs and other implications, a zonal strategy has distinct merits.[10] That is, in the first instance and on an experimental basis, one zonal representative will be appointed to cover a small group of contiguous countries; based on the experience the next steps would be determined. The Council decided in 2004 to adopt this approach depending on the outcomes of its experiment with representation in a few selected countries.

The opposing school of thought maintains that rather than create new structures the constraints confronted by existing structures should be frontally attacked in order to improve on their performance. This is particularly true of the national units which, if meaningfully reoriented and reinforced, would better perform whatever roles and functions are envisaged for the Representative. 'Africa should not be a place where we are always creating new structures,' was the caution expressed by one Head of Unit. The governments themselves adopted the resolutions not only for the creation of these units but for upgrading them. Yet, the units are invariably ignored by them; they are mere adjuncts to larger structures, lacking autonomy, poorly staffed, poorly equipped and poorly financed. Similarly, most countries are yet to create the inter-ministerial committees and sectoral committees.

Shifting the limelight away from the member states this counter opinion argues that, currently, the problems of integration in the sub-region have more to do with the ineffectiveness of the ECOWAS secretariat. There are weighty problems within the secretariat, as regards arrangements for monitoring and coordinating the work of the units which, if resolved, the performance of the totality of the system would vastly improve. The zonal offices for conflict management have been set up in

---

10 The argument is developed in greater detail in Senghor, Jeggan, "The ECOWAS Secretariat: Institutional and Related Issues," IN Senghor, Jeggan (ed), *ECOWAS: Perspectives on Treaty Revision and Reform*, IDEP, Dakar, 2000, pp.64-65.

some countries. Yet where they are, what they do, how they function, what they have achieved, are unknown, even locally. There is a probability that the ECOWAS Representation would suffer the same fate.

Finally, the counter-opinion is concerned about the cost implications. A detailed cost/benefit analysis must first be made by independent experts. In a situation where there are constant complaints about the unavailability of funds, especially for work programme implementation and staffing in the secretariat, is it judicious to devote limited resources to new infrastructures? Member States are overburdened. Rather than continue to depend on external sources, ECOWAS should generate its own resources and one way is to eliminate unnecessary overheads such as would arise if the Representation is created.

A pertinent development is the adoption by the Authority, in December 2002, of the New ECOWAS Information and Communication Policy (A/DEC.7/12/00). The policy provides for the establishment of information/documentation centers in each member State 'to facilitate access to information on the Community by students, researchers, journalists and the general public.' The secretariat is to recruit local journalists to run the centers. Each member State is to provide an office for the centre as part of its contributions to the center's operations and development.

A major argument for the creation of these centers is that the national units have proved themselves unwilling or unable to market the products of ECOWAS, especially through dissemination of its publications. As with other technical fields, they do not have the technical capability and it is therefore considered necessary to set up these centers to do the job. This is an unwelcome development. None of the departments in the secretariat is satisfied with the extent of follow-up and implementation of its sector programmes in the member States. If all were to proceed and set up field offices there would result chaos, disharmony and wanton waste of resources. This has a direct bearing on the proposal for the establishment of an ECOWAS country representation.

The Way Forward

One value of the wealth of empirical material in this and in the larger study is that it has implications for theorizing on organization design and organizational change. Equally valuable is that it is a basis for policymaking aimed at performance improvement and goal-achievement. On this, explicit or implicit in the discussions on various aspects of the subject examined above (particularly on location, structure, functions, resources, inter-sectoral coordination, interface relations with the regional secretariat, etc.) are ideas on new directions for policymaking.

The way forward is equally conditioned by a number of parametric issues. First, unit-level actors must critically evaluate their conceptions of and approaches to regional integration. Based on this, it is imperative that their commitments are redefined and translated into national framework policies and action plans. Furthermore, national policy making on regional cooperation and integration must be coordinated in order that there is greater consistency between government commitments in ECOWAS and national commitments. It is in this context that the appropriate national institutional architecture will be crafted and constructed.

The absence of systems and processes for such exercises explains, to a degree, the myriad weaknesses of national institutional mechanisms reviewed in this chapter. Additionally, and as concluded in an ECA study, they are evidence of the following:

- The failure of governments to translate their commitments under regional treaties and arrangements into substantive changes in national policies, legislation, rules, and regulations.
- The unwillingness of governments to subordinate immediate national political interests to long-term regional economic goals—or to cede essential elements of national sovereignty to regional institutions.
- The absence of monitoring and enforcement mechanisms to ensure adherence to agreed timetables on such matters as reducing tariff and non tariff barriers or achieving more difficult objectives such as macroeconomic stabilization. (ECA, 2004, p. 43)

Second, there are two related priorities in the sequential processes leading to greater regional integration. As regards the central government institutions the commitment of the political leadership must be reflected in the network of national institutions for regional integration, both for reasons of institutional identification and for bureaucratic effectiveness. At a minimum, following the example of five countries in the region, there must be a full ministry for regional integration answerable directly to the Head of State. It should be headed by a senior minister be of Cabinet rank. The selection of the appointee should be guided less by political factors than by professional background, qualifications and experience. As proposed in the earlier article:

> It would ensure that regional policies were integrated into all aspects of national policy and that they were implemented according to plan. The staff would have to be selected with the specific needs of regional integration in mind. They must be both narrowly technocratic and at the same time adopt broad perspectives and a multidisciplinary approach to development and its relationship to regional issues. (Senghor, 1994)

Within the ministry there would be departments dealing exclusively with Africa Continental or Africa Union, ECOWAS/(UEMOA), and Inter-regional Cooperation.

In each relevant sector ministry there will be an officially designated focal point, the Regional Integration Division, which will be structured to liaise directly with the ECOWA/ (UEMOA) Department and headed by a Director.

The next priority would be to enable private sector operatives to participate meaningfully in policy formulation implementation for integration, given the key roles played by trade. If a government is to sustain support for regional programmes long enough for the benefits to accrue it will require a wide base of interest groups throughout civil society.

Another parametric issue is the question of whether the realities on-the-ground as regards level of integration programme implementation do not justify adoption of the variable geometry approach to regional integration based on the subsidiary principle.[11] According to the variable geometry approach some member states can agree to advance towards integration at a faster speed than others, a multi-speed regionalism. Regional integration proceeds at different speeds, on a dual track which allows implementation of region-wide policies to vary by sub-groups of states; others would follow when they are ready to join in.[12] The advantages are, first, that it permits the states that want to accelerate integration to do so and, second, it prevents stalling of progress in integration because some states do not favour particular actions. On the debit side, the approach can undermine unity and common sense of purpose and may give rise to problems as to which actions apply where. The challenge is for the overall programme to be well defined and criteria agreed upon for monitoring implementation in each participating unit.

Another differentiated method deserving of serious consideration is integration *a la carte*, which gives member states the option of selecting policies in which they will be fully involved (as if from a menu), within the framework of a minimum number of common objectives. This accords with the fact that implementation of a particular programme may not be a feasible option for all member state at the same time, due to specific operational particularities or unfulfilled pre-conditions.

In many respects, UEMOA, the cross-border initiative and the growth triangle project management in Southern Africa exemplify the flexibility, openness, and dynamism which are the trademarks of the variable geometry and integration *a la carte* approaches.

The real concern is whether for the participating units the integration agenda in West Africa is not over congested, given, in particular, the already burdensome national development agendas. As noted in an earlier section, besides macroeconomic integration programmes all development sectors impose unbearable demands on national structures. As if these were not heavy enough, the political and regional security sectors have emerged with their own new demands, as have the Revised Treaty and NEPAD. Consequently, the loads may be beyond the capability of national structures to cope with. New imaginative approaches are called for.

This brings to mind the argument that it is unrealistic for common policies to be adapted instantly at macro or sector levels, as is often prescribed in resolutions and decisions of the ECOWAS policy organs. Rather, a sequenced approach may produce more sustained results and be more manageable by national institutions. It would, for

---

11 As defined in the European Convention this principle 'is intended to ensure that decisions are taken as closely as possible to the citizen and that constant checks are made as to whether action at Community level is justified in the light of the possibilities available at national, regional, and local levels.' See The European Convention at http://european-convention.eu.int/glossary.asp) The regional authority performs only those tasks which cannot be performed effectively at national or local levels. This principle is akin to that of proportionality which stipulates that actions by the Community should not go beyond what is necessary in order to achieve the objectives of the Treaty.

12 For example, the United Kingdom, Denmark and Ireland decided to opt out of the European Community title on Free Movement of Persons, Asylum and Immigration.

example, initially encompass exchange of information progressing to coordination and harmonization of policies and, ultimately, the adoption of common policies. The end result is a synchronization of the sectoral prioritization programme, the adoption process, and the institutional capacity development strategy which would be mutually reinforcing.

Yet another parametric issue is the age-old and ever-present cross-cutting need for sustained and programmed capacity building to which the network of institutions, at the national, regional and interface levels, is subjected. Capacity includes human, technological, organizational, financial and other resources. As conceptualized by the UNDP, capacity building is a process of creating and/or strengthening capabilities to mobilize these resources in order to 'evaluate and address the crucial questions related to policy choices and modes of implementation among development options, based on an understanding of environment potentials and limits, and of needs.' (UNDP, 1992) In addition to training, it involves a mix of activities focused on the improvement of the performance of an organization in relation to its mission, strategic objectives and technical programmes. A fundamental objective of organizational capacity building is to increase the efficiency and effectiveness of an organization to deliver in the context of changing social, economic and political environments.

In the light of the expanded responsibilities in ECOWAS the need for systematic (as opposed to *ad hoc*) institutional assessment and capacity building takes on new dimensions. Capacity building must be systemic, integrated and cost-effective. As in all countries in the region integration tasks spread across several ministries, the central bank and different types of government agencies, and the private sector; these stakeholders should also be engaged in the design and execution of capacity building programmes. Capacity building may be best and more economically programmed and efficiently promoted at the regional than national level, given the scope and magnitude of the tasks involved. The cascading effects of the impact of a unified strategy would lay the foundations for even higher levels of institutional performance in the future.

Finally, ECOWAS now operates in the changed environment of the 'new regionalism' distinct from the 'old regionalism' of the 1970s and 1980s. Bjorn Hette and Fredrik Soderbaum define the new regionalism as:

A comprehensive, multifaceted and multi-dimensional process, implying the change of a particular region from relative heterogeneity to increased homogeneity with regard to a number of dimensions, the most important being culture, security, economic policies and political regimes. (Hette and Soderbaum 1998)

Its distinguishing characteristics are that it emphasizes interlinkages between the regional, inter-regional and global, in place of the almost-total preoccupation with the inward-looking regional focus of the old regionalism. The walls of the fortress have collapsed. This interdependence encompasses 'new actors, new social complexes, and new forms of identity' (Louise Butler, 1977) which go beyond formal state actors to include transnationals, civil society, non-governmental organizations, the informal sector and other non-state actors. It demands a change in mindset, away from dogmatic faith in the musketeer philosophy of all-for-one-and-one-for-all. This evolving environment poses enormous challenges for an ECOWAS that is even yet to cope satisfactorily with the demands of the old.

References

Africa Research Bulletin, Economic, 31 July 1986, p.8264.
Amoako K.Y. (2003), Statement at 27th Ordinary Summit of the Authority of Heads of State and Government of ECOWAS, Addis Ababa, p.9.
Aning, Emanuel K (1999), Security in the West African Subregion: An Analysis of ECOWAS 'Policies in Liberia, Institut for Statskundskab, Kobenhavns Universitet, Copenhagen, p.25.
Asante, S.K.B.(2002), 'ECOWAS and West Africa's Development in the Globalizing World of the Twenty-first Century: The Agenda for Action.' *ECA Sub-Regional Development Centre for West Africa,* Niamey, Niger, p.6 and p.8.
Butler, Louise (1977), 'Regionalism and integration,' IN John Baylis and Steve Smith (eds.) *Globalization of World Politics: An Introduction to International Relations,* 1977, p.418.
ECOWAS (2002), Declaration on the Implementation of NEPAD in West Africa, Summit of ECOWAS Heads of State and Government on NEPAD, Yamoussoukro, p.2.
ECOWAS (2002A), Fostering Regional Integration through NEPAD Implementation, Executive Secretary Annual Report, para. 482.
ECOWAS Secretariat (2005), Status of ratification of the ECOWAS Revised Treaty, protocols and convention as at 30th May 2005, Abuja.
Francis, David (2001), *The Politics of Economic Regionalism: Sierra Leone in ECOWAS,* London: Ashgate Publishers. Francis discusses, in some detail, the national institutional structures in Sierra Leone, see pages 92-96; this is one of the few accounts in the literature dealing with the subject.
Hette, Bjorn and Soderbaum, Frederik (1998) 'The New Regionalism Approach,' *Politeia,* vol.17, no 3, p.7.
Jebuni, Charles (1998), 'The Role of ECOWAS in Trade Liberalization,' IN Z. Iqbal and M.S. Khan (ed.) *Trade Reform and Regional Integration in Africa,* Washington: I.M.F.
Lardner, Tunji, Jnr.(1990), 'The Babangida Blues', *Africa Report,* vol.35, no.3, July-August, p.51.
Okolo, Julius E. and Stephen Wright (1990), *West African Regional Development,* Westview Press, Boulder, CO., p.4.
Senghor, Jeggan, C. (1994), 'Cooperation in Africa: Generating Action at the Unit-Level,' *ECDPM Bulletin,* Maastricht, Vol. 1, no.1.
UNDP (1992), Agenda 21, Chapter 37, UNCED.
UN Economic Commission for Africa (2004), Assessing Regional Integration in Africa, Addis Ababa, p. 203.

Chapter 7

Vassal States, Development Options and African Development

Anthony V. Obeng

Status as Destiny, Challenge or Opportunity: An African Problematic Revisited

The bi-polar or multi-polar world order[1] that preceded the collapse of the Soviet Union and the end of the cold war was, in more ways than one, a world of relative political, economic, cultural and even ideological diversity. Reflecting this relative diversity and accompanying freedom of expression many African countries gave themselves a variety of revolutionary names, making "Peoples' Republics", "Socialist Republics" and "Democratic Republics" a familiar feature on the political map of Africa. In retrospect the subsequent return to conventional "western names" – after "regime change", the disappearance of the Soviet Union as patron or development model or an autocrat's change of heart – was predictable. For the "revolutionary" posturing was generally infantile, opportunistic or a mere reflection of an illusion of the times: that the brand-new independence or sovereignty of "the new states", by itself, gave them the freedom to pursue their own development paths and partnerships. As is now generally acknowledged the constraints on their freedom were many, severe and firmly rooted in their "colonial" or semi-colonial heritage.

Heritage does not always amount to destiny, of course. But it often has the potential to do so. And today's African states are nothing if not products of colonial cartography and political, economic, social, cultural and even spiritual manipulation. In assessing Africa's development opportunities, challenges and options, therefore, it is essential to evaluate the independence status of the colonial artefacts that currently present themselves as independent states and, in particular, the extent to which they have or have not freed themselves from their colonial heritage.

It is proposed in the following pages to do just that, and to outline the African peoples' development options and challenges, without the complexes, fear or blinkers that have too often distorted visions of Africa's development, but without neglecting the realities of the states that dominate important aspects of their lives either.

---

1 Different observers have characterised that world as "bi-polar" or "multi-polar", depending on whether or not they count the "medium powers" of the era, with their own shrinking colonies to administer, as independent powers or as satellites of their lead super power.

The Vassal States of Africa, Independence and the Colonial and Semi-Colonial Trap

When Kwame Nkrumah, the leading twentieth century Pan-Africanist, thinker and statesman exposed neo-colonialism in his 1965 on it (Nkrumah 1965) as a device by which colonial or imperial powers controlled and administered subject territories behind the façade of independence he was roundly condemned as a neurotic danger to his people in Africa and the Diaspora; a tool of "Communism"; and an enemy of the "free world".[2] The country he then led was accordingly declared a danger to "the West", subjected to political, economic and diplomatic pressure and, eventually, to Regime Change.[3]

The hostility that greeted Nkrumah's exposure of neo-colonialism was, of course, driven by the ignorance of some among his "non-Western" critics and the cynicism of those who thought he had crossed a security red line. For the latter Nkrumah had, by his book, committed the unforgivable sin of exposing and endangering an administrative tool which the colonial Establishment had long known about and which Lord Luggard had, in a different context, described and commended to friendly audiences as *indirect rule*.[4] Little did Luggard realise, apparently, that he had, in doing so, also exposed a British colonial subterfuge: informal colonial rule,[5] or the perfidious art and science which Nkrumah preferred to denounce as neo-colonialism. Nkrumah's use of "Leninist language" to denounce neo-colonialism and couple it with imperialism also caused understandable offence to existing and aspiring imperialists who did not want to see a "dual use" colonial tool discredited, and who objected just as strongly to his continuation of the Leninist tradition of linking colonialism and imperialism to capitalist expansionism.

In what students of the politics of language and the language of politics may find fascinating "neo-colonialism" virtually disappeared from the vocabulary of Euro-African relations after the overthrow of Nkrumah in 1966. The resulting linguistic void led some African political economists to borrow the concepts and language of "centre-periphery" and "patron-client" relationships, and "dependency"

---

    2   Otherwise known then as "the West" the "free world" was defined by its spokespersons to include Portugal under Salazar's fascist and die-hard colonial regime, apartheid South Africa and "former" colonial masters exercising indirect rule over their "former" colonies and other "dependencies" by force or subterfuge.

    3   In Milne (1977) the author reminds us that the US Government took such strong exception to the book that they protested to the Ghana Government, formally, about it – and stopped the delivery to Ghana of US$35 million previously promised. It is also now generally acknowledged that the coup d'etat which overthrew Nkrumah in February 1966, was CIA sponsored.

    4   Lord Luggard had been a British colonial Governor whose claim to fame was, precisely, his elevation of "indirect rule" to the status of an imperial governance art.

    5   For a brilliant analytical use of the concept of "informal colonialism" see Sideri (1970). Many are the current African states that looked like "informal colonies" before and after "independence". It is far from certain, however, that those who objected to the exposure of neo-colonialism would have looked more kindly on the exposure of disguised colonialism as "informal colonialism", in Africa or anywhere else.

– derived principally, though not exclusively, from studies of capitalism and underdevelopment in Latin America by Gunder Frank (1975) and others in their analyses of the development of underdevelopment in Africa, the state in Africa and informal colonial relationships between African states and their "former colonial masters" after independence.

Nuances and sometimes critical differences between the African and the Latin American underdevelopment experiences meant that the analytical tools of the dependency school were not perceived to be fully applicable to Africa, however. That, and other difficulties about the suitability of the word "dependency" and its derivatives (popularised by social policy and welfare professionals to describe entirely different entities that the informal colonies of Latin America and Africa were not) meant that if Africa had to find a replacement for the word "neo-colonialism", with its unfortunate history as well as boundary difficulties with "indirect rule" and other forms of informal colonialism, the language of the Latin American inspired dependency school was not the answer.

Other possible substitutes for "neo-colonialism" – such as peripheral states, marginal states, puppet states, client states, Bantustans, and ghettoes in the "global village" – do not seem immune from controversy either. In truth there does not appear to be an objection-free way of describing informal colonies and informal colonial relationships where key and influential stake holders prefer to cover what should be revealed about asymmetrical and unequal relationships between "former colonies" and "former colonial masters".

Against this background and as a matter, purely, of convenience such states, African and non-African, will be referred to in this essay collectively as *vassal states*, but also as informal states, neo-colonial states, peripheral states, marginal states, puppet states, client states, etc, as necessary – with the understanding, however, that as and when globalisation takes on the characteristics of a new imperialism the term may be applied to informal colonies under the new imperialism.

For identification, if not for the purposes of definition, therefore, states would be regarded as "vassal states" if they maintain the structures of a colonial economy; bear the marks of stunted intellectual, technological and cultural development, or appear to submit future development or growth in these sectors to the institutionalised leadership of another state or group of states; bear the telltale signs of past or ongoing philosophical and spiritual vandalisation; and are pointedly burdened by local elites which depend on external patrons for social, professional, psychological or spiritual validation and important benefits.

Suspect states which, having been vassalised at some point in their history, can be said to have graduated out of vassal state status would be those that would have since:

- Achieved and maintained economic self-reliance, and the freedom to choose their development goals and methods;
- Transformed themselves into intellectually, technologically, culturally, socially, spiritually and generally independent states; and
- Acquired, and are it in a position to assert: the freedom to choose their place in the world; the freedom to choose their friends and identify their enemies

in accordance with their own definitions of their peoples' short, medium and long-term interests; and the freedom to avoid or repudiate unequal or unfair treaties, contracts and other vassalage forming political, economic, commercial, diplomatic or cultural entanglements.

Vassal or Free States? The States of Africa Some Half a Century After Post-Colonial Independence

African countries have undoubtedly undertaken and witnessed many movements and changes in the half a century or so of the accession of the former colonies among them to independence. The changes have been driven by a variety of forces, benign and otherwise. The self-interested pursuit of private capital accumulation by the political and bureaucratic branches of the governing elites is certainly one such force. Changes have also been initiated or pursued as a means of grabbing, keeping or legitimising power for other honourable or dishonourable purposes. Development commands, prescriptions and fashions from "development partners"; the need to respond to what was known in the immediate post-colonial era as the "revolution of rising expectations"; the messianic visions of politicians and nationalists whose ambition for their countries was to get them to "catch up" with the East or West; the availability of pork-barrel hand-outs from East and West within the cold war context of competition for the hearts and minds of Africa; and the emergence of a United Nations Development System as a third force in the postcolonial development industry, with management and staff pursuing their careers or ideals, are rapidly identifiable among the other post-colonial driving forces for change.

"The Washington consensus", a complex of "reform" measures and conditionalities designed to "free" economies and "markets" in target countries for globalisation, has, by its ascendancy as the pre-eminent economic management instrument of choice for the "global village", succeeded lately in redefining the "westernisation of Africa" as an American, rather than a European project. Besides consolidating Pax Americana as a result (through the US controlled World Bank and related international and regional institutions, bilateral agreements and unilateral measures) the effective transfer of overlordship control of Africa from Europe to the United States is keenly felt on the continent as intolerance of welfare or "nanny" state habits, institutions and "benefits". The casualties of this intolerance have included subsidised health care, education and utility services; the disengagement of the state in Africa from direct economic production through the avoidance of state participation in industrial and commercial activities and the privatisation of state enterprises ; and market deregulation. Each of these clusters of "economic" measures has had its political consequences, of course. But the privatisation of state enterprises, along with the replacement of the service culture by the business culture in public administration in the new dispensation, has been particularly remarkable, and resented, for turning state service into an avenue for the illicit acquisition of public assets at bargain prices by kleptocrats for themselves, their families and their cronies. The original colonial state in Africa has thus been reportedly transformed into a "crony capitalist" state and a theatre of institutionalised corruption.

Other modernisation, development or economic reform tools, mantras, programmes, projects, systems, policies and by-products that have changed the socio-economic and political profiles of the state across Africa, for good or ill, over the past fifty years or so of Africa's independence include:

- "Human resources development" (often reduced to "education" or "training" for "development", but sometimes broadened to include issues of health and "cultural development" to modify African cultural practices to suit European tastes or projects in or for Africa);
- "Technical Assistance" – to assist the "poor" continent with the macro and micro planning, programming, implementation, monitoring and evaluation aspects of "development" administration and management, pending the education and training of a critical mass of natives to assume their developmental responsibilities;
- Technical assistance aided plans and programmes for wages and salaries administration, with professionalisation packages designed to motivate key indigenous development administrators and managers and enhance their professional competence;
- Development finance mobilisation through, *inter alia:* super-taxation of peasant producers; fiscal, monetary and other policy changes to meet aid, debt service and debt forgiveness conditionalities; prioritisation of donor driven projects, whether or not they fit into national priorities; expansion of traditional exports and diversification of export production and markets; labour laws and incomes policies designed to promote countries as competitive destinations for foreign investment, along with investment codes and practices which lead African states generally "racing to the bottom"; *de jure* or *de facto* expropriation of native lands to make way for foreign direct investors, notably in alcoholic and non-alcoholic beverage production, mining and petty industrial production; investor-friendly tolerance of polluting industries and environmentally irresponsible manufacturing and mining practices; and revival or desecration of sacred institutions and rituals as "tourist attractions";
- Continuation and indeed intensification of the "proletarianisation" processes first began by colonial regimes to create labour for the colonial state;
- Expansion or modernisation of roads, railways, ports and airports, as countries seek to reposition themselves in the ruling world order;
- Community Development style projects, to: stem the tide of rural-urban migration; extend the benefits of "development" to the rural poor; mitigate the deleterious effects of colonial style development and/or donor conditionalities on the underprivileged; and make the rural areas less forbidding to public servants and others needed there for public and development administration purposes;
- Creation and/or modernisation of national, regional and district administrative capital cities and towns, for administrative convenience, expected "growth pole" effects or the management of internal migration;
- Emergence of inner city ghettoes and dormitory suburbs;

- Administrative reforms, to position the inherited colonial bureaucracies to manage the post-colonial "revolution of rising expectations";
- Military rule, promoted by influential "development experts" in and around the 1960's, as a means of bringing the modern outlooks, discipline, professionalism and bureaucratic virtues of "the men on horseback" to bear on the modernisation of Africa and other developing continents;
- "Scientific socialism"; "African socialism"; "liberal democracy"; and multi party, single and no party rule;
- Demand based development strategies;
- Basic needs based development strategies;
- Structural Adjustment and its various phases, sub-programmes and conditionalities;
- Regional cooperation and integration; and
- Preferential and general agreements on tariffs, trade and investment guarantees.

Changes and the Illusion of Change

The "development" landscape of Africa cannot be said to have been entirely static in the face of the programmes, projects, processes, activities and developments partially summarised above. But they have not, by any means, transformed Africa from a mass of poverty-stricken vassal states into the collective of even modestly developed and self-reliant ones visualised by African Heads of State in the *Lagos Plan of Action for the Economic Development of Africa, 1980 – 2000, (LPA)* (OAU 1980). Nor were they designed to. As Claude Ake (1996, 2001) and others have repeatedly pointed out, development planning and development interventions in postcolonial Africa have remained firmly within the colonial paradigm – despite the transformational and revolutionary rhetoric, posturing and experiments of the 1960s to the mid-1980s.

The Development Paradigm in Postcolonial Africa and the Development in Vassalage Syndrome

The strategic conservatism of the paradigm that has governed independent Africa's so-called development efforts was never a secret to astute observers, such as Samir Amin and many others, including, a once reform-minded but Afro-centric United Nations Economic Commission for Africa,[6] of course. But beyond the obvious replications by independent Africa of the forms and substance of colonial development, extensively described by Ake and many others[7] the monotonous regularity with which various "development recipes" have been repeated, recycled, reworded and served as new panaceas as and when the failures of previous versions have been exposed would seem to be a clear enough indication that the paradigm

---

6   See, for instance, Economic Commission for Africa (1990).

7   For an in-depth review of the linkages and continuities between the colonial and postcolonial development paradigms see Ake, op. cit.

is as intellectually bankrupt as it is operationally suspect. In addition, the fact that, after half a century of development dead-ends and failure the development mission itself has been effectively abandoned by those who were inextricably bound to the vassalage framework – and replaced by "Market worship" as the solution to Africa's underdevelopment and poverty – is a powerful admission not only that the paradigm has run its course but that it is no longer marketable.

Other Pointers

In his brilliant account of democracy and development in Africa Ake's includes some telling facts and figures about the financial, manpower and planning limitations of the post-colonial states in Africa – consequences of deliberate colonial actions and omissions – which conspired with other factors to trap even independent-minded African Governments into "making token gestures to development while trying to pass on the responsibility for development to foreign patrons", thus guaranteeing that the development interventions conceived and pursued in Africa's name could only be extensions of colonial development.

As Ake puts it:

> While African leaders talked about the fragility of political independence and the need to buttress it by self-reliant development, they eagerly embraced economic dependence. In time, this frame of mind led to the conception of development as something to be achieved through changes in the vertical relations between Africa and the wealthy countries: a greater flow of technical assistance to Africa, more loans on better terms, more foreign investment in Africa, accelerated transfer of technology, better prices for primary commodities, greater access to Western markets, and so forth.
>
> In this spirit, African governments expected a large portion of their development budget to be financed externally. That was true even for those countries such as Tanzania whose leaders seemed conscious of the need for self-reliance. For instance, Tanzania's first post independence plan of 1964, the first phase of an ambitious fifteen-year development plan, projected an expenditure of $285.7 million for the plan period, of which $222.7 million, or 78 percent, was to come from external sources. (Ake 1996, 2001, 7-8)

Ake is generous with other eye openers. As he points out:

> Manpower shortages, especially the dearth of economists, was part of the problem. Few African countries had a pool of economists to support public policy. Some countries had no Universities. In Zambia, where per capita income had been one of the highest at independence, the ratio of expatriates (mostly macroeconomists) to Zambians on the National Commission for Development Planning in 1975 (a decade after independence) was 21 to 4. The Zambians were largely junior, both in qualifications and position. In this respect Zambia was typical. The dearth of native economists and planners led to a reliance on expatriate staff, which in turn caused the reproduction of neo-colonial notions of development. Not surprisingly, the first-generation development plans in Africa, such as Kenya's Development Plan, 1964 (the Red Plan), its Development Plan, 1966 (the Green Plan), Tanzania's First Five-Year Development Plan, 1964, and Nigeria's First National

Development Plan, 1962-68, simply followed the rhythm of the colonial economy." (Ake 1996, 2001, 19)

Manpower constraints appear to have been a minor problem, however, compared to the poverty of ideas and palpable dependency, not to say inferiority, complexes that appear to drive all but a very tiny minority of Africa's governing politicians and bureaucrats.

These complexes are most recently manifest at the regional or continental level in the *New Partnership for Africa's Development (NEPAD)*. This ostensible tool of African development in the twenty-first century has, of course, been widely touted as African owned. But it is more accurately described as an unabashed plea for the accelerated globalisation of the continent. The rhetoric and conduct of *NEPAD*'s African promoters also confirm, for good measure, their implacable hostility to the spirit of African self reliance which animated the *Lagos Plan of Action*, a developmental monster in World Bank eyes which was killed at birth by a combination of African naivety and neglect and World Bank orchestrated international hostility (OAU op. cit.).[8] Samir Amin was, of course, right to dismiss the *LPA* itself as politically naïve in its eccentric expectation that the "international community" would pay to free the continent from dependency, as the *Plan* supposed,[9] and may well have added that the expectation was another measure of the gravity of the dependency complex of those who harboured it. But the eccentricity of the *LPA* does not make less pathetic *NEPAD*'s alternative of founding Africa's development on the renewal of the very "partnerships" that have trapped Africa in dependent underdevelopment and poverty for over two centuries. Between the *LPA* and *NEPAD* the degree of entrenchment of dependency in the psyche of Africa's governing elites was also manifest in the story of the mutation of *Africa's Priority Programme for Economic Recovery, 1986 – 90 (APPER)*, itself a case study in dependency thinking, into a *United Nations Programme of Action for African Economic Recovery and Development, 1986 – 1990 (UNPAAERD)*, after a *Special Session of the United Nations General Assembly on Africa's Economic and Social Crisis* convened in 1986 at Africa's request to transfer responsibility for the implementation of APPER to the international community.

Meanwhile the forward match of economic dependency continued at the country level, driven by African Governments and their development partners and fuelled by the intellectual, technological, cultural, philosophical and spiritual dependency of the African intelligentsia in general.

---

8   NEPAD is also remarkably similar in thrust and tone to those of the World Bank's 'Accelerated Development for Africa: An Agenda for Action', popularly known as the "Berg Report", after its principal author, which the World Bank commissioned as an avowed counter to the 'Lagos Plan of Action'.

9   Verbal critique of the Plan by the distinguished Third World political economist.

Intellectual, Technological, Cultural, Philosophical and Spiritual Manifestations of the Dependent Underdevelopment Syndrome

Intellectual Manifestations

None but those who deny the very humanity of Africans and available historical, sociological and anthropological evidence can fail to credit pre-colonial Africa with an intellectual heritage, of course. There is no natural or logical reason, moreover, to suppose that Africans were more limited in their ability to create, process, store and transfer knowledge – i.e. philosophy, science, technology and culture – than other peoples. Not even Africa's reputed inability to produce written languages, also used by some apologists of colonialism to justify it as a vehicle that was needed to endow Africans with "the alphabet", is supported by logic or the facts. Such myths belong to the category of the many others invented by colonialism's apologists to justify colonialism in Africa as a selfless gift to an inferior race. Their claim to serious attention derives from the fact that they have succeeded in entering the psyches of a good number of influential and powerful Africans, with serious consequences for Africa's situation and future.

Among Africans the view that Africans owe their humanity to their colonisation by Europe and, further, that civilisation equals "Europeanisation" has succeeded over the years in raising a class of people whom Fanon (1967) called *black skins, white masks*. This breed of Africans was, of course, instrumental in maintaining colonialism especially in territories where unfavourable climatic and other conditions rendered permanent white settlements unfeasible and extensive use of expatriate administrators problematic. With rare exceptions, the tailor-made roles of these empire assets also limited their capacity and inclination to question received dogmas, however. And, "authorised wisdom" for most of them, in the colonial era and beyond, includes the entrenched belief that colonisation was, and neo-colonialism is, a blessing to Africa.[10]

Meanwhile, at the other end of the intellectual divide, the producers, repositories and teachers of native wisdom, knowledge and insights who should have provided the intellectual energies for resistance against colonial and neo-colonial control, and for national development, were and remain confined in limbo where their numbers and quality continue to suffer decline from neglect, attrition, defection and suffocation.

---

10 "Resistance" or "progressive" African intellectuals like Nkrumah, Amilcar Cabral, Patrice Lumumba, Archie Mafeje and Samir Amin from the continent and W.E.B. Du Bois, George Padmore, Franz Fanon and intellectual artists like Bob Marley, from the African Diaspora are among the notable exceptions. Though by no means alone among Africans at home or in the Diaspora such resistance intellectuals as Africa has produced, against the odds, have, needless to add, lacked the numbers or the influence, so far, to change the continent's dependent underdevelopment course. African "nationalists" whose "nationalism" was fuelled by resentment of unequal treatment for "civilised natives" and demands for equal rights for educated natives, i.e. themselves, are not counted as "resistance" or "progressive" intellectuals.

Technological Underdevelopment and Dependent Underdevelopment

As may be expected, Africa's dependent elites, products of colonial education and miseducation, promote technological dependency as a "development tool". The most frequently heard excuse for this promotion is that the continent is technologically backward and would be economically and culturally even more backward without the benefit of imported technology and industrial products.

The excuse is doubly pathetic: it fails to trace Africa's technological backwardness, as institutionalised since colonial times to its vassal status, and perpetuates a myth about "technological transfer" which makes it another contributor to the institutionalisation of dependency – namely that technologies are value-free and socially, culturally, economically and politically neutral tools whose social and developmental effects are essentially universal, give or take minor adjustments and adaptations for appropriateness. The myth does so by promoting an international division of technology power based on established track records and resulting "comparative advantage".

As a matter of practical politics – and because access to technology and the products of technology is dependent in technologically dependent countries on the decisions of foreign governments, foreign contractors, foreign direct investors, foreign suppliers, foreign logistics infrastructures and systems and foreign controlled means of exchange – the vast majority of African countries that live with technological dependency do more than suffer the vulnerabilities of buyers in suppliers' markets, including the much decried "unfair trade". They, more seriously, allow the superstition to be reinforced among the susceptible masses that the producers of the "magic technologies" that define and dominate their lives, livelihoods and lifestyles are superior to themselves and their race; perpetuate the cycle of inferiority complex among the elites who know no better; and complete the surrender of the lives and destinies of Africans and African states to the power of the foreign states, bodies and entities that control the technologies that rule them.

A dramatic illustration of the nexus between Africa's general dependency posture, technological dependency in particular and underdevelopment is provided by the continent's response to the human need for vitamin C.[11] While the need for vitamin C is physiologically determined for all members of the human race, vitamin C tablets are not determined by the laws of nature as the essential or preferred source of this nutrient. On the contrary, established expert opinion is that all things being equal citrus fruits, the natural source of this vitamin, are also its best source. Yet vitamin C tablets – which Africa procures almost exclusively by direct importation, imported technologies or imported factories, all of which reinforce the continent's dependency – have long dominated African health promotion and delivery systems.

The promotion in colonial and neo-colonial Africa of rice at the expense of indigenous cereals, such as millet and sorghum, is another case in point.[12] The

---

11 The credit for this example is due to Samir Amin, the distinguished Third World political economist, who used it to unforgettable pedagogical effect in various fora.

12 Note, for instance, that in a country like Senegal, where rice is regarded by many as a traditional or national food, rice consumption as a "national" phenomenon was engineered by

crushing defeat of valiant attempts in the last decades of the twentieth century to introduce composite flour – from, for instance, a combination of wheat flour and local cereal flours – for bread making in some African countries, using locally developed and otherwise available technologies, is yet another.

These relatively recent examples of the enforced separation of Africa's natural resources and Africa's production from African consumption are, of course, but continuations, replicas or modern versions of the mechanisms employed by Europe after the slave trade for the integration of subsistent African peasants and peasant societies into empire economies, in the initial period of what Kwame Nkrumah and Walter Rodney (1972), among others, have identified as the underdevelopment of Africa for the development of Europe. Such "disconnections" are, unfortunately, replicated in other critical areas of human and social life, such as clothing and shelter.

Add to the above examples, and the infinite number of other examples that can be given, Susan George's observation that "anyone who buys Western technology should understand that he is not just buying a product, but rather a distinct set of social relationships which have now become so embedded in the technology that they are nearly invisible" (Geoge 1984, 1990) and the virtually boundless capacity of technological dependency to broaden and deepen political, economic and cultural dependency, for instance, becomes that much more difficult to ignore.

The Economic Costs of Cultural Bondage

The conventional wisdom that prevailed during the colonial and immediate post-colonial periods was that there were two Africa's: a primitive Africa remaining to be "modernised" according to colonial concepts of modernisation, and a modernised, westernised or western oriented Africa created by the grace of European colonialism. As is well known the African inheritors of colonial power accepted with their inheritance responsibility for completing the integration of Africa into the prevailing colonial or neo-colonial order. In doing so they also clearly accepted the definition of the responsibility given them by the "modernization intellectuals" of the day as "westernization" (Apter 1965, Rustow 1960, Shils 1962), including the reform of governance and culture, in the broadest senses of the words, to suit evolving European interests and tastes.[13]

No reflection on the economic choices and development options available to Africa's vassal states will be complete, in these circumstances, without an accounting for the economic costs of the continent's cultural submission to "western" interests, tastes and norms. Some of these costs can, no doubt, be estimated for particular countries at particular times, but not without yet to be developed methodologies to address this issue of the economic costs of cultural bondage which "development experts" have paid little or no attention to so far.

---

an imperial France in need of markets for "French rice" from its Asian colonies.

13 "Globalisation" has, of course, merely added an American super-layer to the hierarchy of external politico-economic and cultural controls.

If and when "developmental accounting" becomes the developmental concern that it ought to be it would, no doubt, be realised that the costs to Africa, and to directly affected African communities, of any loss of economic and cultural autonomy arising from any "development intervention" must be weighed against its actual as opposed to ostensible benefits, to determine its acceptability or otherwise. Developmental accounting, with rigorous and broad based developmental cost/benefit analysis as a vital tool, should also help avoid negative development interventions while, on the positive side, facilitating the identification of ways of increasing the developmental benefits and reducing the negative effects of proposed or ongoing development initiatives.

In this connection, it is worth pointing out that while examples are not far to seek of economically and developmentally inappropriate imported technologies examples are not lacking of developmentally positive imported technologies either. One such positive example, arguably, is motorised transport. But even this relatively uncontroversial colonial European injection into African cultures has had the effect of compounding homegrown snobbery by adding access to types of cars, for instance, to the catalogue of status symbols, worsening snobbery and even the incentives for corruption as a means of acquiring illegitimate access to this new status symbol. The total dependence of African countries on importation for finished cars, car factories and imported parts to meet the need and demand cars, and their operation and maintenance, has also increased dependency in obvious ways.

Similar cultural damage is observable in the housing sector where home ownership status, access or lack of access to official or company housing, and the "standing" of housing where available, double as ego and image defining symbols of "success" or "failure". Clothing has become yet another imported, or "re-mixed" measure of "success" or "failure", courtesy of the neo-colonial or global order: in much of contemporary Africa it has become accepted practice for the dictates of the "fashion capitals of the world" to be used to determine sartorial elegance and socio-economic status.

Even the traditional arts, sacred and profane, have been pressed into the service of dependency, at considerable spiritual, cultural and psychological costs to Africa and Africans – as traditional paintings, handicrafts, music, poetry, rituals, ceremonies and dances have remained demonised, marginalized or, alternatively, reduced to curios for the titillation of "detribalised natives" on ceremonial occasions, tourists and visiting dignitaries. Finally, the economic and related costs to African countries of the compulsory or blind importation of elements of the "permissive society", sometimes disguised or excused as the a widening of the frontiers of freedom, would also seem to require estimating and factoring into the economic costs of cultural bondage.

Costs of Africa's Philosophical Vandalisation, Past and Present

Africa's indigenous philosophical heritage, and the value placed on it, or discounted, by Africans themselves and their "development partners", have an obvious bearing not only on the self esteem and dignity of Africans but on the sourcing of the continent's development philosophies, assessments of its development options and the direction and control of its development future. The repatriation of responsibility for Africa's development future cannot be conceived, let alone proceed, without a determination by Africans themselves that they have independent philosophy for development resources; that those resources are not inferior to those pushed on them by their various conquerors, protectors and friends; and that in creating and re-creating their own development philosophies and paradigms they have the same right as every other peoples to tap from the world's philosophical heritage where necessary, without interference from "friends", "development partners", creditors or other development mentors. The caution is, of course, warranted by Africa's costly experience with well intentioned as well as cynical philosophical interference.[14]

A look at the political and development scene in Africa in the first decade of the twenty-first century, that is some fifty years after independence, confirms that the negative effects of the continent's philosophical vandalisation on its development are as present and disabling as ever. The widespread misrepresentation of kleptocratic rivalries[15] as democracy in action on the basis, simply, that the exotic rituals of "free and fair elections"[16] have been performed, and Africa's acceptance of the travesty, or failure to resist it, is a measure, surely, of its political and philosophical impotence. African acquiescence in the charade is, of course, secured through an outlandish philosophy which deifies democracy and presents it as a composite of freedom of expression, "multi-party systems", "free and fair" elections and an "independent" judiciary.[17]

The divestiture, privatisation and commercialisation waves that have battered Africa since the last decades of the twentieth century are another example of costly alien philosophical and ideological invasions and vandalisation of the continent. It is no secret, of course, that these waves are carried by Structural Adjustment and Globalisation. What is less well known is the fact that behind them are the alien and, in Africa at any rate, untested dogmatic offshoots of Social Darwinism, a perversion by Herbert Spencer of Charles Darwin's theory of evolution by natural selection and struggle, and Adam Smith's laisser-faire economic theory. The surreptitious introduction into Africa of these quasi-philosophical and ideological dogmas, under the cover of economic reform, is thus not only a case of philosophical abuse but one of reckless economic engineering as well.

---

14 For a sample of indigenous African philosophies readers may wish to consult Abraham (1962), Gbadegesin (1991), Gyekye (1995, 1996), Mbiti (1978), and Wiredu (1980).

15 By "kleptocratic rivalry" is meant competition for state power for illicit gain under cover of politics, revolution, liberation, redemption, democratisation and other false pretences.

16 The point, of course, is that as a matter of verifiable practice "the people" have little or no influence on the processes by which the competing "barons" are selected or on the barons themselves – and the victorious rivals in these competitions are principally, if not exclusively, responsible to their external patrons or "development patrons", who also double as economic philosopher-kings of the world, not to "their people".

17 The romanticisation of democracy as "government of the people by the people for the people", a necessarily good thing, is, of course, routinely exposed as such by the more common reality that it is, or has become, a system for the containment of the people.

The "christianisation" of Africa, a philosophical as well as religious process which began modestly in the "pre-colonial" era and was expanded under colonial patronage[18] is, yet another ongoing philosophical and cultural "westernisation" project with known and sometimes obvious spiritual, psychological and even economic costs.

A Continent in Spiritual Bondage

The political, economic, cultural, intellectual, philosophical, psychological and other bonds with which the colonial masters tied their subjects would ordinarily have sufficed to guarantee their spiritual enslavement as well. And so they appear to have done – with "saved" Africans joining their colonial mentors in condemning traditional African religions as superstitions and joining their spiritual mentors in fishing for additional "converts". "Christianisation" of the natives was not confined to indoctrination on purely spiritual matters, of course. The package included the substitution of Christian, predominantly white, saints for revered African ancestors as role models and intercessors; Christian or baptismal names as adjuncts or substitutes for African names; displacement of native religious icons, rituals, rites, feasts, festivals and ceremonies by Christian ones; and selective bans on the wearing of native cloth. Such was the success of the brainwashing and "spiritual rebirth" achieved through these colonial tactics and missionary activity that one Central African country is reported to have chosen at independence a national anthem which included the words, unofficially translated: "little by little we are leaving our savage state"!

The programmed self-denigration exemplified by this episode may not be conclusive evidence that "political independence" does not translate directly into spiritual liberation, of course. More evidence that spiritual bondage has persisted in Africa after political independence is, however, unfortunately available. For more of such evidence one needs to look no further than the reckless arrogance often displayed by Fanon's famous "black skins, white masks". In a recently reported example of such arrogance a Christian church leader called for a ban on traditional religious rituals at official ceremonies in his officially lay country – on the grounds that they are unchristian! And in the globalising or "globalised" Africa that Fanon did not live long enough to see large sections of the semi-literate and immature youth, and the denizens of the urban slums and rural settlements, who would almost certainly not have qualified as "black skins, white masks" in his book, appear to seek and find spiritual fulfilment in the sub-cultures of America, Europe and the Caribbean.

Development as Alienation: Necessity, Choice or Accident?

The African and non-African proponents of vassalage-driven development have touted that model since colonial times as the continent's only possible hope of

---

18 The Portuguese state reportedly paid for the subsistence of Catholic priests on posting in "Portuguese Africa".

salvation from underdevelopment, backwardness and poverty. There can be no stronger propaganda for colonialism, formal or informal, and colonial development than that. But that also amounts to the promotion of alienation as a development tool, for, as Ake (op. cit.) rightly puts it, the colonial development paradigm is inherently alienating.

It is perhaps, a sign of the times that in the age of globalisation the "partners" for African development take no steps to hide, but rather flaunt the fact, which was once elaborately concealed by its proponents and just as painstakingly exposed by its opponents, that the operating development paradigm in the age of globalisation is the colonial development one – and that the "development partnership" behind it is just as "traditional". Public lectures, and flaunted "conditionalities", by "donors" and their agents on governance, economic management and development issues – and recipient Governments' compliance, including pre-emptive compliance, with donor demands and "recommendations" would seem in this context to be but demonstrations of a new transparency about colonial relationships and colonial development.

If then the persistence of the colonial development paradigm in independent Africa is not in doubt and the paradigm is recognised as alienating the remaining question is whether Africa is stuck with it by accident, choice or necessity. Beyond the political, economic, social, cultural, spiritual, philosophical and technological chains to "development partners" discussed across the essay the content of Africa's "development" policies, programmes and practices from the colonial era to date suggests a continent "hooked" on dependency.

In the agricultural sector it is a notorious fact that African commercial farmers continue, under independent Governments, to produce essentially for overseas factories and supermarkets under buyers' terms; "independent" peasant farmers are compelled to continue to feed workers cheaply, so that their employers can continue to pay them starvation wages; and "cash crop" peasants retain their status as *de facto* wage earners or share croppers through administrative and pricing mechanisms designed by the state, marketing boards and licensed companies to exploit or super-tax them.[19] With the exception, indeed, of amputations, corporal punishment and imprisonment initially used in some African colonies to push previously independent peasants into the "modern" or "cash" economy as workers or commodity producers the instruments employed by colonial regimes to procure cheap African labour remain substantially in place.[20]

The conversion of mining in Africa from a local needs driven activity to a sector in which the continent is systematically undermined to satisfy the needs and greed of "foreign investors" and "overseas markets" has followed a similar pattern of "development" by alienation. And just as the previous phase of colonialism distorted power and economic and social relations in the rural sector for its ends the mining industry has continued the creation or reinforcement of industry-friendly socio-economic and political structures, functions and attitudes, including inequalities, in

---

19 See for instance Bernal (1988), Gakou (1987), and Mkandawire and Naceur (1987).

20 For an overview of those instruments see, for instance, Ake (1996 and 2001) and Rodney (1972).

its areas of operation. With state connivance some mining companies in independent Africa have even reportedly constituted themselves into states within the states, with the equivalents of "mines police" and mines prison services to secure their concessions. To add insult to injury many mining communities and their populations suffer the indignity of finding the jewellery, cement, fertilisers, silver and copperware, roofing sheets and machine tools produced from their minerals typically priced beyond their reach. Industrial manufacturing, a novelty in Africa which followed independence, was also alienating without delivering the contributions to the continent's economic liberation expected by leaders like Kwame Nkrumah before its virtual death at the hands of incompetent and corrupt managers and supervising politicians and the forces and agents of globalisation.[21]

More explanations of the ease and speed of Africa's recent de-industrialisation processes should not be difficult to find. But none of these can beat the weak political base and the alienating nature of the industrialisation strategy adopted in importance. Internal resource mobilisation for the new industries was much too dependent, for a start, on the same alienating practices of overtaxing already impoverished workers and peasants. Fatal dependence on foreign technologies, foreign capital and foreign investors, a consequence of the industrialisation model itself, was bound to alienate a whole constituency of local artisans, inventors, professional managers, aspiring national capitalists and the more nationalistic sections of the professional classes and intelligentsia[22] who should have been moulded, strengthened and mobilised to provide the engine for national industrialisation.

The above summary of independent Africa's development adventures within the colonial paradigm would no doubt confirm that the colonial development paradigm is materially and structurally incapable of developing the continent and is thus not a serious development option.

Development as Liberation: Utopia or Development Imperative?

Between Alienation and Liberation: The Reformist Blueprints

It would appear from the discussions above – but more importantly from the dismal failure of the colonial development model to deliver development – that dependent development is long overdue for the dustbin of history. Does the persistence of the international Development Establishment – represented by the

---

21 Nkrumah's faith in industrialisation as the continent's engine of growth and development was so central to his life and work that it would be invidious to single out any of his declarations, publications or works as evidence of his vision in this regard. But perhaps his Government's *Seven Year Development Plan* (launched in March, 1964) and his *Africa Must Unite* (1963) provide enough clues about his thinking on the industrialisation of Ghana and Africa as a force for the liberation of Africa and Africans from the humiliations of poverty and political and economic dependence.

22 For the social and professional backgrounds of those elites see Ake, op. cit; and Coleman, James S. 1958. *Nigeria: Background to Nationalism.* University of California Press.

likes of Tony Blair and his friends on his *Commission for Africa*, the G8 and the African voices of *NEPAD* – in continuing to treat African development as "the white man's burden" suggest a conscious or unconscious inclination to consolidate and perpetuate its underdevelopment, an unwillingness or inability to countenance an independent development option for Africa or total lack of trust in the ability of African Governments or the peoples of Africa or both to develop the continent independently? Do those who work to keep Africa within the colonial development framework do so merely by force of habit, out of a clinical inability to think outside "the box, that is? Or are Africans and the world being subliminally brainwashed by the constant repetition of dependency as Africa's development necessity or destiny to think of Africans as the "children", small brains or lower animals they were once openly said to be?

These questions may or may not be fully answerable, even if the patronising arrogance and insensitivity of some of the posturing about African development is reminiscent of the dark days of the initial period of colonial developmentalism. It is possible, perhaps, to give Mr. Blair and company the benefit of the doubt, and to evaluate their development project for Africa without "undue" attention to its presentation. But their development themes and the posturing around them – notably debt cancellation, market access, aid and trade and " good governance" under carefully designed conditionalities – place their project firmly within the same centre-periphery/patron-client framework which has been at the heart of Africa's vassalisation and dependent development/underdevelopment over the centuries. They also betray the supervising "development partners" as unwilling or unable to conceptualise Africa and African development outside the dependency framework.

Significantly, the "good governance" conditionalities – "democracy", transparency and the curbing of corruption – do not suggest a high regard for the recipient Governments concerned, or their peoples who, perhaps not unreasonably, appear in the new developmentalism as villains and victims respectively. The problem with the new scenario is that it, too, is all too familiar – and just as contemptuous of, and inimical to, Africa's independent and democratic development option. In particular the "new scenario" is familiar in privileging the accountability of benefits receiving Governments to the international community over their accountability to their own peoples. It thus continues the cynicism of adopting the posture of promoting democracy, as "the new partnership" does, while submitting governments more firmly to external control, as it also does.[23]

Unblocking Africa's Independent Development Option: A Mental Liberation Struggle for Africa and its Friends

The fact that after centuries of economic vassalisation and mental colonisation Africa's Governments and mainstream intelligentsia continue to entrust the continent's development future to the very people, institutions, partnerships, mechanisms, processes, strategies, programmes, projects and instruments that have governed its development destiny, with results which most people recognise as disastrous, is both

---

23 See, for instance, chapter on *Blocked Options* in Ake (1996, 2001).

understandable and paradoxical. It is understandable for some of the reasons outlined across this paper and by other observers. And paradoxical because two centuries of dependent underdevelopment do not appear to have concentrated enough African minds on the dangers of the dependency syndrome and the need to develop and apply appropriate remedies for it.

Freeing otherwise intelligent Africans from the dependency complex that prevents their consideration of "alternative development" would necessarily require identifying and overcoming the following effects of colonial and neo-colonial conditioning, among others:

- Adherence to the proposition that in an "inter-dependent" world any attempt at independent development amounts to mad and dangerous secessionism from an essentially benign world order, which deserves to be, and will surely be, punished by "the international community";
- Belief that Africans would be crushed by the international community's retaliation if the continent took the "irresponsible" and "suicidal" path of attempting to regain control over its resources and development;
- Explicit or implicit acceptance that Africans are, in any case, incapable of managing their own economic affairs and development and need foreign assistance and supervision to survive, grow and develop;
- Internalization of the idea that independent development for Africa is, furthermore, utopian or undesirable;
- Faith in dependency as a mutually beneficial relationship for Africa and its "development partners";
- Faith in dependent development as a sustainable, as well as desirable, development option for Africa – based on faith in the altruism of the continent's external patrons, or the assumption that they will act fairly towards the continent out of "enlightened self-interest"; and
- Internalization of the insult that dependency and dependent development are necessary to prevent Africa's "return" to backwardness and savagery.

For inspiration and guidance in the struggle to overcome the above and similar conditions the likes of Nkrumah, Nyerere, Cabral, Du Bois, Fanon and George Padmore are, as usual, a precious mine. Too much intellectual energy appears to have been wasted, on the other hand, by other intellectuals and activists who were, and have been, more preoccupied with proving their humanity to the purveyors of racist ideologies than with the liberation of their own or other colonised minds. African liberation thought and action will hopefully be dominated in future by recognition that African liberation is first and foremost a struggle for the mental decolonisation of Africans.

Unblocking Africa's Independent Development Option: An Operational Agenda for Africans

Unblocking Africa's independent development potential is, of course, impossible without recognition of the absurdity of continuing to pursue a development philosophy and process – dependent development – which has been proved in some two centuries of Africa's history as, charitably speaking, naïve and, arguably, a veritable weapon for the conquest and control of the continent for imperialist gain. In the struggle, therefore, for an alternative to the development catastrophe that dependent development has proved itself to be Nkrumah's exhortation to "seek ye first the political kingdom…" seems as relevant as ever.

Liberation Politics: Reclaiming African Politics as a Development Tool

Of all the structural and functional weaknesses of the vassalised continent that Africa is the most disabling is, arguably, the subordination of its politics at all levels to the interests, controls, manipulation and tastes of external forces. Indeed that is not a mere disability: it is, indisputably, the essence of colonial domination itself.

It is also indisputable, however, that as and when the need arises some powers seek, acquire or retain imperial control over target peoples through formal colonialism, neo-colonialism or informal colonialism: through systems, by whatever name that is, of exercising power with or without responsibility, for the defense and advancement of imperial interests. Indeed the fact that Nkrumah did not invent a bogeyman with his warnings against neo-colonialism when formal colonialism seemed no longer tenable has been more than amply confirmed by the history of Africa since his overthrow. Nor are the interests to be defended or advanced through formal or informal colonialism; the rationalisations for the perpetuation of colonialism, formal and informal; and the instruments of colonial and neo-colonial control secret: they are the same in substance if not in appearance as those that have driven, rationalised and administered colonial and indirect rule in Africa for two centuries. That should give an advantage to those who would struggle to reclaim African control over African development and African politics: the adversary has virtually no tricks or surprises left!

Social Transformation for Independent Development

The colonial project for the transformation of African societies, which has demonstrably and often blatantly continued into the neo-colonial and globalisation eras, has been traditionally described as "westernisation". The description is only partially correct. In fact, while "westernisation" remains a convenient code word the European led transformation of Africa over the past two centuries is perhaps best and more accurately understood as the molding of Africa to suit the imperial needs and tastes of "the West", another misleading word. Some of the effects of westernisation have been undoubtedly positive. But its negative effects have, by several reckonings, including that of Walter Rodney (1972), overridden the positive. Suffice it to say that globalisation, the current phase of imperialism, has increased, not lowered, the costs to Africa of westernisation – and has, moreover, *not* altered the balance of the costs and benefits of imperialism in favour of Africa.

Conventional statistics and cost/benefit analyses would not, of course, verify this observation meaningfully – for the good reason that they are not designed to measure the costs, and benefits, if any, of subjugation by imperialist forces. Pending the development of scientific measures for such matters the observation is made on the basis that globalisation does not appear to have increased Africa's economic, political, social, technological and cultural independence. There are, on the contrary, ample indications that Africa has become more dependent, under globalisation, in these departments of life. This should not be surprising. The greater peripheralisation of weak or peripheral states and the simultaneous strengthening of the pulling power over them of powerful or central states that globalise the weaker ones would seem, indeed, to be the very essence of globalisation. History, and the limited carrying capacity of the earth's resources, suggest, of course, that globalisation is less likely to make the states at the centre of the "global system" its "growth poles" than to empower them to "cannibalise" the weaker states. Continental and local struggles for the socio-economic transformations required to achieve and sustain Africa's independent development remain, therefore, at least as vital as ever.

From Dependency Economics to Liberation Economics: An Agenda for Action

For an agenda of action to guide the possible rescue of Africa from institutionalised underdevelopment one needs look no further than the many constructive ideas embedded in available critiques of "dependency economics", and the proposals for alternative development that usually follow the critiques.[24] It may not be redundant to remind African economic freedom fighters and their international allies here, however, that the struggle is *against* an economic system which has trapped the continent in poverty and underdevelopment for centuries, and *for* a new Africa in which "development" is about the mobilisation and application of every resource at the continent's disposal for the enhanced and sustainable security, welfare, growth, dignity and happiness of Africans everywhere. That, it is submitted, is the foundation for a true agenda for an African renaissance – or transformation of the continent from formal or informal colonial status to independence, self-esteem and respectability.

An Agenda for the Psychological Liberation Imperative

Psychological liberation is no easier to propose to an enslaved mind than it is to suggest a visit to a mental health professional to a mentally sick individual. To the extent that the enslaved mind is not aware of its servitude it cannot, of course, be liberated. And those who profit from the servitude of the mentally enslaved can be counted on to encourage or reinforce the misrepresentation of efforts to liberate their slaves as destabilisation, brain washing, indoctrination or intoxication by other names, with dire consequences for the "agitators". The call for the psychological liberation, also known as the mental decolonisation, of African victims of mental slavery is no more and no less than a call for the freeing of afflicted African minds from the low self esteem and inferiority complexes created by colonial indoctrination or brain washing.[25]

---

24 See, for instance, Ake (1996, 2001), Amin (1976), and Frank (1975).
25 For a refreshing contribution to this process see Kebede (2004).

Agenda for Cultural Liberation and Cultural Reconstruction for Development

Thanks to the work of Mafeje (1988) and other distinguished African scholars and writers on the cultural dimensions of Africa's liberation and development such as Samir Amin, Willie Abraham, Franz Fanon, Kwame Nkrumah, Ngugi wa Thiong'o and Wole Soyinka a solid foundation exists for reflections by free Africans on the cultural dimensions of Africa's liberation and development. For the record and as an *aide-memoire* we summarise the challenges on this front as: combating the ideology that cultural development for Africans means turning them into a "black skin, white masks"; the promotion of African cultures as a means of satisfying the spiritual, physiological, social and ego needs of Africans through their self-improvement and self realisation; the rescue of these cultures from their degrading treatment as commodities for sale to tourists and other curio hunters; and the protection, renewal and development of African cultures and environmental resources for the benefit of present and future generations of Africans and humanity at large.

The Liberation of African Minds: The Philosophical Dimension

The racist insult that Africans were incapable of philosophical thought is rarely broadcast in its original, crude, form in recent years. But ongoing westernisation and globalisation of Africa projects – in the areas of governance and "democracy", economic management, religious practice, "sexual freedom", for instance – necessarily imply the persistence of the image of Africa as philosophically and culturally empty, backward or stupid. The imposition on Africa of the weird definition of democracy outlined above – without noticeable African resistance, be it noted, except by a few African oligarchs who oppose it with romantic accounts of supposedly more relevant African governance traditions, to mystify everybody – is an example of this contempt for Africa's ability to work out appropriate governance norms and institutions for itself. The smuggling into Africa of Social Darwinism on the wings of Structural Adjustment, also cited above, against some of the still most deeply held cultural, economic and social solidarity principles of "unspoiled" Africa, is another. Structural Adjustment itself, perhaps still the flagship of the globalisation forces in Africa, has been more than massively reinforced in recent decades by social, cultural and other change forces and weapons that the original armies of neo-colonial change agents, and their intellectual auxiliaries, could only dream about.[26]

But the fact that Structural Adjustment was not transported into Africa in a vacuum but as a follow-up to the Reagan/Thatcher counteroffensive against Third World demands in the 1970's for a just New International Economic Order (NIEO) is a sobering reminder that in submitting to Structural Adjustment and its social, cultural and philosophical by-products and appendages Africa has, in effect, bent once again to the forces of the unequal world order. It also confirms, once again, that the liberation of Africa would be impossible without the liberation of African

---

26 The classics of modernisation theory, whose analyses and prescriptions, though hardly referred to in recent times, appear to inform contemporary globalisation or reform projects, include Hagen and Everett (1962), Lerner (1958) and Levy (1952).

minds and, arising from that, the strengthening of Africa's capacity to detect and resist social, cultural and philosophical manipulation against the supreme interests of its own peoples. The intellectual foundations exist, fortunately, for such an enterprise.[27]

After the Spiritual Vandalisation: Towards an African Spiritual Revival

After the spiritual vandalisation outlined above, a first step in the spiritual rehabilitation of Africa has to be acknowledgement that the very existence of Fanon's "black skin, white masks" is a spiritual disaster for those human specimens themselves, as Fanon, a professional psychiatrist by training, recognised; an affront to decent Africans; and a disservice to humanity. The challenge goes beyond rehabilitation, however: it is about the self-esteem of the direct victims; the dignity of a continent and its peoples, at home and in the Diaspora; and the replacement of cultural imperialism by a world in which cultural diversity is respected, the strengths of world cultures serve to promote the development of all and democratically identified weaknesses in individual cultures are democratically and sensitively corrected.

Meeting these development and growth challenges would require, *inter alia*, the development of the intellectual and institutional capacity to detect and counter signs and threats of the spiritual domination of any group or groups of people by another. The development of this capacity can only benefit from an understanding of the nexus between the continent's spiritual vandalisation and its economic, political and cultural domination and poverty.

Back to Basics: African Development Without the Familiar Obscurantism and Cynicism

The reality and image of Africa as a "scar on the conscience of the world", to quote British Prime Minister Tony Blair again – or as a living humiliation – as many Africans and people of African descent would describe it, is, by and large, a familiar one. What Blair and his kind, African and non-African, also fail or refuse to see, but free Africans see all too clearly, is the fact that the continent's catastrophic poverty is the proven result, not exclusively or even principally, of accident, African weaknesses, neglect of the continent or its exclusion from "developed" or "rich" country largesse – as their moral posturing suggests – but of the continent's vassalisation and exploitation for the benefit of countries such as Blair's. Proposals for revitalising "development partnerships" with Africa that do not recognise and denounce this fact but seek instead merely to give a more humane face to Africa's "traditional relationships" with its so-called development partners deserve, therefore, to be rejected as obscurantist at best, and cynical at worst. The alternative to the Blairite project for the modernisation of Africa's dependency is, of course, the continent's liberation from dependency itself and dependent development or underdevelopment.

---

27 For a recent overview of some of the resources already available see *Special issue on 'Philosophy and Development'* in *Africa Development*, Vol. XXIX, No.1, 2004.

Epilogue

The following principles, ideas and notes are offered for consideration in the formulation of guidelines and strategies for rescuing Africa from its dependency and dependent underdevelopment trap.

1. No Apologies for an Afro-Centric Development Perspective: As the history of Africa's dependent underdevelopment shows, and free Africans and their true friends know, colonialism, neo-colonialism and globalisation have created a mass of "educated" and influential Africans who have felt obliged or proud to deny, denounce, renounce or apologise for their Africanness. The very idea of an Afro-centric development perspective, or African development on the basis of a self-reliant or independent development strategy, is bound to be opposed by this group of Africans. They did so in their responses to the relatively timid and self-defeating LPA. That, however, need not prevent the pursuit of an Afro-centric development strategy based on *coherent* plans for national and collective self-reliance.

The necessary conditions for such a strategy would be the political commitment of a critical mass of free Africans, from the continent and the Diaspora, to the project; recovery of African responsibility for, and control, of African development, with recognition that an Afro-centric development strategy requires the sourcing of the human and material resources required for its development and implementation from Africa and Africans; and an iron determination, backed by all necessary measures, to overcome all obstacles to success.

2. Africa Does Not Owe the World its Underdevelopment: One of the more bizarre, if enduring, results of the vassalisation of Africa in recent centuries is the mostly unwritten and unspoken but palpable assumption that Africa has, by its history and status, incurred an obligation to remain dependent and underdeveloped. This widespread assumption was, of course, more brazenly proclaimed as a matter, virtually, of course during the formal colonial era. But it reappears in the age of neo-colonialism and globalisation in hardly more subtle assertions by latter-day imperialists, who proclaim their strategic or national security interest in Africa's natural and other resources; in hardly veiled threats to African and non-African competitors for those resources to keep off them or face their wrath; and in the deployment of the classic and new economic, military, political and diplomatic tools of imperialism to enforce their "interests".

Latter-day imperialism and bullying need to be identified and resisted by Africans and all freedom, justice and peace loving peoples, of course – whether they manifest as the defence of "strategic" or "national security" interests abroad, or under other cynical banners": no war on terrorism, a current "global" preoccupation, can be credible or legitimate in this day and age, in any case, unless it targets the terrorism of "rogue states"[28] as well as non-state terrorism.

---

28 For case studies of "rogue state terrorism" see Chomsky (2000).

3. Africa's Peoples Do Not Owe their Rulers Their Vanities: Global studies, reports and direct observation suggest that African rulers, ancient and modern, were and are no more or less prone to acquisitiveness, pomposity, exhibitionism and general vanity than their counterparts elsewhere.[29] But the contrast between the spectacular poverty of Africa's peoples and the profligate incomes, legal and illegal, and lifestyles which too many African rulers extract from their subjects suggests an anachronistic contempt for their peoples. The peoples of Africa need to resist and punish such anachronistic arrogance – for their own self-respect and well being, and the respects of others.

Towards Afro-centric and Democratic Development in Africa

The Challenge to Africa's "Traditional" Governance Institutions and Rulers

For the benefit of Africa's peoples free Africans have a responsibility to de-romanticise all "traditional" governance institutions and all but a very tiny few of Africa's rulers before, during and after colonial rule. Intellectual and political honesty would seem to rule out undue glory to institutions and rulers that failed, and continue to fail, in their duty to protect their peoples from formal or informal colonialism and exploitation. The challenge to Africa's traditional institutions of government and rulers who aspire to greatness would seem accordingly obvious: reclaim legitimacy and greatness by positioning themselves as forces for the liberation and Afro-centric and democratic development of their communities, countries and Africa.

The Challenge to Africa's "Modern" Governance Institutions and "Politicians"

To the extent that the continent's "modern politicians" and their support systems continue the tradition of selling, condoning the sale or failing to prevent the sale or theft of their peoples' interests, for any reasons whatsoever, they can claim no greater legitimacy than the "tribal chiefs" who did the same before them. This would, technically and objectively, put the Nkrumahs, Nassers, Nyereres, Modibo Keitas and Sekou Toures in the same basket with the likes of Mobutu, Kamuzu Banda and other unabashed puppets of colonialism and neo-colonialism. Legitimate distinctions can, and ought to be drawn, however, between "leaders" who tried and failed, for reasons they did not understand or due to factors they could not control, to disengage their countries from colonial or semi-colonial economic relationships from those, on the other hand who made no such effort, basked in them or actually reinforced their countries' informal colonial status.

There can be no "benefit of the doubt", however, for any contemporary African politicians, in government or opposition, who collaborate with imperialist forces in the colonial exploitation of the continent and their peoples: the readily available benefits of hindsight, blinding contemporary evidence and an abundance of popular and academic critiques of neo-colonialism deny present day collaborators the excuse

---

29 See, for instance, Gigantes (2003).

of ignorance or naivety. By the same token the peoples of Africa lose any excuses they might have had for failure to punish "leaders" who surrender them to, or keep them in, formal or informal colonial bondage.

Challenge to Africa's Peoples

While popular resistance to colonial and neo-colonial penetration, control and exploitation is not unknown in Africa identifiable weaknesses among the African masses, including some active collaboration with colonial and neo-colonial masters and their agents, have also served colonial interests on the continent.

Some of these weaknesses are:

- Docility or instinctive submission to authority and power;
- The cynicism of the oppressed - manifest in, for instance, readiness to betray or brutalise other oppressed people on behalf of the oppressor, for direct personal benefit;
- Participation in the "legitimisation" of corruption through their own corrupt practices;
- Own misuse, as initiator or collaborator, of ethnicity, religion, regionalism and socio-economic and "cultural differences" for personal or sectional advantage;
- Irrational faith in local "charismatic leaders" and their "development partners", rather than in themselves, as architects of their economic and political salvation;
- Tendency to pray and beg for, rather than demand, justice and their rights;
- Extreme vulnerability to ideological manipulation;
- Collaboration with exploiters who abuse "community development", religion, sex, pornography, alcohol, drugs, sports, etc, to tranquillise them or misdirect their energies;
- Indulgence in degrading, inefficient, divisive, counter-productive and ultimately unsustainable practices like begging, stealing, petty corruption, fraud, prostitution, robbery and sale of brutal force to "war lords", "political" gangsters and common crime bosses for income and other survival assets; and
- Low self esteem.

Without exception, all the above-mentioned weaknesses, which are by no means mutually exclusive, reflect the mindset of "the wretched of the earth" – a product of indoctrination, miseducation, neglect, exploitation and poverty which makes its victims susceptible to more manipulation, marginalisation, exploitation and impoverishment. For the democratic and sustainable development of Africa overcoming this mindset in the wretched majority of its people would be undoubtedly essential. It cannot be achieved, however, without their active participation in the process spontaneously, under the leadership of "peer educators" or with the support of free and selfless Africans outside their ranks. But that requires painful acknowledgement by them of the above and similar weaknesses as contributors to their plight.

The Challenge to Non-African Supporters of the Continent's Independent and Democratic Development

It was standard practice for leaders of Africa's "post-war" nationalist movements, particularly in the British colonies, to be required to establish their own and/or their peoples' democratic credentials, as a condition for considering the "granting" of independence to them. To some of those leaders, Nkrumah among them, this was just another imperialist ruse for delaying independence, given that the regimes making those demands had never previously placed democratisation of the colonies on their political agenda, were guilty of very undemocratic practices themselves in the colonies and had shown no great love for decolonisation previously.

Evidence of manipulation or attempted manipulation of the "democratisation" processes themselves in favour of "conservative", "moderate" or "friendly" forces, when "independence" became inevitable, also fuelled suspicions that the "independence" being delivered was a fraud aimed at transferring the shadows of power and sovereignty to the natives, while the "former" colonial or occupying power retained the substance of both. President Bush George W. Bush's oft-repeated claim that the "democratisation" of the Middle East is driven by the need to protect America's homeland security and interests in that region is, in that sense, an eerie reminder that "plus ca change, plus ca reste la meme chose"!

The arrogant cynicism of the likes of George Bush, his European allies and their forebears, and their propaganda organs, past and present, has not always succeeded in knocking idealistic internationalists, who understand that democracy and colonial servitude are incompatible, out of business, however. The examples of the likes of Fenner Brockway of Britain's *Movement for Colonial Freedom*[30] and other Europeans, and indeed Americans, who supported, and support, Africa's struggles for genuine independence and true democracy provide encouraging signs that freedom and justice loving peoples everywhere can join forces with their African counterparts to oppose dependency and construct free and mutually beneficial development partnerships.

Non-African supporters of the continent's independent and democratic development have also always understood, to their credit, that their struggles in this regard are not another patronising initiative for Africa's ostensible development but part of a global struggle for freedom from oppression and want everywhere. Being mostly, fighters for greater freedom and justice at home as well they have operated, in any case, on the basis that freedom's "battlefield" is wherever oppression and poverty exist. And they know from secondary sources and participant and non-participant observation that oppressors and freedom fighters alike come in all shapes, colours and forms, and are not identifiable by the superficial criteria of colour, "race", nationality, gender, ethnicity, class or geographical origin.

---

30 A group formed in 1954 to campaign for the right of all people to full independence and international mutual aid.

Vassal States, Development Options and African Development: Closing Summary

It would have been observed from above and elsewhere, and directly by most readers, that the weapons used by the enemies of Africa's freedom and independent development to fight against it are many. In this closing summary two of these weapons are singled out for special attention – because, as weapons of elite and mass miseducation and propaganda warfare, they are particularly vicious and central to this essay's concerns. Denying or obscuring independent development as an available or desirable option for Africa, and thus disarming some among those would work for its realisation, is one of them. It may be termed as the "weaponisation pragmatism". The nonsense that tracing Africa's underdevelopment to the continent's formal and informal colonial subjugation amounts to unproductive indulgence in a so-called "blame game" is another. It is tantamount to denying Africans a vital tool: a "road map" for a necessarily long journey made hazardous by the predictable ambushes of entrenched opponents of Africa's independent development.[31]

Against these two weapons this essay offers the proposition that Africa does not have to project, or allow others to prolong, its miserable "development" history into an indefinite future. Whether Africa continues or escapes its development history is, in other words, a matter of choice, not of destiny. It is further suggested that Africa's development future would be determined by whether the continent chooses to:

- Continue the path of submission to external "overlords", "protectors", "development partners"; external markets, foreign direct investors, the "international community" and other willing and able destiny makers; or
- Reject servitude as a "development" resource, and dedicates its human and natural resources to independent and independently sustainable development.

These messages are not new.

But another reminder that Africa's dependent underdevelopment is not divinely ordained and the continent's development future would remain subject to external manipulation and control if and only if Africa wills it so is, from all indications, not redundant. The bias in this essay in favour of the second option derives from the following related beliefs: that for Africans, as for everyone else, freedom and development are inseparable; dependency is a negation of freedom; and dependency is not, has not been, and cannot be a development resource for Africa.

---

31 This is not to be confused with the age-old propaganda that colonialism was good for Africa, which finds current expressions in new attempts to whitewash colonialism and even calls from some quarters for the "re-colonisation" of Africa.

References

Abraham, W.E. (1962), *The Mind of Africa* (Chicago: University of Chicago Press).

Ake, C. (1996), *Democracy and Development in Africa* (Washington DC: The Brookings Institution).

Amin, S. (1976), *Unequal Development* (Sussex: Harvester Press and Monthly Review Press).

Apter, D.E. (1965), *The Politics of Modernisation* (Chicago: University of Chicago Press).

Bernal, V. (1988), 'Coercion and Incentives in African Agricultural Development: Insights from the Sudanese Experience', *African Studies Review* 31 (September).

Chomsky, N. (2000), *Rogue States, The Rule of Force in World Affairs* (London: Pluto Press).

Economic Commission for Africa (1976), 'Revised Framework of Principles for the Implementation of the New International Economic Order in Africa, 1976 – 1981 – 1986. E/CN.14/ECO/90/Rev.3, 25 June' (Addis Ababa: United Nations Economic Commission for Africa).

Fanon, F. (1967), *Black Skin, White Masks*, trans. C.L. Markmann (New York: Grove Press).

Frank, A.G. (1975), *On Capitalist Underdevelopment* (Oxford: Oxford University Press).

Gakou, M. (1987), *The Crisis in African Agriculture* (London: Zed Books).

Gbadegesin, S. (1991), *African Philosophy: Traditional Yoruba Philosophy and Contemporary African Realities* (New York: Peter Lang).

George, S. (1984, 1990), *Ill Fares the Land* (London: Penguin Books).

Gigantes, P. (2003), *Power & Greed: A Short History of the World* (London: Constable and Robinson).

Gyekye, K. (1995), *An Essay on African Philosophical Thought: The Akan Conceptual Scheme* Revised edition (Philadelphia: Temple University Press).

Gyekye, K. (1996). *African Cultural Values: An Introduction* (Accra: Sankofa Publishing Company).

Hagen, E. (1962), *On the Theory of Social Change: How Economic Growth Begins* (Homewood, Ill: Dorsey Press).

Lerner, D. (1958), *The Passing of Traditional Society: Modernising the Middle East* (Glencoe, Ill: Free Press).

Levy, M. (1952), *The Structure of Society* (Princeton, NJ: Princeton University Press).

Mafeje, A. (1988), 'Culture and Development in Africa: The Missing Link', Codesria Bulletin, No.1 (Dakar: CODESRIA).

Mbiti, J.S. (1978), *African Religions and Philosophy* (New York: Doubleday).

Milne, J. (1977), *Forward Ever: The Life of Kwame Nkrumah* (London: Panaf Books).

Messay K. (2004), 'African Development and the Primacy of Mental Decolonisation', Special Issue on "Philosophy and Development", *Africa Development*, Vol.XXIX, No. 1.

Mkandawire, T., and Bourenane, M. (eds.) (1987), *The State and Agriculture in Africa* (Dakar, Senegal: CODESRIA).

Nkrumah, K. (1965), *Neocolonialism, the Last Stage of Imperialism* (London: Heinemann).

OAU (1980), 'Lagos Plan of Action for the Economic Development of Africa, 1980 – 2000', Adopted by the Heads of State and Government of the Organisation of African Unity (OAU), meeting in its Second Extraordinary Session devoted to economic problems in Africa, held in Lagos, Nigeria, from 28 to 29 April.

Rodney, W., (1972), *How Europe Underdeveloped Africa* (Dar-es-Salaam Bogle-L'Ouverture Publications, London and Tanzania Publishing House).

Rustow, W.W. (1960), *The Stages of Economic Growth, A Non-Communist Manifesto* (Cambridge: Cambridge University Press).

Shils, E.A. (1962), *Political Development in the New States* (The Hague: Mouton).

Sideri, S. (1970), *Trade and Power – Informal Colonialism in Anglo-Portuguese Relations* (Rotterdam: Rotterdam University Press).

Wiredu, K. (1980), *Philosophy and an African Culture* (Cambridge: Cambridge University Press).

Chapter 8

Instabilities and Development in Africa

Augustin Kwasi Fosu

Introduction

Various forms of instabilities have been observed to adversely affect economic growth in African countries (see, e.g., Fosu, 2002a, 2001a, 2000c, 1992a, 1991; Guillaumont et al., 1999; Gyimah-Brempong, 1999, 1991). In particular, there is a long history of studies that analyze the impacts on growth of economic instabilities, especially of exports, in developing countries (for a review see, for example, Fosu, 2001a). More recently, there has been increasing attention towards the role of political economy, with some emphasis on political instability. Alesina and Perotti (1994) survey the literature on the importance of political economy generally, while Alesina et al. (1996) explore the impact of PI on growth based on a large sample consisting of both developing and developed countries.

The scope of the present chapter will be limited primarily to those studies focusing on Africa, especially sub-Saharan Africa (SSA). The chapter explores the evidence on the importance of instabilities – economic and political – for development in African countries by reviewing the literature related to growth. It also reviews studies that bear on the role of instabilities, specifically political, in the transformation of growth to development.

From a production-function perspective, instabilities may have important economic growth implications due to two major reasons. First, they can influence the levels of production inputs, such as capital and labor. For example, social or political instabilities tend to reduce the levels of productive investment and labor available in a given country. Fewer investment projects are likely to be undertaken by risk-averse firms for a given marginal efficiency of investment schedule, since firms associate the greater uncertainty with increased variability of profits. Risk-neutral firms, on the other hand, may prefer the "waiting option" and instead invest in information acquisition in order to reduce the source of uncertainty. In either case, investment is likely to be curtailed, at least for the short run.[1] (Fosu, 1992a)

With respect to labor, greater political or social instabilities could reduce the supply of skilled labor, for workers tend to emigrate in search of better economic opportunities elsewhere – "brain drain" (ibid.). For example, Collier, Hoeffler and Pattillo (2004) empirically find that PI in the form of a civil war increases brain drain. However, the cause of the brain drain need not be limited to this form of PI.

---

1 Instabilities may lead to policy uncertainty, which in turn acts as a tax on investment and thus reduces private investment (Rodrik, 1991).

Uncertainties created by the events of military coups d'etats, especially characteristic of the post-independence era in Africa,[2] for instance, can be very destabilizing in terms of future prospects for the highly educated, who may then opt to flee, given their relatively large expected returns from emigration. Moreover, by engendering greater uncertainty, such instabilities are likely to further decrease investment in human capital, as risk-averse individuals curtail their investment in human capital. (Fosu, 1992a)

Second, instabilities may reduce the level of efficiency of the production process itself through the diminution of the productivities of the production inputs. For instance, in the case of physical capital, as future returns become more uncertain, the supply of investible funds is likely to decrease in response to higher capital flight and costs due to increased probability of loan defaults.[3] This outcome would in turn ration out longer-term more productive, but riskier, investment projects. A similar argument could be made for human capital as well, for brain drain often entails the emigration of generally relatively productive individuals with better opportunities elsewhere, thus depleting the country of relatively productive labor. (Fosu, 1992a)

Furthermore, rampant stops and starts in investment projects usually accompany instabilities, political or economic, hence lowering the marginal efficiency of investment. Political instability would particularly foster an atmosphere of uncertainty regarding the appropriate long-term rules of business operation. This could diminish the quality, as well as quantity, of investment projects undertaken. For example, in addition to its tendency to decrease the level of investment, the increased uncertainty of the investment environment would promote relatively inefficient short-term investments over longer-term projects. This is because the rate of time preference tends to rise with instabilities, with the greater risk of a capital loss associated with the longer horizon. (Fosu, 1992a)

Types of Instabilities

Two types of instabilities are usually identified: economic and political. "Economic instability" is traditionally associated with high inflationary uncertainty, and hence the usual reference to a "stabilization" program to cure an inflationary ill in a country. This inflationary phenomenon was particularly characteristic of many African economies, especially in the latter part of the 1970s, eighties and the earlier 1990s. High inflationary uncertainties are generally believed by economists to be deleterious to growth.[4] However, economic instability generally also entails other forms of macroeconomic instabilities, such as those involving investment or the external sector: exports, imports, international terms of trade, and the exchange rate.

---

2   The post-independence period in SSA has been characterized by over 300 coup events, comprising 80 "successful", 108 abortive and 139 officially reported plots (McGowan, 2003).

3   Collier, Hoeffler and Pattillo (2004) empirically find that PI in the form of a civil war, for instance, increases financial capital flight.

4   For an exposition of this view, see for instance Friedman (1977).

It is these types of economic instabilities that are being considered in the present chapter.

"Political instability" comprises the elite form, primarily the incidence of military coups d'etat, actual or potential, as well as mass insurrections as in the case of open civil war conflicts. The elite form has been particularly dominant in the African historical context. The roughly 46-year post-independence period has experienced some 188 incidents of coups, 108 of them abortive (McGowan, 2003). As it will become apparent below, these attempted but unsuccessful events constitute the most deleterious type of coups. There have also been a total of 139 officially reported incidents of coup plots. While the frequency of successful coups has declined since 1980, that of failed coups has actually increased. Specifically, there were 46 and 47 abortive and successful coups, respectively, during 1956-1979; however, while the frequency of successful coups decreased to 33 during 1980-2001, that of abortive coups actually skyrocketed to 62 over the same period. (Ibid.)

The present chapter does not deal with the microeconomic form of instability, such as weather conditions that affect certain farmers, or prices received by individual producers. It is worth noting, though, that such instabilities may also be translated to the macroeconomic form, which is the primary type of EI considered in the current chapter.

What is "Instability"?

By "instability" we mean fluctuations of a given variable from the norm. For instance, a peaceful political environment is assumed to be the norm. Hence, the occurrence of a coup, successful or abortive, or its plot that distorts the perceived political environment, would constitute instability. And so would the incidence of open warfare.

Similarly, the deviation of the level of investment, exports, or imports from trend would be considered instability. Thus, this definition excludes secular changes. In theory, the delineation between the secular and the deviation around trend is rather straightforward. In practice, though, it may be difficult for economic agents to separate out these two forms of changes. For example, farmers might notice only that prices have decreased by a certain amount. As to which portion can be considered as a secular change and which as actual deviation may not be easily identified. Nonetheless, for policy purposes, it is important to be able to identify the types of changes that are at work. For instance, if governments are to appropriately plan development programs requiring regular levels of payments, then knowledge of the secular vis-à-vis transitory changes in revenues becomes critical. The optimal choice of policy measures, furthermore, would depend on the ability to delineate between these two forms of changes. In the case of secular trends, the appropriate policy would involve ensuring that such trends are well captured. On the other hand, if it is deviations around trend that are consequential, then some sort of insurance scheme would be required based on the distribution of the perturbation.

Effects of Economic Instabilities on Growth[5]

One variable whose instability has long been suspected to be deleterious to economic growth of developing countries generally, and African economies in particular, is export earnings. For African countries these earnings are derived mainly from primary exports, which are especially sensitive to shocks. Uncertainties associated with such earnings tend to make it particularly difficult for private economic agents or governments to plan, and could negatively influence production. Gyimah-Brempong [1991], for example, presents cross-country evidence in support of the hypothesis of a negative effect of export instability on GDP growth in SSA countries over 1960-86.

As several authors have argued, however, export instability need not be growth-inhibiting, for relevant economic agents would take account of the uncertainty by increasing capital accumulation appropriately (e.g., Savvides, 1984; Moran, 1983). Several studies, including these two (ibid.), have supported the view empirically, based on samples of developing countries, suggesting that instability in export earnings exert little or no adverse effects on economic growth. Using a similar sample of African countries and period as Gyimah-Brempong's, Fosu [1992b] estimates a statistically insignificant, though negative, coefficient for the export instability variable, measured as the variance of the export share about its "best" trend. In contrast, a significant negative coefficient of export instability is estimated for non-African countries (ibid.). Thus, the evidence in support of the negative impact of export instability does not seem robust, especially in the case of African countries.

According to Fosu [1991], export instability is consequential for growth only when it is transmitted into capital (investment) instability. There is no guarantee that such a transmission is automatic, however, since "substantial portions of export proceeds may be channeled into consumption rather than investment" (ibid, p. 82). It may also be the case that other investible funds other than export proceeds, such as domestically generated funds and foreign direct investment as well as external aid, are available and may be used to compensate for export earnings instabilities. Hence, it would seem reasonable that countries experiencing significant instability in their export earnings would diversify away from this to other sources of funding investments. It is argued (ibid., p. 75):

> That is, a higher EI [export instability] would render export earnings a less reliable source for funding investment projects. Hence, for precautionary reasons, it would be rational for countries with larger values of EI to diversify their set of funding sources away from export earnings and toward other sources, such as domestic savings or international bodies, in order to smooth out potential fluctuations in capital flow attributable to export proceeds. Whether or not EI actually depresses economic growth, then, will depend upon the extent to which these efforts are successful in tapping alternative sources. In effect, it is the instability in capital formation, rather than EI per se, that is likely to influence economic growth, especially in sub-Saharan Africa where high EI itself could render export proceeds a relatively unreliable source for funding investment projects.

---

5   This section and the next borrow significantly from Fosu [2001b].

Using a 1967-1986 cross-country sample of SSA countries, Fosu (1991) finds support for the hypothesis of an adverse impact of investment instability on GDP growth, but observes little evidence in favor of the negative impact of export instability. Moreover, the investment instability effect is estimated to be rather large. Its magnitude is nearly twice that of the estimated impact of export growth, for example. Specifically, "a reduction in GDP growth of 5 percent would be associated with a 10 percent increase in capital instability, while a similar improvement in export performance would result in a smaller GDP growth of 3 percent." (Fosu, 2001b, p. 299)

Impact of Terms of Trade Instability

As reported above, the instability of real exports may have only a weak negative effect on growth in African economies. Might export price instability exert a significant negative impact on growth, though? This is a relevant question, because the quantity of exports itself may be dependent on the export price, which is exogenous generally to decision making in African countries. It is possible, therefore, for export price instability to influence both the growth and instability of exports, as well as investment and its instability.

Existing evidence for SSA suggests, however, that export price instability has little correlation with either export or investment instability (Fosu, 1997).[6] Hence, the observed adverse effect of capital instability on GDP growth in African economies is unlikely to be traceable to the instability of export prices or terms of trade. Furthermore, neither export price instability nor volatility[7] in the barter terms of trade appears to exert a negative direct impact on GDP growth (ibid.). What remains to be explored, however, is whether there is an indirect effect of export price instability through exports growth or the level of investment.

Although he does not provide direct evidence on African economies directly, Lutz (1994) presents 1970-1988 panel-data results on terms of trade volatility that appear to support the above view that instability in neither the price nor quantity of exports per se is deleterious for growth in Africa, particularly SSA. The author reports estimates based on several sub-samples of developed and less developed countries (LDCs), including "low income" and "LDC primary product exporters". He finds that for both of these subgroups, the coefficient of the volatility in the net barter terms of trade (NBTT) present in the GDP growth equation was positive, while that of income terms of trade (ITT) volatility was negative; however, neither was significant. Hence, neither the volatility in NBTT nor in ITT appears to exert a negative impact in GDP growth. The author concludes: "The low-income countries and primary exporters are the only subgroups for whom ITT fails to explain changes in output growth." (p. 1970)

The Lutz results on NBTT suggest that there are no apparent negative consequences for GDP growth of the volatility in the relative price of exports. Furthermore, the

---

6   The first-order correlation coefficients are 0.192 and -0.078, respectively.
7   "Volatility" is hereby defined synonymously with instability.

results for ITT, coupled with those for NBTT, point to the lack of potency for the instability of the volume of exports.

The above findings, then, support the above results for Africa and SSA reported in Fosu [1991, 1992b, 1997], as these subgroups in the Lutz sample are characteristic of African economies. That is, the evidence is in concert with the hypothesis that neither the instability in real exports nor in the export price seems to help explain the low growth experienced in African countries generally.

Import instability is another variable of potential concern for growth in Africa. Based on a cross-country study involving a sample of 24 SSA countries over 1960-80, Helleiner (1986) finds a strong negative effect of import instability on economic growth. According to Helleiner (p. 143), "the principal external instability problems faced by African policymakers can plausibly be taken as those of import volume instability." Using a 1967-1986 cross-country sample of 33 SSA countries, Fosu [2001a] corroborates the Helleiner result and further observes that import instability (MI) was an even greater deterrent, than either export instability (XI) or capital instability (KI), for GDP growth in SSA. More specifically, "the study finds that although KI is still a relevant argument of the production function, MI appears to be more important, while XI is extraneous." (Ibid. p. 71) Thus, "for economies that are heavily dependent on imports for productive investment, such as those of sub-Saharan Africa (SSA), a stable flow in imports may be a critical factor in promoting production efficiency and growth." (Ibid., p. 80)

It must be stressed, nonetheless, that all these three forms of instability are correlated. The first-order correlation coefficients of MI with XI and with KI are, respectively, 0.44 and 0.61, while the correlation coefficient between XI and KI is 0.69, all of which are significant at the .01 level (ibid., table 2). Hence, it is possible for XI, even though not independently negatively related to GDP growth, to result in higher MI or KI, neither of which is inconsequential for growth. Indeed, the lack of significance of XI for growth might be explained by the possible intermediation via other financial flows, such as remittances and external aid that help mitigate the transmission of XI into MI or KI.

As observed above, this finding of inconsequential independent adverse implications of XI for economic growth appears to be limited to low-income and primary-exporting economies such as those of SSA (Lutz, 1994). Furthermore, Fosu (1992b) corroborates this finding, observing that XI had a substantial adverse impact on non-African countries, despite its insignificance for African economies. In the case of Latin America (LA), moreover, even when the effect of KI is controlled for, the impact of XI remains negative and large, though statistically insignificant. "Unlike the case of SSA, however, XI appears to be non-extraneous for growth in LA, that is, accounting for it improves the goodness of fit of the growth equation." Fosu (2002c, p.13)

Therefore, despite the above observation of an insignificant independent effect of export instability on GDP growth, a stable flow of export earnings could help to increase growth, that is, to the extent that it mitigated instabilities in investment or imports. And so could instability-reducing flows of other financial resources, as well as the maintenance of sufficient levels of international reserves to help stabilize the flow of (capital) imports, in order to engender a more reliable and efficient production process (Fosu, 2001a). Unfortunately, the lack of such an inter-temporal capital-smoothing mechanism has engendered anti-growth "inter-temporal syndromes" that have contributed to the dismal growth records of many African countries, especially since the 1980s. (Fosu and O'Connell, 2006)

The Role of Real Exchange Rate Instability

Instability in the real exchange rate (RER) has been observed to also adversely affect economic growth. For example, on the basis of 1972-87 data on 33 SSA countries, Ghura and Grennes [1993] find a negative relationship between RER instability, on the one hand, and exports and investment, on the other. They do not, however, uncover a direct effect of RER instability on growth once the effect of RER misalignment is controlled for. Hence, the impact of RER instability on GDP growth appears to be indirect, that is, via investment, exports, or RER misalignment.

RER misalignment, synonymous with overvaluation of the real exchange rate in most African countries particularly in the early 1970s and in the 1980s, is now rare in Africa, thanks to the Bretton Woods-administered economic reforms in many of these countries. It seems reasonable to assume, therefore, that the direct effect on GDP growth of RER instability is less potent today than in previous years. Nonetheless, the indirect effects via investment or exports may still be consequential.

Instability of External Aid and Economic Growth

Recent studies suggest that through generating uncertainty in economic planning by domestic governments, the instability of external aid exerts adverse effects on economic growth. For example, Lensink and Morrissey (2000) uncover that the uncertainty of aid receipts reduces the growth effectiveness of external aid in developing countries generally. More importantly, this finding holds for their sub-sample of African countries as well. The predictability of external aid is, therefore, a salient dimension together with the actual level of aid in defining the development partnership agenda for Africa.

Secular Change versus Instability

Whether it is real exports, investment or imports, the evidence seems incontrovertible that secular declines in any of these variables would have negative effects on GDP growth.[8] Of greater concern for policy-making purposes, though, is the delineation between the implications of secular changes vis-a-vis instability of the international barter terms of trade (TOT), which are often exogenous to these countries' policies. The foregoing account suggests that instability in the terms of trade would have only weak implications for GDP growth. Might this result hold as well for the secular decline in terms of trade?

---

8 For African countries, many studies have estimated positive impacts on GDP growth: of exports (e.g., Fosu, 1990; Lussier, 1993); of imports (e.g., Savvides, 1995); and of investment (e.g., Fosu, 1990, 1991, 1992a, 1997; Gyimah-Brempong, 1991; Ojo and Oshikoya, 1995).

Studies reporting positive effects of TOT on African economic growth include: Rodrik (1998), Deaton and Miller (1996), Ghura (1995), Skinner (1987), and Wheeler (1984). For example, in a model where a large number of variables are controlled, including export growth and investment, Ghura (1995, table 5) estimates the impact of the growth of TOT on per capita GDP growth in a 1970-90 annual panel of 33 SSA countries as 0.059. This estimate represents one-half of the export growth effect reported therein, and suggests that a 10-percent deterioration in TOT would lead to per capita growth of about 0.6 percent. Furthermore, 0.6 percent is not paltry especially when compared with the 0.3 percent average per capita GDP growth over the sample period. With TOT also falling by 2.3 percent annually on average over the same period, the effect of this deterioration is estimated at 45 percent of the per capita GDP growth. The "direct" impact of the terms of trade is therefore considerable (Fosu, 2001b).

Deaton and Miller [1996, table 13] also estimate for SSA countries a contemporaneous elasticity of output with respect to international commodity prices of 0.4, and a three-year cumulative lag elasticity of about 0.6. They find further that the greatest impact of international commodity prices is on investment (Deaton and Miller, table 5).

Furthermore, based on a sample of SSA countries, Rodrik (1998) estimates from a per-capita-GDP growth equation a TOT coefficient of 0.17, which includes both the direct and indirect effects of TOT. Meanwhile, there was deterioration in SSA's TOT at an average of 2.0 percent per year over Rodrik's 1965-94 sample period. Thus, it is estimated that the diminution of growth attributable to TOT deterioration over this sample period constituted as much as 85 percent of the observed growth. (Fosu, 2001b, p. 298) That is, per capita growth could have nearly doubled in the absence of TOT deterioration.

The above findings clearly indicate that international terms of trade shocks are consequential for GDP growth in Africa. However, it is the secular changes in TOT that apparently matter. This trend impact is both direct and indirect via investment. In contrast, TOT instability (deviation from trend) has had little effect on growth in Africa.[9] The implication is that measures of instability that do not adequately remove the secular trend, at least in the case of TOT, would likely exhibit a negative impact on growth. Hence, it is important to properly delineate between these two components of price fluctuations. If secular price trends are what matter for growth, as observed above, then the appropriate policy would be to provide measures that limit such price declines, rather than those that minimize instability per se. For example, appropriate policies for reducing secular export price declines might entail supply limitations over time. In contrast, policies to smooth out export revenue inflows would help mitigate the potential effects of TOT instabilities.

---

9 This finding is further corroborated by Dehn (2000).

Effect of Political Instability

Consistent with the above definition, political instability (PI) exists if the political atmosphere deviates from an orderly government change.[10] Hence, the occurrence of coups d'etat, successful or abortive, connotes PI. Officially reported coup plots, by perturbing the normalcy of the perceived political environment, could similarly be viewed as PI as well. Furthermore, coups constitute "elite" PI, which is defined as: the forceful removal, or attempt or plot to remove, from office those holding leadership positions in a nation's political institutions (Morrison and Stevenson, 1971).

As observed above, African countries have experienced over 300 coup events during the post-independence period. This rampancy has not been benign to Africa's economic growth or development. For example, using an index of the above three forms of coup events, Fosu (1992a, 2001c) finds that elite PI has a deleterious impact on GDP growth of SSA. African countries classified as high-PI suffered a reduction in their annual GDP growth rates by an average of 1.2 percentage points, which constituted about one-third of the mean growth over the 1960-1986 sample period (Fosu, 1992a).

The PI impact is non-monotonic, however; though negative overall, it can actually be positive at sufficiently low levels of investment (Fosu, 2001c, 2002a). Furthermore, the effects on growth differ among the three types of elite PI. By far, the impact of the frequency of abortive coups is the most deleterious, followed by "successful" coups, and then by coup plots. Moreover, while the effect of the incidence of abortive coups is monotonically negative, that of successful coups may be positive at very low levels of investment (Fosu, 2002a). As argued (ibid, p. 341):

> One possible explanation is that, under depressed economic conditions, an attempted coup that fails is unlikely to ameliorate the negative expectations associated with such conditions, so that no positive expectations are generated. In contrast, a successful coup may engender the anticipation that the economic woes will probably improve, or the coup could effect an actual change in the status quo. Such improved expectations or change can be a stimulus to growth.

Because the above three types of coups are inter-related, however, it might be preferable to treat them jointly. Theoretically, a potential investor would likely formulate his/her decisions on the basis of the perceptions of the political atmosphere, which would reflect the cumulative presence of all three forms of coups. Based on 31 SSA countries over 1960-1986, Fosu (2001c) finds that a specification that includes the first principal component of the three types of coups is statistically superior to those containing them separately. Thus, the cumulative effect of these coup events is likely greater than the sum of their individual effects.

The above studies on the impact of PI on GDP growth employ the augmented production function that usually includes export growth as well as investment and

---

10 The present definition of PI deviates from that used by Alesina et al. (1996), for instance, who define PI as the propensity to change the executive by "constitutional" (orderly) as well as "unconstitutional" means.

the growth of labor as functional arguments. Therefore, to the extent that PI also adversely influences the levels of these variables, the above reported PI impacts may have been underestimated. For example, Gyimah-Brempong and Traynor (1999) find that PI reduces the level of investment.[11] Indeed, based on annual contemporaneous estimates, the authors find only a slightly larger direct growth effect than the indirect impact via investment.

Using a longer-run period of estimation,[12] however, Fosu (1992a) observes that much of the PI impact is via the productivity, rather than the level, of investment. Similarly, one would expect the adverse effect of PI on labor to be primarily on its productivity, as much of the human capital flight engendered by PI is likely to be the highly educated who enjoy relatively large expected values of marginal product of emigration.

PI and Export Performance

Exports may be particularly vulnerable to PI. The evidence is clear that African exports have not performed well since the 1980s, especially when compared to exports from developing countries generally. To what extent has PI contributed to this outcome? Fosu (2003) reports results showing that not only has elite PI adversely affected export performance in SSA, but also that the impact on export growth is substantially higher in magnitude than on GDP growth. Specifically, the effect of a unit change in an index of the three types of coup events would result in a reduction of GDP growth of 0.3 percent per year, compared with a decrease of 1.0 percent for exports (ibid., table 3). The estimated partial elasticities are 0.35 and 0.73, respectively (ibid.). That is, a 10 percent increase in elite PI would lead to a decrease of 3.5 percent in GDP growth, but as much as 7.3 percent in the rate of growth of exports. The relatively large export impact may be attributable to the competitive nature of exports coupled with the tendency for PI to raise the inefficiency and cost of production (Fosu, 2003). It seems reasonable to infer, therefore, that elite PI was an important culprit for the historically dismal performance of exports, as well as for GDP growth, in SSA.

Impacts of Other Forms of PI

Other forms of PI include open conflicts, in the form of armed insurrections such as civil wars, which have been relatively frequent in Africa since the early 1990s. Some 19 major conflicts ensued in Africa between 1990 and 2000 (Wallensteen and Sollenberg, 2001). The incidence of this type of PI has also been observed to account for a significant reduction in growth. For example, per capita GDP growth is estimated

---

11 Gyimah-Brempong and Traynor employ as a measure of PI that comprises more components than just coups d'etat, such as riots, strikes and mass insurrections. The strength of their measure is that it is relatively comprehensive. On the potential downside, however, it is unclear for policy purposes as to what components are actually driving the potency of the measure.

12 The estimation involves a twenty-year average.

to have fallen on average by 2.2 percentage points per year on average during civil wars, and by a mean of 2.1 percentage points annually over the consecutive five years thereafter (Collier, 1999).

It is also estimated that avoiding a "state breakdown", defined as primarily the incidence of open conflicts such as civil wars or, in rare cases, of extreme elite political instability, is a near-sufficient condition for preventing growth collapse.[13] The absence of a state breakdown is a necessary condition for sustainable growth, and could add as much as 2.5 percentage points per year to per capita GDP growth. (Fosu and O'Connell, 2006) These estimates are indeed huge, for per capita growth in SSA since independence in African countries has averaged less than 1 percent (Fosu, 2001b). As this form of instability is relatively recent,[14] however, the current review focuses on elite PI in the form of coups, which have historically received greater attention in the literature on African political and economic development.

PI and Aid Effectiveness

The reigning hypothesis has been that external aid succeeds in raising economic growth in only good-policies environments (Burnside and Dollar, 2000). More recent evidence, however, suggests that PI may actually constitute the mediating variable between external aid and growth. Islam (2005, p. 1467), for example, finds that "aid promotes growth only in a politically stable environment irrespective of the quality of the country's economic policies." Consequently, the role of PI is likely to transcend the traditional one of adversely influencing growth through the levels or productivities of traditional factors of production, and to serve as a conduit for the transmission of the effect of external aid.

An important lesson from this emerging evidence on the impact of aid is that in trying to enforce the practice of good governance, should donor conditionalities exacerbate the political situation and lead to higher PI, then aid may be ineffective in its objective to promote growth. Aid donors should, therefore, weigh the potential PI that may be engendered by conditionalities, at least in the short run, against the expected benefits in the long run from improved governance emanating from the conditionalities.

---

13 This condition is actually associated with a "syndrome-free" status; however, the most deleterious syndrome appears to be a state breakdown (Fosu and O'Connell, 2006; table 7).

14 Except for the immediate period around the time of independence, there were relatively few civil wars in African countries until the early 1990s. For example, according to the classification of the AERC Growth Project, the frequency of the episodes of state breakdown in 46 SSA countries, primarily in the form of civil wars, more than tripled after 1990 (Fosu, 2005). Thus, this type of conflict has now become a more important feature to contend with in the development process (Fosu and Collier, 2005). See also this study for both analytical and case studies on this form of PI in the context of post-conflict economies.

Instabilities and Development

The bulk of the evidence on the role of instabilities in economic development is through their impact on economic growth. Instabilities tend to reduce growth, and hence economic development. For example, a 10 percent reduction in the growth rate of GDP is estimated to reduce human or economic development, measured as an algebraic change in the Human Development Index (HDI), by as much as 3.6 percent (Fosu, 2004).

Instabilities may additionally affect the extent to which growth itself is transformed to development, however. The available evidence is on elite PI. Using cross-section data on SSA, for example, Fosu (2004) finds that elite PI, measured as a principal component of the frequencies of successful coups, abortive coups and coup plots, reduces the rate at which growth is transformed to human/economic development. Similarly, when development is measured by non-income components of HDI,[15] a similar result emerges (Fosu, 2002b).

As observed above, a country classified as high-PI could have its GDP growth reduced by about one-third, even when the levels of the production inputs were controlled (Fosu, 1992a, p. 836). Furthermore, GDP growth has a positive impact on human development (Fosu, 2004, 2002b, 2004). PI could, therefore, reduce human development directly by attenuating the rate at which GDP growth was transformed to human development, and by decreasing GDP growth itself. Taken together, it is estimated that PI could cumulatively reduce development by roughly 27 percent on average (Fosu, 2004). Thus, elite PI reduces human development in two ways. First, it could decrease the impact on growth either through the level of investment or directly through investment productivity. Second, elite PI might adversely influence the rate at which growth was transformed to human development.

Conclusion

The present chapter has reviewed the literature on instabilities and development in Africa. It finds that economic instabilities, particularly of investment and imports, tend to reduce economic growth and hence economic development. While the evidence is weak for the independent adverse implications of export instability, a more stable flow of export earnings could, nevertheless, help promote growth by reducing import and/or investment instability.

One way to ensure such an outcome of a stable flow of export earnings, as is usually advised, is for African countries to reduce their dependence on primary products that are more vulnerable to global demand shocks. Such export diversification is, however, realistically a long-term proposition. In the meantime, it would be judicious to create the institutional mechanism that built up international reserves in response to favorable terms of trade in order to insure against future inevitable deterioration in the trade terms. The lack of such a mechanism is believed to have resulted in "inter-

---

15 That is, human development (HD) is defined to exclude the income component and to comprise literacy and life expectancy (see Fosu, 2002b, footnote 7, p. 17).

temporal syndromes" in many African countries, contributing to their dismal growth records. (Fosu and O'Connell, 2006).

Also helpful would be other stabilizing international flows, such as inflows of remittances and external aid. Domestic polices to channel the former into more reliable capital accumulation would be particularly desirable. That would entail a greater stabilization of the investment environment generally for foreign investors, as well as policies that entice the Diaspora to renew their affinity to their respective countries of origin. Furthermore, as part of the currently evolving development partnership under "mutual accountability", ensuring a more predictable external aid flow would help to reduce both import and investment instabilities.

Additionally deleterious to growth is elite political instability (EPI), in the form of the rampancy of coups d'etat – successful, abortive or plots – that have afflicted most African countries since independence. Such events have adversely affected GDP growth mainly through their deleterious implications for both the level and productivity of investment. EPI could also entail the diminution of human capital, via emigration for instance. Indeed, a country classified as high-PI could result in a reduction by as much as one-third of a country's GDP growth rate.

Moreover, emerging evidence supports the view that EPI may also retard the rate at which growth is transformed to human development. The cumulative reduction of human development by EPI is estimated to be nearly 30 percent of the observed level of human development. The role of other forms of instabilities in the transformation process of growth to development requires additional research investigation.

Thus, the role of EPI in African development is large, and measures to attenuate it are indeed in order. Sadly, as observed above, the more recent period since 1980 has not necessarily been characterized by a reduction of the overall event levels of EPI. While the incidence of successful coups has decreased, that of abortive coups has actually increased. Unfortunately, this latter form of EPI may be even more insidious to growth than successful coups, as observed above.

The African Union seems to have been playing an important role recently through its legislative provision not to recognize governments that seize office via coups rather than by constitutional means. While this is a step in the right direction, the efficacy of such a provision, even if effectively enforced, would depend critically on its ability to deter coup attempts, to begin with. If it instead led to a greater frequency of coup attempts that fail, then the consequence for economic growth might be even more disastrous. Besides, it must be recalled that the historical ascendancy of the military in the political affairs of many African countries was itself necessitated, in the first place, by the lack of democratic processes to change governments (Fosu, 2005).

Recent attempts at democratization in most African countries will certainly help to minimize the tendency of the military to seize executive power. Yet, we must also guide against distributive politics that might lead to state failure (Bratton and van de Walle, 1997). As observed above, the incidence of state failure, the relatively recent and most extreme and deleterious form of political instability, has deprived Africa of the sustainable growth needed for poverty reduction and human development. Unfortunately, this form of political instability has assumed increased ascendancy since the early 1990s as other forms of anti-growth syndromes have waned in importance. The solution, then, is to ensure that all forms of PI are minimized.

Appropriate measures might include a democratic process that assures smooth government succession, which is more likely to keep the military at bay. In addition, the measures must obviate distributive politics and minimize the likelihood of civil wars. As we have observed, avoiding this form of political instability is necessary for the sustained growth required for economic development on the African continent.

References

Alesina, A., S. Ozler, N. Roubini, and P. Swagel, 1996. "Political Instability and Economic Growth," *Journal of Economic Growth* 1 (June), 189-211.

Alesina, A. and R. Perotti, 1994. "The Political Economy of Growth: A Critical Survey of the Recent Literature," *World Bank Economic Review* 8(3)(September), 351-371.

Bratton, Michael and Nicolas van de Walle (1997). *Democratic Experiments in Africa* (Cambridge: Cambridge University Press).

Burnside, C. and D. Dollar, 2000. "Aid, Policies and Growth," *American Economic Review* 90(4), 847-68.

Collier, Paul, 1999. "On The Economic Consequences of Civil War," *Oxford Economic Papers* 51, 168-83.

Collier, Paul, Anke Hoeffler and Catherine Pattillo (2004). "Africa's Exodus: Capital Flight and the Brain Drain as Portfolio Decisions," *Journal of African Economies*, Supplement 2, 13(0), ii15-54.

Deaton, Angus and Ron Miller, 1996. "International Commodity Prices, Macroeconomic Performance and Politics in Sub-Saharan Africa," *Journal of African Economies*, Vol. 5, No. 3, supplement, pp. 99-191.

Dehn, J., 2000. "The Effects on Growth of Commodity Price Uncertainty and Shocks," World Bank Policy Research Working Paper Series No. 2455, Washington, DC.

Fosu, A. K., 1991. "Capital Instability and Economic Growth in Sub-Saharan Africa," *Journal of Development Studies* 28(1), 74-85.

_____, 1992a. "Political Instability and Economic Growth: Evidence from Sub-Saharan Africa," *Economic Development and Cultural Change* 40(4)(July), 829-841.

_____, 1992b. "Effect of Export Instability on Economic Growth in Africa," *Journal of Developing Areas* 26(3)(April), 323-332.

_____, 1997. "Instabilities and Economic Growth in Contemporary Africa: The Role of Export Price Instability," in Thomas D. Boston, ed., *A Different Vision: Race and Public Policy*, London and New York: Routledge, 401-409.

_____, 2001a. "Economic Fluctuations and Growth in Sub-Saharan Africa: The Importance of Import Instability," *Journal of Development Studies* 37(3), 71-84.

_____, 2001b. "The Global Setting and African Economic Growth," *Journal of African Economies*, 10(3), 282-310.

_____, 2001c. "Political Instability and Economic Growth: Some Specification Empirics," *Economics Letters* 70(2), 289-294.

_____, 2002a. "Political Instability and Economic Growth: Implications of Coup Events in Sub-Saharan Africa," *American Journal of Economics and Sociology* 61(1), 329-348.

_____, 2002b. "Transforming Growth to Human Development in Sub-Saharan Africa: The Role of Elite Political Instability," *Oxford Development Studies* 30(1)(February), 9-19.

_____, 2002c. "Economic Volatilities and Growth in Latin America: Comparative Evidence with Sub-Saharan Africa on Export versus Capital Instability," *Economia Internazionale/ International Economics*, 55(1), pp. 1-16.

_____, 2004. "Mapping Growth into Economic Development: Has Elite Political Instability Mattered in Sub-Saharan Africa?" *American Journal of Economics and Sociology* 63(5), 137-156.

_____, 2005. "Anti-Growth Syndromes in Africa: A Synthesis of the Case Studies," paper presented at the AERC/Weatherhead Center Workshop on Explaining African Economic Growth, Harvard University, Cambridge, MA, March 18–19.

Fosu, A. K. and P. Collier, eds., 2005. *Post-conflict Economies in Africa*, New York: Palgrave Macmillan.

Fosu, A. K. and S. A. O'Connell, 2006. "Explaining African Economic Growth: The Role of Anti-growth Syndromes," *Annual Bank Conference on Development Economics (ABCDE)*, (Francois Bourguignon and Boris Pleskovic, eds.) Washington, DC: World Bank, 31-66.

Friedman, M., 1977. "Nobel Lecture: Inflation and Unemployment," *Journal of Political Economy*, June, 451-472.

Ghura, Dhaneshwar, 1995. "Macro Policies, External Forces, and Economic Growth in Sub-Saharan Africa," *Economic Development and Cultural Change* 43(4)(July), 759-778.

Ghura, Dhaneswar and Thomas J. Grennes, 1993. "The Real Exchange Rate and Macroeconomic Performance in Sub-Saharan Africa," *Journal of Development Economics* 42(1), 155-174.

Guillaumont, P., S. Jeanneney-Guillaumont and J-F Brun, 1999. "How Instability Lowers African Growth," *Journal of African Economies*, 8(1), 87-107.

Gyimah-Brempong, Kwabena, 1991. "Export Instability and Economic Growth in Sub-Saharan Africa," *Economic Development and Cultural Change*, 39(4) (July), 815-828.

Gyimah-Brempong, Kwabena and Thomas Traynor, 1999. "Political Instability, Investment and Economic Growth in Sub-Saharan Africa," *Journal of African-Economies* 8(1), 52-86.

Helleiner, G. K., 1986. "Outward Orientation, Import Instability and African Economic Growth: An Empirical Investigation," in S. Lall and F. Stewart, eds, *Theory and Reality in Development*, London: Macmillan, Chapter 9, 139-153.

Islam, M. N., 2005. "Regime Changes, Economic Policies and the Effect of Aid on Growth," *Journal of Development Studies* 41(8), 1339-1368.

Lensink, R. and O. Morrissey, 2000. "Aid Instability as a Measure of Uncertainty and the Positive Impact of Aid on Growth," *Journal of Development Studies* 36(3), (February), 31-49.

Lussier, M., 1993. "Impacts of Exports on Economic Performance: A Comparative Study," *Journal of African Economies*, 2: 106-127.

Lutz, Matthias, 1994. "The Effects of Volatility in the Terms of Trade on Output Growth: New Evidence," *World Development* 22(12), 1959-1975.

McGowan, Patrick J., 2003. "African Military Coup d'etat, 1956-2001: Frequency, Trends and Distribution," *Journal of Modern African Studies*, April.

Moran, C., 1983. "Export Fluctuations and Economic Growth: An Empirical Analysis," *Journal of Development Economics* 12(1-2), 195-218.

Morrison, Donald G. and Hugh Michael Stevenson, 1971. "Political Instability in Independent Black Africa: More Dimensions of Conflict Resolution Within Nations," *Journal of Conflict Resolution* 15 (September), 347-368.

Ojo, Oladeji and Oshikoya, Temitope, 1995. "Determinants of Long-Term Growth: Some African Results," *Journal of African Economies*. 4(2), 163-91.

Rodrik, D., 1991. "Policy Uncertainty and Private Investment in Developing Countries," *Journal of Development Economics*, 36, 229-242.

_____, 1998. "Trade Policy and Economic Performance in Sub-Saharan Africa," NBER Working Paper No. 6562, Cambridge, MA.

Savvides, A., 1984. "Export Instability and Economic Growth: Some New Evidence," *Economic Development and Cultural Change* 32, 607-14.

_____, 1995. "Economic growth in Africa," *World Development* 23(3), 449-458.

Skinner, Jonathan, 1987. "Taxation and Output Growth: Evidence from African Countries," NBER Working Paper No. 2335.

Wallensteen, P. and M. Sollenberg, 2001. "Armed Conflict 1989-2000," *Journal of Peace Research*, 38(5), pp. 629-644.

Wheeler, David, 1984. "Sources of Stagnation in Sub-Saharan Africa," *World Development*, Vol. 12, pp. 1-23.

Chapter 9

Trade Regimes, Liberalization and Macroeconomic Instability in Africa

Chantal Dupasquier and Patrick N. Osakwe

Introduction

The role of trade policy in economic development has been the subject of recent studies and vigorous debates among economists and policymakers. The prevailing, and still popular, view is that countries with more liberal or open trade policies have better economic performance than those with restrictive trade policies (Sachs and Warner 1995; Krueger 1998). Proponents of this view argue that liberal trade policies enable countries to produce and allocate resources more efficiently, access new ideas and technologies, and have access to cheap foreign consumption goods.[1] Recently, this view has been questioned by prominent economists. For example, Stiglitz (2002) stresses that there is no conclusive evidence that more open economies have higher growth rates. Rodriguez and Rodrik (2000) have also argued that methodological problems with the empirical strategies used in examining the link between trade policy and growth make it difficult to argue that there is a systematic inverse relationship between trade barriers and economic growth. They stress, however, that their analysis or interpretation of the evidence does not mean that trade protectionism is good for growth. It simply means that, contrary to the claims of proponents of trade liberalization, it is hard to find any systematic relationship between trade policy and economic performance in regressions. This reflects largely the fact that the relationship between the two variables differs across countries and so is difficult to pick up in cross-section or panel data.

In Africa, there is a renewed and increasing interest in the role of trade policy in economic performance (Rodrik 1998a). This is due largely to the disappointing economic performance of most countries in the region in the last two decades and attempts to explain why they have not done well relative to developing countries in Asia and Latin America. For example, between 1980 and 2002 Sub-Saharan Africa's share of world trade fell from 4.6 percent to less than 1.8 percent. Real

---

1   Despite the theoretical or potential advantages of a liberal trade policy, it is common knowledge that countries are generally hesitant to embark upon aggressive trade reforms. For example, the Fifth WTO Ministerial Conference held in Cancun, in September 2003, collapsed in part because trade Ministers, from both developed and developing countries, were reluctant to make serious and binding commitments on eliminating existing trade barriers (see Evenett 2003).

Gross Domestic Product (GDP) per capita declined by 1.2 percent over the period 1981-1990 and by 0.4 percent over the 1991-2000 period. In contrast, in East Asia, real GDP per capita grew by 5.7 percent from 1981-90 and by 6.4 percent from 1991-2000 (World Bank 2003). Various explanations have been adduced for Africa's dismal economic performance. These include poor domestic economic policies, geography, colonial legacy, political instability, weak institutions, and an inhospitable external environment. While it is generally acknowledged that the inward-looking trade policies pursued in the region since independence contributed to its poor export performance, the link to growth performance is not well established (Rodrik 1998a).

That said, it is often argued that African countries are very reluctant to open up their economies.[2] Sharer (1999) points out that most countries in Sub-Saharan Africa have not implemented trade reforms on a sustained basis as in other developing countries, particularly those in East Asia and Latin America. Oyejide (1998) and Rodrik (1998b) argue that trade reforms in the region are replete with policy interruptions and reversals. This largely reflects the fact that policymakers have not accepted that opening their economies to trade is the best way to achieve their development aspirations.

Among the reasons why governments have this attitude towards international trade a first is that as trade taxes account for a significant portion of government revenue developments in the external sector affect government finance and spending and the overall economy.[3] For the period 1999-2001, in the Least Developed Countries in Africa import duties as a percentage of total revenue was 34 percent compared to 20 percent for the same category of countries in Asia and 15 percent for developing countries as a whole.

Second, because of the small and underdeveloped nature of African economies as well as the power imbalances in the multilateral trading system there is apprehension that they will not be able to compete in the international market. Third, trade reforms harm the interests of some groups while generating positive welfare benefits for others.[4] In the absence of domestic safety nets and mechanisms to compensate

---

2 Mayda and Rodrik (2005) provide an interesting analysis of why some individuals and countries are more protectionist than others. They show that pro-trade preferences are positively correlated with an individual's level of education and relative economic status. They are, however, negatively correlated with the degree of nationalism/patriotism and the trade exposure of the sector in which an individual is employed. Guisinger (2003) argues that diffusion mechanisms provide a good explanation of the trade policy choices of countries. The paper treats diffusion as a competitive process where countries emulate the trade liberalization of similar countries.

3 This is related to the idea that multilateral trade reform and the associated obligations will deny African governments the policy instruments and space needed to address pressing development problems.

4 Davidson and Matusz (2004) explore the best way to compensate those who lose from trade liberalization. They focus on four labour market policies: wage subsidies, employment subsidies, unemployment assistance and training subsidies. They argue that a temporary targeted wage subsidy is the best way to compensate those who bear the cost of adjusting to

potential losers policymakers tend to be hesitant about increasing the pace of reforms for fear of triggering political unrest.

Third, most African countries rely on the export of a few commodities and so are wary that the more open their economies the more exposed they would be to external shocks, with potential consequences for the stability of key macroeconomic variables such as output, consumption, investment, and government revenue. Pindyck (1991) provides mechanisms through which uncertainty and volatility can have negative effects on investment. Several other studies show that volatility has consequences for economic performance in developing countries (Basu and McLeod 1992; Bleaney and Greenaway 2001). Clearly, African countries are concerned about macroeconomic volatility and vulnerability to external shocks because they do not have good markets to insure agents against risk and they also do not have well-diversified production structures. Available data indicate that in 2002 the export concentration index for Africa was 0.49, which is twice the figure for developing countries and four times that for developed economies (see Table 9.1). Other features that make the region vulnerable to external shocks include the heavy dependence on agriculture and the high degree of indebtedness (see Table 9.2).

Table 9.1 Selected Indicators on African Economies

Indicator	Africa	Developing economies	Developed economies
No. of commodities exported			
• 1992	116	199	231
• 2002	123	210	231
Export concentration index			
• 1992	0.57	0.25	0.10
• 2002	0.49	0.23	0.12
Export diversification index*			
• 1992	0.82	0.60	0.35
• 2002	0.79	0.55	0.35

Source: UNCTAD (2004a)
* Note that this index is constructed such that values close to 1 represent less export diversification.

---

reform while a temporary targeted employment subsidy is the best way to compensate those who are trapped in the previously protected sector.

Table 9.2 Structure of African Economies (% of GDP)

Variable	1980	1990	2000
Agriculture	16.9	17.3	15.3
Industry	41.1	33.0	33.3
• Manufacturing	11.7	14.1	12.7
Services	38.5	44.0	45.7
Merchandise Exports	24.4*	23.1	28.2
Merchandise Imports	23.9*	21.5	24.8
External Debt	29.1	59.0	53.4

Source: World Bank (2004)
* Data for 1984

The idea that trade liberalization could lead to macroeconomic instability is not new in the literature. What is surprising, however, is that there is, so far, limited empirical evidence dealing with the subject. Razin and Rose (1992) examined the impact of openness on volatility of macroeconomic variables using data for 138 countries spanning the period 1950-88. They found no relationship between openness and volatility. On the other hand, Rodrik (1998c) found that the volatility of national income is higher in more open economies. This is consistent with the recent empirical finding of Easterly and Kraay (2000) that small states have higher volatility of national income due in part to their higher volatility of terms of trade shocks. They ascribe the high volatility of terms of trade shocks in small states to their greater openness. It should be noted that a common feature of the abovementioned studies is that they use data for both developed and developing countries and so do not specifically address issues of interest to African countries.

There is a small body of literature on the sources of macroeconomic volatility in African economies. Using a vector autoregression (VAR) framework, Deaton and Miller (1996) provide evidence on the importance of commodity-based terms of trade shocks. Their study suggests that these shocks play an important role in macroeconomic fluctuations in Africa. Hoffmaister, Roldos, and Wickham (1998) use a structural VAR model to examine the relative importance of external and domestic shocks in macroeconomic fluctuations in Africa. They conclude that domestic shocks account for the bulk of movements in output. They also show that although external shocks play a minor role in output fluctuation, they tend to be more important in CFA compared to non-CFA African countries, reflecting the fact that the former has a fixed exchange rate regime and so the exchange rate cannot respond to terms of trade shocks. Using a stochastic, dynamic, general equilibrium model, Kose and Reizman (2001) present evidence that a large fraction of the volatility of macroeconomic variables in African countries is attributable to trade shocks. They also show that trade shocks account for 87 percent of the variation in investment, 45 percent of the variation in output, 79 percent of the variation in consumption, and 80 percent of the variation in labour supply. Furthermore, their analyses suggest that in contrast with other types of disturbances, adverse trade shocks cause prolong recessions in Africa.

In this chapter the hypothesis that a more open trade regime leads to higher instability or volatility in macroeconomic variables in Africa is tested for a panel of 33 African countries for which data is available. The study contributes to the existing literature in several ways. First, in contrast to Deaton and Miller (1996) and Hoffmaister et. al. (1998), we consider instabilities in consumption and investment; this because instabilities in output do not imply instabilities in other macroeconomic variables. For example, a country with a very volatile output may not experience instabilities in consumption if consumers can borrow to smooth over consumption. Besides, output instability is of less concern and consequence to households than consumption instability.[5] Kose and Reizman (2001) also considered instabilities in consumption and investment, but they used a different framework and did not examine explicitly the role of trade regimes. Our research does that. In particular, we considered three measures of trade policy regimes: one based on outcome or practice (trade/GDP ratio); one based on policy incidence (tariff and non-tariff barriers); and one based on the conventional wisdom that African countries have been relatively more open since the 1990s (Hinkle, Herrou-Aragon, and Kubota 2003).

The second contribution is that we account for key potential sources of macroeconomic instability in Africa. In the discourse on Africa's economic performance some authors argue that institutional quality, climatic disasters (for example, high incidence of drought), severity of debt and geography play important roles in explaining differences in macroeconomic outcomes across countries (Collier and Gunning 1999; Rodrik 1999; Sachs 2003). Unlike previous studies, we control for these factors in our estimations. Third, we use both single and system statistical estimation techniques and conduct a battery of sensitivity analysis to examine the robustness of our results.

The organization of the chapter is as follows. The next section presents stylized facts on macroeconomic instability in Africa over the 1986-2000 period whilst the section following provides brief background information on Africa's experience with trade liberalization. Standard theoretical explanations for the link between trade liberalization and macroeconomic instability are then analysed, followed by a presentation and discussion on the results of the estimations. The final section examines the policy implications of the analyses and offers some recommendations on how to deal with vulnerability to external shocks and reduce macroeconomic instability in African countries.

---

5   There is also a literature on revenue instability. See for example, Bleaney, Gemmell and Greenaway (1995). They argue that tax revenue instability is high in Less Developed Countries (LDCs) and are highest in open economies with low per capita income, high output variance, and inflationary problems.

Macroeconomic Instability in Africa

This section focuses on instability in three key macroeconomic variables for which we have data: real output per capita; real consumption per capita; and real investment per capita. Instability is measured by the standard deviation of macroeconomic variables. For ease of analysis, we have classified the countries in the sample into three categories depending on whether they have high, moderate, or low macroeconomic volatility. More specifically, for each variable of interest, a country is classified as high volatility if it has standard deviation greater than 5. It is classified as moderate volatility if it has standard deviation less than 5 but greater than 2. Countries with standard deviation less than or equal to 2 are classified as low volatility. The results based on this classification of the data are presented in Tables 9.3 to 9.5.

Table 9.3 Output Volatility

Country Classification*	1986-90	1991-95	1996-2000
High volatility	Swaziland, Gabon, Mozambique, Ethiopia, Cameroon, Mali, Sierra Leone	Rwanda, Cote d'Ivoire, Togo, Malawi, Ethiopia, Sierra Leone, Morocco, Zimbabwe, Mozambique, Comoros, Zambia	Guinea-Bissau, Sierra Leone, Rwanda, Lesotho, Morocco, Zimbabwe
Moderate volatility	Morocco, Burkina Faso, Botswana, Nigeria, Cote d'Ivoire, Tunisia, Lesotho, Congo Rep, Guinea-Bissau, Comoros, Rwanda, Zimbabwe, Zambia, Mauritania, Togo, Uganda, Senegal, Malawi, Algeria	Mali, Congo Rep, Gabon, Madagascar, Uganda, Burkina Faso, Cameroon, Senegal, Algeria, South Africa, Tunisia, Kenya	Togo, Gabon, Congo Rep, Ethiopia, Mozambique, Cote d'Ivoire, Zambia, Burkina Faso, Comoros
Low volatility	South Africa, Egypt, Mauritius, Gambia, Madagascar, Kenya, Ghana	Botswana, Nigeria, Guinea-Bissau, Egypt, Mauritania, Swaziland, Gambia, Ghana, Mauritius, Lesotho	Malawi, Uganda, Algeria, Mali, Kenya, Gambia, South Africa, Nigeria, Botswana, Madagascar, Mauritania, Tunisia, Mauritius, Swaziland, Egypt, Ghana, Senegal, Cameroon

* A country is classified as high volatility if it has standard deviation greater than 5. It is classified as moderate volatility if it has standard deviation less than 5 but greater than 2. Countries with standard deviation less than or equal to 2 are classified as low volatility.

Table 9.4 Consumption Volatility

Country Classification*	1986-90	1991-95	1996-2000
High volatility	Guinea-Bissau, Gabon, Swaziland, Zimbabwe, Mauritania, Zambia, Cameroon, Sierra Leone, Ethiopia, Togo, Burkina Faso, Cote d"Ivoire, Malawi, Gambia, Nigeria, Botswana, Rwanda, Morocco, Mali, Kenya, Madagascar, Mozambique, Algeria	Malawi, Comoros, Sierra Leone, Zambia, Guinea-Bissau, Zimbabwe, Togo, Ethiopia, Mozambique, Mauritania, Swaziland, Nigeria, Morocco, Congo Rep, Rwanda, Gabon, Botswana, Kenya, Cameroon, Cote d'Ivoire, Lesotho, Burkina Faso, Mali	Sierra Leone, Congo Rep, Ghana, Malawi, Nigeria, Guinea-Bissau, Zimbabwe, Togo, Lesotho, Mauritania, Rwanda, Botswana, Gambia, Comoros, Burkina Faso, Morocco, Kenya, Ethiopia, Mozambique, Swaziland
Moderate volatility	Congo Rep, Lesotho, Mauritius, Tunisia, Uganda, Egypt, Senegal	Uganda, Gambia, Algeria, Senegal, Ghana, South Africa	Cameroon, Cote d"Ivoire, Zambia, Senegal, Mali, Uganda
Low volatility	South Africa, Ghana, Comoros	Madagascar, Tunisia, Egypt, Mauritius	Algeria, Madagascar, South Africa, Gabon, Egypt, Tunisia, Mauritius

* A country is classified as high volatility if it has standard deviation greater than 5. It is classified as moderate volatility if it has standard deviation less than 5 but greater than 2. Countries with standard deviation less than or equal to 2 are classified as low volatility.

Table 9.5 Investment Volatility

Country Classification*	1986-90	1991-95	1996-2000
High volatility	Sierra Leone, Gabon, Swaziland, Ethiopia, Zambia, Nigeria, Guinea-Bissau, Congo Rep, Malawi, Mauritania, Tunisia, Lesotho, Uganda, Ghana, Botswana, South Africa, Zimbabwe, Cameroon, Mali, Gambia, Madagascar, Morocco, Togo, Algeria, Mauritius, Senegal, Comoros, Burkina Faso, Cote d'Ivoire, Egypt, Rwanda, Kenya	Rwanda, Sierra Leone, Ghana, Comoros, Guine-Bissau, Togo, Congo rep, Zambia, Madagascar, Malawi, Nigeria, Ethiopia, Cote d'Ivoire, Burkina Faso, Uganda, Mauritania, Morocco, Swaziland, Mali, Cameroon, Mozambique, Egypt, Zimbabwe, Gabon, Kenya, Tunisia, Gambia, South Africa, Lesotho, Algeria, Senegal	Swaziland, Congo Rep, Ghana, Mozambique, Cote d'Ivoire, Gabon, Guine-Bissau, Mauritania, Togo, Zimbabwe, Gambia, Mali, Nigeria, Rwanda, Morocco, Comoros, Malawi, Senegal, Ethiopia, Burkina Faso, Uganda, South Africa, Botswana, Madagascar, Egypt, Lesotho, Zambia
Moderate volatility	Mozambique	Mauritius, Botswana	Kenya, Mauritius, Sierra Leone, Cameroon, Tunisia
Low volatility			Algeria

* A country is classified as high volatility if it has standard deviation greater than 5. It is classified as moderate volatility if it has standard deviation less than 5 but greater than 2. Countries with standard deviation less than or equal to 2 are classified as low volatility.

The first point to be made from these tables is that for most countries in the sample, the volatility pattern has changed significantly over time. For example, over the 1986-90 period Algeria had moderate output volatility but highly volatile consumption and investment. However, over the 1996-2000 period it had low volatility in output, consumption and investment.

Second, investment is generally more volatile than consumption and output. For example, while Egypt and South Africa had highly volatile investment over the 1996-2000 period, the volatilities of output and consumption over the same period was low. This is in line with the results of several studies that investment is the most volatile component of aggregate demand.

Third, more countries seem to have lower output and, to a lesser extent, consumption and investment volatility in the 1996-2000 period compared to 1986-90. In the former period, 7 countries had low output volatility while in the latter period there were 18 countries. As for consumption, a change is also noticeable although to a much lesser degree. While 3 countries had low consumption volatility over the 1986-90 period, the number increased to 7 over the 1996-2000 period. Investment seems to be the only variable where there has not been any significant change in the number of countries with low volatility. It is interesting to note that in 10 of the 18 countries that had low output volatility over the 1996-2000 period, there was a significant reduction in tariffs over the same period. For example, in Uganda average tariffs was 25 percent in the 1986-90 period but fell to 10.9 percent in 1996-2000. Similarly, over the same period, average tariffs fell from 22.3 to 15.9 percent in Mauritania whilst in Kenya they fell from 40.3 to 17.7 percent. These facts suggest that the reduction of trade barriers do not necessarily lead to greater volatility in macroeconomic variables. The pace and sequencing of trade liberalization as well as the nature of domestic economic and social policies may play a role in determining the extent of macroeconomic instability in an economy.

Trade Policy and Liberalization in Africa

In the 1970s, most countries in Africa used trade restriction as an important instrument for protecting domestic industries and for economic development in general. Since the mid-1980s, some countries in the region have adopted a more outward-looking development strategy. Efforts have been made to reduce and or eliminate exchange controls, export taxes, and import-export monopolies. The move from quantitative controls to tariffs as the main instrument of protection was also a key component of the trade reform programmes. In general, trade reforms in the region have been implemented under three platforms. First, countries that sought assistance under the IMF/World Bank Structural Adjustment Programmes were compelled to embark on unilateral trade liberalization as a major component of macroeconomic stabilization. There was also unilateral liberalization in response to positive external shocks, as occurred in Kenya and Tanzania during the commodity booms of 1976-77. The second source of reforms is membership of regional economic groupings.[6] As members of regional economic groups several countries had to implement certain trade reforms, although the scale or extent of liberalization is quite small. Finally, African countries have also taken part in multilateral trade reforms as a result of their membership of the World Trade Organization (WTO).

Trade reform in Africa occurred in three stages. The first involved the rationalization of tariffs; a number of countries in the region have completed this process. The second focused on the reduction of tariff dispersion. This typically means reducing high tariffs and increasing the lowest tariffs, as done in several countries. The final stage, which is still on-going, is the reduction of average tariffs.

Ancharaz (2003) provides evidence on the determinants of trade reforms in Sub-Saharan Africa. His study suggests that larger aid flows, higher levels of urbanization, a strong current account position, economic crises, and a relatively large manufacturing sector enhance the probability that trade reform is adopted. In

---

6 There are several economic communities in the region. These include the Economic Community of West African States (ECOWAS), Common Market for Eastern and Southern Africa (COMESA), Southern Africa Development Community (SADC), West African Economic and Monetary Union (WAEMU), Southern Africa Customs Union (SACU), and Communaute Economique et Monetaire de l'Afrique Centrale (CEMAC).

addition, heavy dependence on trade taxes, greater import competition, and a large government make trade reform less likely.

Although most trade reforms in Africa were initiated in the second half of the 1980s, substantial progress was not observed until the 1990s (Hinkle, Herrou-Aragon, and Kubota 2003).[7] This is illustrated by the fact that in 1980-85 average tariffs in sub-Saharan Africa was 30 percent. But by 1996-98 it had declined to roughly 18 percent (Martin 2003). Table 9.6 presents information on trade liberalization episodes in selected African countries.

Table 9.6 Trade Liberalization Episodes in Selected Countries

Countries	Liberalization starting year	Liberalization episodes
Benin	1988	1990-1994
Burkina Faso	1991	1992-present
Burundi	2002	2002-present
Cape Verde	1987	1997-2001
Ethiopia	1992	1996-present
Gambia	1985	1985-1988
Guinea	1985	1985-1997
Lesotho	1984	1994-1999
Madagascar	1988	1988-1996
Malawi	1988	1997-2001
Mali	1986	1991-2000
Mauritania	1992	1992-1997
Mozambique	1987	1992-1993
Senegal	1986	1994-present
Sudan	1992	1996-2000
Togo	1988	1988-1996
Uganda	1981	1991-1996
Tanzania	1984	1990-present
Zambia	1982	1992-1995

Source: UNCTAD (2004b)

---

7   For example, in 1990 no country in the region had trade regimes that could be classified as open based on the IMF's Index of Aggregate Trade Restrictiveness. By 2001, however, 43 percent of African countries' trade regimes were classified as open (Sharer 2001).

Table 9.6 shows that the pace of reform differs across countries. In the fast liberalizers, reforms occurred within 1-5 years. Countries in this category include Benin, Cape Verde, Gambia, Malawi, Mozambique, Sudan and Zambia. On the other hand, in countries such as Guinea, Lesotho, Mali, and Togo it was gradual and occurred within 6 to 15 years. In countries such as Burkina Faso, Burundi, and Ethiopia the process is still ongoing.

While there is agreement that countries in Africa made substantial progress in opening up their economies in the 1990s, trade policy is still regarded by some analysts as more protectionist than those of its trading partners and competitors (Sharer 1999; Hinkle, Herrou-Aragon, and Kubota 2003). This conclusion is based on the fact that average tariffs are higher than the world average. For example, in 2004, average tariff in African countries was 17.1 percent compared with the world average of 12.1 percent. However, one must be very cautious in using tariff changes alone as an indicator of changes in trade regimes because a country may achieve tariff reduction by simply substituting non-tariff barriers for tariffs. This is an important point because although average tariffs in Africa are high, recent evidence indicates that core non-tariff barriers in Africa are lower than for several developing countries. For example, in 1995-98 core non-tariff barriers in sub-Saharan Africa was 10.4 percent while it was 58.3 and 16.3 percent respectively for South Asia and East Asia and the Pacific (Martin 2003).

Transmission Mechanisms and Empirical Methodology

There are two standard explanations for the relationship between trade liberalization and macroeconomic instability (McCulloch, Winters and Cirera 2001). The first is based on the fact that trade liberalization enables countries to exploit economies of scale and specialize in the production of goods in which they have a comparative advantage. The increase in specialization results in more competitiveness as countries are forced to reallocate resources to sectors where they can be utilized more efficiently given existing resource endowments. Although the increase in specialization raises national income, it also increases a country's vulnerability to industry-specific shocks and so may lead to more macroeconomic instability. The problem is even more acute for countries that specialize in the production of primary commodities whose prices experience wide fluctuations. It is also compounded in economies that do not have domestic insurance markets for risk.

The second explanation for the alleged relationship between trade liberalization and macroeconomic instability is that liberalization exposes countries to external shocks and so increases the importance of foreign, relative to domestic, shocks. The idea is that if foreign shocks are large relative to domestic shocks, and if there is either positive or no correlation between the two shocks, trade liberalization will increase the overall risk faced by a country. If however foreign shocks are either relatively small or are negatively correlated with domestic shocks, trade liberalization is likely to reduce overall risk.

One simple method to examine the relationship between trade liberalization and macroeconomic instability is to identify periods in a country's history in which trade policy was restricted and periods in which trade policy was liberal and then compute the variances of the relevant variables across the two samples and test whether or not they are significantly different. This is similar to the "before and after" type of analysis employed by some authors to study the impact of economic policies, programmes, and events in developing countries (Killick 1995; Crafts 1999). The key drawback of this approach is that it implicitly assumes that trade liberalization is the only source of macroeconomic instability. In general, this is not the case. Volatilities in inflation and terms of trade as well as political instability, the nature of fiscal policy, and financial depth, may also affect macroeconomic volatility.

Another approach is to run a regression with volatility as the dependent variable and a measure of trade policy regimes as one of the explanatory variables. This is the standard approach employed in the literature. Its strength is that it allows the researcher to control for factors, other than trade policy, that affect macroeconomic instability. This is the approach we adopt. In particular, we estimate versions of the following equation:

$$V_{it} = \alpha + \beta TP_{it} + \sum_{j} \lambda_j X_{jt} + \varepsilon_{it} \tag{1}$$

where i denotes a country, t denotes time, and:

- V is a measure of instability,
- TP is a measure of trade policy or regime,
- X is a set of control variables,
- α and λ are nuisance coefficients, and
- ε is a well-behaved residual.

In the equations we estimate, the coefficient of interest is β. If this coefficient is significantly different from zero then we have evidence that trade liberalization has a significant impact on macroeconomic instability. Given that the dependent variable in each equation is a measure of instability and this can only be estimated over time, all variables used in the analysis are computed over non-overlapping five-year intervals from annual data spanning the period 1986-2000. More specifically, the five-year intervals are 1986-90, 1991-1995, and 1996-2000. This approach yields three observations for each of the 33 countries in the sample.[8] Each of the dependent variables used in the estimation is defined in terms of real per capita growth. Following Ramey and Ramey (1995), we define instability as the standard deviation of the annual growth rate of the variables of interest. For example, for output it is the standard deviation of the growth rate of real output per capita. Instability can also be defined in terms of the level of each variable as in Gavin

---

8 Note that Nigeria and Swaziland have two observations instead of three due to missing data.

and Hausman (1996) or the coefficient of variation as in Rose (2004).[9] Equation (1) is estimated using OLS with robust standard errors. It is also estimated using a system approach—the Seemingly Unrelated Regression (SURE) technique—which accounts for contemporaneous correlation across errors of equations in the system. Furthermore, we include dummies for oil exporters as well as severely indebted countries to control for the fact that oil importers and indebted countries may be more vulnerable to external shocks.

A very contentious issue in the literature on trade liberalization is how to measure the degree of restrictiveness of trade policy. This controversy has led to the development of various measures. Sachs and Warner (1995), Harrison (1996), and Edwards (1998) provide examples of these measures. Rodriguez and Rodrik (2000) present detailed but interesting critique of these measures. Given the lack of consensus on the most appropriate measure of trade policy regimes, it would be misleading to use one approach. This is particularly important because most of these measures are uncorrelated (see Pritchett (1996)). Our way of getting around this problem is to use three representative measures in the analysis. The first measure we use is the trade/GDP ratio, which is an outcome-based measure and so is referred to as openness by practice. The second measure is based on tariffs and non-tariff barriers and so is referred to as an incidence-based measure of openness. The final measure used is based on the popular view that African countries have been relatively more open to trade since the 1990s (Sharer 1999; Hinkle, Herrou-Aragon, and Kubota 2003). We call this openness based on conventional wisdom. Detailed information on the exact definition of variables used in the estimations is in the data appendix.

Another issue that needs to be addressed is the choice of control variables in the regressions. The approach we adopt is to include a broad set of potential explanatory variables suggested either by theory or by recent empirical literature.

- *Level of development*: The first control variable in the regression is per capita GDP, which was included to capture the size or level of development of the economy. Theory suggests a negative relationship between country size and volatility because large economies tend to have more diverse sectoral structures and so are more immune to sector-specific and external shocks (Head 1995; Acemoglu and Zilibotti 1997).
- *Distortionary macroeconomic policies*: As reflected in high inflation and exchange rate misalignment have been emphasized by several authors as sources of instability (see for example, Agenor et al. 2000). Since the volatility of inflation in our sample is highly correlated with that of the real exchange rate, to avoid multicollinearity we cannot include both variables in the same regression. Consequently, we use inflation volatility to capture the impact of distortionary macroeconomic policies.
- *Terms of trade volatility*: Based on the work of Razin, Sadka and Coury (2003) we include terms of trade volatility as a variable in the regressions. Deaton and Miller (1996) have also emphasized the importance of commodity-based

---

9 In the empirical analyses we tried these measures of volatility and found that there was no significant difference in the results.

terms of trade shocks in explaining macroeconomic volatility in Africa. Note that the terms of trade captures the effect of commodity prices since most African countries are exporters of primary commodities.

- *Fiscal policy*: Economic theory suggests that fiscal policy could be used to cushion the impact of shocks on macroeconomic variables (Kose, Prasad, and Terrones 2003). We examine whether or not fiscal policy is used in a manner that dampens macroeconomic volatility by including the ratio of fiscal deficit to GDP in our regressions.
- *Institutional quality*: Acemoglu et al (2003) and Rodrik (1999) emphasize the role of institutions in explaining macroeconomic outcomes. The idea is that institutional weaknesses make countries more vulnerable to external shocks. In other words, countries with very weak institutions have limited ability to cushion the impact of shocks and so are likely to have higher macroeconomic volatility. In the regressions, we use the type of political regime in a country—democratic or autocratic—as our proxy for institutional quality. Almeida and Ferreira (2002) present evidence that democracy is associated with less variable macroeconomic outcomes than autocracy. On the link between democracy, governance and growth see Rivera-Batiz (2002).
- *Geography*: There is a recent literature suggesting that geographic barriers to trade have implications for economic performance (Sachs 2003). For example, it has been suggested that countries that are landlocked or separated from large markets, are likely to have more concentrated export structures and so are predisposed to experience more macroeconomic volatility (Malik and Temple 2005). There are two reasons why landlocked countries may have less diversified exports. The first is that they tend to have high transport costs and this limits their ability to develop competitive manufacturing industries. Radelet and Sachs (1998) show that there is a strong link between high shipping costs and low manufacturing export growth. The second reason is that their limited access to external markets forces them to specialize in a few export commodities. To capture the impact of geographic barriers we include a dummy variable for landlocked countries.
- Climatic disasters such as droughts, floods, and extreme weather conditions have also been identified as possible sources of macroeconomic instability in poor countries (Raddatz 2005). To control for this potential source of instability in the regressions we include the incidence of severe drought as a proxy for climatic disasters.
- *Financial development*: we also control for the degree of domestic financial development, as measured by credit to the private sector as a proportion of total domestic credit. Theory suggests at least two ways in which the degree of financial development can affect the volatility of macroeconomic variables. The first is that it makes diversification possible and the second is that it allows agents to share risk as well as smooth consumption (Easterly et al. 2001). Consequently, theory suggests that countries with good financial systems are in a better position to cushion the impact of shocks and so there should be a negative link between domestic financial development and macroeconomic instability.

At this stage it is necessary to justify why we do not include a direct measure of export diversification in the benchmark regressions. There are two reasons. The first is that several countries in the sample do not have long and reliable time series on measures of diversification and so if this variable is included in the regressions it will reduce the sample size significantly, and result in imprecise coefficient estimates. The second is that the volatility of the terms of trade is one of the explanatory variables in the regressions and studies suggest that it is highly affected by the degree of export diversification of an economy (Deaton and Miller 1996; Bleaney and Greenaway 2001). Consequently, the terms of trade volatility variable is a good proxy for the degree of diversification. Recall that one of the reasons why African countries are vulnerable to terms of trade shocks is that they export relatively few export commodities. Given this link between terms of trade volatility and specialization, the inclusion of export diversification in addition to the measure of terms of trade volatility would be inappropriate and also create problems of multi-collinearity.

The Evidence

In this section, we present results of OLS estimations of equation 1 for each of the three dependent variables of interest—output, consumption, and investment. The standard errors of each equation were corrected for heteroskedasticity and autocorrelation. Furthermore, the estimations involve the use of three measures of trade policy regimes in addition to the set of control variables identified in the previous section. Table 9.7 presents results of the estimations using the first measure of trade regimes—openness based on policy incidence (tariff and non-tariff barriers).

The regressions have a reasonably good fit as indicated by the fact that the R-squared for each equation is above thirty per cent. The results show that there is no systematic relationship between trade regimes and macroeconomic instability. The trade regime measure is insignificant in the equations for output, consumption and investment. In the output equation, the variables that are significant at conventional levels and have the expected signs are inflation volatility, volatility of the terms of trade, the ratio of fiscal deficit to GDP, and climatic disasters. The results suggest that distortionary macroeconomic policies, as reflected in the volatility of inflation, lead to more volatility in output. Furthermore, an increase in terms of trade volatility increases output volatility. This is consistent with the findings of Deaton and Miller (1996) that commodity-based terms of trade shocks play an important role in output fluctuations in Africa. Climatic disasters, such as an increase in the incidence of drought, also increase output volatility. Interestingly, an increase in the ratio of fiscal deficit to GDP leads to a reduction in output volatility.

In the consumption equation, output per capita, the ratio of fiscal deficit to GDP, volatility of the terms of trade, and the severity of debt have the expected signs and are significant at conventional levels. The significance of the ratio of fiscal deficit to GDP in both the output and consumption equations suggest that fiscal policy has a role to play in dampening macroeconomic volatility in Africa. Finally, in the investment equation, the variables that have the expected signs and are significant at conventional levels are the volatility of inflation, the volatility of terms of trade and the severity of debt.

Table 9.7 Benchmark Estimation Using Trade Regime Measure 1

	Output volatility	Consumption volatility	Investment volatility
Openness based on policy incidence (Tariff and non-tariff barriers)	-0.780 (0.295)	0.334 (0.845)	-0.951 (0.707)
Volatility of inflation	0.127 (0.010)**	0.161 (0.109)	0.457 (0.053)***
Output per capita	0.144 (0.282)	-0.465 (0.056)***	-0.471 (0.328)
Fiscal deficit (% of GDP)	-0.186 (0.000)*	-0.180 (0.062)***	-0.192 (0.221)
Volatility of terms of trade	0.046 (0.044)**	0.142 (0.040)**	0.177 (0.095)***
Climatic disaster	4.676 (0.017)**	3.956 (0.103)	-1.063 (0.811)
Political regime	-0.021 (0.752)	-0.061 (0.568)	-0.223 (0.246)
Credit to private sector (as % of total credit)	0.002 (0.851)	0.005 (0.664)	-0.047 (0.161)
Landlocked countries	-0.605 (0.442)	0.153 (0.913)	-2.635 (0.263)
Oil exporters	-0.281 (0.793)	-1.709 (0.328)	-3.916 (0.182)
Severity of debt	0.670 (0.305)	3.214 (0.030)**	4.198 (0.035)**
R-squared	0.372	0.365	0.322
F-statistic	5.30 (0.000)*	4.45 (0.000)*	9.75 (0.000)*
No. of observations	97	97	97

Figures in parentheses are p-values
* Significant at the 1% level
** Significant at the 5% level
*** Significant at the 10% level

Table 9.8 Benchmark Estimation Using Trade Regime Measure 2

	Output volatility	Consumption volatility	Investment volatility
Openness by practice (trade/GDP)	-0.120 (0.889)	4.987 (0.026)**	5.797 (0.033)**
Volatility of inflation	0.124 (0.013)**	0.161 (0.091)***	0.452 (0.049)**
Output per capita	0.111 (0.428)	-0.342 (0.097)***	-0.380 (0.394)
Fiscal deficit (% of GDP)	-0.190 (0.000)*	-0.242 (0.012)**	-0.272 (0.076)***
Volatility of terms of trade	0.046 (0.058)***	0.162 (0.027)**	0.201 (0.062)***
Climatic disaster	5.012 (0.013)**	5.056 (0.021)**	0.845 (0.860)
Political regime	-0.034 (0.643)	-0.112 (0.303)	-0.305 (0.141)
Credit to private sector (as % of total credit)	0.003 (0.807)	0.014 (0.225)	-0.035 (0.186)
Landlocked countries	-0.552 (0.500)	-0.230 (0.867)	-3.003 (0.190)
Oil exporters	-0.045 (0.965)	-2.093 (0.197)	-3.969 (0.126)
Severity of debt	0.785 (0.253)	3.057 (0.018)**	4.209 (0.037)**
R-squared	0.365	0.412	0.340
F-statistic	4.84 (0.000)*	5.76 (0.000)*	6.77 (0.000)*
No. of observations	97	97	97

Figures in parentheses are p-values
* Significant at the 1% level
** Significant at the 5% level
*** Significant at the 10% level

Table 9.8 presents results of the estimations using our second measure of trade regimes—openness by practice (trade/GDP). The use of this measure does not change the key results of the output equation. However, for the consumption and investment equations, the trade regime measure is now significant at 5 per cent level. This suggests that the more open the trade regime is the higher is the volatility in consumption and investment. The other change that we notice in the consumption equation is that the volatility of inflation is now significant unlike in the previous estimation. As for the investment equation, the measure of fiscal policy is now significant at 10 per cent level. Results for the other variables are pretty much the same as in the previous estimation.

Table 9.9 Benchmark Estimation Using Trade Regime Measure 3

	Output volatility	Consumption volatility	Investment volatility
Openness based on conventional wisdom	1.107 (0.165)	1.111 (0.433)	2.484 (0.408)
Volatility of inflation	0.119 (0.008)*	0.157 (0.117)	0.442 (0.054)***
Output per capita	0.123 (0.363)	-0.443 (0.054)**	-0.487 (0.256)
Fiscal deficit (% of GDP)	-0.196 (0.000)*	-0.183 (0.064)**	-0.210 (0.186)
Volatility of terms of trade	0.047 (0.033)**	0.143 (0.039)**	0.180 (0.084)***
Climatic disaster	4.686 (0.018)**	3.441 (0.191)	-1.416 (0.765)
Political regime	-0.073 (0.386)	-0.094 (0.361)	-0.325 (0.115)
Credit to private sector (as % of total credit)	0.006 (0.645)	0.007 (0.538)	-0.040 (0.217)
Landlocked countries	-0.566 (0.494)	0.128 (0.928)	-2.593 (0.265)
Oil exporters	-0.178 (0.866)	-1.933 (0.273)	-3.918 (0.183)
Severity of debt	0.732 (0.286)	3.114 (0.023)**	4.221 (0.037)**
R-squared	0.380	0.370	0.328
F-statistic	5.66 (0.000)*	4.73 (0.000)*	7.77 (0.000)*
No. of observations	97	97	97

Figures in parentheses are p-values
* Significant at the 1% level
** Significant at the 5% level
*** Significant at the 10% level

Table 9.9 presents the results of estimations using the measure of trade regime based on conventional wisdom. It shows that the results are qualitatively similar to those of the estimation using the measure of trade regime based on policy incidence.

Table 9.10 Excluding the Terms of Trade

Output Equation	Openness by policy incidence	Openness by practice	Openness by conventional wisdom
Trade regime	-0.807 (0.272)	-0.343 (0.699)	1.078 (0.171)
Volatility of inflation	0.151 (0.016)**	0.147 (0.019)**	0.144 (0.013)**
Output per capita	0.170 (0.207)	0.131 (0.343)	0.149 (0.270)
Fiscal deficit (% of GDP)	-0.187 (0.000)*	-0.189 (0.000)*	-0.198 (0.000)*
Volatility of terms of trade	–	–	–
Climatic disaster	4.820 (0.017)**	5.111 (0.013)**	4.858 (0.016)**
Political regime	-0.036 (0.603)	-0.046 (0.537)	-0.088 (0.315)
Credit to private sector (as % of total credit)	0.004 (0.764)	0.004 (0.747)	0.008 (0.556)
Landlocked countries	-0.721 (0.372)	-0.648 (0.440)	-0.685 (0.419)
Oil exporters	-0.147 (0.891)	0.108 (0.918)	--0.027 (0.980)
Severity of debt	0.883 (0.214)	1.005 (0.180)	0.960 (0.195)
R-squared	0.357	0.351	0.365
F-statistic	5.49 (0.000)	4.94 (0.000)*	5.73 (0.000)*
No. of observations	97	97	97

Figures in parentheses are p-values
* Significant at the 1% level
** Significant at the 5% level
*** Significant at the 10% level

Table 9.11 Sub-Saharan Africa

Output Equation	Openness by policy incidence	Openness by practice	Openness by conventional wisdom
Trade regime	-0.552 (0.414)	-0.384 (0.661)	0.838 (0.369)
Volatility of inflation	0.126 (0.016)**	0.124 (0.018)**	0.121 (0.012)**
Output per capita	0.092 (0.529)	0.065 (0.682)	0.083 (0.575)
Fiscal deficit (% of GDP)	-0.223 (0.000)*	-0.222 (0.000)*	-0.228 (0.000)*
Volatility of terms of trade	0.050 (0.070)***	0.050 (0.083)***	0.050 (0.066)***
Climatic disaster	5.822 (0.012)**	6.015 (0.012)**	5.643 (0.017)**
Political regime	0.006 (0.929)	0.003 (0.971)	-0.031 (0.715)
Credit to private sector (as % of total credit)	0.0003 (0.981)	0.0003 (0.986)	0.003 (0.825)
Landlocked countries	-0.455 (0.562)	-0.380 (0.639)	-0.404 (0.623)
Oil exporters	1.315 (0.340)	1.511 (0.266)	1.303 (0.342)
Severity of debt	0.411 (0.503)	0.510 (0.475)	0.499 (0.477)
R-squared	0.401	0.400	0.406
F-statistic	7.08 (0.000)*	6.51 (0.000)*	7.05 (0.000)*
No. of observations	85	85	85

Figures in parentheses are p-values
* Significant at the 1% level
** Significant at the 5% level
*** Significant at the 10% level

Sensitivity Analysis

We conducted a battery of sensitivity analyses to determine whether or not our results are robust to changes in some of the assumptions made in the analysis. In this section, we use the output equation to demonstrate the robustness of our results. The full estimation results are summarized in the charts presented in the next subsection. The first sensitivity analysis we conducted was to exclude the volatility of the terms of trade as an explanatory variable in the regressions. This is important because one might argue that the mechanism through which the trade regime affects macroeconomic volatility is the terms of trade; including this variable in addition to the trade regime will make the latter insignificant. Table 9.10 shows the results of this sensitivity analysis for the output equation across the three measures of trade regimes. Clearly, the exclusion of this variable does not change the key result that the trade regime has no systematic relationship with output volatility.

The second sensitivity analysis involved the exclusion of North African countries in the sample. The idea is that one may argue that countries in Sub-Saharan Africa (SSA) have a different production structure than those in North Africa and, as such, the relationships may be different. Results of this sensitivity analysis for the output equation are presented in Table 9.11. The key message from this is that there is no qualitative change in the results. The trade regime variables continue to be insignificant in the output equations.

Finally, we conducted sensitivity analyses using a system as opposed to a single equation method. The system approach we employ is the Seemingly Unrelated Regression (SURE) technique which allows us to account for contemporaneous correlation across equations of the system. For each dependent variable of interest, we estimated three equations capturing the three measures of trade regimes. We also did a Breusch-Pagan test to determine whether or not there is evidence of contemporaneous correlation across residuals of the equations in the system. The test rejects the assumption of independence of the residuals at the 1 percent level, thereby providing justification for the use of the SURE technique. The estimation results are presented in Table 9.12. Once again, the results indicate that the trade regime has no systematic impact on output volatility in the region. In addition, there is no qualitative change in the results for the other variables.

Table 9.12 System Estimation (SURE)

Output Equation	Openness by policy incidence	Openness by practice	Openness by conventional wisdom
Trade regime	-0.013 (0.861)	0.002 (0.981)	0.033 (0.758)
Volatility of inflation	0.124 (0.011)**	0.124 (0.012)**	0.124 (0.011)**
Output per capita	0.114 (0.411)	0.114 (0.415)	0.114 (0.409)
Fiscal deficit (% of GDP)	-0.191 (0.000)*	-0.191 (0.000)*	-0.191 (0.000)*
Volatility of terms of trade	0.046 (0.133)	0.046 (0.135)	0.046 (0.130)
Climatic disaster	5.036 (0.004)*	5.043 (0.004)*	5.032 (0.004)*
Political regime	-0.035 (0.565)	-0.035 (0.564)	-0.036 (0.548)
Credit to private sector (as % of total credit)	0.003 (0.718)	0.004 (0.718)	0.004 (0.709)
Landlocked countries	-0.562 (0.452)	-0.561 (0.455)	-0.561 (0.450)
Oil exporters	-0.056 (0.951)	-0.052 (0.955)	-0.056 (0.951)
Severity of debt	0.781 (0.254)	0.783 (0.255)	0.781 (0.251)
R-squared	0.365	0.365	0.366
F-statistic	56.39 (0.000)*	55.81 (0.000)*	57.26 (0.000)*
No. of observations	97	97	97

Figures in parentheses are p-values
* Significant at the 1% level
** Significant at the 5% level
*** Significant at the 10% level

Summary of Results

For ease of comprehension, we have summarized the results of all the estimations in Figures 9.1-9.3. For each dependent variable, the figures show the percentage of estimations in which an explanatory variable was significant and of the expected sign. Starting with the output equation, Figure 9.1 shows that openness based on the three measures was not significant in any of the estimations. This suggests that the trade regime is not a major source of instability in real output in the African region. Inflation volatility is significant and of the expected sign in 100 percent of the estimations, indicating that instability in domestic macroeconomic policy as reflected in inflation volatility results in instabilities in the growth of real output per capita. The results also suggest that volatility of the terms of trade leads to instability in the growth of real output per capita. The terms-of-trade variable was significant and of the expected sign in 67 percent of the estimations. Climatic disasters, as reflected in the incidence of drought, was significant and of the expected sign in 100 percent of the estimations, suggesting that extreme weather conditions contribute to real output instability in the region.

Another variable that emerged as important in explaining output instability is the ratio of fiscal deficit to GDP. This is particularly interesting because it suggests that fiscal policy has a role to play in dampening the effects of shocks. Interestingly, variables such as output per capita, credit to the private sector, the political regime, and dummies for oil exporters, landlocked and severely indebted countries were not significant in the estimations.

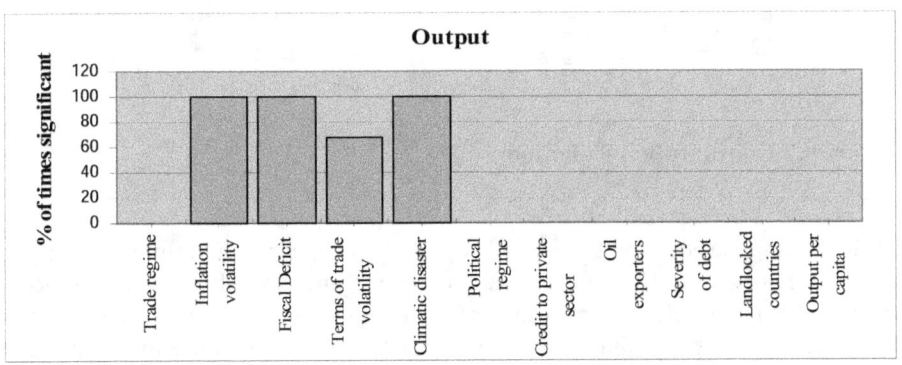

Figure 9.1 Output Equation

Turning to the volatility of the growth of real consumption per capita, we see that the variable capturing our measures of trade regimes is significant and of the expected sign in less than 20 percent of the estimations. This indicates that there is weak evidence that trade liberalization is a source of instability in consumption. It is pertinent to note that the trade/GDP ratio is the measure of trade regime that accounts for the significant relationships observed. The other measures were insignificant in all the estimations.

Fiscal policy and the volatility of terms-of-trade growth are the most important drivers of instability in the growth rate of real consumption per capita. The two variables are significant and of the expected signs in all the estimations. In other words, volatile terms of trade lead to more instability in the growth of real consumption per capita whereas more expansionary fiscal policy dampens instability in consumption. In contrast to the output equation, the level of development of an economy as measured by real output per capita is also important in explaining instability in consumption. This variable was significant and of the expected sign (negative) in 75 per cent of the estimations. The volatility of inflation is also significant in 67 per cent of the estimations while climatic disasters and the severity of debt were significant in 50 per cent of the estimations. The other variables were not significant in the regressions.

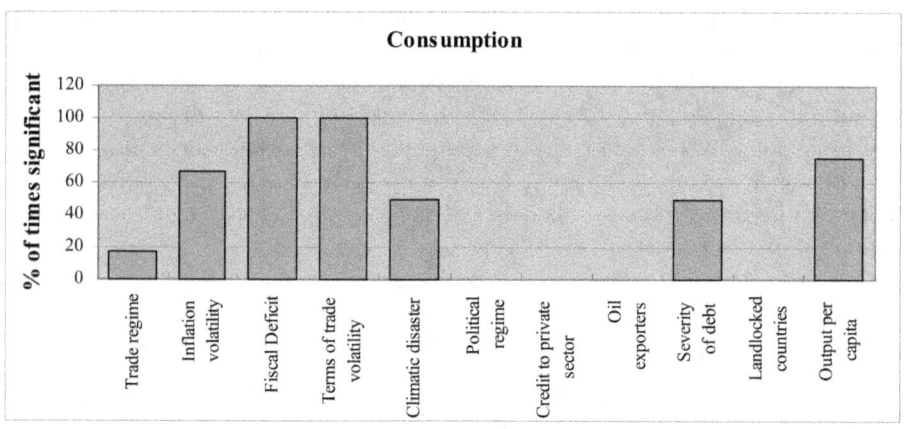

Figure 9.2 Consumption Equation

Regarding the equation for instability in the growth of real investment per capita, the results provide weak evidence that the trade regime contributes to instability in the dependent variable. The measures of trade regime were significant and positive in 17 percent of the estimations, suggesting that trade liberalization contributes mildly to instability in the growth of real investment per capita.

The most important factors explaining instability in investment are the volatilities of inflation and terms-of-trade growth. The two variables were significant and of the expected sign (positive) in 100 percent of the estimations. The results also suggest that severely indebted countries have more volatile growth of real investment per capita. It was significant and of the expected sign in 75 percent of the estimations. Furthermore, the political regime variable which is a proxy for institutional quality was significant and of the expected sign (negative) in 17 percent of the cases. The fiscal policy variable was also significant in 17 per cent of the cases. Climatic disasters, the dummy for oil exporters, credit to the private sector as a percentage of total domestic credit, and the dummy for landlocked countries were insignificant in all the estimations.

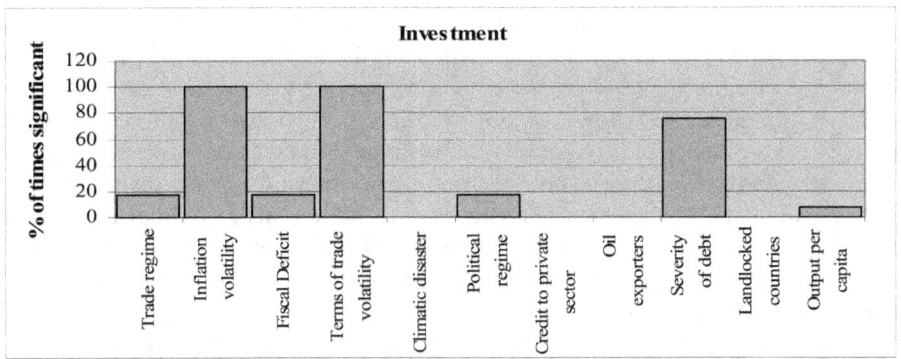

Figure 9.3 Investment Equation

Policy Implications and Recommendations

In this chapter, we examined the effects of trade liberalization on macroeconomic instability using a reasonably-sized panel of annual data on 33 African countries spanning the 1986 to 2000 period. In all specifications, we find no evidence that trade liberalization has any systematic effect on output instability. However, there is some, albeit weak, evidence that liberalization increases instability in consumption and investment. The evidence is weak because it is sensitive to the method of estimation adopted as well as the measure of trade policy used. In particular, the impact of liberalization on consumption and investment volatilities is significant when we use the trade/GDP as a measure of openness. It is not significant when we measure openness by tariff/non-tariff barriers or by conventional wisdom. In sum, there is no compelling evidence that trade liberalization is a major source of macroeconomic instability in African countries. Any impact that liberalization has on macroeconomic instability in the region is subtle and weak. Factors such as the volatility of inflation, the volatility of terms of trade, the nature of fiscal policy, climatic disasters, and the severity of debt are more robust determinants of macroeconomic instability in the region.

The results of our empirical analyses have serious implications for government policy in African countries. Specifically, although countries can use trade restriction as an important instrument for protecting domestic industries and enhancing their industrialization efforts, it is not the most appropriate way to deal with vulnerability to external shocks or macroeconomic instability. These shocks could be more effectively dealt with through other means. In particular, we see at least three ways of dealing with vulnerability to external shocks in the region: reducing terms of trade volatility through diversification of the production and export structure; using fiscal policy in a countercyclical manner; and financial sector development.

Diversification: Our empirical results show that terms of trade volatility contributes to macroeconomic volatility in the region. And one of the reasons African countries have high terms of trade volatility is that they have highly concentrated production and export structures. In particular, their exports are concentrated in primary commodities with very unstable and volatile prices. Consequently, one effective method to reduce the region's vulnerability to trade shocks is to expand its export base through diversification of the production structure. For diversification efforts to be successful, however, policymakers must find ways to deal with the problems posed by supply constraints. They must also create appropriate domestic conditions and capacity for export of dynamic products. It is clear that inadequate human and physical capital as well as infrastructure inhibits export development in the region. In this regard, there is an urgent need for African countries to intensify regional integration efforts in the area of infrastructure so as to reduce transactions costs and make exports more competitive.

Fiscal policy: Another mechanism for dealing with external shocks available to African policymakers it to use fiscal policy in a countercyclical manner. In other words, governments can run fiscal surplus in periods of positive external shocks and deficit in bad times. This will enable them to cushion the effects of these shocks and reduce macroeconomic volatility.

Financial sector development: Enhancing access to credit for firms and consumers will also help African countries to reduce the impact of negative external shocks. In some of these countries, the financial sector is not developed. Consequently, access to credit is not as easy as it is in a well-functioning society. Furthermore, consumers have serious difficulties obtaining loans from banks to smooth over consumption temporally and firms also face severe credit constraints. Policy makers in the region can increase financial depth and minimize the impact of shocks by improving the efficiency and functioning of the financial sector.

Data Appendix

The data used in the analysis were obtained from the 2004 World Bank's Africa Database, and the 2003 International Financial Statistics published by the IMF. The variable used to proxy political stability was obtained from the Polity IV database available at: http/www.cidcm.umd.edu/inscr/polity. The 33 African countries in the sample are: Burkina Faso, Botswana, Ivory Coast, Cameroon, Congo, Comoros, Algeria, Egypt, Ethiopia, Gabon, Ghana, Gambia, Guinea-Bissau, Kenya, Lesotho, Morocco, Madagascar, Mali, Mozambique, Mauritania, Mauritius, Malawi, Nigeria, Rwanda, Senegal, Sierra Leone, Swaziland, Togo, Tunisia, Uganda, South Africa, Zambia, and Zimbabwe.

The variables used in the estimations are defined as follows:

1. Openness by practice is defined as the ratio of trade to GDP.
2. Openness based on policy incidence is a dummy variable capturing the extent of tariff and non-tariff barriers. In any year, the dummy takes the value 1 if average tariffs are below 20 percent and the coverage ratio for non-tariff

barriers is not more than 20 percent. It is zero otherwise. If the dummy is 1 the country is said to be open and if it is zero it is said to have a restricted trade regime.
3. Openness by conventional wisdom is a dummy capturing the popular view that African countries have been relatively more open to trade since the 1990s. The dummy takes the value 1 for any year greater than 1990. It is zero otherwise.
4. Volatility of inflation is defined as the standard deviation of inflation as computed using the GDP deflator.
5. Output per capita is defined as real GDP divided by population.
6. Volatility of terms of trade growth is the standard deviation of the growth rate of the net barter terms of trade.
7. Landlocked country is a proxy for geographic barriers. It is a dummy which takes the value 1 if a country is landlocked and zero otherwise.
8. The incidence of drought is used as a proxy for climatic disasters. This variable is a dummy capturing severe shortage of rainfall available in the World Bank Africa Database.
9. Institutional quality is measured by the type of political regime in a country as depicted by the Polity IV database. This variable takes the value -10 for strongly autocratic regimes and 10 for strongly democratic regimes.
10. Credit to the private sector is defined as claims on the private sector as a percentage of total domestic credit.
11. Fiscal deficit is the ratio of fiscal deficit to GDP.
12. Dummy for oil exporters is equal to 1 if the country is oil exporter.
13. Dummy for severely indebted countries is equal to 1 for countries classified as severely indebted in the World Bank Africa database.
14. Output instability or volatility is defined as the standard deviation of the growth rate of real GDP per capita.
15. Investment instability or volatility is defined as the standard deviation of the growth rate of real investment per capita.
16. Consumption instability or volatility is defined as the standard deviation of the growth rate of real consumption per capita.

References

Acemoglu, D., and Zilibotti, F. (1997). "Was Prometheus unbound by chance? Risk, diversification, and growth". *Journal of Political Economy*, Vol. 105, 1167-1200.

Acemoglu, D., Johnson, S., Robinson, J., and Thaicharoen, Y. (2003). "Institutional causes, macroeconomic symptoms: volatility, crises, and growth". *Journal of Monetary Economics*, Vol. 50.

Agenor, P. R., McDermott, C. J., and Prasad, E. S. (2000). "Macroeconomic fluctuations in developing countries: some stylized facts". *World Bank Economic Review*, Vol. 14, 251-285.

Almeida, H., and Ferreira, D. (2002). "Democracy and the variability of economic performance". *Economics and Politics*, Vol. 14, 225-257.

Ancharaz, V. D. (2003). "Determinants of trade policy reform in Sub-Saharan Africa". *Journal of African Economies*, Vol. 12, 417-443.

Basu, P., and McLeod, D. (1992). "Terms of trade fluctuations and economic growth in developing economies". *Journal of Development Economics*, Vol. 37, 89-110.

Bleaney, M., Gemmell, N., and Greenaway, D. (1995). "Tax revenue instability, with particular reference to sub-Saharan Africa". *Journal of Development Studies*, Vol. 31, 883-902.

Bleaney, M., and Greenaway, D. (2001). "The impact of terms of trade and real exchange rate volatility on investment and growth in sub-Saharan Africa". *Journal of Development Economics*, Vol. 65, 491-500.

Collier, P., and Gunning, J. W. (1999). "Why has Africa grown slowly?" *Journal of Economic Perspectives*, Vol. 13, 3-22.

Crafts, N. (1999). "East Asian growth before and after the crisis". *IMF Staff Papers*, 46, 2, June, 139-166.

Davidson, C., and Matusz, S. J. (2004). "Trade liberalization and compensation". Mimeo, Michigan State University.

Deaton, A., and Miller, R. (1996). "International commodity prices, macroeconomic performance and politics in sub-Saharan Africa". *Journal of African Economies*, Vol. 5, 99-191.

Easterly, W., and Kraay, A. (2000). "Small states, small problems? income, growth, and volatility in small states". *World Development*, Vol. 28, 2013-27.

Edwards, S. (1998). "Openness, productivity and growth: what do we really know?" *Economic Journal*, Vol. 108, 383-398.

Evenett, S. J. (2003). "The failure of the WTO ministerial meeting in Cancun: what implication for future research on the world trading system". *CESifo Forum*, Vol. 4, Autumn, 11-17.

Gavin, M., and Hausman, R. (1996). "Securing stability and growth in a shock prone region: the policy challenges for Latin America". In R. Hausman and H. Reisen (Ed.), *Securing stability and growth in Latin America.* Paris: OECD.

Guisinger, A. (2003). "Patterns of trade protection and liberalization: is there a role for diffusion?" Mimeo, Yale University.

Harrison, A. (1996). "Openness and growth: a time series, cross-country analysis for developing countries". *Journal of Development Economics*, Vol. 48, 419-447.

Head, A. (1995). "Country size, aggregate fluctuations, and international risk sharing". *Canadian Journal of Economics*, Vol. 28, 1096-1119.

Hinkle, L., Herrou-Aragon, A., and Kubota, K. (2003). "How far did Africa's first generation trade reforms go? An intermediate methodology for comparative analysis of trade policies" (World Bank Africa Region Working Paper No. 58a).

Hoffmaister, A. W., Roldos, J. E., and Wickham, P. (1998). "Macroeconomic fluctuations in sub-Saharan Africa". *IMF Staff Papers*, Vol. 45, 132-160.

Killick, T. (1995). *IMF programmes in developing countries: design and impact.* London: Routledge.

Kose, A., Prasad, E., and Terrones, M. (2003). "Financial integration and macroeconomic volatility". *IMF Staff Papers*, Vol. 50, 119-42.

Kose, M. A., and Reizman, R., (2001). "Trade shocks and macroeconomic fluctuations in Africa". *Journal of Development Economics*, Vol. 65, 55-80.

Krueger, A. (1998). "Why trade liberalization is good for growth". *The Economic Journal*, 108, 1513-1522.

Malik, A., and Temple, J. R. (2005). "The geography of output volatility". (CSAE Working Paper No. WPS/2005-07).

Martin, W. (2003). "Developing countries' changing participation in world trade". *The World Bank Research Observer*, Vol. 18, 187-203.

Mayda, A. M., and Rodrik, D. (2005). "Why are some people and countries more protectionist than others". *European Economic Review*, Vol. 49, 1393-1430.

McCullock, N., Winters, L. A., and Cirera, X. (2001). *Trade liberalization and poverty: a handbook*. London: DFID.

Oyejide, A. (1998). "Trade policy and regional integration in the development context: emerging patterns, issues and lessons for sub-Saharan Africa". *Journal of African Economies*, Vol. 7, 108-145.

Pindyck, R. S. (1991). "Irreversibility, uncertainty and investment". *Journal of Economic Literature*, Vol. 29, 1110-1148.

Pritchett, L. (1996). "Measuring outward orientation in LDCs: can it be done?" *Journal of Development Economics*, Vol. 49, 307-335.

Raddatz, C. (2005). "Are external shocks responsible for the instability of output in low-income countries?" (World Bank Policy Research Working Paper 3680).

Radelet, S., and Sachs, J. (1998). "Shipping costs, manufactured exports, and economic growth". Paper presented at the American Economic Association annual meeting.

Ramey, G., and Ramey, V. (1995). Cross-country evidence on the link between volatility and growth. *American Economic Review*, Vol. 85, 1138-1151.

Razin, A., and Rose, A. K. (1992). "Business cycle volatility and openness: an exploratory cross-sectional analysis". In L. Leiderman and A. Razin (Ed.), *Capital mobility: the impact on consumption, investment, and growth*. Cambridge: Cambridge University Press.

Razin, A., Sadka, E., and Coury, T. (2003). "Trade openness, investment instability and terms of trade volatility". *Journal of International Economics*, Vol. 61, 285-306.

Rivera-Batiz, F. L. (2002). "Democracy, governance, and economic growth: theory and evidence". *Review of Development Economics*, Vol. 6, 225-247.

Rodriguez, F., and Rodrik, D. (2000). "Trade policy and economic growth: a skeptic's guide to the cross-national evidence". *NBER Macroeconomics Annual*, 261-338.

Rodrik, D. (1998a). "Trade policy and economic performance in Africa". (National Bureau of Economic Research, Working Paper No. 6562).

Rodrik, D. (1998b). "Why is trade reform so difficult in Africa?" *Journal of African Economies*, Vol. 7, Supplement 1, 10-36.

Rodrik, D. (1998c). "Why do more open economies have bigger governments?" *Journal of Political Economy*, Vol. 106, 997-1032.

Rodrik, D. (1999). "Where did all the growth go? External shocks, social conflict, and growth collapses". *Journal of Economic Growth*, Vol. 4, 385-412.

Rose, A. (2004). "Does the WTO make trade more stable?" (National Bureau of Economic Research Working Paper No. 10207) forthcoming Open Economies Review.

Sachs, J. D. (2003). Institutions don't rule: direct effects of geography on per capita income. (National Bureau of Economic Research Working Paper No. 9490).

Sachs, J. D., and Warner, A. (1995). "Economic reform and the process of global integration". *Brookings Papers on Economic Activity*, 1-118.

Sharer, R. (1999). "Trade: an engine of growth for Africa". *Finance & Development*, Vol. 36, 26-29.

Sharer, R. (2001). "An agenda for trade, investment, and regional integration". *Finance & Development,* Vol. 38.

Stiglitz, J. (2002). *Globalization and its Discontents*. New York: W. W. Norton and Company.

UNCTAD (2004a). *UNCTAD Handbook of Statistics*. Geneva: United Nations Conference on Trade and Development (UNCTAD).

UNCTAD (2004b). *The least developed countries report 2004*. Geneva: United Nations.

Wolf, H. (2004). "Accounting for consumption volatility differences". *IMF Staff Papers*, Vol. 51, 109-125.

World Bank (2003). *Global Development Finance: Striving for Stability in Development Finance*. Washington, DC: World Bank.

World Bank (2004). *World Bank Africa Database*.

Chapter 10

Civil Society Organizations: The Search for Empowerment

Amy S. Patterson

During the past twenty years, scholars, policy-makers, and development practitioners have paid great attention to the topic of 'civil society' in African politics and development. Bilateral and multilateral donor officials have trumpeted civil society as the solution to the continent's economic woes, while democracy advocates have praised the potential of civil society to bring about long-needed change to Africa's political landscape. Patrick Chabal and Jean Pascal-Daloz refer to civil society as 'ideology,' indicating how the concept has taken on a life of its own, particularly in a global environment defined by neoliberalism that values a minimal African state.[1] Because definitions of the concept abound, it is easy to get caught up in what is (or is not) civil society, instead of clearly examining its possibilities and limitations.

Since this chapter is predominantly concerned with the variables that shape how civil society organizations achieve their goals, it utilizes Michael Walzer's broad definition of civil society. Civil society includes all public, non-state activity occurring between government and the family. It is 'the space of uncoerced human association and also the set of relational networks—formed for sake of family, faith, interest and ideology—that fill this space'.[2] To be clear, this chapter refers to the broad political space as civil society and the groups working within that space as civil society organizations (CSOs). Walzer's definition has four advantages: (1) it acknowledges that informal, social relations such as religious or ethnic identities constitute civil society; (2) it does not define CSOs based on their ability to meet their goals; (3) it includes a wide variety of reasons that networks exist, from material interests, to political ideology, to religious motivations, to mutual support; (4) it includes individual actions within social movements, though this chapter does not focus on such actions. In contrast, more narrow definitions of civil society have included only CSOs that confront the state, that meet their goals, and/or that are internally democratic. In reality, these definitions ignore much collective and individual action outside the realm of the African state.[3]

---

1 Chabal, Patrick, and Daloz, Jean-Pascal (1999), *Africa Works: Disorder as Political Instrument*, Indiana University Press, Bloomington, p. 22.

2 Walzer, Michael (1991), 'The Idea of Civil Society: A Path to Social Reconstruction', *Dissent*, Vol. 38(2), p. 293.

3 Kasfir, Nelson (1998), 'The Conventional Notion of Civil Society: A Critique', in Nelson Kasfir (ed.) *Civil Society and Democracy in Africa: Critical Perspectives*, Frank Cass

Walzer's definition includes a wide array of social formations as CSOs, more adequately reflecting what Naomi Chazan refers to as 'Africa's rich associational life'.[4] CSOs include ethnic groups, voluntary associations, village self-help clubs, political interest groups, religious bodies, women's support groups, nongovernmental organizations (NGOs) that focus on development (both within African societies and across national borders), academic research organizations, private foundations, and political parties that are outside of the state. I include opposition parties because they are non-state entities, they have ideological and/or material interests, and they often reflect social formations based on class, ethnicity, and/or region. (Once an opposition party controls the state apparatus, however, some of these conditions are not met.) CSOs are autonomous from the state, but they may not necessarily seek to confront the state. At times, CSOs may cooperate with the state in order to meet their goals. For example, women's organizations may register with the state to gain access to project grants. I consider such groups to be CSOs. Other CSOs, such as private media organizations, opposition parties, or interest groups, serve as intermediaries that link the state and citizens. CSOs may have explicit political objectives, such as protecting human rights or changing economic policy, or non-political goals, such as materially supporting their members.

As the list above illustrates, CSOs are diverse; they vary in their relationships with the state and their levels of formal institutionalization. They differ in their available resources and the issues they address, and they operate within unique political and cultural contexts. Overall, though, many African CSOs lack crucial attributes of power: wealth, size, reputation, and an ability to write and/or rewrite the rules.[5] While some CSOs have some of these attributes, most do not have all of them. This is particularly true about the ability of CSOs to shape both policy outcomes and the policy-making process (i.e., the rules of the game). A small membership makes it difficult to acquire resources and achieve a reputation. Yet reputation and resources attract members. Without size, wealth, and reputation, it is more difficult to challenge the processes for decision making within civil society, government, or partnerships with external donors.

Some CSOs either have been able to wield power or have the potential to do so. This chapter examines three understudied types of CSOs to analyze what factors give or potentially may give them power: faith-based organizations (FBOs), African CSOs that are part of global movements, and African research institutes (or 'think tanks'). To be clear, I do not argue that all CSOs in these categories are powerful; instead, I analyze select organizations in order to raise questions for further research. The chapter first examines general findings about CSOs in Africa. Next, it investigates

---

and Co., London, pp. 4-5.

4   Chazan, Naomi (1993), 'Africa's Democratic Challenge', *World Policy Journal*, Vol. 9(2), pp. 280-311.

5   van de Walle, Nicolas (2004), 'Economic Reform: Patterns and Constraints', in E. Gyimah-Boadi (ed.), *Democratic Reform in Africa: The Quality of Progress*, Lynne Rienner Publishers, Boulder, p. 43; Michael, Sarah (2004), *Undermining Development: The Absence of Power among Local NGOs in Africa*, Indiana University Press, Bloomington, pp. 23-37.

the potential sources of power for select FBOs, CSOs in global movements, and think tanks. Finally, the chapter concludes with some policy suggestions.

What We Know about CSOs in Africa

CSOs play multiple roles in African society, politics, and economics. At the most basic level, they provide social services such as education and health care which the state cannot (or will not) supply.[6] Since the1980s, as African states have increasingly been unable to meet demands for social services because of debt, structural adjustment policies, and economic mismanagement, rural and urban CSOs have stepped in to assist their members. For example, small-scale women's microfinance organizations have provided their participants with credit to start businesses. In the rural village of Ndoulo in Senegal, the fifty-member *gennaaw rail* women's organization gives its members monthly loans of less than $5. Women invest this money in vegetables and fish which they sell at the weekly market. From their meager profits, the women pay their children's school fees, buy extra food for the household, and repay their loans. This informal CSO builds on existing gender networks within the community, and it operates outside the realm of state activities. Although it would like to cooperate more closely with the state to meet its members' material goals, local officials have practically ignored the group.[7]

Multilateral and bilateral donors have long recognized the capacity of local and multinational CSOs to promote public health, environmental protection, and small business endeavors. Donors have relied on multinational NGOs and their local partners to develop and implement AIDS prevention, support, and orphan care programs on the continent. US President George W. Bush's $15 Emergency Plan for AIDS Relief (PEPFAR), which targets twelve African countries with high HIV prevalence rates, demonstrates this point. Multinational NGOs, a specific type of development CSO that stretches across national borders, have received large grants under the 2003 policy, but they have been encouraged to include African CSOs as sub-recipients of grants. The US Office of Global AIDS Coordinator reported in 2005 that 80% of its more than 1,200 partners working on the continent were African CSOs.[8]

The belief that CSOs can help fight the AIDS pandemic is also evident in the institutions of the Global Fund to Fight AIDS, Tuberculosis, and Malaria (GFATM). Formed in 2001, the GFATM provides grants to governments (and some

---

6   Bratton, Michael (1994), 'Civil Society and Political Transitions', in John Harbeson, Donald Rothchild, and Naomi Chazan (eds), *Civil Society and the State in Africa*, Lynne Rienner Publishers, Boulder, pp. 55-56.

7   Patterson, Amy S. (1996), *Participation and Democracy at the Grassroots: A Study of Development Associations in Rural Senegal*, Ph.D. Dissertation, Indiana University, Bloomington.

8   Office of Global AIDS Coordinator (2005), *Engendering Bold Leadership: The President's Emergency Plan for AIDS Relief*, First Annual Report to Congress, US State Department, Washington, DC, http://www.state.gov/documents/organization/43885.pdf (accessed May 25, 2005), p. 13.

NGOs) worldwide to address AIDS, TB, and/or malaria. In order to be eligible, governments must set up a country coordinating mechanism (CCM), which must have representatives from government, bilateral and multilateral donors, and local CSOs. CSO representatives come from FBOs, business associations, women's groups, academic institutions, and organizations of people living with AIDS, TB and/or malaria. CCMs build consensus as they design health programs; they write grant proposals to the GFATM; and they oversee any grant money that is awarded to the country. Through the CCM requirement, the GFATM has institutionalized CSOs into Africa's AIDS fight. Likewise, CSOs are represented on the Technical Review Board of the GFATM that makes funding decisions about country grants.[9]

However, this emphasis on CSOs in Africa's socioeconomic development may ignore some of these groups' limitations. Michael Bratton cautions: '[CSOs] in Africa face the danger of being oversold... Enthusiasm for [civil society] must be tempered by the recognition that the organized voluntary sector in Africa is still extremely weak and dependent'.[10] Many CSOs lack the capacity to do large-scale development projects. As detailed below, they may be internally divided, hampering their ability to meet their objectives.

Other African CSOs have played a direct role in politics. Specifically, some CSOs were crucial in the democratic transitions that spread across the continent in the early 1990s. Student organizations and civil servant unions protested and demanded the end to authoritarianism in Benin, Togo, and Mali. While these activities initially focused on economic issues, such as unemployment and high inflation, protesters soon demanded political accountability, multiparty elections, and the end to corruption. Independent media outlets and election monitoring organizations have played a watchdog role in new democracies such as Nigeria, Ghana, South Africa, Senegal, Kenya, and Mali.[11]

Through their roles in economic, political, and social development, CSOs may foster empowerment, teach democratic values, and build networks of trust among group members. They can help people learn to participate in politics, to voice their opinions, and to hold leaders accountable. CSOs may create 'rich networks of nonmarket relationships that build a generalised sense of trust and reciprocity [or] "social capital;" [these networks also] increase the efficiency of human relationships

---

9 Patterson, Amy S., and Cieminis, Dave (2005), 'Weak and Ineffective? African States and Recent International AIDS Policies', in Amy S. Patterson (ed.), *The African State and the AIDS Crisis*, Ashgate Publishing, Aldershot, p. 175.

10 Bratton, Michael (1989), 'The Politics of Government-NGO Relations in Africa', *World Development*, Vol. 17(4), pp. 569-87.

11 Smith, Zeric Kay (1997), '"From Demons to Democrats": Mali's Student Movement, 1991-1996', *Review of African Political Economy*, Vol. 24, pp. 249-63; Bratton, Michael, and van de Walle, Nicolas (1992), 'Toward Governance in Africa: Popular Demands and State Responses', in Michael Bratton and Goran Hyden (eds), *Governance and Politics in Africa*, Lynne Rienner Publishers, Boulder, p. 31; Heilbrunn, John R. (1993), 'Social Origins of National Conferences in Benin and Togo', *Journal of Modern African Studies*, Vol. 31, pp. 277-99; Gyimah-Boadi, E. (2004), 'Civil Society and Democratic Development', in E. Gyimah-Boadi (ed.), *Democratic Reform in Africa: The Quality of Progress*, Lynne Rienner Publishers, Boulder, pp. 100-105.

in both market and governmental affairs'.[12] These intangible outcomes may be as crucial for Africa's long-run development as CSO activities that directly confront government institutions and policies. Stephen Ndegwa shows how the Undugu Society of Kenya, an urban organization that provides housing for poor citizens, has empowered its participants through community organizing experiences and leadership training. By working together on home-building projects, participants have gained confidence in their abilities.[13] Even CSOs that are relatively apolitical may build the confidence and layers of trust among members for future cooperation in politics.

Trust enables members, who operate in a world of incomplete information, to better predict the actions of others in the marketplace and in politics. Yet, trust does not arise in a vacuum. It must be nurtured from repeated interactions, and CSOs provide an arena in which those interactions can occur. For example, the repeated public giving and repaying of loans in the *gennaaw rail* association fostered transparency and mutual confidence among the women. The trust among members spilled over into the marketplace and social sphere: the women bought vegetables from each other, instead of other merchants, because they trusted their co-members to charge a fair price. Group members helped each other in times of sickness and death, because they believed that in the future such help would be reciprocated. The 'economy of affection' facilitated small-scale economic development in Ndoulo and made life survivable during difficult periods.[14] Through this reciprocity and trust, members achieved their objectives of material benefits and nonmaterial friendship and support.

Social capital may facilitate several outcomes: democracy, holistic development, and more efficient governance. Robert Putnam finds that Italian communities with strong social networks that resulted from CSOs were better equipped to address corruption than those without such networks.[15] In the inner-cities of the United States, community groups that have fostered social capital across racial, ethnic, and religious lines have effectively advocated for pro-working class policies.[16] CSOs can promote the values, morals, and networks necessary for social, economic, political, environmental, physical, and spiritual development. However, it would be simplistic to assume that all CSOs play such roles.

CSOs provide an avenue for citizen participation, which is particularly important in African political systems which often *de facto* (or *de jure*) concentrate power in the executive branch and central government. This avenue is particularly crucial for citizens such as women, migrants, and the poor who are often excluded from

---

12 Korten, David (1998), *Globalizing Civil Society: Reclaiming Our Right to Power*, Seven Stories Press, New York, p. 55.

13 Ndegwa, Stephen (1996), *The Two Faces of Civil Society: NGOs and Politics in Africa*, Kumarian Press, West Hartford, p. 70.

14 Patterson, Amy S., *Participation and Democracy at the Grassroots*; Hyden, Goran (1983), *No Shortcuts to Progress*, University of California Press, Berkeley, p. 18.

15 Putnam, Robert (1993), *Making Democracy Work: Civic Traditions in Modern Italy*, Princeton University Press, Princeton, p. 87.

16 Warren, Mark (2001), *Dry Bones Rattling: Community Building to Revitalize American Democracy*, Princeton University Press, pp. 13-14, 20-30.

formal political institutions such as legislatures, the bureaucracy, and subnational governments. Though they have achieved high levels of representation in South Africa, Mozambique, Uganda, and Namibia, and although Africa now has its first female president, Liberia's Ellen Johnson-Sirleaf, women still are underrepresented in African politics. Women's CSOs have sought to fill this gap by lobbying for policies to benefit women and children, and by advocating for increased female representation in government. For example, because of their crucial support for President Yoweri's National Resistance Movement in the mid-1980s, women's CSOs in Uganda were able to demand quotas for women's representation on local councils.[17] However, Nelson Kasfir cautions that society's marginalized members are still less likely to participate in CSOs than society's more powerful individuals. And the CSOs such poorer individuals form are more likely to have inadequate resources.[18]

While CSOs have played a crucial role in Africa's development and democratization, it would be naïve to ignore the obstacles many of these associations face. Some CSOs are hierarchical, authoritarian, and elitist. They may be divided along class, gender, ethnic, and religious lines. Leaders may refuse to be accountable to members, financial activities may not be transparent, and participants may not actively involve themselves in decision making.[19] Such divisions make it more difficult for CSOs to facilitate compromise, build consensus, and foster trust. In the long term, such divisions complicate the achievement of economic or political goals. Two examples illustrate this problem. One is a village youth group in central Senegal that existed between 1994 and 1995; the other is Zimbabwe's opposition party, the Movement for Democratic Change (MDC). At first glance, these associations seem very different. The youth group lacked resources; its leaders had little education or political experience; before its demise, its goal was to earn money from a garden; and it had minimal interaction with state officials. In contrast, the MDC has financial resources; its leaders have political and educational experiences; its goal is to get its members elected; and it has experienced confrontation with and repression from the state. Despite these differences, these two CSOs illustrate the negative impact of internal divisions.

The youth group's members were young women and men, many unmarried. The group hoped to provide income-generating opportunities for young people, so that they would not have to migrate to the cities during the dry season. Since the village had a new well, the group planned to complete a dry-season garden and then use the profits to buy cattle, sheep, and goats. In reality, the group never harvested the garden, because of miscommunication between the men and women and because of distrust between the leaders and members. Female members were unaware of project tasks or

---

17 Tripp, Aili Mari (2001a), 'New Political Activism in Africa', *Journal of Democracy*, Vol. 12(3), pp. 141-55; Tripp, Aili Mari (2001b), 'The Politics of Autonomy and Cooptation in Africa: The Case of the Ugandan Women's Movement', *Journal of Modern African Studies*, Vol. 39(1), pp. 101-28.

18 Kasfir, Nelson, 'The Conventional Notion of Civil Society', p. 5.

19 Patterson, Amy S. (1998), 'A Reappraisal of Democracy in Civil Society: Evidence from Rural Senegal', *Journal of Modern African Studies*, Vol. 36(3), pp. 423-41; Fatton, Robert (1995), 'Africa in the Age of Democratization: The Civic Limitations of Civil Society', *African Studies Review*, Vol. 38(2), pp. 67-110.

group resources. Male leaders rarely held meetings to discuss these issues, and when they did, female members were rarely told about meetings. Lack of communication was detrimental, particularly because the project's success relied on the women to water the garden. By the end of 1995, the youth group had disbanded.[20]

Similar problems can exist in national-level, political organizations, as actions in 2005 within Zimbabwe's MDC illustrate. As part of what Walzer defines as civil society, the MDC is a non-state entity, formed for the sake of material interest and/ or political ideology, and rooted in urban networks and labor union experiences. Formed in 1999, the MDC quickly became the major opposition to the authoritarian regime of President Robert Mugabe. The MDC helped to defeat a constitutional proposal in 2000, and won almost half the legislative seats in that year's election. Soon after, state repression increased, though the MDC did compete in the 2002 presidential and May 2005 legislative elections. After President Mugabe's party ZANU-PF won the majority of seats in the 2005 election, government forces turned on urban citizens, a majority of whom had voted for the MDC. Police and ZANU-supported youth cleared slums, destroyed businesses, and jailed individuals; the United Nations estimated that 700,000 people were left homeless.

After these actions, the MDC divided over whether it should compete in the November 2005 Senate elections. President Mugabe had reinstated the Senate in order to increase his power and to provide more patronage avenues for his cronies. MDC founder Morgan Tsvangirai wanted the party to boycott the elections, claiming they were too costly and a sham. In contrast, five of the party's six top officials voted to run in the elections. Tsvangirai overrode that decision and demanded MDC supporters boycott the election; his spokesman then insisted that the twenty-six MDC members who had registered their candidacies under the MDC party name had done so in fraud. In late December 2005, party leaders expelled Tsvangirai from the MDC, though Tsvangirai said he would ignore what he termed this 'illegal' expulsion decision.[21]

Some observers argue that the MDC split manifests the Shona-Ndebele ethnic group division found in the country, with Tsvangirai from the majority Shona group and his opponents from the minority Ndebele group. As such, the MDC is partly rooted in the ethnic social networks found in Zimbabwean society. Others argue that the division reflects larger questions about what strategy the opposition can effectively use in an increasingly repressive state. Party insiders maintain that the regime has exploited the divisions in the MDC, and possibly even helped to foment them by infiltrating the party. The immediate outcome of the MDC divide was that ZANU-PF won 59 of the 66 Senate seats in an election with only 15 percent to 20 percent voter turnout. The larger issue, though, is that the conflict has harmed the MDC's long-term prospects and its ability to mount a successful challenge to Mugabe's one-party dictatorship: 'Observers say divisions within the party are unlikely to be healed

---

20 Patterson, Amy S., *Participation and Democracy at the Grassroots*.
21 Wines, Michael (2005), 'Zimbabwe's Opposition Party "Expels" Its Leader (but Not for Sure)', *New York Times*, December 26, http://www.nytimes.com/2005/12/26/international/africa/26zimbabwe.html (accessed December 29, 2005).

and the MDC is now on its deathbed'.[22] Like the Senegalese youth group, the MDC illustrates that it is difficult for CSOs to achieve their goals without some level of internal unity. However, unlike the youth group, the MDC faced external pressures from state repression that exacerbated its internal divisions.

Even CSOs that are unified may lack such mundane but necessary resources as funding or skilled leadership. The tenuous nature of some CSOs means that their life spans may be short; the lack of resources makes it more difficult for these associations to achieve their long-term goals. There are thousands of small African CSOs like the *gennaaw rail* women's group, whose members have no literacy or numeracy skills, and whose leaders have little, if any, education. These limitations prevent such groups from directly applying for grants from bilateral or multilateral donors or from keeping the detailed financial records that donors, governments, or private investors require. In general, African CSOs have fewer sources for funding than similar groups in the West. They cannot engage in massive fund-raising drives, like many citizens' groups in the West do, because of the general poverty of African populations. There are few African foundations, like the Ford or Rockefeller Foundations, to provide large grants to nonprofit groups. And few African CSOs have received grants directly from Western foundations. While some African CSOs have sought to raise funds by providing services such as consultancy work to multinational NGOs, this approach has two drawbacks. First, it may distract the organization from its original mission; and second, the vast majority of small-scale CSOs in Africa cannot engage in this type of activity because of lack of capacity. Instead, CSOs often must rely on the state, multinational NGOs, or bilateral and multilateral donors for funds.

Groups that autonomously decide to cooperate with the state to achieve their material, faith, and/or ideological objectives are part of civil society. For example, a parent association may cooperate with school officials and local government leaders to obtain state funds for a new classroom. However, I do not consider organizations that the state, or the ruling party, sets up to generate support for the regime and its policies to be CSOs. For example, Ghana's 31st December Movement, which former President Jerry Rawlings' wife headed, was ostensibly set up to foster women's empowerment but really worked to mobilize women to support the regime.[23] Such an association did not autonomously decide to cooperate with the state, because in reality, it was an arm of the state.

As the following examples illustrate, there are a variety of CSO-state relationships. These may change over time, as the state and CSOs jockey for political hegemony. At times, this jockeying requires cooperation, at other times, confrontation.[24] First, CSOs may operate independently from the state. For the most part, the *gennaaw rail* women's group exemplified this model, since its activities were outside the realm of state control or concern. Second, CSOs may cooperate with the state to achieve their goals. During the regime of Daniel arap Moi, the Undugu Society worked closely

---

22 'Mugabe's Party Wins Zimbabwe Poll' (2005), *BBC News*, November 28, http://newsvote.bbc.co.uk/mpapps/pagetools/print/news.bbc.co.uk/2/hi/africa/4475640.stm (accessed December 14, 2005).

23 Gyimah-Boadi, E., 'Civil Society', pp. 108-110.

24 Chabal, Patrick, and Daloz, Jean Pascal, *Africa Works*, p. 21.

with local government officials on housing projects. This cooperation with the state was essential for Undugu to meet the socioeconomic needs of its members. But, it meant that Undugu could not challenge the underlying structures such as land tenure laws that hampered the material advancement of its poor, urban members.[25] Third, CSOs may confront the state. With its formation in 1999 and its opposition to the 2000 constitutional changes, the MDC confronted the Mugabe regime.

Fourth, the state may co-opt CSOs in order to increase its legitimacy or to limit challenges to its policies. In doing so, the CSO may gain material benefits and/or a voice in policy making. Many AIDS activists in South Africa assert that the South African state (particularly the ministry of health) has coopted the National Association of People with AIDS (NAPWA). The ministry of health provides NAPWA with funding and positions on AIDS decision-making bodies; NAPWA officials have closely allied themselves with the health minister Manto Tshabalala-Msimang to support nutrition and vitamins instead of antiretroviral drugs for people living with HIV/AIDS.[26] The linkage between NAPWA and the state may have an immediate health cost for its HIV-positive members.

Fifth, the state may repress CSOs by cutting off resources, limiting opportunities for CSO advancement, or using violence. Events after the 2005 elections in Zimbabwe illustrate state reaction to MDC challenges and the state's loss of hegemony. But events in the *gennaaw rail* group shows that state repression may be less violent, but still effective. In 1995, group leaders fell out of favor with local party bosses from the ruling *Parti Socialiste* because some of them had supported a younger candidate in party elections. (The group, on the other hand, had not taken an official position in the election.) The old *Parti Socialiste* leaders continued to control local politics and maintained ties to state officials. Because state officials had the power to recognize women's associations, allocate state funds to them, and recommend these groups for donor-financed development projects, the *gennaaw rail* organization lost opportunities to expand its activities.[27]

Instead of looking to the state for resources, some CSOs may turn to multinational NGOs or to bilateral donors such as the US Agency for International Development (USAID) or the United Kingdom's Department for International Development (DFID). Yet even reliance on these external actors may not mean that CSOs can explicitly oppose state policies. International donors have a propensity to 'depoliticize' their activities and view their assistance for CSOs in terms of short-term, discrete, technical projects. In doing so, donors are more likely to avoid some issues that some CSOs, particularly those working on human rights, gender equality, legal reform, or democracy, hope to address.[28] Reliance on funds from external sources raises questions about accountability. CSOs may have divided loyalties: they must balance

---

25 Ndegwa, Stephen, *The Two Faces of Civil Society*, p. 78.

26 Heywood, Mark (2004), 'Condemn the Threats by NAPWA Against AIDS Activists', *TAC Newsletter*, March 30, http://www.tac.org.za/newsletter/2004/ns30_03_2004.htm (accessed December 1, 2005).

27 Patterson, Amy S., *Participation and Democracy at the Grassroots*.

28 Uvin, Peter (2004), *Human Rights and Development*, Kumarian Press, West Hartford, p. 93.

accountability to bilateral donors or multinational NGOs who finance them with accountability to their members, their partners, their staff, and the group's mission. These webs of accountability may require CSOs to choose, for example, between clients' needs and donor's goals. Power inequalities shape these relationships, since the donor has the financial resources the indigenous CSO needs. In such a situation, a partnership in which both the donor and recipient listen to and learn from each other is difficult. One outcome is that some indigenous CSOs have become merely the conduits of First World development assistance.[29]

In summary, African CSOs are complex and differ widely in their relations with the state and external actors. At times, African CSOs have helped to foster democracy, encourage development, and promote accountability. CSOs may empower citizens, teach participation, and help individuals develop leadership skills. In contrast, some have been co-opted by repressive governments, and others have lacked financial resources or human capacity to be effective players in politics, economics, or society. The next three sections examine how CSOs in particular categories have sought empowerment. First, FBOs call into question the role of mission-orientation in shaping civil society's power and effectiveness. Second, the specific organization of the Treatment Action Campaign (TAC) raises questions about the role of African CSOs in global coalitions. Third, African research institutions highlight the potential power of ideas. But while mission, international coalitions, and ideas are important, the cases also illustrate that organizational attributes, such as resources, leadership, and political context also matter.

Faith-Based Organizations: Mission-Driven Rule Changers?

FBOs are not new to the African continent. Muslim organizations, Christian associations, and traditional religious communities have played a key role in the continent's political, economic, and social development. For example, churches spoke out against authoritarian rule in Kenya in the 1990s. Yet, the literature on FBOs as a particular type of CSO is relatively limited. There are three reasons FBOs deserve greater attention as part of African civil society. First, examining FBOs acknowledges the fact that African culture is intensely spiritual. Lamin Sanneh writes:

> According to Africans . . . we are not alone in the universe, which is inhabited by the devil and by a host of spirit forces that are ever attentive to us. We should also be ever attentive to them if we are sensible. The stripped-down universe of a post-Enlightenment Christianity is a small fit for this larger world that Africans live in.[30]

---

29 Garilao, Ernesto (1987), 'Indigenous NGOs as Strategic Institutions: Managing the Relations with Government and Resource Agencies', *World Development*, Vol. 15 (supplement), pp. 113-20.

30 Sanneh, Lamin (2005), 'The Changing Face of Christianity: The Cultural Impetus of a World Religion', in Lamin Sanneh and Joel Carpenter (eds), *The Changing Face of Christianity: Africa, the West and the World*, Oxford University Press, London, p. 7.

Second, by ignoring FBOs, scholars are applying a Western secular understanding of religion and politics to Africa. In this view, religious faith is relegated to the private realm and has no impact on political participation, decision making, or resource allocation. Yet, as I illustrate below with the case of Senegal's Muslim brotherhoods, FBOs have played an important public role in politics.

Third, scholars often define CSOs in instrumental and worldly terms: as groups that seek to represent their members material interests, to lobby for more resources for their projects, or to get their participants elected to office. FBOs may do these things, but they also often provide another set of intangible benefits. The mission of these CSOs, which is rooted in theological understandings of the world, motivates the participation of most members. Of course, there also are cultural, economic, and social reasons that individuals may join FBOs. But my point is that FBOs offer another layer of belonging to members: a sense of identity rooted in a larger worldview the community shares. These larger beliefs can motivate action inside and outside of the community. The Muslim belief that the world belongs to Allah, and not to people, is manifested in almsgiving. The Christian obligation to care for the hungry, the needy, and the stranger is demonstrated in development efforts to reduce poverty or educate children.[31] For many adherents, participation in FBOs is rooted in more than the goal of achieving material benefits in this life; rather, it is based on the believer's hope for eternal life and salvation.

The shared worldview among participants and their long-term motivation for action means that FBOs tend to have a longer life-span than many other CSOs. Though some are 'fly-by-night' organizations, many are not. This institutionalization means they have the opportunity to socialize members into norms and values, and they provide a collective attempt to live out these moral teachings. By fostering social capital, FBOs may give participants the skills, confidence, and motivation to participate in politics. For example, American church goers are more likely than non-church goers to engage in a variety of political activities.[32] Of course, it takes more than a church or a mosque to foster social capital. African mainline churches have been more likely to support democratization, but less likely to be able to socialize their members into a new sense of personal and social efficacy; in contrast, Pentecostal churches have been better at socialization and mobilization, but less likely to support democracy.[33]

Because of their mission orientation, these FBOs have the potential to put forward new visions for politics and development. Organizational capacities, resources, leadership, legitimacy, and the larger political context help determine if that potential is met. Here I provide three examples of FBOs that are 'rule changers'. In each, I note how these associations' power rests partly on their ability to change the way

---

31 Cnaan, Ram A. (1999), *The Newer Deal: Social Work and Religion in Partnership*, Columbia University Press, New York, pp. 98-105.

32 Thomas, Scott (2005), *The Global Resurgence of Religion and the Transformation of International Relations: The Struggle for the Soul of the Twenty-First Century*, Palgrave MacMillian, New York, p. 239.

33 Kassimir, Ronald (1998), 'The Catholic Church in Uganda', in Tom Young (ed.), *Readings in African Politics*, Indiana University Press, Bloomington, pp. 148-60.

problems are viewed and partly on the resources they possess and the context in which they operate.

First, over the last twenty years, international FBOs such as World Vision and Catholic Relief Services (CRS) have shaped how policy makers, practitioners, and scholars understand the development process. While we traditionally think of World Vision or CRS as multinational, development NGOs, they are also rooted in faith traditions. These traditions—Protestantism for World Vision and Catholicism for CRS--continue to shape their policies and programs. World Vision's goal of promoting holistic development is situated in biblical understandings of sin and redemption.[34] Catholic teachings on birth control shape CRS policies on family planning. Even more 'secular' groups such as Christian Children's Fund and American Jewish World Service receive support from Western FBOs and frame their development messages in light of larger religious teachings. For this reason, it is appropriate to include these multinational NGOs as FBOs.

Because of their views of human nature and eternal life, these development-focused FBOs have advocated for social progress that includes spiritual, mental, and physical well being. Rather than espouse a development agenda based on modernization's narrow view of capitalism and progress, which has been 'increasingly recognized... as a type of secular, "global faith", religious organizations have argued [that development] can no longer be thought of as a positivist, value-free, activity led by economists and technicians'.[35] There is evidence that this perspective is shaping the policies of some multilateral and bilateral donors. For example, World Bank staff has been meeting formally for over twenty years to discuss the role of religious and ethical values in development. One staff member, Michael Woolcock, has advocated for a distinctly religious view of development, in which poverty reflects a world in which the social relations between individuals are 'wrong'.[36] FBOs have been able to shape the development dialogue because their resources and large memberships enable them to hire staff to advocate in Washington for such viewpoints. Because many of these FBOs are among the largest private development organizations, and because they have years of experience in poor countries, they have legitimacy on development issues.

The second example is Senegal's major Muslim organizations (or brotherhoods), the Tijaniyaa and the Mourides. The larger of the two, the Tijaniyya is divided into several orders, while the Mourides tend to be more cohesive and dynamic. Over 90 percent of Senegalese is Muslim, with most belonging to either the Tijaniyya or Mourides. Religious leaders, or *marabouts*, play a central role in the brotherhoods, and individuals tend to have a close relationship with their *marabouts*. The hundreds of Senegalese who call themselves *marabouts* serve as patrons to their followers, providing them with spiritual guidance and at times, material assistance. They often

---

[34] Myers, Bryant (1999), *Walking with the Poor: Principles and Practices of Transformational Development*, Orbis Books, Maryknoll, New York, pp. 5-19.

[35] Thomas, Scott, *The Global Resurgence of Religion*, pp. 223-25.

[36] Woolcock, Michael (2004), 'Getting the Social Relations Right: Towards an Integrated Theology and Theory of Development', in Peter Heslan (ed.), *Globalization and the Good*, Eerdmans, Grand Rapids, pp. 41-51.

act as intermediaries between the state and their followers, negotiating access to patronage, particularly for rural citizens. Each of the brotherhoods also utilizes local associations, or *daaira*, to organize their followers and create common identity among members. *Daaira* often organize ritual pilgrimages and religious ceremonies; some *daaira* support Koranic schools or engage in local-level development projects.[37]

The brotherhoods form a 'religiously based civil society' in Senegal, and in many rural areas, they have superseded the development structures of government and traditional NGOs.[38] French colonialists and post-independence politicians capitalized on the *marabout*-disciple relationship by rewarding the religious leaders with patronage in return for their mobilizing disciples to produce cash crops or to support the ruling party. Until recently, there has been an implicit social contract between the brotherhoods and the state. The state provided benefits to the *marabouts* and their followers and in return, the *marabouts* supported the state. The *marabouts* used their religious injunctions, or *ndigals*, to encourage their followers to vote for particular candidates. However, one should emphasize that the *marabout*-disciple relationship has always been conditional on the community's ability to meet its obligations to its members and the *marabouts'* influence has varied significantly from one context to another.[39] In the 1990s, neoliberal economic policies made it more difficult for the state to guarantee patronage to the *marabouts* and their followers; in turn, the religious leaders were less likely to encourage their followers to vote for the ruling party. Because fewer disciples have followed political *ndigals* since the 1990s (in contrast to *ndigals* on family, marriage, or community life), the *marabouts*, particularly at the national level, have become less likely to issue these injunctions for elections.[40]

Since the 1990s, the traditional *maraboutic* system has suffered pressure from within, as younger, university students have tried to 'modernize' and 'rationalize' the *daaira* model and some have questioned the hereditary nature of *maraboutic* power. These movements have sought to integrate Islamist themes, including a strong anti-Westernization stance, into their identity, and they have contributed to a growing respect for intellectuals with religious and Arabic language education. For example, the *Dahiratoul Moustarchidina wal Moustarchidaty* (or Moustarchidine) emerged in the early 1990s and directly attacked the close relations between the traditional *maraboutic* authorities and the political elite.[41]

---

37 Villalón, Leonardo (1994), 'Sufi Rituals as Rallies: Religious Ceremonies in the Politics of Senegalese State-Society Relations', *Comparative Politics*, Vol. 26(4), pp. 415-38.

38 Villalón, Leonardo (1995), *Islamic Society and State Power in Senegal*, Cambridge University Press, Cambridge, p. 12; Michael, Sarah, *Undermining Development*, p. 91.

39 Coulon, Christian, and Cruise O'Brien, Donal B. (1989), 'Senegal', in Donal B. Cruise O'Brien, John Dunn, and Richard Rathbone (eds), *Contemporary West African States*, Cambridge University Press, Cambridge, pp. 149-50.

40 Patterson, Amy S. (1999), 'The Dynamic Nature of Citizenship and Participation: Lessons from Three Rural Senegalese Case Studies', *Africa Today*, Vol. 46(1), pp. 15-20.

41 Villalón, Leonardo (2004), 'Islamism in West Africa: Senegal', *African Studies Review*, Vol. 47(2), p. 67.

Despite these challenges, the historic state-*marabout* relationship has made the holy men, the *daaira*, and the Muslim brotherhoods powerful actors in Senegalese politics. Through their reciprocal relationship with the political elite, including Senegal's first president Léopold Sédar Senghor who was Christian not Muslim, the brotherhoods have achieved patronage benefits and positive policy outcomes such as agricultural implements and land for their leaders and members. The *marabouts* have controlled peanut production in rural areas and, since the 1970s, have gained import licenses and control of many urban businesses.[42] At the grassroots level, developmental NGOs realize the necessity of cooperating with the local *marabout* to ensure project success. More broadly, because they have linked the state with citizens, the religious orders have helped to foster stability in Senegal, even during the country's democratic transition that culminated in the 2000 election. While some would argue that the brotherhoods have tended to promote the status quo to the detriment of Senegal's poorest citizens, it cannot be denied that these FBOs have used their relationship with the state to wield power in Senegalese politics.[43]

The power of Senegal's brotherhoods comes from these groups' roots in rural society through the *daaira* and their ability to meet citizens' spiritual and material needs. The brotherhoods also have links to resources, particularly rural production and urban trade. Because of their large number of adherents, these FBOs have power, making these organizations a difficult force to ignore. And political elites do pay considerable attention to them: on the day of the 2000 election, opposition party candidate Abdoulaye Wade traveled to the Mouride holy city of Touba to receive a blessing from the brotherhood's highest leader.[44]

The final example of an FBO is the Inter-Religious Council of Sierra Leone, which played a highly visible role building bridges between warring factions and shaping the 1999 Lomé Agreement to end that country's civil war. Because other CSOs had been repressed or remained silent out of fear of repression, the Council—and its various constituent religious group members—formed a unique voice in the peace process. In Sierra Leone's divided society, the Inter-Religious Council modeled cross-group collaboration and advocated for peace and justice that was inclusive and participatory. The organization's larger vision of a peaceful society gave it legitimacy with citizens. But the power of the organization also rested with more worldly factors. First, Council members had boldly stood up against violence, often at great risk to themselves. Second, the Council mobilized citizens to support peace through its leadership training and peace building activities, and the education it provided citizens and the media about the war's atrocities.[45] Third, these FBOs were rooted in communities and formed a moral authority based in society.

---

42 Cruise O'Brien, Donal B. (1988), 'Charisma Comes to Town: Mouride Urbanization 1945-1986', in Donal B. Cruise O'Brien and Christian Coulon (eds), *Charisma and Brotherhood in African Islam*, Clarendon Press, Oxford, p. 139.

43 Markovitz, Irving Leonard (1970), 'Traditional Social Structure, the Islamic Brotherhoods and Political Development in Senegal', *Journal of Modern African Studies*, Vol. 8(1), pp. 73-96.

44 Villalón, Leonardo, 'Islamism in West Africa', p. 66.

45 Brima, Abu, Hasselblad, Wyva, et al. (2002), 'The New African Liberation Movement: A Case Study of the Implications of Civil Society in the Sierra Leone Peace Process', in

Fourth, the Council demonstrated its goodwill to all sides through concrete actions: providing clothing, blankets, and sanitary kits to surrendered soldiers and giving food to displaced civilians: 'These activities helped to consolidate real confidence and thus marked the beginning of actual dialogue between the Revolutionary United Front (RUF) and the government of Sierra Leone through the facilitation of the Council'.[46]

The Council played a role that the government, RUF, and international mediators could not, with one of its biggest policy goals—the formation of a Truth and Reconciliation Commission for Sierra Leone—being achieved. The Commission was formalized and began operations in 2002. Of course, the Sierra Leone conflict also shows that the efforts of FBOs such as the Council may not be sufficient for ending conflict, if all parties are not willing to lay down arms and if the perceived material benefits to aggressors outweigh the costs. The continuation of the fighting despite the Lomé accords until 2002 was clearly a set back for the Council and its efforts to build trust among all parties. Yet, to its credit, the organization continued its peacebuilding efforts during this period.

Each of these three cases illustrates that FBOs can bring new visions to development, conflict resolution, and state-civil society relations. But for these new visions to be accepted, FBOs must have legitimacy, leadership, resources, and connections to society. Because of the *potential* of FBOs, policy-makers have paid more attention to this type of CSO in recent years. These organizations increasingly are shaping the agendas of bilateral and multilateral donors, and they are receiving more donor resources as a result. For example, FBOs are urged to compete for grants for AIDS prevention, care, support, and treatment projects as part of the US PEPFAR program. In many African countries, FBOs sit on the CCMs that devise programs to fight AIDS, TB, and malaria and write grants to the GFATM.[47]

But this attention and funding may obscure the fact that FBOs can face the same challenges that other CSOs do. They may be under-funded: the *New Republic* quoted Martin Ssempa, a well-known Ugandan evangelical leader, who reported that 99 percent of his church's funding comes from US churches.[48] Some FBOs face internal challenges based on race, class, gender, or generation, as seen with Senegal's Muslim brotherhoods. Many FBOs have not adequately faced Africa's pressing challenges such as HIV/AIDS, poverty, and gender inequalities. And religious leaders have not always challenged authoritarianism or human rights violations. Some of the worst massacres during the 1994 Rwandan genocide occurred in churches, demonstrating how Tutsi-Hutu ethnic identities overshadowed believers' religious unity.[49]

Roland Hoksbergen and Lowell M. Ewert (eds), *Local Ownership, Global Change: Will Civil Society Save the World?* World Vision, Monrovia, pp. 32-56.

46 Turay, Thomas Mark (2000), 'Civil Society and Peacebuilding: The Role of the Inter-Religious Council of Sierra Leone', *Accord*, Vol. 9, http://www.c-r.org/accord/s-leone/accord9/society.shtml (accessed January 2, 2006).

47 Patterson, Amy S. (2006), *The Politics of AIDS in Africa*, Lynne Rienner Publishers, Boulder, pp. 74-75.

48 Rice, Andrew (2004), 'Enemy's Enemy', *New Republic*, Vol. 231(5), pp. 18-21.

49 Katongole, Emmanuel (2005), 'Christianity, Tribalism, and the Rwandan Genocide: A Catholic Reassessment of Christian "Social Responsibility"', *Logos*, Vol. 8(3), pp. 67-93.

While the mission-centered nature of FBOs may help these groups change views of justice, human rights, equality, peace, reconciliation, and development, many questions remain about this type of African CSO: How have the increased attention and funding these groups have received shaped their power, autonomy, character, mission, and internal dynamics? What types of organizational structures facilitate or hinder FBOs? How can FBOs work with the state? And given recent inter-religious conflicts in Nigeria and Uganda, how can FBOs create social capital *across* ethnic, religious, and regional divides?

CSOs and International Coalitions: The Case of TAC

In an era of globalization, CSOs can reach across international boundaries to shape domestic and international politics. As mentioned above, FBOs have worked across international lines to influence definitions of development. Similarly, organizations such as Jubilee 2000 successfully built global coalitions to advocate for debt relief for poor countries. But African and Middle Eastern organizations are often underrepresented in these transnational coalitions.[50] This section examines one particular CSO—South Africa's Treatment Action Campaign (TAC)--to argue that transnational networks have the potential to bolster civil society's influence, but that alone, such networks are insufficient for increasing an organization's power.

Formed in 1998 and greatly influenced by the anti-apartheid activism of South Africa community groups, TAC's mandate is to 'campaign for greater access to [antiretroviral] treatment for all South Africans, by raising public awareness and understanding about issues surrounding availability, affordability and use of HIV treatments'. TAC also 'campaigns against the view that AIDS is a "death sentence"'.[51] It uses multiple strategies to achieve its goals: lawsuits, civil disobedience, protests, a treatment literacy campaign for those undergoing antiretroviral (ARV) treatment, and projects to demonstrate that treatment can work on a large scale in poor communities. Three policy issues illustrate the different factors that have made TAC influential.

In the first case, TAC supported the South African government when pharmaceutical companies sued the government for passing the South African Medicines Act of 1997. The law allows South Africa to engage in compulsory licensing of medicines in health emergencies, a process by which a patent owner provides a license to manufacture a product at a negotiated price. Compulsory licensing enables South Africa to produce generic ARVs at a lower price than brand-name drugs. The United States supported the companies in the lawsuit and threatened trade sanctions against South Africa if it did not rescind the legislation.

---

50 Florini, Ann M. (2000), *The Third Force: The Rise of Transnational Civil Society*, Carnegie Endowment for International Peace, Washington, DC.

51 Mbali, Mandisa (2004), 'The Treatment Action Campaign and the History of Rights-Based, Patient-Driven HIV/AIDS Activism in South Africa', Research Report no. 9, University of Kwazulu-Natal Centre for Civil Society, http://www.nu.ac.za/ccs/files/RReport_29.pdf (accessed December 7, 2005), p. 2; Treatment Action Campaign (2005a), 'About TAC', http://www.tac.org.za (accessed November 7, 2005).

Health Global Access Project (Health GAP), an ad hoc coalition formed in 1998, reacted by pressuring the pharmaceutical industry and the Clinton Administration. Health GAP's founding members included the AIDS Coalition to Unleash Power (ACT UP), Search for a Cure, Health Action International, *Médecins Sans Frontières* (Doctors Without Borders), Partners in Health, TAC, the AIDS Treatment Data Network, and Ralph Nader's Consumer Project on Technology. At the 2000 International AIDS conference in Durban, South Africa, activists led by TAC demanded treatment access and their actions received global media attention. In the United States, Health GAP members held loud, raucous protests at presidential campaign events for then Vice President Al Gore, actions that embarrassed the Clinton Administration.[52] These protests targeted pharmaceutical companies that set high prices and Western governments that enforced the strong patent protection of the Trade Related Intellectual Property Rights (TRIPS) Agreement of the World Trade Organization (WTO). The protests were also framed as part of a larger anti-globalization movement, which viewed the WTO and its neoliberal policies as elite-driven.[53] TAC's coalition with Western AIDS and anti-globalization groups helped the South African government win the public relations war against the drug companies. In 2001, the companies dropped their lawsuit.

The global treatment movement demonstrates the ability of TAC to forge international ties to achieve its objectives. This does not mean that Western AIDS organizations or donors control TAC. Instead, TAC has added a unique African voice to the movement, particularly since it represents citizens in a country with one of the highest HIV prevalence rates in the world.[54] But TAC has modeled some of its civil disobedience campaigns on those used by ACT UP, particularly when it charged the Minister of Health Manto-Tshabalala Msimang with culpable homicide in 2003. This action echoed ACT UP protests in the late 1980s that charged pharmaceutical companies and the US Food and Drug Administration with killing AIDS patients because of their slow approval of AIDS drugs.[55] Thus, there is reciprocal learning and information sharing within the movement. Easy internet communication and relatively cheap transportation have facilitated the efforts of this loosely knit movement.

In 2001, TAC successfully sued the South African government to provide the drug nevirapine for prevention of mother-to-child HIV transmission (PMTCT). The government has consistently argued that the drug is too expensive and unsafe

---

52 Behrman, Greg (2004), *The Invisible People: How the U.S. Has Slept Through the Global AIDS Pandemic, the Greatest Humanitarian Catastrophe of Our Time*, Free Press, New York, pp.151-59.

53 Smith, Raymond (2002), 'Bridging the Gap: The Emergence of a US Activist Movement to Confront AIDS in the Developing World', Paper presented at the Annual Meeting of the American Political Science Association, Boston, MA, August 30-September 2.

54 UNAIDS estimated in 2004 that HIV prevalence among South African women attending antenatal clinics was 29.5%. UNAIDS (2005), *UNAIDS/WHO AIDS Epidemic Update: December 2005*, http://www.unaids.org/Epi2005/doc/report_pdf.html (accessed December 28, 2005), p. 21.

55 Mbali, Mandisa, 'The Treatment Action Campaign', p. 17.

and that South Africa lacks the health care infrastructure to deliver the drug.[56] The South African High Court ruled that the government must provide nevirapine or a comparable drug such as AZT (zidovudine) to all HIV-positive pregnant women at public hospitals. As the government dragged its feet on nevirapine distribution and continued to question the scientific findings about the drug, TAC increased its pressure on the government through lawsuits, public relations efforts, and public protests.

The nevirapine issue has received considerable international press attention and official and unofficial spokespeople for bilateral and multilateral donors have criticized the South African government for its delays. For example, UN Envoy Stephen Lewis has made pointed comments urging the government to do more on PTMCT. TAC has helped to cultivate these media relations through its timely and well-written press releases issued domestically and internationally to its coalition partners. But the nevirapine case demonstrates additional factors beyond global coalitions that have helped TAC achieve its goals. First, TAC has benefited from the democratic environment of a post-apartheid South Africa. The organization has used South Africa's independent judiciary, its free media, and its liberal constitution that permits free assembly and free speech to the organization's advantage. Second, TAC has financial resources that have helped it achieve its objectives. Unlike many CSOs, TAC has successfully applied to Western foundations and donors for grants for its advocacy and treatment projects. It had a budget of R18 million for 2004-2005, double the income it had two years earlier. It has used its resources to bring lawsuits, to issues press statements, and to maintain an informative website. It also has roughly forty staff members, a fact which further empowers it in the policy process. These personnel and financial resources have enabled TAC to publicize scientific studies supporting nevirapine and to counter the government's position on ARVs in easy-to-understand language.[57]

In the third policy case, in late 2003, the South African government announced it would provide ARV treatment for all HIV-positive South Africans who needed it at public hospitals, a policy shift that reflected TAC influence. This case highlights TAC's use of resources, its ties to international coalitions, its ability to utilize South Africa's new democratic structures, and its successful mobilization of citizens. In terms of mobilization, it is important to know that TAC's roots lie in anti-apartheid community organizations. Its leaders, such as Zackie Achmat and Mark Heywood, have long histories of social activism and strong ties to legal and human rights organizations within South Africa. Since its founding, TAC has grown in size, though its roughly 9,500 membership is a very small percentage of the estimated five million people living with HIV/AIDS in South Africa. No doubt, the unique

---

56 Furlong, Patrick, and Ball, Karen (2005), 'The More Things Change: AIDS and the State in South Africa', in Amy S. Patterson (ed.), *The African State and the AIDS Crisis*, Ashgate Publishers, Aldershot, p. 143; LaFraniere, Sharon (2004), 'South Africa Rejects Use of AIDS Drug for Women', *New York Times*, July 14, p. A11.

57 Friedman, Steven, and Mottiar, Shauna (2004), 'A Moral to the Tale: The Treatment Action Campaign and the Politics of HIV/AIDS', Paper presented for the Centre for Policy Studies, University of KwaZulu-Natal, Durban, p. 5.

nature of the disease affects membership: individuals may not join because of the AIDS stigma and other members die from the disease. Leaders acknowledge that the relatively small size of its base may constrain its activities, but TAC has been able to mobilize nonmembers for its marches, with as many as 15,000 turning out for some events.[58] What is probably more important than sheer numbers is that the membership (as well as the funding and staff size) has continued to grow as the organization has achieved policy successes.

TAC has been able to mobilize large numbers of supporters because of its legitimacy, its ties to human rights and democracy movements, and its work in some of the poorest South African communities such as the Khayelitsha Township. Mass mobilization enabled TAC to put pressure on the South African government prior to the 2003 announcement. TAC engaged in civil disobedience during public speeches made by the health minister and other government officials. It leaked internal government reports to the media that estimated the number of South Africans who would die without government-provided ARVs. TAC provided a wealth of scientific research demonstrating that ARVs could be effectively administered and that the cost of *not* doing so for business profits, labor productivity, and South Africa's long-term economic development was higher than the cost of universal ARV access. It teamed up with multinational NGOs such as Doctors Without Borders to engage in treatment pilot projects, which provided further evidence that ARVs could be administered in South Africa's poorest neighborhoods.[59] As it had in the nevirapine case, TAC mobilized international public opinion and activists globally. Former US President Jimmy Carter spoke about the government's stubbornness in providing ARVs. And, former President Nelson Mandela, after meeting with Achmat and South African treatment advocates, publicly supported universal ARV access.[60]

TAC is a powerful organization, because it has used its resources, international ties, and local legitimacy to gain a reputation and to reformulate the ways the South African government and the international community view AIDS policies. Before 2001, the conventional wisdom among multilateral and bilateral donors, many development officials, and the South African government was that AIDS treatment was impossible in poor countries. TAC, working in a global coalition, changed that view. It built on the success of Doctors Without Borders and Partners in Health, which showed that ARV distribution was possible in Haiti. These groups demonstrated that treatment was not only a human right, but that it also was feasible.[61] This new perspective generated further momentum for AIDS treatment programs internationally. Even with this attention, though, progress on achieving universal access to treatment is slow; the Joint United Nations Programme on HIV/AIDS (UNAIDS) reported in 2005 that only 10 percent of HIV-positive people needing

---

58 Friedman, Steven, and Mottiar, Shauna, 'A Moral to the Tale', p. 5.

59 Johnson, Krista (2004), 'The Politics of AIDS Policy Development and Implementation in Postapartheid South Africa', *Africa Today*, Vol. 51(2), pp. 107-28.

60 Cameron, Edwin (2005), *Witness to AIDS*, I.B. Tauris & Co., London, pp. 127-29.

61 Farmer, Paul (2005), *Pathologies of Power: Health, Human Rights, and the New War on the Poor*, University of California Press, Berkeley, p. 19.

ARVs in Africa were receiving them.⁶² And despite TAC's efforts, only about 70,000 of the 500,000 South Africans who needed ARVs in 2005 were getting them.⁶³

TAC raises several questions about African CSOs. Specifically, what is the relationship between internal assets, such as membership, leadership, financial resources, and legitimacy, and external assets, such as participation in global coalitions? How do the two factors interact to create, or stifle, powerful organizations? In terms of external factors, what type of long-term challenges do African CSOs face as they participate in global coalitions? As global movements achieve successes, how do they—and their constituent organizations—reformulate goals? Though TAC prods us to ask such questions, it also raises a more fundamental point: Why have other African CSOs not be able to emulate TAC's successes?

Think Tanks: The Power of Ideas?

Independent research think tanks are another element of African civil society that has received limited attention. Because of the relative newness of this CSO type, it is difficult to say such groups are 'powerful'. E. Gyimah-Boadi claims these organizations help 'break the monopoly African governments have held over the production and dissemination of information'.⁶⁴ Examples include the Institute for Democracy in South Africa (IDASA), the Center for Democratic Development (CDD) in Ghana, the Center for Basic Research in Uganda, and Kenya's Research on Poverty Alleviation. Many of these organizations have teamed up with research institutions in the West to produce in-depth reports on democratic transitions, citizen attitudes, poverty, and economic policies. These CSOs have benefited from the global flow of information on the internet, and they routinely publish their research on their websites. Their in-depth studies have helped to put pressure on domestic governments. For example, IDASA routinely evaluates the South African budget in particular areas and advocacy groups use this information in their work. Additionally, some groups such as CDD, have helped to train judges and legislators about their role in democratic political systems. The emergence of these particular CSOs demonstrates a deepening of democracy in some African countries.

Think tanks have several potential sources of power. First, the spread of democracy in many African countries since the early 1990s has created an open environment in which they can engage in policy debates. Open political systems promote free media, which can expose the ideas of think tanks, and interest groups, which can use the research that think tanks conduct when they lobby government. Second, ties to the global academic community can increase these organizations' access to resources and augment their legitimacy. For example, the close links that the CDD has with the Afrobarometer project at Michigan State University in the United States empower that Ghanaian CSO; it has gained recognition for its research

---

62 UNAIDS, *UNAIDS/WHO AIDS Epidemic Update*, p. 6.
63 Treatment Action Campaign (2005b), 'Joint COSATU, SACC, TAC Press Statement', November 23, http://www.tac.org.za/COSATUTACSACCStatement23Nov05.html (accessed December 30, 2005).
64 Gyimah-Boadi, E., 'Civil Society', pp. 106-7.

on African public opinion and democratization. Moreover, the relationship between the African institution and Western organization often is reciprocal, since Western academics are eager to forge ties with African research institutions in order to more accurately and efficiently conduct research on the continent. The mutual benefits that drive African-Western academic cooperation have the potential to increase the voice of African research institutes.

A third source of power is the fact that ideas matter in policy making. Because of their in-depth analysis of problems and the expertise of their staff/members, think tanks have the long-term potential to change how society and political leaders view political and socioeconomic problems. For example, the rise of neoconservative beliefs about the power of the United States contributed to President George W. Bush's decision to invade Iraq in 2003.[65] In the African context, Nicolas van de Walle illustrates that the lack of acceptance of neoliberal economic theories among African intellectuals is one reason why structural adjustment policies have not been fully implemented in most sub-Saharan African countries.[66] Overall, policy ideas in Africa have tended to come from the state and donors. Think tanks provide a potentially powerful means for breaking this duopoly in the African policy dialogue.

Yet, this type of CSO also faces obstacles. Under-resourced think tanks may have to rely on external donors, a fact that may drive their research agenda in subtle ways. More investigations are needed to better understand how resources and dependence shape relations between think tanks and their partners. Second, there are relatively few African think tanks. If they are to generate a plethora of ideas, as pluralist views of policy making would assert, their numbers, size, and prestige must increase. Third, how do these organizations get their ideas accepted? That is, in African societies with relatively low levels of literacy and internet access, how do think tanks educate citizens about their proposals? These questions are important if part of the power of CSOs lies in their ability to link the state and citizens. Finally, how do these research institutions operate in a policy environment shaped by neopatrimonialism and the demands of bilateral and multilateral donors? The arbitrary nature of decision making in many African state institutions, and the fact that civil service advancement often does not reward new policy suggestions, make it more difficult for the best ideas from independent, non-state actors to affect executive decisions.[67] Additionally, bilateral and multilateral donors may curtail policy options. While donor influence has been most apparent in macroeconomic policy-making, other policy arenas have not been immune. For example, in return for loans and grants, multilateral and bilateral donors have required the establishment of AIDS commissions and the acceptance of particular HIV prevention policies.[68] In this donor-conditioned environment, think

---

65 Fukuyama, Francis (2006), *America at the Crossroads: Democracy, Power, and the Neoconservative Legacy*, Yale University Press, New Haven.

66 van de Walle, Nicolas, 'Economic Reform', pp. 47-49.

67 van de Walle, Nicolas (2001), *African Economies and the Politics of Permanent Crisis, 1979-1999*, Cambridge University Press, New York, pp. 118-29.

68 Putzel, James (2004), 'The Global Fight Against AIDS: How Adequate Are the National Commissions?' *Journal of International Development*, Vol. 16(8), pp. 1129-40.

tank influence may be more 'on the margins' through policy implementation and/or assessment.

CSOs and the Way Forward

As E. Gyimah-Boadi writes, 'Civil society is a mixture of good and bad'.[69] African CSOs are a potentially powerful force to hold government accountable, provide needed services to citizens, teach democratic values, and foster social capital. Yet, these groups can face challenges: limited resources, internal divisions, authoritarian decision-making processes, and a lack of autonomy from the state or donors. These obstacles curtail the power of CSOs, preventing their influence on political decision-making, service provision, or policy conversations.

This chapter illustrated how the obstacles and opportunities that CSOs face are played out in three different types of associations. First, some FBOs have utilized their mission, and the legitimacy and group identity that stems from it, to mobilize citizens, represent their members, and shape how problems are viewed. For the FBOs examined here, mission alone was insufficient to promote success: resources, context, and internal dynamics mattered too. For example, multinational FBOs engaging in development work have resources and legitimacy that have helped them shape development policies. Senegal's *marabouts* have close relations with their followers, a fact that has enabled them to generate support, legitimacy, and, at times, material resources.

Second, some CSOs, such as TAC, have become part of larger global movements. In doing so, they have added important African voices to debates on international problems. Yet, few African CSOs play such a global role, and the reasons TAC has been able to do so relate to its internal cohesion, its roots in South Africa's struggle against apartheid, its institutionalization, and its growing membership. These internal dynamics have enabled TAC to become an international actor; its global reputation, in turn, has helped the organization to raise funds. Third, as a relatively new type of CSO, think tanks gain power from their ability to shape policy options, both domestically and internationally. Their ties to Western institutions provide them legitimacy, resources, and important connections to international political and economic institutions. Yet, we know precious little about the long-term ability of these CSOs to control their research agenda and to get their ideas accepted among African citizens and policy-makers.

Using the lessons from FBOs, TAC, and think tanks, I suggest several policies to empower African CSOs. FBOs demonstrate that CSOs with communal roots, legitimate leaders, and resources such as social trust and shared identity may be able to shape the rules of the game. Donors that want to support CSOs must encourage groups with deep foundations and legitimacy, and they must question their support for newly formed organizations that may lack such assets. Part of the power of the FBOs presented here lies in their ability to set their own agenda. Donors must be willing to let organizations define their own problems and devise their own solutions.

---

69 Gyimah-Boadi, E., 'Civil Society', p. 116.

For CSOs, their leaders and members must learn to recognize the power that their organizations may already possess. For example, until quite recently few church leaders in Nigeria realized the important role these religious institutions could play on the AIDS issue, despite their relatively large membership and their already-existing structures of communication.[70]

TAC illustrates the power of global ties, but it is unrealistic to assume that all African CSOs can (or should) forge international coalitions. For applicable groups, donors and multinational NGOs can seek to enhance the communication technologies available to CSOs to facilitate contact between Western and African organizations. In order for these coalitions to be long-lasting, structures that encourage honest dialogue will need to emerge. Western groups and their African partners must be conscious about how they build relationships in order to foster long-run equality and participation. Finally, think tanks must seek to integrate their work with the activities of other African CSOs, in order to more effectively disseminate their ideas. CSOs may provide opportunities to 'test' the theories that think tanks advocate in particular policy arenas. Western academic institutions may be able to support such partnerships with resources or communication technologies.

While there are many reasons the richness of Africa's associational life has not been fully tapped, one is that many CSOs have yet to attain the necessary power to become legitimate, long-run players in Africa's social, economic, and political development. Although not every CSO should be powerful—racist groups and sexist organizations are the negative part of civil society—Africa's future at least partly relies on CSOs that care for the sick and elderly, that push the state and donors with new ideas, and that represent their members' interests in policy discussions. While CSOs should not be viewed as a panacea to all Africa's complex problems, their empowerment is one piece of the puzzle in forging a path forward for the continent.

---

70 Representative of multinational FBO working with twelve Protestant denominations in Nigeria on AIDS education programs, conversation with author, March 9, 2006, Grand Rapids, Michigan.

Chapter 11

Gender and Development

Christine Obbo

Introduction

Gender, the social and cultural construction of men and women; and Development, the global instrument of change; cannot be understood as givens without examining the framing social and analytical paradigms and practices. An analytical understanding of gender dynamics and development agenda ownership requires a consideration of their influences on the social and economic relations resulting from the roles of men and women clearly spelling out class, age and generation. Science grows by accretion until a residue of anomalous data forces overthrow of the old and establishment of a new paradigm (Kuhn, 1962). Paradigms are "patterns of ideas, values, methods and bahaviour which fit together and are mutually reinforcing, to co-exist, overlap, coalesce and separate." (Chambers, 1995:32). The extractive model of development practised by most African countries has not solved the critical development problems of poverty, ignorance disease and injustice. There can be no development without equity, and no equity without addressing gender inequalities in household and community. Equitable development is people-centred and sustainable. Some insist that in development, we are all trapped in the prison of power in which the power of expertise and patronage money define the reality of development (1984-5, Escobar; Chambers, 1996). This chapter reviews some development paradigms, the UN as the midwife of gender equity and human rights, and the obstacles to eradicating gender inequalities.

Campaigns for Change and Resistance

Since 1945 the UN has addressed itself to people's civil and legal rights in general, and those of specific groups (UN, 1996). UN declarations, conventions and instruments now cover rights in every aspect of life. The 1995 Copenhagen World Summit for Social Development Declaration and Programme of Action called for strengthening the UN's role in promoting people-centred development and included among ten the specified commitments, human rights and a "new paradigm" for achieving equity and equality between men and women.

UN conferences symbolically legitimise women's concerns thus forcing national leaders to address issues. Feminist writers, researchers and practitioners have been the driving forces behind the UN Conferences on women, and shifts in global development policies on women.

The UN energised the Women Movement by designating 1975 International Women's Year and organising the first Conference on Women in Mexico to assess the situation, and to highlight strategies and goals for women's advancement. The conference Plan of Action: Equality, Development and Peace reflected the broad interests of Northern, Southern and Eastern Block women respectively. It also focused on women's access to education, employment, political participation, health care services, housing, nutrition and family planning. Years 1975-1985 were designated the Decade for Women.

Northern women activists lobbied their lawmakers to ensure that foreign aid to the global South strove to increase the roles of women in decision making and economic participation. Boserup's (1970) research and assertive conclusions that modernisation had marginalised women inspired considerable scholarship that exposed male domination (Elson, 1991), and the fallacy of gender neutral development and lead to a paradigm shift to Women in Development (WID) (Buvinic et al 1978; Staudt, 1985; Tinker, 1991). Planners were criticised ignoring and undermining women by privileging male views on women's activities, and thereby overlooking considerations of time budgeting, the operative local knowledge and the acceptability of projects to proposed beneficiaries. Earlier intensive, large-scale and infrastructural interventions had unintentionally harmed and sidelined women. The emphases on "human capital", "basic needs", and technological development overlooked women's need for appropriate technology which they could afford and operate (Dauber and Cain, 1981; Stamp, 1989), and failed to address the pressing development issues women's health, education and employment. WID demanded separate projects to enable women to develop their human capital and to meet their basic needs.

Boserup had reported that the African farmer, was not the "he" of the official development policies but a woman doing most of the agricultural work. The introduction of cash crops increased work burdens on food producers. Women worked, and men, in their role as de jure household heads, appropriated the cash. Researchers argued that the work of African women who constitute 60-80% of agricultural workers had been undercounted and undervalued in official demographic and economic statistics. Women's work was a valuable resource but wastefully rendered "invisible" (Bay et al, 1976). When women migrate to cities to escape the restrictive rural economic opportunities and ideological controls, their lack of schooling qualifies them for underpaid jobs and self-employment in the informal economy. Urban dwellers depend on women in their various capacities as food growers, traders processors, hawkers, servants and municipal public workers.

The 1980 Copenhagen UN Women's Conference assessed the progress of the Mexico Plan of Action. Research reported that women's rights under the law did not match women's ability to exercise them. Women's interests were not being integrated in development programmes because their projects were afterthought additions. This denied women the incentives of improving and applying skills and knowledge (Rogers, 1980). The adopted plan for action called for national measures to integrate women into all areas of development by according them rights to inheritance, children and control over property.

The 1985 Nairobi Conference concluded UN Women's Decade by reviewing and appraising the achievements towards Equality, Development and Peace. The general verdict based on regional reports was that changes and benefits had been minimal. A summary document: The Forward Looking Strategies for the Advancement of Women (UN 1985) provided guideline for national and international action. Specific guideline proposals included: employment, health, education, food, water, agriculture, industry-trade-commerce, science and technology, communication, housing and settlement, community development, transport, energy, environment and social services (Rathgeber, 1995:208). The Nairobi Strategies were adopted by 157 countries.

The UN Women's Decade was concurrent with the Second UN Development Decade which promoted a unified approach to development and planning that would result in social and economic equity (UNRISD, 1980). The problems of environment, population, hunger, women, habitat, and employment became prioritised (Esteva, 1992:14). A new paradigm "another development" was proposed as the route to achieving genuine "integrated" development that would be "human-centred" (Dag Hammarskjold1975), and "endogenous" (UNESCO,1977). Sustainable development depended on people being stakeholders. WID proposed "another development with women" using organisational collective action in order to achieve the economic and political empowerment of women (DAWN 1985).

In the 1970s and 1980s development agencies incorporated WID in human capital development policies to provide training opportunities through either adding women components to existing projects or creating women's projects. Women's projects created additional work for women and jobs for men. Women continued to do their domestic productive and reproductive work in addition to income generating activities such as horticulture, animal husbandry, craft making and co-operative labour at grain-mills. But because women lacked education, technical and marketing know how, it is men who became empowered with marketing and managerial skills as they became project middle men and salaried employees.

WID research and interventions had successfully served as antidote to gender neutral policies that assumed men's and women's needs and responses to opportunities to be identical. But WID efforts to provide women with opportunities to participate in male-defined, male dominated social and economic structures produced minimal changes in the conditions and situations of women. The prevailing cultural norms that privileged men with preferential treatment at the expense of women were an obstacle to changes promoted by WID. Objection to "women's development exceptionalism" became common and is still manifested in constant reminders that women's human rights should not be achieved "the expense of antagonising men" (Nyerere, 1984; Uganda AIDS Commission, 2000).

When women-only projects are successful, families are fed and clothed, children are schooled and husbands' social and business ventures supported. In some cases husbands abandon all economic responsibilities to women. But whether women's projects are successful or not, they invoke male jealousy and backlash (Obbo, 2005; Momsen 2001) blamed for increasing violence against women.

In the global North, the legal, educational and employment gains achieved by the women's movement led to male backlash by the late 1980s. This was reflected in searches for new approaches of dealing with women and development aid in the South. Because WID had become synonymous with "women only", a short lived reconciliatory approach, Women and Development (WAD) came into use. WAD advocated the studying and understanding of masculinities as a starting point for involving men in the development process. However, critics argued that this would undermine the struggle to achieve gender equality (Cornwall and White 2000). Tackling problem of women's exclusion from development required an analysis of the process of exclusion.

Gender and Development (GAD) became a new paradigm, advocating a holistic assessment of the needs and strategies of both women and men when planning and evaluating the success of development programmes and projects. GAD development interventions calls for fundamental reassessment of gender relations and ideology (Marchand and Parpart, 1995). Advocates assert that economic improvement is impossible without political empowerment; and suggest policy solutions to the intractable unintended results of development such as the "feminisation of poverty" particularly associated with female headed households (Fhh). Fhh are disproportionately concentrated among low income groups and tend to suffer extremes of poverty compared to their male-headed counterparts. Fhh are the result of the predominance of men in rural-urban migration, male desertion, divorces, and wars. Furthermore, female wage employment, however low, exacerbates declining employment for men in the lower end of the societal hierarchy and increases women's responsibilities and male resentment.

GAD focuses on the "condition" and "situation" of women in the development process. The condition of women is defined by their legal and economic statuses that determine their access to health, education, technology and credit. The position of women pertains to the power driven social relations between men and women (Young, 1988; Rathgeber, 1995:206). Thus informed policies on gender cannot ignore the multiple power relationships in households and between social groups. GAD advocates the creation of a change enabling environment through gender empowerment and mainstreaming. Empowerment entails the accessing and exercising of power by marginalised peoples. Power is a complex relational process. It is both a concept and a practice and its meaning changes according to the circumstances and perspectives of different people. Power is always imbedded in local, regional, national and global contexts of dominance and subordination. Power has been studied from many perspectives. Kabeer (1994) has made three distinctions: power to; power over and power within . The WID paradigm was based on the assumption that women had the "power to", the capacity to make decisions and act. Policy interventions played the enabling role for women's economic engagement without challenging the structural inequalities. The GAD paradigm insists structural transformation through participation in process of political and economic structures of the decision making. This is imperative because even when people have exercised their agency in wielding and yielding power, those with the "power over" them may successfully use institutional factors to exclude certain issues from the agenda. However, the greatest hindrance to achieving empowerment is the "power within" which through psychological suppression, self-censorship and de-politicization inhibits individuals or groups from confronting conflicting interests. Conceptualising empowerment of women in practice requires distinguishing between practical and strategic gender interests (Molyneux, 1985). Women can organise collective actions to achieve immediate practical interests but may need consciousness raising to organise for long-term gender equality and liberation. A useful educational tool in this case is Participatory Action Research, an empowering culturally sensitive methodology that enhances the capacity of existing community groups and networks to organise, learn and develop means of analysis, reflection and problem solving. The group becomes the vehicle of collective learning and action (Schoepf, 1993). The nature and content of women's powerlessness varies according to age, class and ethnicity. Powerlessness is manifested in the general failure of women's capacity to secure their needs. Action Research can be used to understand how power can be enabling or incapacitating; and to deconstruct male bias that resides in the deep structures of society and is reflected in the day to day intimate behaviours that deny women power and control. Participatory analysis reveals the processes by which male power gains legitimacy and forces women to tolerate behaviours that are harmful to their well being.

Participatory paradigms evolved as correctives to general failure of "trickle down", the dominant assumption in development policies, to raise the standards of living. Gender neutral planning assumed, benefits would naturally "trickle down" to women in the "private sphere" from the targeted "public", mainly elite male sphere. If "trickle down" failed then state power would be strengthened in order to guarantee the proper functioning of market forces and the success of capitalism (Payer, 1982). Demands for "people centred" and "participatory" development led to the broadening of economic growth indicators to include quality of life.

In the late 1970s and 1980s. the development establishment declared war on poverty by adopting the "basic needs" paradigm. The rural poor and small farmers were targeted with the aim of achieving certain specific minimum standards of living before the end of the century. Women who were identified then by WID as the vulnerable poor continue to be disproportionately so. The opportunities SAP sought to provide for market based agriculture benefited men who profited from having access and entitlement to women's uncompensated labour, land and bank credit loans. Although land reform issues are recognised as central to rural development, yet women still lack control over land. Development policies have ignored economic changes manifested by non-farm employment activities: [de-agrarianisation] (Bryceson, 1997). Women's responsibilities for food production, processing and child rearing, make them less mobile than men. Most women combine farming with off farm activities. Women earn less than men and are often forced to pool their incomes with their husbands compromising their bargaining for rights.

The 1990s saw a concerted search for a workable marriage between development and politics. Focus turned to how development aid could tap the potential of private and voluntary efforts to achieve greater economic growth; and institutional and capacity building. NGOs initiated, encouraged and promoted the formation of intermediary local organizations to pressure and nudge governments towards transparent and accountable forms of democratic governance. Some new "pressure groups" had their roots in the economic crises of the 1970 and 1980s when local communities formed "development associations in response to the decline in the standards of public services. Neighbourhood Associations collected money to buy medicines to keep clinics and dispensaries open. Schools functioned because Parent/teacher associations made it possible to commute students' fees and pay teachers' salaries. Organised voluntary communal labour ensured the construction, maintenance and expansion of schools and roads; ensured garbage disposal and local security. These poverty coping strategies betrayed the failure of governments and the development enterprise.

The 1980s was a lost decade because development efforts in general had failed to improve economic performance and to raise the standard of living in Africa. Structural Adjustment Programmes (SAP) were imposed on African government with mismanaged economies as a condition for future aid loans. Focus was on growth oriented adjustment. Poverty alleviation projects were not placed in the broader social and economic policy frameworks that critically defined possible economic opportunities and existing constraints on men and women. Critics point out that SAP policies exacerbated poverty by narrowly focusing on market forces, while overlooking "non-price factors" such as quality of education, transportation and credit affecting rural areas (Schatz, 1994). The 1986 UN World Survey on the Role of Women in the global economy and the 1989 update both recorded limited progress during the decade for Women and in Africa noted the negative impact of policies on women. Under SAP women have borne increasing workloads and their unpaid labour has heavily subsidized cuts in social services, and civil service retrenchment (Staudt, 1985; WB 1989a). SAP has inadvertently underscored the fact that gender is a co-factor in development.

Projects for women were frequently started without feasibility studies with the result that they sometimes proved to be unsustainable (Buvinic, 1986). The dominant criterion in the implementation of development projects has been efficiency or cost effectiveness. It continues to be used as an evaluative tool because "efficiency and "productivity" are regarded as value neutral and objective (Kardam, 1991:116). In the early 1980 mainstream development agencies favoured initiatives that linked efficiency and human resources development allowing them to target women under the broad policies of education, population, health and nutrition (Chawdhry, 1995:32). The WB adopted this approach after its 1979 World Development Report acknowledged the invisibility of women in development (1979:83-84). Anti-poverty programmes promoted income generating activities for rural women. Education projects focused on women because their influence on family health and size is greater [than that of the father]; and may also have a greater effect on children's learning (Chowdhry, 1995; WB, 1990:5).

The integration of women's needs in agency planning and programming is still problematic. Minimal gains have been made in access to education, credit and legal services. Progress towards the implementation of gender issues into programmes depends on the efforts of a few progressive individuals. North and South hostile male technocrats often collude to block out WAD discourses on solving women's needs (Braxton, 1999). This explains why mission statements using fashionable jargons do not translate into concrete results.

In 1993 an internal World Bank evaluation of WID programs (WB Report 1993) observed that most staff were convinced that if integrating women's concerns into programme delivery makes projects more economically efficient then ultimately they will be included without special effort or manipulation (Rathgeber, 1995:210). This argument overlooks the fact that routinely, donor agencies as "brokers of development and modernisation have served the priorities of male dominated host governments. Agencies' capacity to effect societal changes in recipient countries are limited by the constraints of their governments' policies, and their dependence on the co-operation of local officials. The sexual division of labour, the social relations of gender, with all the in built power and economic inequalities, "are reified as culture and placed out of the mandate of development" (Parpart 1995:228, Goetz, 1991, Stamp, 1989). Sovereign rights are sacred and social transformation is not a development issue (Young et al 1981; Parpart, 1995:235; Kleeber, 1991). This reasoning finds resonance in the attitudes of local male leaders who are offended by the suggestions of women's development (WB, 1989c:x). Projects that attempt to operate outside mainstream government positions are doomed to failure.

In the 1990s donor countries advocated increase in aid effectiveness while reducing budgets. This approach was promoted by many governments and experts (Esteva, 1992:15). Under the push to 'get development right', projects would be kept small, government intervention would be minimal and expert knowledge would not be privileged over local knowledge. NGOs became the preferred mode of delivering aid to ensure that development reached the intended beneficiaries. At the turn of the 20th century, there were an estimated 30,000 NGOs working in the South. However, the expectations of sensitivity, reliability and, were often unfulfilled. In Burkina Faso for example, an NGO funded Primary Health Care project not only increased the power of bureaucrats in village affairs but sidelined local knowledge and health practices as PHC experts with imported scientific knowledge became dominant. Women opted out and continued with traditional practices.

The real problem was still knowledge production and dissemination by experts. Development plans are not conceptually holistic and earlier experiences and information are irrelevant. Planners rationalize decisions with reference to expatriate derived knowledge. Repetitive reference to consultant reports reaffirms its superiority over the knowledge of nationals (Crewe, 1997:71; Crewe and Harrison, 1998; Escobar, 1995). In the 1980s it was noted that advising Africa was a major industry with Europeans and north Americans consulting firms charging as much as much as US $ 180,000 for a year of an expert time. More than $7-8 billion was spent yearly by donors to pay at least 80,000 expatriates working for public agencies under official aid programmes (Timberlake, 1986:8). Even an NGO could spend £900 a day on a very expensive consultant (Crewe, 1997:61). Reportedly 60 percent of US foreign aid never leaves the US. Money is spent on American office and travel equipment, travel, housing and salaries, conferences and other allowances. The money that arrives is spent on ill conceived projects based on the expert knowledge of foreign bureaucrats and consultants (Epstein, 2005). Africa is dying from ill advice and projects designed for the wrong problems (Nindi:1990:59; Timberlake, ibid).

Implementing the 1990s espoused agenda of empowering, enabling and sustainable development became impossible because the aid industry is replete with rituals, such as participatory appraisals and project evaluations, and specialized development jargons. These create and recreate development ideologies, which reinforce the legitimacy of donors as powerful but benign benefactors (Crewe and Harrison, 1998:24). The control of money and the construction of public knowledge about development make the donors unchallengeable. At all encounters the dominance of the donors and the subordination of the locals are reaffirmed (ibid:189; Chambers, 1994).

GAD campaigns have sought to influence the agenda of institutions both in donor and recipient countries. In Africa GAD advocates seized the historical "moment" in the 1990s to push the agenda of "mainstreaming" women after SAP made politics and development openly intertwined. Donors were insisting upon political reform as a condition for receiving funding. Reforms included: democratic elections, transparency and accountability in public actions. Donors promoted "civil society" development to monitor the actions of states. In Africa NGO mushroomed to campaign for debt relief, women's political participation, women's property rights, human rights, and girls' education. The conditions seemed right for the GAD agenda to become reality with women's organisations pressuring for social and political change, the universities providing the research support for policy planning in gender bureaux, parliamentary women working for legislative reform, and women lawyers defending the civil and human right of women. The proliferation of women's groups rather than being a strength, undermined efforts at forging strong national feminist movements. Elites spoke for and not with the ordinary women, competition over jobs and prestige created divisive jealousies. Gender ministries were often lumped with culture, youth and sports, sometimes headed by indifferent men, and important decisions taken by male bureaucrats. Constitutional affirmative action allocating 30% parliamentary seats to women provokes male resentment. Some women have successfully competed for their seats and Rwanda has a total of 45% women in Parliament. But in general women parliamentarians have failed to articulate the interests of women and are accused of looking pretty and doing nothing. Several countries have had female vice-presidents and prime ministers, women are ministers and judges but few fail to be rewarded with intimidating male ridicule. The press, colleagues and electorates constantly remind women that their place is at home bearing children ad cooking for their husbands. Most women who make it to the top are not emancipated and lack the support of other women. Women need to organize themselves to increase their own self reliance, to assert their independent right to make choices and to control resources which they need to eliminate their subordination (Keller and Mbwere). Grassroots based women's movements are needed to put more women in politics in order to achieve that critical mass that will make them an effective empowered voice and force for demanding governments' commitment to development, empowerment, human rights, political participation. African women have made a start with an intellectual, bureaucratic and activist President being elected in Liberia.

Gender and Change Agents

According to GAD changes in the institutional decision making structures and cultures of national and international development agencies should reinforce the empowerment process of women's collective actions to gain effective voices and transform themselves into agents of social change.

It has been noted that development agencies are negotiation arenas of strategic groups. Progressive individuals in development agencies struggle to ensure that gender remains on the agenda. Gender officers proliferate. Few development interventions pass without a check list scrutiny to their possible impact on gender relations Gender mainstreaming has failed because a high proportion of male staff in donor agencies neither see what is wrong with existing gender relations nor the need to privilege women's issues. The male perspective still dominates the development discourse (Crewe and Harrison, 1998:49). All measures of economic success are male oriented with occasional acknowledgement of the real and value-adding contributions of women. When "women" become the shorthand for gender analysis, the political implications of gender analysis are blunted. Men often use organisational efficiency arguments to absorb the business of gender sections in general operations. This leads to women-only-projects (Williams, 1999:67-68). Men deal with the technical matters while gender issues are assigned to women. Realization that their analyses and recommendations can be dismissed as too negative or threatening, leads individuals to suppress data on political and economic gender inequalities. Possible policies for empowering women, when weighed against the practical exigencies of project realities, end up being inapplicable, or recreating gender inequalities through misapplication. While on paper gender has become "an essential uncontestable component of the development agenda", gender analysis rarely leads to gender sensitive practices. To explain why changes have been minimal, donors blame lack of information as the biggest barrier to addressing gender issues. The real problem, some argue, is that of incorporating feminist knowledge and insights during the process of data production (Goetz, 1994).

Women's researchers insists that men need to be aware and analyze the interests, needs and rights of women in relation to male identities and power. This is a prerequisite for mainstreaming gender in policy and institutions.

A "transformed partnership based on equality between women and men is a condition for people centred development" was the mission statement of the 1995 Beijing Women's Fourth Conference (UN, 1996:652). The platform for Action renewed the global commitment to women's empowerment through the mainstreaming of gender equality, and affirmed that women's advancement is a matter of fundamental human rights and a prerequisite for justice. The Platform was unanimously adopted by 191 member states.

The June 2000 UN General Assembly New York conference on "Women 2000: Gender, Equality, Development and Peace in the 21st Century" assessed the progress and readopted areas of concern from the Nairobi and Beijing platforms: poverty, environment, conflict migration and empowerment. The role of men and boys in achieving gender equality and demands for greater access to HIV/AIDS treatment by women and girls were highlighted focus.

At a September 2000 UN conference in New York, 191 nations were represented, including (147 heads of states) and the Millennium Development Goals (MDGs) were adopted. MDGs are a set of internationally agreed targets of development efforts that form the basis for much of the international development effort in the

21st Century. Delegates declared a commitment to engage politicians, civil society and the media in efforts:

i. primary education
ii. promote gender equality and empower women
iii. reduce child mortality
iv. to improve maternal health
v. combat HIV/AIDS, malaria and other diseases
vi. ensure environmental sustainability and
vii. develop a global partnership for development.

UN General Assembly Conferences, have an atmosphere of pomp and circumstances which forces attending government officials and delegates sign empty commitment. The damning proof is that after several official recommitments in 2000, the UN Commission on the Status of Women's 2005 report on the progress of the Beijing platform revealed that there had been little progress in twelve critical areas including poverty and economic empowerment, human right, health and violence. These conclusions formed the background theme to the annual March 8th International Women's Day and the 2005: "The Role of Women in Wealth Creation at the Household Level".

The HIV/AIDS epidemic has further highlighted how women's poverty makes them vulnerable to infections, stretches their coping strategies as care givers with limited resources, and compromises them as producers unable to feed and take proper care of their families. The HIV/AIDS crisis is a medical problem fueled by poverty, injustice, inequalities, ignorance, wars and migration as well as gendered cultural expectations. Many see this as systemic violence (Schoepf, 2001; Farmer, 1996). The number of infected girls and women in Africa is high and rising in all countries affected. Infection rates among young women aged between 15 and 24 years are four times higher than those of men of the same age. It is estimated that 76 percent of infected Africans are women.

HIV prevention is one of the MDGs which African Governments are committed, yet many are shifting the prevention strategies to ABC (Abstinence, Be faithful and Condomise as a last resort). This accommodation of the current US government no condoms prevention funding policy promoting AB as social vaccines is a backward move. It took three decades of massive funding and relentless educational efforts for people to adopt condom use. Until a cure is found, condoms offer a safer sex option to anyone who is sexually active. Condoms also stop the infected from infecting others. The strong argument that men have an important role in HIV prevention (Obbo, 1993; Setel, 1996; Baylies and Bujra, 200), is neutralized by condom denigrating which minimizes their involvement.

Fidelity is the wrong sermon when evidence shows that no African country has effective laws to protect women against male violence. There is inadequate protection for young girls against abuses of apparently responsible adults such as teachers, guardians, employers and stepparents. All rapists are not strangers. Women are raped in wars and in refugee camps. Married women are battered and marital rape does not exist as a social concept worthy of legislation. Their husbands in monogamous marriages and relationships infect the majority of African women. Women are unable to confront men's rights by demanding sexual abstinence because it leads to beating or divorce. Women submit to unsafe sex for the economic security it guarantees them and their children. Cultural prescriptions dictate that a good wife is a mother and does not demand condom use because she is neither promiscuous nor suspicious of her husband's fidelity. Abstinence is not a choice for women because they are constrained from exercising sexual and reproductive choice. Women need the power to use the ABC prevention methods individually or in combination as they best suit their circumstances. 'We will not achieve progress against HIV until women gain control over their sexuality', Dr Brundtland, Director General of WHO, has observed. Defilement, rape and forced early marriages that subject young women to statutory rape require aggressively enforced legal measures. Women as citizens in modern states have a right to live free of violence, rape and sexual harassment. Kofi Anan has lamented that as long as violence against women, the most shameful human rights violation, continues no progress is being made towards equality, development and peace. Gender equality and the empowerment of women are fundamental factors in the reduction of the vulnerability of girls and women to specific and systemic violence.

Development agencies support education for because of the influence it has on family size and health as well as children's learning. Children of literate mothers are more likely to attend school. Thus while women's contribution to agriculture is not in doubt, their exclusion from rights to property such as land, limited access to loan schemes, and limited education means that they are generally unable to access knowledge of improved agricultural methods. Yet when female farmers have access to micro-credit schemes that do not charge high interest rates, have some education and access agricultural inputs, they not only raise yields but the well being of the family improves because they invest in better nutrition, education and health. Education fights poverty by empowering women in many other areas. Even in countries with universal primary education, there is need for gender aware affirmative action policies to improve enrolment, retention and quality of education for girls. Educating women helps to make societies and communities healthier, wealthier and humane.

The political platform of many African countries when they attained political independence was nation building through fighting poverty, ignorance and disease. In the past decades the march forward has led African countries to adopt numerous policies and programmes; passing resolutions and making recommendations; and signing UN treaties and conventions. However, there is lack of political will to effectively invest in social development and to implement national, regional and international policies. Research suggests that development has failed largely because policy makers adopt gender blind policies that ignore the differing opportunities, achievements and constraints faced by men and women.

The African Union (AU) is committed to not only achieving but exceeding the MDGs according to a review of the African Union Commission (2005). AU is further committed to the principle of gender equality and equity. It was formed on a 50/50 gender parity basis and one in every five national members of its parliament is a woman including its first Speaker. In 2004 the Protocol to the African Charter on

Human and people's Rights of Women in Africa was adopted by heads of states and 17 countries have signed it. The New Partnership for Africa's Development (NEPAD) is expected to enhance women's human rights through the social development indicators included in its African leaders Peer Review Mechanism.

A joint ECA and AU meeting of Ministers in charge of gender and women's affairs was held in Dakar on 14th October 2005. The ministers' agenda included reviewing and approving the joint EAC/AU strategy for implementing, monitoring and evaluation of progress on the Solemn Declaration on Gender Equality in Africa, adopted by African Heads of State in 2004, which obliges states to respect normative standards on women's rights; and Outcome and the Way Forward, a set of recommendations resulting from their 2004 meeting in Addis Ababa which reviewed the progress on implementing the Dakar and Beijing Platforms of Action on gender equality, equity and women's empowerment. The conference of ministers was assisted by the Committee on Women and Development (CWD). This statutory body of experts, was set up in 1977 both to advise ECA and to provide leadership in Africa on gender-related issues.

The AU and Economic Commission for Africa review documents, and regular conferences leave the impression that progress on gender equality is gaining momentum. However, the majority of women are still trapped in ignorance, poverty and disease. There are many proposals to achieve the MDGs but it all sounds top heavy with expert ideas about what to do *for* not *with* the women. MDGs represent input targets for development practice, but their achievability, or the political will to achieve them by 2015 is in doubt.

In 1981 the UN Convention on the Elimination of All Forms of Discrimination Against Women (CEDAW), the international treaty that provides international standards for the protecting and promoting women's rights, was adopted in 1979 and by 1996 had been ratified by 152 (including 51 of the 53 African) countries. CEDAW sets standards for women's political, social economic, legal and cultural rights. It establishes women's right to vote, hold public office, be employed, establish contractual relations, and to reproduce and to determine the nationality of their children. UN proposals for the Advancement of Women were restated at the 1993 Vienna Conference on Human Rights. The UN and governments were urged to ensure the full participation of women 'as both agents and beneficiaries of development' in addition to according them 'the full and equal enjoyment' of human rights' (UN, 1996:60). Women's rights and gender equality in development have, since the UN Women's Decade (1975-85), been emphasized by the 1994 Cairo Conference on Population and Development, the 1992 Copenhagen World Summit for Social Development, and the 1995 Fourth World Conference on Women in Beijing. The implementation CEDAW principles requires regular reporting of sex-disaggregated data on many indicators. Progress is monitored using the UN Gender-related Development Index and Gender Empowerment Measure. This confronts planners with the results of their policies.

Progress in gender empowerment and mainstreaming is slow because among all human rights instruments negotiated under the auspices of the UN, CEDAW provokes the highest expressed reservations among governments (UN, 1996:72). African women continue to face violence which is rooted in personal and institutional discrimination. CEDAW (1979) articles acknowledge that social and economic norms that deny women equal rights with men also render women more vulnerable to physical, sexual and mental abuse. The success of gender mainstreaming crucially depends on educating women and men to be committed to the agenda of changing gender relations and the structures that maintain them. Women must get involved in the interpretation of cultural practices since they play a big role in the socialising of children. Women whose consciousness has been raised in participatory debates on governance and development analysis processes will lose the current voicelessness and be ready to demand their human rights to education, to sexual and reproduction health, to health and to political leadership.

Despite mobilization, advocacy and increased representation in governance, normative gains are not yet reflected in substantial changes in women's lives. A wealth of research examples through centuries and across the globe dividing resources relatively equally and guaranteeing property rights are more important in explaining the economic success and failure of a country (WB, 2006). Every aspect of human, social and economic development requires the co-operation of women (Sullerot, 1974:248). Comparative evidence suggests that societies that discriminate on the basis of gender pay a price in more poverty, slower growth and lower quality of life. The best recipe for progressive development is equity. If capitalist development is "modernizing poverty" (Illich, 1971), and "social obstacles" blamed for increasing gender inequalities, then gender equity in development planning and policy is the solution to future prosperity and well being of Africa. Gender equity is good common sense in search of political will for realization. "The price of transformation is eternal vigilance" (Roche, 1999: 210).

References

African Charter on Cultural and Human Rights and People's Right (1986) Addis Ababa: Organization of African Unity.
African Union (2005), Review of Progress towards the Millennium Development Goals in Africa. AU: Addis Ababa.
Armstrong, A. (1987) "Tanzania's Expert-led Planning: An Assessment", *Public Administratiuon and Planning 7:261-7.*
Bay, E., Hafkin, N. (1976) eds. "Women in Africa" *African Studies Review.* Vol. XV111:3.
Baylies, C. and Bujra, J. (2000), *AIDS, Sexuality and Gender in Africa: Collective Strategies and Struggles in Tanzania and Zambia.* Routledge.
Boserup, E. (1970) *Women's Role in Economic Development,* New York: St. Martin's and George Allen and Unwin.
Braxton, G. (1991) "Designing Projects as if Mattered" *paper presented at the Canadian Association of African Studies Conference, Toronto, 16-18 May.*
Bryceson, D.F. (1997) "De-agrarisation in Sub-Saharan Africa: Acknowledging the Inevitable": Introduction. *Farewell to Farms: De-agrarinasation and Employment in Africa.* D.F. Byceson (ed.) Leiden: African Studies Centre.

Buvinic, M. (1986) "Projects for Women in the Third World: Explaining their Misbehaviour," *World development 14, 5:653-64.*

Chambers, R. (1996) Whose Reality Counts?, London: Intermediate Technology Publications. (1995) "Paradigm shifts and the practice of participatory research and development." N. Nelson & S. Wright (eds.) *Power and participatory Development*, London: Intermediate Technology Publications.

Chowdhry, G. (1995) "Engendering Development? Women in Development in International Development Regimes." *Feminism, Postmodernism and Development*, M.H. Marchand & J. L. Parpart (eds.) New York: Routledge.

Cornwall, A. and White, S. (2000) "Introduction: Men, Masculinities and Development: Politics, Policies and Practice". *IDS Bulletin* 31:21.

Crewe, E. (1997) "The Silent Traditions of Developing Cooks," Oxford: Berg. *Discourses of Development: Anthropological Perspectives.* Grillo, R.D. & Stirrat, T.L. (eds).

Crewe, E. & Harrison, E. (1999) *"Whose Development?" An Ethnography of Aid.* London: Zed Books.

DagHammarskjord Foundation (1975) "What Now? Another Development" a special issue *Development Dialogue*, Uppsala.

Dauber, R. and Cain, M. (1981). (eds) *Women and Technological Change in Developing Countries*, Boulder: Westview Press.

DAWN (1985) *Development Alternatives with Women for a New Era.* Oslo.

Derbyshire, H. (2002) "Gender Manual: A Practical guide for Development Policy Makers and Practitioners". London.

Elson, D. (ed. 1991) *The Mal Bias in the Development Process*, Manchester: Manchester University Press.

Epstein, H. (2005) *The Lost Children of AIDS.* New York Review of Books. New York.

Escobar, A. (1984-5) "Discourse and Power in Development: Michael Foucault and the Relevance of His work to the Third World," *Alternatives 10,3:377-400.*

Escobar, A. (1995), *Encountering Development: The Making and Unmaking of the Third World.* Princeton: Princeton University Press.

Esteva, G. (1992) "Development" *The Development Dictionary.* (ed.) Wolfgang Sachs London: Zed Press.

Farmer, P.E. and Connors, M. and Simmond, J. (eds.) (1996) *Women, Poverty and AIDS: Sex, Drugs and Structural Violence.* Monroe, ME: Common Courage.

Illich, I. (1971) "Planned poverty: The End Result Of Technical Assistance," *Celebration of Awareness*, London.

Goetz, A.M. (1988) "Feminism and the Limits of the Claim to Know: Contradictions in the Feminist Approach to Women in Development. *Millennium 17, 3:477-96.*

Kabeer, N. (1994), Reversed Realities, Gender hierarchies in Development Thought. London: Verso.

Kardam, N. (1989) "Women and Development Agencies", R. Gallin, M. Aronoff and VII. Ferguson (eds.) *The Women and International Development Annual*, vol. 1, Boulder: Westview Press.

Keller, B and Mbwewe, B.C. (1991), "Policy Planning for the Empowerment of Zambia's Women Farmers." Canadian Journal of Development Studies Vol.12, 1:75-88.

Kuhn, T. (1962) *The Structure of Scientific Revolution.* New York.

March, C. "Gender means doing things differently: Lessons from Oxfam' Women's Linking Project". Gender works: OXFAM Experience in Policy and Practice (eds.)

Marchand, M.H. and Parpart, J.L. (1995) eds. *Feminism, Postmodernism and Development*, London/New York: Routledge.

Molyneux, M. (1998) "Analysing Women's Movements," Feminist Visions of Development. Routledge. (1985) "Mobilization Women's Interests, the State, and Revolution in Nicaragua". Feminist Studies 11, 2:227-54.

Momsen, J. (2001) "Backlash: Or How To Snatch Failure from the Jaws of Success in Gender and Development Progress", in *Development Studies.* 1:151-56.

Nindi, B. (1990) "Expert Donors, Ruling Elites and the African Poor: Expert Planning, Policy Formulation and Implementation: A Critique. *Journal of East African Research and Development*, 20:41-67.

Nyerere J. (1984) "Preface" *Forward Looking Strategies For the Advancement of Women in Africa.* Arusha.

Obbo, C. (1995) "Gender, Age and Class: Discourses on HIV Transmission and Control in Uganda" *Culture And Sexual Risk: Anthropological Perspectives on AIDS.* Han ten Brummelhuis and Gilbert Herdt (eds.) Gordon and Breach Publishers.

Obbo, C. (2005) Cultural and Religious Sensibilities and Behavioural Change. *UNAIDS project paper. AIDS in Africa Scenarios.* "Women in Development" *Women's Studies Encyclopedia*, Vol. 111: pp. 17-19. New York: Greenwood Press. 1993, Theorizing Black Feminisms (eds.) S.M. James and A.PA. Busia. Routledge.

Payer, (1982) *The World bank: A Critical Analysis*, New York: Monthly Review Press.

Porter, F., I. Smyth, C. Sweetman. OXFAM GB.

Rathgeber, E.M. (1995) "Gender and Development in Action" *Feminism, Postmodernism and Development*, M.H. Marchand & J. L. Parpart (eds.) London/ New York: Routledge. (1990) "WID" "WAD" "GAD": Trends in Research and Practice", *Journal of Developing Areas 24, 4: 489-502.*

Rogers, B. (1981) *The Domestication of Women.* Tavistock.

Schatz, S.P (1994) "Structural Adjustment in Africa: A Failing Grade So Far". *Journal of Modern African Studies 32, no.4:679-692.*

Schoepf, B.G. (1993), "AIDS Action Research with Women in Kinshasa, Zaire." Social Science and medicine 37, 11:1404-1413.

Schoepf, B.G. (2001) "International AIDS Research in Anthropology: Taking a critical Perspective on the Crisis". *Annual Review of Anthropology*, 30:335-61.

Setel, P. (1996) "AIDS as paradox of Manhood and Development in Kilimanjaro, Tanzania". Social Science and Medicine 43, 8: 1169-1178.

Shell/UNAIDS (2005) *AIDS in Africa: Three Scenarios.* Geneva: UNAIDS.

Stamp, P. (1989) "Technology, Gender, and Power in Africa" Technical Study 63E, Ottawa: International Development Research Centre.
Staudt, K. (1985) *Women, Foreign Assistance and Advocacy Administration.* New York: Praeger.
Sullerot, E. (1974) *Woman, Society and Change.* New York: World University Press.
Timberlake, L. (1986) *Africa in Crisis.* Earthscan.
Tinker, I. (1990) "The Making of a Field: Advocates, Practitioners and Scholars," *Tinker (ed.) Persistent Inequalities: Women and World Development.* Oxford: Oxford University Press.
Uganda AIDS Commission (2002) *The Role of Men in HIV Prevention.* Entebbe: Ministry of Health.
United Nations (1962) *The UN Development Decade: Proposal for Action.* New York.
United Nations (1996) *The United Nations and The Advancement of Women, 1945-1996.* New York.
Unesco (1977) Plan à moyen terme (1977-1982), Document 19 c'4.
UNRISD (1980) *The Quest for A Unified Approach to Development.* Geneva: UNRISD.
Williams, S. "Chronicle of a Death foretold: The birth and death of Oxfam GB's Gender and Development Unit," Porter, F., Smyth & Sweetmeat, (eds.) *Gender Works: Oxfam Experience in Policy and Practice.* Oxford: Oxfam.
World Bank (1989a) *Women in Development: Issues for Economic and Sector Analysis.* Policy Planning and Research Working Paper No. 269. Washington DC.
World Bank (1989b) *Sub saharan Africa: From Crisis to Sustainable Growth.*
World Bank (1993) "Paradigm Postponed: Gender and Economic Adjustment in Sub-Saharan Africa' *Technical Note, Human Resources and Poverty Division.* Washington, DC.
Young, K., Walkowitz, C., and McCallogh, R (eds. 1981) *Of marriage and the Market*, Berkeley: University of California Press.

Chapter 12

Migrants' Remittances and the Nigerian Economy: Theoretical and Impact Issues

Siyanbola Tomori and Michael A. Adebiyi

Introduction

Poverty is as present in Nigeria as in most other African countries. The Human Development Index for 2002 was 0.46, the Human Poverty Index was 35.1 percent, life expectancy at birth was 51.6 years, the proportion of the population living below $1 a day from 1990 to 2002 was 0.2 percent, while GDP per capita was only $328 (Nwajiuba, 2005). The proportion of the population without access to water sources was 38 percent, and the urban population was 45.9 percent rising to 55.5 percent in 2005. High rates of poverty, low human development, and low per capita income are important incentives for international migration, particularly from developing countries This chapter partly examines the consequences of international migration for development in Nigeria in terms of remittances from nationals who have migrated. It is structured as follows. The section following discusses the theoretical underpinnings, which include microeconomic theory of income remittances; migrant remittances, economic growth and poverty; determinants and the uses of remittance. A detailed examination of empirical findings is presented next and on direct investment income remittances as they affect the Nigerian economy. The final section concludes with a summary consideration of some policy options which would make for increased benefits from remittances to the Nigerian economy.

Theoretical Issues: A Review

Theories on Remittances

The theoretical literature on remittances distinguishes between two motives, altruistic and exchange. Becker was among the first economists to model altruistic behaviour in the context of household through allowing the utility of migrant to be effected by the well-being of the household (Becker, 1974). The basic prediction here is that a rise in the income gap between the sender (migrant) and recipient (household) will increase the probability and the size of transferred income, whereas a reduction in the income gap reduces both. The other conceivable motive is exchange.

Cox presents a model where private transfers are payments for services rendered. (Cox, 1987) Under such a model, a rise in the income of the migrant is associated with an increase in both the probability and size of transfer. However, if the recipient's income increases, the opportunity cost of providing the service rises, and the recipient thus requires a higher price for providing services. Thus, a negative correlation between the size of transfer and recipient's income is consistent with both hypotheses, whereas a positive correlation is consistent with exchange only.

Stark came up with a new theory of remittances, known as Tempered Altruism or Enlightened Self-Interest (Stark, 1991). It views remittances as part of an intertemporal, mutually beneficial contractual arrangement between the migrant and the household in the country of origin. Such contractual arrangements are based on investment and risk; they are voluntary and, hence, must be self-enforcing. Initially, the rural household insures the migrant against the early uncertainties associated with migration but subsequently the migrant adopts the role of insurer to allow the rural household to undertake riskier, higher expected yield ventures. The mechanism for self-enforcement can be mutual altruism that explains why such arrangements are usually struck between members of a household. The aspiration to inherit, the desire to return home, and the need to have reliable agents to assist in the accumulation and maintenance of assets are additional considerations for self-enforcement.

Poirine (1997) outlines a theory of remittances based on the notion that informal financial markets function within families. Migrants receive loans to invest in human capital and remittances constitute the repayments of these loans. The model is more applicable to the case of international migration and one of the main conclusions that Poirine draws from his model is that remittances will not necessarily decline over time, as loan repayments come to be replaced by loan advances.

Micro theories focus on factors influencing individual decisions to migrate, analyzing how potential migrants weigh the various costs and benefits of migrating (Boswell, 2002). The economic theory of migration seems to be supported by Crisp and Russell. Crisp's analysis is based on the scenario of people leaving low or middle income countries and seeking refuge in more prosperous states (Crisp, 1999). From this perspective, further questions arise: how are migrants and others able to raise the large amount of cash needed to pay for their journey? To what extent are these resources mobilized by means of remittances sent by members of the diaspora community? The economic perspective is reinforced by Russell, who examines the macro-economic effects of remittances on receiving countries (Russell, 2002). She highlighted the fact that with declining foreign aid and foreign direct investment, the importance of remittances as main sources of foreign exchange becomes visible.

Another relevant subject that has been under considerable discussion is the brain drain, that is the emigration of qualified professionals from developing countries and the subsequent loss of skills more rapidly than it can be replaced. In the contemporary literature, especially in the African developmental context, two aspects have become increasingly important, namely, remittances to relatives staying behind and the long-term impacts on Africa's human resource base, which is so critical for the continent's development. For instance, according to the United Nations Development Programme (UNDP), there were more than 21,000 Nigerian doctors in the United States alone, while, at the same time, Nigeria's health system suffers from an acute lack of medical personnel. Some 60 percent of all Ghanaian doctors trained locally in the 1980s had left the country while, in Sudan, in 1978 alone 17 percent of doctors, 20 percent of university lecturers and 30 percent of engineers alone had gone to work abroad (Nwajiuba, 2005).

While the brain drain remains problematical, emphasis has shifted from its negative impact to the recognition of the potential positive effects on the development of the country of origin. Some scholars recognize that the patterns of international migration have changed from uni-directional and permanent to temporary, seasonal and circular (Usher, 2005). Moreover, new information and communication technologies facilitate contacts between migrants and those they have left behind. Some countries have also made it possible for migrants to maintain dual citizenship, that is, to maintain close affiliations to both countries of origin and of residence. Consequently, migrants become directly involved in the economic development of their countries of origin. In short, migrants are now being increasingly considered as agents of development, who can strengthen co-operation between home and host societies. They can contribute to development, not only through remittances, investment and entrepreneurial activities, but also through the transfer of newly developed skills and knowledge, or through fostering democratization and the protection of human rights in their countries of origin (Nwajiuba, 2005; Usher, 2005).

Migrants' Remittances, Poverty and Economic Growth

There has been a growing literature on how migrant workers' remittances can affect households and some have documented how migrants have contributed to economic and social development in their country of origin. Thus, evidence suggests that remittances from abroad are increasingly crucial to the survival of communities in many developing countries, as indicated in an IMF Country Analyses Report (Russell et. at., 1990). One benefit expected from labour emigration was that migrants would bring increased investments and transfer of technology, skills and entrepreneurship. Thus, Russell et.al. conclude that once subsistence needs are satisfied; migrants do use remittances for investment purposes, including education, livestock farming and small scale enterprises'. Taylor has also argued that remittances have multiplier effects that work to increase national income (Taylor, 1996). In a study on Senegal, Diatta and Mbow found that remittances were a substantial source of revenue for families with migrant members, and were also used to promote development in migrants' home communities (Diatta and Mbow, 1999).

Remittances significantly affect welfare. A study on their impact on the standard of living of left-behind families in Turkey showed that they have a positive effect on household welfare, and have both direct and indirect income effects (Quartey, 2005). The study also showed that 12 percent of households used about 80 percent of remittances to improve their standard of living, though it is argued that dependency on the same leaves households vulnerable to changes in migration cycles (Quartey, 2005).

Migrant remittances also serve as a source income for savings and investment and this has been confirmed by Taylor. He found that remittances contribute to savings and investments, thereby leading to growth and development of an economy (Taylor, 1999). In fifteen developing countries studied by the International Monetary Fund

(IMF), remittances account for more than 10 percent of Gross Domestic Product (Ruiz-Arranz, 2006). This is true for some islands in the Caribbean and the Pacific, and for several labour-exporting countries such as Albania, El Salvador, Jordan, Lesotho, Moldova, and the Philippines.

Despite their increasing importance in total international capital flows, the relationship between remittances and economic growth has not been adequately studied. This contrasts sharply with the extensive research on the relationship between growth and other sources of foreign capital, such as foreign direct investment (FDI) and official aid. The accepted view seems to be that because remittances are used mostly for consumption by individual households, they have a minimal impact on long-term growth.

The biggest challenge is to understand why remittances do not seem to boost growth in countries with well-functioning credit markets, and to work out how policies could address this. A recent IMF working paper examined how local financial sector development influences a country's ability to take advantage of remittances (Ruiz-Arranz, 2006). In theory, the impact of remittances on growth can work either through the financial system or parallel to it. Relatively developed financial systems would presumably treat remittances like any other form of savings and, by reducing transaction costs, allocate them to projects that yield the highest returns. This might be expected in some emerging Asian countries where banking sector development is high.

In countries with less developed financial systems (most of Sub-Saharan Africa and some post-Soviet central Asian states), remittances might become a significant complement for inefficient or nonexistent credit market by helping local entrepreneurs bypass lack of collateral or high lending costs to start productive activities. Using data covering 100 developing countries from 1975 to 2002, the IMF study finds strong evidence that the second theory works: remittances boost growth in countries with less developed financial systems by providing an alternative way to finance investment. Remittances act as a substitute for the domestic financial system. They boost growth in countries with less developed financial systems by providing alternative ways to finance investment and they act as a substitute for the domestic financial system.

There is no evidence, however, that the first channel works: even after allowing for differences in the level of income among countries, remittances do not seem to have an impact on growth in countries with well-functioning domestic financial markets. Specifically, research findings show that: (i) while more developed financial systems seem to attract more remittances (due to lower transaction costs and fewer restrictions on payments), they do not seem to increase their impact on growth; and (ii) remittances substitute for financial development in countries with less developed financial systems (Ruiz-Arranz, 2006).

Determinants of Migrants' Remittances

In recent decades, remittances have become an important source of income for many developing countries. Remittances are not only used as a mechanism for the survival of the poor in developing countries, but also as a risk sharing mechanism, a stable source of investment and for future consumption smoothing (Ratha, 2003). The increase in the value of remittances flows around the world has made the study of its determinants and socio-economic consequences important for understanding a broad array of issues from migration to terrorism.

In a presentation prepared for the Federal Reserve Bank of Atlanta, John Taylor, Secretary of Treasury for International Affairs in the George W. Bush administration, outlined why the U.S. government considers remittances to be important (Taylor, 2004). First, the U.S. wants to increase the amount of remittances going to developing countries because it can promote economic growth in these countries, as remittances are commonly used for investment. Furthermore, sending remittances through formal channels is a business that may attract the banking industry in developing countries. Also, the U.S. government wants to track remittances flows to deter money laundering and financing of terrorist activities.

Lucas and Stark discuss the determinants of remittances in Botswana. Emigrants enjoy remitting home because they care about household consumption, but pure altruism is not enough to explain the dynamics of remittances (Stark, 1985). There is also the case of pure self-interest. Three examples provided by the authors. First, an emigrant may remit because he/she is expecting to inherit from the household's fortune. Second, the emigrant remits because he/she is investing in assets in his/her home area and expects the household to take care of them. Third, the emigrant expects to return home in the future and can benefit from the household gratitude from having sent remittances.

Lucas and Stark also proposed enlightened self-interest as a complementary alternative to pure altruism and pure self-interest. Here the emigrant and the household have a contractual agreement in which they share risk. The emigrant supports the household in bad economic times in the rural areas (or home country) and the household supports the emigrant if he/she becomes unemployed in the urban area (or host country).

One of the first studies to use macro-level data to test for the determinants of remittances is Swamy. Using data from Greece, Turkey and Yugoslavia, he finds no significant impact of most home and host country macroeconomic variables on remittances (Swamy, 1981). Straubhaar, using data of remittances, from Germany to Turkey, obtains similar results. He finds that only variables like the wage level in Germany (indicator of the host country economic situation) are significant (Straubhaar, 1986). These two research find no evidence that exchange rates or interest rates have an effect on remittances (FN below see Sayan (2004) and Tuncay et al. (2004) for other studies related to Turkey).

However, few studies find that macroeconomic variables have an impact on remittances. For example, El-Sakka and Mcnabb, in a study for Egypt, find that the black market premium and interest rate differentials are important variables explaining remittances (El-Sakka and Mcnabb, 1999) (FN below see Feiler (1987) and Wahba (2003) for other studies related to Egypt). In the same way, Elbadawi and Rocha, using data for six countries show that macroeconomic variables play an important role in determining remittances. In their study they used fixed effects panel estimation techniques (Elbadawi and Roacha, 1992). Recently, also using fixed effect panel estimation techniques, Higgins *et al.*, found that exchange rate uncertainty (a measure of risk) is an important determinant of remittances (Higgins et al, 2004). Their results also show that unemployment in the host country and the exchange rate are significant determinants of remittances.

Faini, concentrates on the issue of the effect of real exchange rate depreciation on remittances. His main contribution is that real exchange rate depreciation of the home currency has a positive effect on remittances (Faini, 1994) (FN below, see also Garson, 1994). Other findings indicate that home country income is negatively related to remittances.

Katseli and Glytsos, in a study using data from Greece, found that remittances are negatively related to inflation in the home country, host country income and host country interest rates (Karseli and Glytsos, 1986). In another study, Glytsos, distinguishes between remittances sent by temporary migrants and remittances sent by permanent migrants. His results suggest that temporary migrants are more likely to remit for investment and future consumption smoothing. Permanent migrants are more likely to remit for altruistic purposes (FN below see Glytsos (1988) and Djajic (1989) for more on temporary vs. permanent migration).

Remittances are influenced by the following factors: number of workers; wage rates; economic activity in the host country and in the sending country; exchange rates; relative interest rate between the labour-sending and receiving countries; political risk; facility for transferring funds; marital status; level of education of the migrant; whether accompanied or not by dependents; years since out on migration and household income level (Puri and Ritzema, 1999). Russel provides a framework for clarifying the intermediate relationships between the determinants and effects of remittances. According to him, factors that affect migrant workers' choice between the formal banking system and informal channels in remitting their earnings include: individual socio-economic characteristics of their household members, levels and type of economic activity in the sending and host countries, differential interest and exchange rates and the relative efficiency of the banking system compared with informal channels (Russell, 1992; Straubhaar, 1986).

In analyzing the determinants of remittance levels, Swami examined the effect of several of these variables on remittance flows to Greece, Yugoslavia and Turkey. She found that the *level of and the cyclical fluctuations in economic activity* in the host countries explain 70 to 95 per cent of the variation in remittances flowing into labour-exporting countries. A more detailed analysis by Swami showed that the number of migrant workers abroad and their wages together explained over 90 per cent of the variation in inflow or remittances into these countries. Looking at per capita remittances instead of total remittances, the study found that the length of actual or expected stay of the migrant abroad and the number of dependents at home appeared to have some influence on remittances (Puri and Ritzema, 1999).

Another econometric analysis of remittances data from Turkey, over the period 1963-82, confirmed Swami's earlier findings. Based on secondary time-series data, Straubhaar showed that 'neither variations in exchange rates (reflecting government intention to attract remittances by premium exchange rates) nor changes in the real return of investments (reflecting government intention to attract remittances by foreign exchange deposits with higher returns) turned out to affect the flow of remittances' (Straubhaar, 1986).

While these incentives do not appear to have a significant impact on *total* remittances they might have an effect on the magnitude of unrecorded remittances. It is suggested that differences in the rates of devaluation and inflation over the 1986-87 periods explain much of the differences between remittance inflows into several Asian countries (Puri and Ritzema, 1999). In India, repatriable deposits grew at a fast rate in response to interest rate differentials created by the drop in international capital market rates (Puri and Ritzema, 1999).

Use of Remittances: Micro and Macroeconomic Perspectives

Puri and Ritzema pointed out that while much of the literature focuses on how remittances are used by recipients (generally spouses, children, parents and siblings), their study emphasized the implications of remittances on the overall economy, without limiting it exclusively to migrant households (Puri and Ritzema, 1999).

For the most part, remittances are used for daily expenses such as food, clothing and health care and they make up a significant portion of the income of those households. Funds are also spent on building or improving housing, buying land or cattle, and buying durable consumer goods such as washing machines and televisions. Generally, only a small percentage of remittances are used for savings and what is termed "productive investment". For example, income and employment-generating activities, such as buying land or tools, starting a business and other activities with multiplier effects (Puri and Ritzema, 1999; Russell 1986; Taylor 1996).

There is, however, an opposing view which sees remittances as a household strategy for improving recipients' standard of living, providing resources for food, housing improvements, education and small household appliances (Puri and Ritzema; 1999). These researchers feel that the criticism of consumption patterns ignores the personal circumstances as well as structural conditions in which migrants make their decisions, as well as the inherently private nature of the transfers, and the limited opportunities for small-scale investment in the community as well as the social and financial capital needed for a new business. Thus, given the circumstances in the various countries (poor infrastructure, lack of access to credit, etc) the migrants are making rational decisions about the use of their remittances.

On macroeconomic factors, the literature describes two opposing perspectives on this issue, with studies supporting both. One school of thought states that at a macroeconomic level, remittances often provide a significant source of foreign currency, increase national income, finance imports and contribute to the balance of payments. Remittances also have economic, social and political life and contributed to the expansion of wire transfer and courier companies as well as money exchanges (Puri and Ritzema, 1999; Russell 1986; Taylor 1996).

Others, however, believe that remittances not only fail to help the economy but also reduce the likelihood of an improved economy. The inflow of funds can be deceptive if it creates dependence among the recipients, encourages the continued migration of the working age population, and decreases the likelihood of investment by the government or foreign investors because of an unreliable workforce. Moreover, these researchers view remittances as unpredictable and as a cause of increasing inequality. Also, remittances are frequently spent on imported consumer goods, rather than locally produced ones, decreasing the potential multiplier effect of the money and increasing import demand and inflation (Russell, 1986). In Korea and Pakistan, for example, it has been observed that inflation, together with specific skill shortages resulting from migration, has led to rising wage rates and dramatic changes in the relative price of labour. The availability of foreign exchange, together with growing demand for consumer goods not available in the domestic market, has been linked with a rising demand for imported goods (Puri and Ritzema, 1999).

Empirical investigation on the use of informal remittances conducted by Alburo and Abella, using information from a questionnaire-based survey of a sample of 600 returns migrant workers in the Philippines, showed how workers' informal remittances impact on the economy (Alburo and Abella, 1992). On the one hand, they found that informal remittances, in the form of foreign exchange, are used to finance trade, leading to the same impact as formal inflows. On the other hand, if the remittances are made in the domestic currency, the net effect of the remittances is on the domestic economy and not on trade (Puri and Ritzema, 1999).

Migrants Remittances in Nigeria: Empirical Findings

The remittances of migrant workers to Nigeria were empirically investigated by Nwajiuba in relation to the following issues: destination of migrants; distribution of migrants by countries/regions; ethnic composition of Nigerian migrants; determinants of migration destination; motivation for migration; effects of migration on the people and economy (Nwajiuba, 2005).There are migrant Nigerians in countries of the Economic Community of West African States (ECOWAS) such as Ghana, Niger, Chad and Ivory Coast. They are also found in other African countries, including South Africa, Cameroon and Gabon. Outside Africa, they are found in the United States, United Kingdom, Ireland, USA, Canada, Saudi Arabia, Japan, Korea, Brazil, among other places. According to Nwajiuba, the distribution of the international migrants shows that 1.81 percent migrated to Europe, 1.06 percent migrated to the United States of America and 0.95 percent migrated to Asia.

International migration is not a recent phenomenon in Nigeria. Before independence in 1960, Nigerians traveled to the United Kingdom, United States and France to obtain higher education and the tendency, then, was to return immediately after completing their studies (Nwajiuba, 2005). The turning point seems to be the collapse of the petroleum boom in the early 1980s, and the attendant economic hardship faced by Nigerians. Subsequently, they started seeking employment opportunities in other countries, while many who did not necessarily study outside the country began to leave. This is the phenomenon of brain drain. According to Nwajiuba and Takoungang, the severe economic difficulties, increased poverty and political instability that have plagued many African countries in the last two decades have also resulted in the large-scale migration to Europe and the United States. Unlike their counterparts in the 1960s and 70s, an overwhelming majority of recent immigrants are more interested in establishing permanent residency (Nwajiuba, 2005; Takoungang, 2004).

Many less educated youths may also have migrated, legally or illegally. Illegal migrants have become noticeable on the streets of Europe and North America doing menial jobs. The role of immigrants in the US has become a major political issue. Foreign workers, many of whom are illegal immigrants, do much of the relatively unskilled work. However, both legal and illegal migrants earn wages which are much higher than what they could have earned in Nigeria. The illegal migrants may remain abroad until they obtain documents that will enable them to regularize their stay; or they may relocate to a country whose resident permits are easier to obtain; or they await deportation. The population of Nigerian migrants abroad has been on the increase: Nwajiuba and Komolafe observed an increase in Nigerians of various ethnic groups in Ireland from 1996 to 2000 (Nwajiuba, 2005; Komolafe, 2002). In this case, the Yoruba of southwest Nigeria outnumbered other ethnic groups, probably because its people had earlier contacts with the western world.

According to Komolafe, Southeast Nigeria is comparatively less developed in terms of infrastructure than other parts of Nigeria, which may be a constraint to economic development and employment opportunities. This situation creates a condition of poverty in the zone. Poverty and its socio- economic constraints are major causes of population movements (Komolafe, 2002). Other factors affecting migration and destination of choice of migration are reflected in the fact that some Nigerian women of fairly wealthy backgrounds travel to Europe to deliver their babies. These babies would have the citizenship of the country in which they were born, and their parents can eventually migrate there to make a better living. The opportunities for overseas migration have also been improved by the visa lottery policy of some countries, such as those of the United States and Canada.

Migrants are influenced by a number of factors in the choice of destinations; these include economic, social, education, climatic and language. The perception of an economically buoyant Europe and North America fuels the desire to migrate to those countries. In addition, social factors, including similarity in education and language, also impact on a migrant's choice of destination – for example, the English-speaking United Kingdom and United States. However, there is overwhelming evidence that economic factors are the major reasons for international migration from Nigeria.

Motivation for migration stems from a search for self and household or family improvement and this is usually to a place where opportunities are perceived as better – usually where comparatively more natural and or man-made resources are vied for by relatively few people. Further examination of the role of economic factors in migration revealed that 75 percent of international migrants have left Nigeria since 1989. What is remarkable about this is that in 1986 Nigeria introduced the Structural Adjustment Programme (SAP), a key element of which was reduction of employment in the public service as well as the reduction in employment in thee economy as a whole. Rural and agricultural sector desertion increased after the introduction of the SAP, irrespective of the country and the degree of implementation of he adjustment programmes. A study of the same southeast Nigeria by Akinsanmi and Nwajiuba shows that up to 100 percent of rural inhabitants have diversified into non-farm economic activities (Akinsanmi, 2005; Nwajiuba, 2005). Reduced real earnings through the inflationary impact of devaluation and trade liberalization as part of the SAP may have reduced living standards and, therefore, led to massive rural out-migration and the desertion of agriculture. The negative side effects of SAP on the agricultural sector arose from increased interest rates, constraints to input purchase and a fall in real farm gate prices. This has contributed to the significant illegal immigration of young Africans into Europe, especially since 1996.

Migrants contribute to the social and economic wellbeing of their families and communities by remitting funds regularly. A study on Southeastern Nigeria reported that although most respondents declined to reveal specific amounts, all agreed that remittances were an important means of meeting family needs and that 50 percent of these needs came from their family members in Europe and the United States (Nwajiuba, 2005). With the perception of differences in wellbeing of families with migrants and non-migrants, Nwajiuba reported significant differences in the living standards of migrant and migrant families in Nigeria. He indicated that migration was perceived as leading to clear improvements in the wellbeing of families with migrant members, which further fuels the desire to migrate.

With regards to the uses of remittances Nwajiuba also (2005) reported that remittances were put to some household and community uses which impact on livelihoods. The predominant use of remittances was partly for farm purposes and non- agricultural activities. Sponsorship of migrants tends to be closely knit with significant degrees of communality. The high degree of communality informs the perception of migration as an investment from which the family expects returns. The major asset of rural families in southeast Nigeria is land. The seriousness of the desire for migration is demonstrated by family willingness to sell land to raise funds to sponsor the migrant's journey. In return for sponsorship, family members have some expectations from the migrants, including money, gifts and support/training (Nwajiuba, 2005).

Nwajiuba estimated that between 20 percent and 65 percent of family needs were met through international remittances (Nwajiuba, 2005). This is a significant contribution to the Nigeria economy. According to Handlin et.al, remittances to Nigeria were valued at 10% of exports. Remittances to Nigeria were about 12 percent of the sender's household income and tended to continue over a long period (Handlin et al. 2002). They play an important role in reducing poverty and income inequality and could affect a wide range of economic decisions.

While, generally, remittances to developing countries have more than doubled in the last decade, they have grown little in Africa. Total remittances to Africa amounted to US$9 billion in 1990 and by 2003 had reached US$14 billion; the continent receives about 15 per cent of flows to developing countries as a whole. In sub-Saharan Africa, Nigeria is the largest recipient, taking between 30 and 60 percent of the region's receipts. Though official figures are not available, economists believe that money sent home by Nigerians in various parts of the world now exceeds US$1.3 billion annually, ranking second only to oil exports as a source of foreign exchange earnings for the country (Mutume, 2005).

Nigeria has liberalized its financial market, allowing foreign denominated accounts and loosening trade in foreign exchange, among other things. This has reportedly led to an increase in remittances through official channels. Unfortunately, there is no data on the nature or amount of flows. According to the World Bank, less than two-thirds of African countries report remittances; flows through informal channels are not recorded. The main sources of official data on migrants' remittances are contained in the annual balance of payments records of Nigeria, which are compiled in *Central Bank of Nigeria Annual Reports and Statement of Accounts*, various years. Annual estimates of official remittance flows based on these balance of payments statistics suggest that remittances increased from US$1,544 million in 1998 to US$2,751 million in 2005 (see Table 12.1). The level of remittances is very significant in proportion to the Nigeria's merchandise exports and imports. As Table 12.1 shows, in 1998 remittances were equivalent to about 17 and 16 percent of total merchandise exports and imports respectively; and they were about 8 and 42 percent of exports and imports respectively in 2001. However, in 2004, remittances as a percentage of exports and imports were about 11 and 23 percent respectively.

Table 12.1 Flow of Workers' Remittances and its Share in Imports and Exports of Goods in Nigeria

Year	Remittances	As a percent of	
	Million US Dollar	Exports	Imports
1998	1544.000	16.7	16.2
1999	1628.000	10.0	15.0
2000	1705.000	8.5	18.7
2001	1303.000	7.6	41.5
2002	1421.000	9.0	13.0
2003	2086.000	6.9	14.8
2004	2751.000	11.4	23.3

Source: *Global Economic Prospects 2006: Economic Implications of Remittances and Migration*, World Bank.
Note: The percentage of remittances to exports and imports were computed from *Central Bank of Nigeria: Annual Reports and Statement of Account*, 2002 and 2004.

The true value of remittances is likely to be much higher as only a portion of total remittances flow through *official* channels. It is now well documented that formally recorded remittances represent only the tip of the iceberg. Remittances sent through informal channels, e.g. self-carry, hand-carry by friends or family members, or in-kind remittances of clothes and other consumer goods, are considerable. It has been noted that such remittances may be quite high, with informal channels responsible for the bulk of all remittances. Osili found that the majority of remittances are sent through informal channels due to advantages such as bypassing the commissions and fees and more favorable exchange rates (Handlin et.al. (2002). In further explaining why remittances are channeled through informal sources, the exchange rate, rates of return on domestic assets, efficient banking facilities and foreign exchange practices are vital factors. Exchange rate overvaluation acts as an implicit tax, low relative rates of return on domestic financial assets induce the retention of money balances in foreign bank accounts, and the lack of adequate and efficient banking facilities and restrictive foreign exchange practices also explain unrecorded remittances.

A discussion on the importance of remittances may be better understood on the basis of three indicators of institutional deficiencies, i.e. the financial intermediation ratio (M_2/GDP), the foreign exchange market premium, and the real interest rate showing the degree of relative incentive for consumption vis-à-vis financial saving in Nigeria (see Table 12.2). Even though the formal remittances increased from US$10 million to US$3200 million between 1990 and 2005, these values would have been higher if the indicators were favourable. It is expected that informal remittances would be higher than formal sources due to its general macroeconomic environment (as reflected in the overvalued exchange rate, low degree of financial development and the negative real interest rate).

Table 12.2 Formal Remittances and Related Macroeconomic Indicators in Nigeria (1990-2005)

Year	M2/GDP (Financial Deepening)	Real Deposit Rate	Foreign Exchange Market Premium	Remittance (in million US Dollar)
1990	19.30000	15.50000	19.50000	10.00000
1991	21.50000	7.100000	31.60000	66.00000
1992	23.80000	-24.00000	15.80000	56.00000
1993	28.50000	-29.18000	64.30000	793.0000
1994	29.40000	-42.00000	173.1000	550.0000
1995	16.30000	-58.53000	3.100000	804.0000
1996	13.30000	-15.75000	2.300000	947.0000
1997	14.80000	-1.070000	3.700000	1871.000
1998	18.50000	0.090000	4.600000	1544.000
1999	20.30000	7.700000	5.600000	1628.000
2000	22.80000	3.540000	9.700000	1705.000
2001	28.10000	-8.810000	18.30000	1303.000
2002	29.60000	-0.290000	19.10000	1421.000
2003	28.60000	-1.740000	9.400000	2086.000
2004	27.40000	-2.500000	5.500000	2751.000
2005	26.80000	-3.000000	4.900000	3200.000

Source: *Global Economic Prospects 2006: Economic Implications of Remittances and Migration*, World Bank; Central Bank of Nigeria: Annual Reports and Statement of Account, various years.

We further examine the determinants of formal remittances in Nigeria using ordinary least square method. The model is specified as follows:

$LR = a_1 + a_2 Er + a_3 FD + a_4 FEP + a_5 INF + a_6 RDR + U$ ....(1)

Where LR is the log of remittances; Er represents exchange rate, which is expressed in Naira to Dollar; FD is ratio of M_2 to gross domestic product; FEP is the foreign exchange market premium, which is the ratio of the difference between parallel exchange and official exchange rates to official exchange rate multiplied by 100; INF represents inflation rate and RDR stands for real deposit rate, which is the difference between nominal deposit rate and inflation rate. $a_1 - a_6$ are parameters and U is the error term, which is assumed to be normally distributed and it is white noise.

The results of the model are presented in Table 12.3.

Table 12.3 Determinants of Remittances in Nigeria, 1990-2005

Variables	Coefficient	Std. Error	t-Statistic	Prob.
Exchange Rate (ER)	0.041103	0.013878	2.961640	0.0159
M2/GDP (FD)	-0.102804	0.085980	-1.195673	0.2624
Foreign Exchange Market Premium (FEP)	0.010504	0.009645	1.089076	0.3044
Inflation (INF)	0.051840	0.099614	0.520413	0.6153
Real Deposit Rate (RDR)	0.042914	0.105086	0.408370	0.6925
C	4.259412	1.612167	2.642041	0.0268
Adjusted R-squared	0.679504			
F-statistic	6.936472			
Durbin-Watson stat	1.550695			

Dependent Variable: Log of Remittances (LR)
Method: Least Squares
Sample (adjusted): 1990 2005
Included observations: 16 after adjusting endpoints

Source: Own Computation.

From Table 12.3, it is obvious that only exchange rate significantly determines remittances at 1 percent level in Nigeria between 1990 and 2005. A 100 percent rise in exchange rate (i.e. depreciation) will raise remittances by 4 percent. The insignificance of other explanatory variables (i.e. inflation, financial deepening, real deposit rate and foreign exchange market premium) indicates the degree of relative incentive for consumption vis-à-vis financial saving in Nigeria. It also justifies the existence of informal remittances in Nigeria.

Direct Investment Income Remittances in Nigeria

We further examine remittances from the perspective of direct investment income remittances. Although capital inflows into a developing country are beneficial under certain circumstances, serious problems arise when the return flow of interest, profits, and dividends on the accumulated investments and repatriation of capital put pressure on its balance of payments. Indeed, heavy dependence on foreign investment may create a situation where the real net export proceeds or real net import savings are low (or even negative) and tolerably insufficient after allowing for remittances of profits, dividends, management fees, salaries of expatriates, and so on (Obadan, 1980: 40). For a developing country remittances may become so substantial relative to capital inflow that foreign direct investment ends up in net capital outflow rather than inflow. Under such circumstances, the benefits of foreign direct investment will become doubtful (Obadan, 2004) (see Figure 12.1).

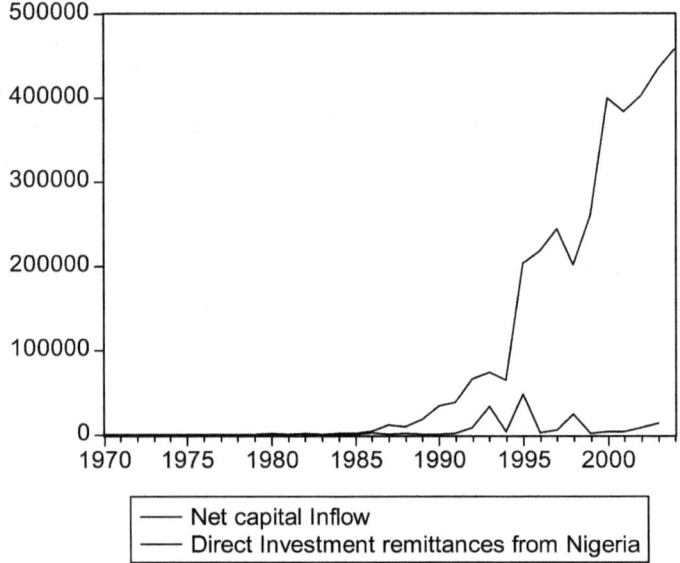

Figure 12.1 Net Capital Inflow and Direct Investment Income Remittances for Nigeria, 1970-2004

Available data shows that direct investment income remittances to and from Nigeria were rather insignificant before SAP. Between 1973 and 1980, direct investment income remittances generally declined. Largely accounting for this phenomenon was the implementation of the Nigerian Enterprises Promotion Decree of 1972, which barred aliens from certain economic undertakings and required indigenous equity participation, ranging from 40 to 60 percent, in other foreign-owned enterprises. The decree, which initially came into effect on 1 April 1974, was later amended in 1997 to broaden its scope.

Direct investment income remittance from Nigeria rose from US$2109.09 million in 1986 to US$3428.67 million in 2004, whereas direct investment income remittances increased from US$48.85 million in 1986 to US$156.73 million in 2004, a relatively small jump (see Figure 12.2).

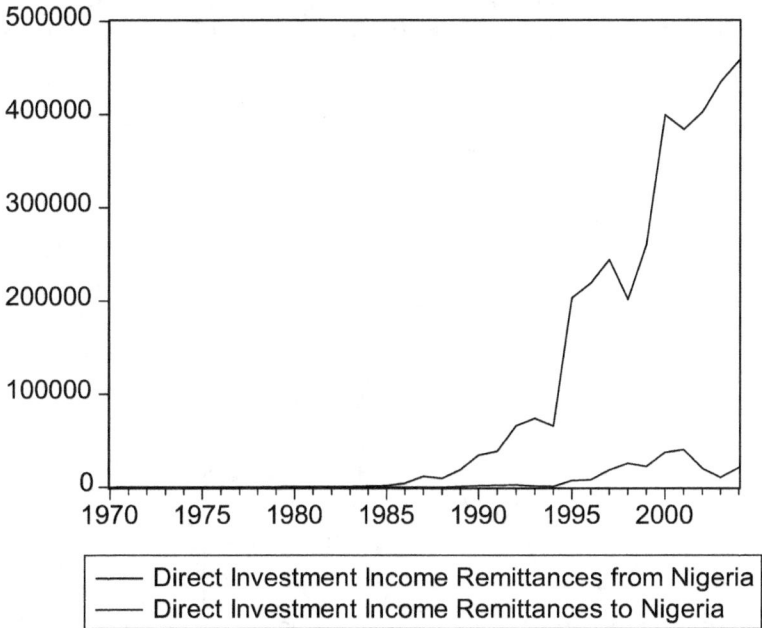

Figure 12.2 Direct Investment Income Remittances to and from Nigeria

The magnitude of direct investment income remittances (DIIR) increased substantially during SAP, which was characterized by foreign exchange market deregulation, exchange rate depreciation, trade and investment liberalization. Accordingly, DIIR rose from 13.6 percent of total merchandise export earnings in 1985 to 47.1 percent of exports in 1986, which was the first year of the adjustment programme. Thereafter, the absolute increase in DIIR was phenomenal. The substantial rise in Naira export earnings largely account for the relative decline in percentage shares. Nevertheless, from 1986 onwards, the percentage of remittances in merchandise exports was generally over 30 percent. As at 2000, remittances stood at 20.5 percent of merchandise export earnings before it fell to 14.6 percent of exports in 2004 (see Figure 12.3).

Figure 12.4 also shows the ratio of direct investment income remittances from Nigeria to net direct foreign investment inflow, GDP, and external reserves. Net inflow of investment funds has grown very much less than profit and dividend remittances. The ratio of direct investment income remittances from Nigeria to net direct investment inflow rose sharply from 97.7 percent in 1970 to 1980. 1 percent in 1974. The ratios became staggering in the last ten years, being as high as 7,446.7

percent in 1990 and 8,023.3 percent in 1996 when net direct investment inflow was quite low – the value in the latter year being 9.3 percent higher than that of 1986 and 94.4 percent lower than the value in 1995 (Obadan, 2004). In the early 1970s, the ratio of direct investment income remittances from Nigeria to external reserves was quite high, rising from 113.6 percent in 1970 to 289.5 percent in 1972. The substantial rise in oil export earnings account for the observed low ratios from 1974 to 1981. From 1982 onwards, the ratios have been quite high, peaking at 474.9 percent in 1992.

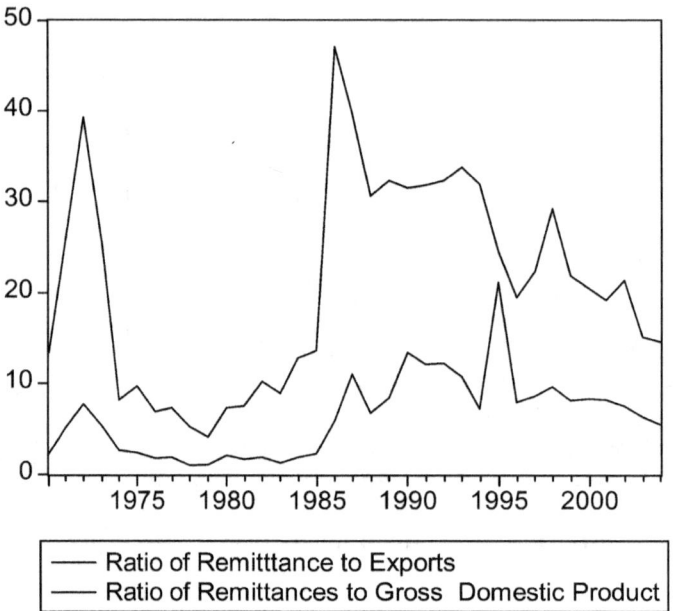

Figure 12.3 Direct Investment Income Remittances from Nigeria as a Ratio of Export and Gross Domestic Product

From the foregoing, it is quite clear that the repatriation of direct foreign investment income from Nigeria has been quite high both in absolute magnitude, particularly in recent years, and in relation to various economic indicators. Given these significant remittances, therefore, the contribution of foreign direct investment to the economic development of Nigeria becomes significantly reduced below whatever it would have been. While foreign investment might have aided the growth of industrial production in the country, part of this growth has become illusory because of the liabilities of repatriating earnings.

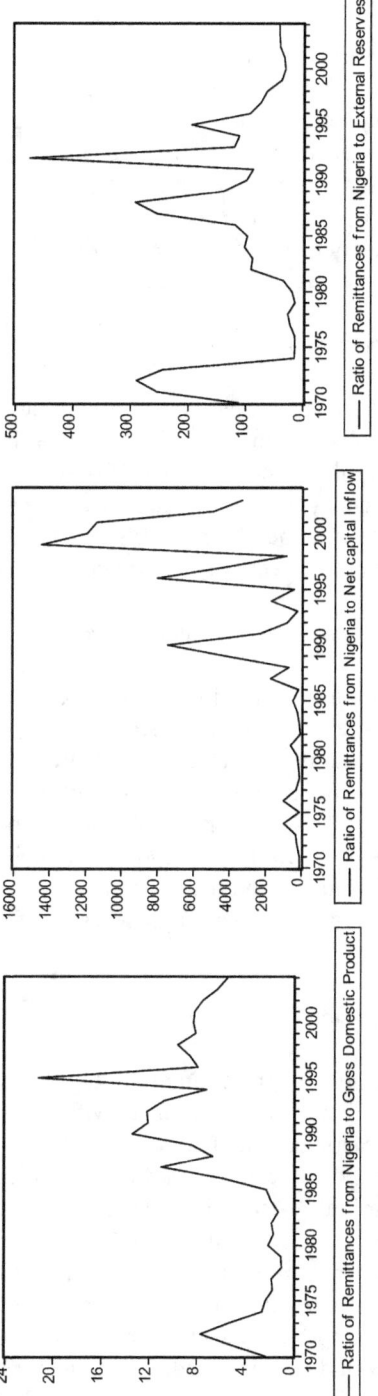

Figure 12.4 Ratio of Direct Investment Income Remittances from Nigeria to Net Direct Foreign Investment Inflow, GDP, and External Reserves

Conclusions and Policy Implications

The subject of remittances is, in the final analysis, virtually inseparable from the broader issues of international migration, such as the number and characteristics of migrants and the rates at which they return home. Despite these close links, the topic warrants focused attention as remittances have grown to become a central factor in the domestic economies of labour-exporting countries. This review had brought out the importance of recognizing the reality of unrecorded remittances in Nigeria.

The following policy options are needed to increase the possibility of remittances having a more positive impact on the Nigerian economy.

Address the Deficiencies in Macroeconomic Policy Regimes

There is need to address the deficiencies in macroeconomic policy regimes. Thus, the "first-best" solution to the problem seems to lie in implementing a wide range of policy reforms aimed at "setting the macro-economic house in order" (Puri and Ritzema, 1999). By setting the exchange rate on a realistic and sustainable course, ensuring a positive real interest rate and liberalizing foreign trade, the conditions for illicit foreign exchange dealings can be effectively destroyed.

Improve Efforts to Collect Data on International Remittance

There is need to improve efforts to collect data on international remittances to Nigeria. Improving remittances data would require not only gathering information, but also studying the relationship between migration stock and remittances flows, remittance behaviour of migrant workers in major remittance-source countries, and the way in which remittances respond to changes in source and destination economies. One way forward would be to conduct surveys on remittance senders and recipients to find out the size of remittances flows, their sources and destinations, the channels used, and their ultimate uses. Major international coordination is necessary for improving the data on remittances.

Strengthening the Financial Infrastructure

The effectiveness of incentive schemes in promoting remittances depends crucially on the ability of the existing banking network to compete with the informal market. Thus, any effective strategy for attracting remittances into the formal banking system should include attempts to expand the branch network further, in order to effectively link overseas workers with the remittance-receiving families and to take on more of the desirable features of the services offered by the informal network.

It is observed that a large number of migrants, especially those who are poor or undocumented, in developing countries like Nigeria, do not have bank accounts. Improving migrant workers' access to banking in the remittance-source countries (typically developed countries) would not only reduce costs of remittances but it would also lead to financial deepening in receiving countries. Maimbo and Ratha have observed that 14 percent to 28 percent of nonmembers who came to credit unions affiliated with World Council of Credit Unions to transfer funds ended up opening an account (Maimbo and Ratha, 2003). The challenges confronting traditional financial institutions and other financial service providers are to integrate unbanked senders and receivers into the financial system. The same authors discuss several approaches such as: prepaid account options, expanded and more flexible card-based services for remittance recipients, increased access to automated teller machines, the IRnet service offered by credit unions, and other modern payment system. The large volume, both of money and potential new clients, makes it attractive to private sector to find ways of providing these services, especially if the appropriate regulatory framework is in place.

Appropriate Financial and Monetary Policies

Sander and Maimbo argue that throughout Africa, financial and monetary policies and regulations have created barriers to the flow of remittances and their effective investment (Sander and Maimbo, 2003). Restrictive licensing of money transfer limits access to remittances and restricts their potential impact in many areas. Other regulations and policies create unattractive environments for investment and block improvements in financial services. Removing those obstacles – and broadening and adapting relevant financial products and services, such as savings and investment instruments – would boost remittance flows and increase their impact on development.

Increasing Transparency in the Informal Financial Infrastructure for Remittances

The regulatory regime governing remittances has to strike a balance between curbing money laundering, terrorist financing, and general financial abuse, and facilitating the flow of funds between hard-working migrants and their families at home, especially for remittances channeled through informal financial systems. It is not entirely clear that personal remittances were an efficient way of laundering or illegally transferring sizeable amount of funds. More importantly, informal channels owe their existence to the inefficiencies in the formal system: informal agents are cheaper, they work longer hours, they often have staff who speak the language spoken by the migrants customers, and they offer anonymity (Maimbo and Ratha, 2003). Strengthening the formal remittance infrastructure by offering the advantages of low cost, flexible hours, expanded reach, and language can induce a shift in flows from the informal to the formal sector. Both sender and recipient countries should support migrants' access to banking by providing them with identification tools. Encouraging funds to flow through formal channels, especially banks, would also help in tracking any illegal use of funds.

Use of Fiscal Incentives

Maimbo and Ratha identified different fiscal incentives used to attract remittances in developing countries. One of them is tax incentive. However, the side effects of such incentives are that remittances may then be used for tax evasion and money laundering. They also identified matching funds for remittance-backed projects and the use of hometown associations to channel aid. One effective policy to measure and encourage remittance inflows is unification of exchange rates and elimination of the black market exchange premium. This policy is being used by Republica Bolivariana de Venezuela (Maimbo and Ratha, 2003).

Ensuring that Foreign Direct Investment is not Counter-Productive.

There is a dire need to ensure that foreign direct investment is an important stimulus to economic growth and social development in developing countries without being counter-productive. Multinational corporations have to cooperate with host countries in the payment of taxes, un-destabilizing investment income remittances, reinvestment of substantial proportions of their earnings in productive activities, improving the efficiency of productive resources – including imported capital, non-political interference, and the avoidance of bribery and corruption. Also, they should conduct their research and development activities in the host countries rather than in their own countries. With such cooperation, it will not be necessary for developing countries to absorb substantial portions of the profits, by fiscal measures, for their economic development.

Concluding Remarks

We conclude the chapter with the words of Maimbo and Ratha:

> While formulating policies on remittances, policy markers should keep in mind that remittances are not public money. They are personal flows, and the decision of how they should be spent is better left to the remitters and recipients. Efforts to tax remittances or direct them to specific investments are likely to prove ineffective. Instead policy makers should try to improve the investment climate in the recipient communities. Remittances are more effective in generating income and investment when they are supported by good policy and public infrastructure. (Maimbo and Ratha, 2003 p.15).

References

Akinsanmi, A. (2005). *Gender relations and food security of rural families in Imo state, Southeast Nigeria*. Ph. D. Dissertation, Institut für agrar- und Sozialökonomie, University of Hohenheim, Germany.

Alburo, F.A. and D.I. Abella (1992) "The impact of informal Remittances of Overseas Contract Workers' Earnings on the Philippine Economy" New Delhi, ARTEP (mimeo).

Baumol, W.J. and A.S. Blinder (1998) "Recent Developments in the U. S. Labour Market". *Economics: Principles and Policy.* The Dryden Press, New York pp. 398-399.

Becker, G.S. (1974) "A Theory of Social Interactions", *Journal of Political Economy*, 82/6, pp.1063-93.

Boswell, C. (2002). "Addressing the causes of migratory and refugee movements: the role of the European Union", New Issues in Refugee Research Working Paper No. 73. *Institute for Peace Research and Security Policy*, University of Hamburg, Germany.

Cox, D. (1987) "Motives for Private Transfers", *Journal of Political Economy*, 195/3, pp. 508-46.

Crisp, J. (1999). "Policy challenges of the new diasporas: Migrant networks and their impact on asylum flows and regimes" *New Issues in Refugee Research*. Working Paper No. 7. http://www. jha. sps. com. ac. uk/c.

Diatta, M.A. and Mbow, N. (1999). "Releasing the Development Potential of Return Migration: The Case of Senegal", *International Migration*, 37 (1), pp. 243-66.

Djajic, S. (1989) "Migrants in a Guest-Worker System: A Utility Maximizing Approach", *Journal of Development Economics*, 31, pp. 327-339.

Elbadawi, I.A. and Rocha, R. (1992) "Determinants of Expatriate Workers' Remittances in North Africa and Europe", *World Bank Working Paper Series* 1038.

El-Sakka, M. and MaNabb, R. (1999) "The Macroeconomic Determinants of Migrant Remittances", *World Development*, 27, pp. 1493-1502.

Faini, R. (1994) "Workers Remittances and the Real Exchange Rate: A Quantitative Framework", *Journal of Population Economics*, 7, pp. 235-245.

Feiler, G. (1987) "Scope and Some Effects of Remittances of Egyptian Working in the Arab Oil-Producing Countries, 1973-1984", *Asian and African Studies*, 21, pp. 305-325.

Garson, J. (1994) "The Implications for the Maghreb Countries of Financial Transfers from Emigrants" in: *Migration and Development: New Partnerships for Cooperation* (OECD), Paris.

Glytsos, N. (1988) "Remittances in Temporary Migration: A Theoretical Model and Its Testing with the Greek-German Experience", *Review of World Economics*, 124, pp. 524-549.

Glytsos, N. (1997) "Remitting Behaviour of 'Temporary' and 'Permanent' Migrants: The Case of Greeks in Germany and Australia", *Labour*, 11, pp. 409-435.

Higgins, M., Hysenbegasi, A. and Pozo, S. (2004) "Exchange-rate uncertainty and workers' remittances", *Applied Financial Economics*, 14, pp. 403-411.

Handlin, E, Krontoft, M. and Testa W. (2002), *Remittances and the Unbanked*, The Federal Reserve Bank, March.

Katseli, L. and Glytsos, N. (1986) "Theoretical and Empirical Determinants of International Labour Mobility: A Greek-German Perspective", *Centre for Economic Policy Research Working Paper* 148.

Komolafe, J. (2002). "Searching for fortune: The Geographical Process of Nigerian

Lucas, R. and Stark, O. (1985) "Motivations to Remit: Evidence from Botswana", *The Journal of Political Economy*, 93, pp. 901-918.

Maimbo, S.M. and D. Ratha (2003). "Remittances: An Overview". In: *Remittances: Development Impact and Future Prospect*, Edited by S.M. Maimbo and D. Ratha. Chapter 1, pp. 1-16.

Meier, G.M. (1995) "Migration and Urbanization". *Leading Issues in Economic Development.* Oxford University Press, New York p. 140.

Migration to Dublin, Ireland" *Irinkerindo: A Journal of African Migration.* Issue 1, September http://www. africamigration.com/archieve_01/j_komolafe_searching. htm

Mutume G. (2005). "Workers' Remittances: a Boon to Development- Money Sent home by African Migrants Rivals Development Aid". *Africa Renewal*, Vol.19, No 3 (October), p. 10.

Obadan, M.I. (1980) "Direct Foreign Investment: A Case Study from Nigeria." *Intereconomics*: January/February.

Obadan, M.I. (2004). *Foreign Capital Flow and External Debt*. Chapter 13, pp. 383-415.

Nwajiuba, C. (2005). "International Migration and Livelihood in Southeastern Nigeria". *Global Commission on International Migration*: Global Migration Perspectives No 50.

Poirine, B., (1997): "A Theory of Remittances as an Implicit Family Loan Arrangement", *World Development*, 25/4, pp. 589-611.

Puri S. and T. Ritzema (1999). "Migrant Worker Remittances, Micro-finance and the Informal Economy: Prospects and Issues". *International Labour Organization*, Working Paper No 21.

Quartey, P. (2005) "Shared Growth in Ghana: Do Migrant Remittances Have a Role?" in *International Conference on Shared Growth in Africa*, ISSER, DFID, USAID and World Bank.

Ratha, D. (2003) "Worker's Remittances: An Important and Stable Source of External Development Finance" in: *Global Development Finance*, pp.157-172 (World Bank).

Ruiz-Arranz, A. (2006). "Boosting Economic Growth". In: *Id21 Insights: Communicating International Development Research*, No 60, January.

Russell, S. (1986) "Remittances from International Migration: A Review in Perspective" *World Development*, 14(6), pp. 677-696.

Russell, S. (1992) "Migrant Remittances and Development" *International Migration Quarterly Review* 30:3/4: 267-287.

Russell, S. et al (1990) "International Migration and Development in Sub-Saharan Africa", Vol. 2 Country analysis, *World Bank Discussion Papers*, No 102.

Sander, C. and Maimbo, S.M. (2003). "Migrant Remittances in Africa: A Regional Perspective" in *Remittances: Development Impact and Future Prospect*, Edited by S.M. Maimbo and D. Ratha. Chapter 2, pp. 53-79.

Sayan, S. (2004) "Guest Workers' Remittances and Output Fluctuations in Host and Home Countries", *Emerging Markets Finance and Trade*, 40, pp. 68-81.

Stark, O. (1991): *The Migration of Labour*, Massachusetts: Blackwell Publishers.

Straubhaar, T. (1986). "The Determinants of Workers' Remittances: The Case of Turkey", *Weltwirtschaftliches* Archiv, 122, pp. 728-740.

Swami, G. (1981) "International Migrant Workers' Remittances: Issues and Prospects", *World Bank Staff Working Paper* 481, Washington, D.C.: World Bank.

Takougabg, J. (2003). "Contemporary African Immigrants to the United States", *Irinkerindo: A Journal of African Migration.* Issue 2, December http://www. africamigration.com/archieve_01/j_komolafe_searching. htm.

Taylor, J. (2004) "Remittance Corridors and Economic Development: A Progress Report on a Bush Administration Initiative" in *Payments in the Americas Conference* (Federal Reserve Bank of Atlanta).

Taylor, J.E. (1996). *International Migration and National Development, Population Index*, Vol. 62(2), pp. 181-212.

Tuncay Aydas, O., Neyapti, B. and Metzin-Ozcan, K. (2004) "Determinants of Workers Remittances: The Case of Turkey", Working Paper, Bilkent University.

United Nations Development Programme (2003). *Human development Report 1993*.

United Nations Development Programme (2005). *Human development Report 2005*.

Usher, E. (2005) "The millennium Development Goals and migration. International Organisation for Migration" (IOM), Geneva. 8-25.

Wahba, J. (2003) "Does International Migration Matter? A Study of Egyptian Return Migrants", Working Paper, University of Southampton.

Wilson, E. (2001). "Urbanization and Agriculture to the Year 2020" in Pinstrup-Anderson, P. and Pandya-lorch, R. *The Unfinished Agenda: Perspectives on Overcoming Hunger, Poverty, and Environmental Degradation*. International Food Policy Research Institute, Washington D.C. pp. 73-77.

Chapter 13

The Nigerian Federation at the Crossroads: The Way Forward

Ladipo Adamolekun

The Nigerian federal system is the oldest on the African continent. It was established in 1954, a few years before the establishment of the short-lived "Mali Federation" comprising Mali and Senegal, 1958-1960. It has been maintained, with various transmutations, longer than the few other federal systems that have emerged in the continent since 1960. However, at age fifty-one, the Nigerian federal system is at a crossroads. Today, many opinion leaders in the country refer to the first twelve years of the federal system (before the advent of military rule) as an era of "true" federalism. Some even refer to the period as a kind of "golden age" of federalism. In reality, it would be more appropriate to refer to the period as one of apprenticeship to true federalism. However, when this period is compared with what happened in the subsequent decades, the laudatory epithets are understandable. Although successive military regimes maintained the "federation" label, the logic of military unitary and centralized command structures meant that the governmental system they controlled was not run along federalist lines. "Military federalism," an expression that has been used in the literature on Nigerian federalism, is a misnomer; what existed in reality under successive military juntas was a "bastardized" federal system.

The fifty-one-month civilian rule interlude of 1979-1983 did not make any serious attempt to reverse the features of the inherited bastardized federal system. The civilian administration was still in a veritable muddling-through mode when the brass hats grabbed power again in January 1984. When civilian rule was reestablished in 1999, a retired general who had served as a military head of state became president. He was reelected in 2003. To date, he has not shown any real interest in dismantling the entrenched unitary and centralized features he inherited from the military. His position contrasts sharply with that of a large number of opinion leaders in the country who advocate a return to the federalism of the premilitary era. What were the salient features of the Nigerian federal system during the era of true federalism, and in what ways was the federal system under the military different from its predecessor? Is a return to the premilitary federalism possible? What would be the desirable way forward for reorienting and strengthening Nigeria's federal system, with a view to turning it into a functioning democratic polity with a well-performing economy capable of assuring an improved quality of life for all the people?

This study seeks to answer these questions. It is in four parts. The article examines the three phases of the Nigerian federal experience: the apprenticeship phase that is also referred to variously as the era of "true" federalism or the "golden age" of federalism, 1954-1965; the federal dominance phase under military rule that I term "bastardized" federalism, 1966-1979 and 1984-1999; and the civilian "muddling-through" phase, 1979-1983 and 1999 to date. In a concluding section, I will argue that the way forward is a choice between devolution and death. Both political power and economic policy and management have to be devolved to the satisfaction of the constituent parts. Failure to devolve will result in a failed state, and the federation will die.

'Golden Age' of Nigerian Federalism, 1954-1965

The following three terms help to summarize the salient features of Nigerian federalism during its first decade: choice, incentive, and competition. Political power was decentralized in a manner that allowed each of the two orders of government (federal and regional) to make choices in both the political and economic spheres. There also was clarity in the allocation of functions and resources between the federal and regional governments. One illustration of the regions' freedom to choose was their selection of different dates for self-governance. The eastern and western regions became self-governing at different times during 1957; the northern region became self-governing in 1959. (All three regional governments and the federal government negotiated and agreed with the British colonial power to make 1 October 1960 the date of independence for the federation.) Because significant political powers were devolved to the regional governments, the leader of each of the three major political parties opted to assume leadership of the regional government it controlled. Within a few years, an informal competition was noticeable among them as they sought to provide "life more abundant" (to use the slogan coined by one of them) for the citizens in their respective regions. The critical incentive factor during the period was a revenue-allocation formula that assigned primacy to the principle of derivation. Each regional government exerted maximum efforts in mobilizing resources within its territorial area. An overview of developments in the areas of governance at the local level and economic and social development is used to illustrate the distinguishing features of the federal system during this phase.

Local Governance

The main point here is the freedom that each regional government had in determining the institutional arrangements for governance at the local level. The federal government had no say on the subject. Local governance as a responsibility of regional governments was already part of the initial steps in the transfer of power from the colonial government introduced in 1951. The 1954 Constitution, which introduced a federal constitution, confirmed the existing reality. Although there was similarity in the movement toward elected local governments in all three regions, the pace differed among the regions. More important, there were significant differences in the manner in which the regions dealt with traditional chiefs who had played a central role in the indirect rule system used by the British colonists to govern at the local level.

In both eastern and western Nigeria, the regional governments rapidly established elected local governments that assumed responsibility for managing local affairs. However, although the inherited "warrant" chiefs in eastern Nigeria (hand-picked by colonial administrators and warranted to act as chiefs) readily adjusted to their new advisory role in local governance, the process in the West was more contentious because some of the traditional rulers had governed large territories before the British colonial era. In the end, the regional government prevailed in subordinating the traditional rulers to elected governments at both the regional and local levels. At the regional level, a House of Chiefs was created, and the senior chiefs were selected as members and assigned an advisory role. Notwithstanding the limited influence of the warrant chiefs in eastern Nigeria, the regional government, too, followed the example of the West by creating a House of Chiefs that was also assigned an advisory role.

In contrast to developments in eastern and western Nigeria, the regional government in northern Nigeria adopted a gradualist approach that maintained the dominance of traditional authorities in the native authorities responsible for local governance for a few more years. When elected councils were eventually established, elected councilors and traditional authorities shared the exercise of power. At the regional level, the House of Chiefs was subordinate to the elected government but was more influential than its counterparts in the two other regions. A key explanation for the gradualist approach and relatively more harmonious relationship in northern Nigeria was the fact that many members of the political class in power at the regional level were former officials of native authorities and were sympathetic to both the native authorities and the traditional rulers. This was not the case in the other two regions.

Economic and Social Development

Economic and social development policies provide illustrations of a combination of the three distinguishing features identified for this phase: choice, incentive, and competition. First, each regional government was free to determine its own economic and social policies. Thus, each region had its own plan for economic and social development. For obvious reasons, there were both similarities and differences in these plans. Second, a strong incentive was built into the revenue-allocation formula, with 50 percent assigned according to the derivation principle. This meant that each region had to mobilize resources that would be used to implement its development plan. Third, because of the desire to provide "life more abundant" for the citizens in their respective regions, an informal competition emerged among them. Consequently, each region cultivated its "garden" by encouraging expansion in the cultivation of both food and export crops (e.g., palm oil in the East, cotton in the North, and cocoa in the West). The entire federation benefited through internal trade in food crops and decent foreign-exchange earnings from the export crops. Education was the priority expenditure item in all the regions, and by 1965 the progress recorded by each region was superior to what the British colonists had achieved during the preceding forty years. The establishment of a university by each regional government was an illustration of competition in a very constructive sense. The most notable success story in education was the universal primary education (UPE) introduced in western Nigeria in 1955 and successfully implemented throughout the period. Furthermore, there were notable achievements in some other areas such as health, housing, and roads in all three regions. It is also important to add that each region developed and nurtured a civil service that served as the main instrument of implementing its development programs and projects.

With the regions occupying center stage in the development of infrastructure and the delivery of public goods and services, the federal government was a distant institution for the average Nigerian. He or she was aware of a common Nigerian currency, and there were occasional newspaper and radio reports of the federal government taking one position or another in international affairs. A small number of students who attended the few secondary schools established by the federal government and the two federal universities also benefited directly from its contribution to educational development. The important point is that the federal government had a lower profile and visibility than the regional governments. It was not in a position to obstruct the regional governments, nor did it have the resources to hijack their functions.

Bastardized Federalism under Military Rule, 1966-1979 and 1984-1999

Based on the Nigerian experience, one can confidently assert that a military junta cannot rule a federation without distorting most of its essential features. The explanation is simple. The logic of the unitary and centralized command structure of the military as an institution and the culture it inculcates in both the leadership and the rank and file are diametrically opposed to the political bargaining, checks and balances, and citizen participation that normally characterize a federal democracy. All three of the main features of the first phase of federal experience--choice, incentive, and competition--were absent under the military. They were replaced by arbitrary diktats, centralism, and uniformity. The decision of the first military government to replace the federal system with a unitary system in 1966 was the supreme illustration of the new military order. Although a federal system was restored within a few months, the actions of successive military heads of state maintained many unitary features. Two key issues that illustrate the bastardization of the federal system under the military are centralized political management and revenue allocation. These two issues are reviewed in turn, followed by an overview of development performance during the entire twenty-eight-year military era.

Centralized Political Management

Following the abandonment of efforts to renegotiate the structure and operations of the federal system through a national dialogue during the second half of 1966 and the stark reality of a looming civil war during the second quarter of 1967, the incumbent military leadership decided in June 1967 to restructure the federation into twelve states: six in the northern part of the country and six in the southern part. The new political structure was a centralized arrangement because it was accompanied by a significant reduction in the powers of the new constituent units. Specifically, the state governments would henceforth need the consent of the federal government to exercise power over any subject in the existing constitution's Concurrent Legislative List, which set out functions that could be performed by both the federal and former regional governments. In practical terms, this meant that all powers in the federal system became concentrated in the federal government and states could handle only matters that the federal government considered appropriate for them to handle. Furthermore, the military officers appointed to head the state governments were hierarchical subordinates of the top military officers who constituted the ruling council at the center.

Subsequent military governments maintained the same arbitrary style of decision making (with only minor differences), and federal dominance became entrenched. Thus, for example, no consultations were carried out before four other increases in the number of states: to nineteen in 1976, twenty-one in 1987, thirty in 1991, and thirty-six in 1996. Another important change to political structure and management was the establishment in 1976 of local governments as a third tier of government (after the federal and state levels) with uniform organizational structure and operational guidelines. This decision was enshrined in the 1979 Constitution and maintained in the 1999 Constitution. As with the number of states, the initial 304 local governments created in 1976 were increased over the years without any consultation by successive military governments to the current 774 that are provided as a schedule to the 1999 Constitution.

In 1967, when the very survival of Nigeria as one country was at stake, the military leader decided to create an equal number of states in the southern and northern parts of the country. In the subsequent exercises of state creation, one or two more states were created in the northern part of the country than in the southern part. (Of the current thirty-six states, nineteen are in the northern part of the country and seventeen in the southern part.) No reasons were given for the departure from the initial "equal" treatment. (Given that Nigeria is yet to conduct a reliable census, the decision was not based on demographic weighting.) Similarly, the determination of the number of local governments created in the different states has been arbitrary. Successive military leaders appear to have reacted to pressures from communities and other vested interests and their own political preferences. As in the case of the states, there are more local governments in the northern part of the country than in the southern part. Evidence that population was not the determining factor is the disparity between Lagos and Kano states, with twenty and forty-four local governments, respectively, although the estimated population of Lagos is larger than that of Kano.

Flowing from this centralized political arrangement, the activities carried out by regional governments during the premilitary era were largely determined by the central government under the bastardized federalism phase. Thus, uniformity replaced diversity. The military heads of the state governments (referred to variously as military governors and military administrators) were only to implement decisions taken by the central military government and were accountable directly to their superiors at the center. There were no checks and balances, and responsiveness to the demands of citizens was at the pleasure of the ruling military men at both the federal and state levels. Examples of centralization during the military era included the following: abolition of regional police forces, a federal takeover of regional universities, and replacement of decentralized development planning with centralized development planning.

Revenue Allocation

With all functions more or less concentrated at the center from 1966 onward, it was logical for the federal government to assign to itself a greater proportion of national revenue than was the case before 1966. Besides the military-style subordination of state governments to the federal government, the financing of the thirty-month civil war required huge resources at the center. In the years immediately after the war, the progressive increase in oil revenues raised by the federal government also increased the revenues available to it. States accepted whatever shares the federal government allocated to them, including shares of grants (outside the revenue-allocation system) that the federal government provided between 1971 and 1979. These federal government grants were "tied" to development activities that it wanted the states to implement, notably, agriculture, housing, and education. However, the discretionary and unpredictable nature of the matching grants limited their development effectiveness. The federal government continued to dominate revenue-raising powers and retained the lion's share of national revenues right up to the end of the military era in 1999. According to one study, between 1970 and 1997, state and local governments accounted for between only 10 and 16 percent of total revenues raised by all three tiers of government during a particular period of six years. During the remaining twenty-two years, they raised less than 10 percent.

Development Performance

The Third National Development Plan (1975-1980) was prepared in a fairly participatory manner, and it contained a vision of Nigeria's future and a bold development strategy aimed at achieving a better quality of life for all Nigerians. Unfortunately, weak implementation capacity resulted in failure to achieve most of the plan's objectives. The next big idea on national economic policy and management under the military was in the form of a "homegrown" structural adjustment program adopted in the late 1980s. This program sought to achieve macroeconomic stability and enhance productive capacity in agriculture, manufacturing, and industry. Again, there was a huge implementation deficit due partly to the diversion of attention to an unending and deceitful program for a transition to civilian rule (1987-1993) and partly to a continuous decline in the capacity of both the federal and the state governments to provide public services. No serious attention was paid to socioeconomic development during the last six years of military rule (1993-1999). Overall, there were only a few achievements in the area of transportation, housing, and agriculture, as well as a significant expansion in tertiary education (although quality declined). By the time the last military ruler left office in May 1999, the country was almost as divided as it was in 1966 (some would say it was more divided); maintenance of law and order was poorer; the civil service was a shadow of the strong and confident institution that it was in 1966 (it suffered severe battering in 1975 and again in 1984); and both corruption and poverty were at levels unknown in 1966. To this negative scorecard must be added the erosion of the independence of the judiciary, institutionalized corruption, periodic assaults on press freedom, and serious dislocations in the social and moral fabrics of society.

Civilian Muddling Through, 1979-1983 and 1999 to Date

There is a real sense in which the adoption of a presidential system of government (under military "guidance") in the 1979 Constitution ensured that the incoming civilian federal government would be more powerful than its predecessor was under the parliamentary system that was operated from independence to the advent of the military in 1966. In contrast to a prime minister who was primus inter pares (first among equals) in a parliamentary system, the constitutional provisions on the position of an elected executive president made him a veritable chief executive officer. Several features of the centralized federal system operated under the military were also enshrined in the Constitution, including formal transfer of functions that were previously performed jointly by the federal and regional governments in the premilitary era to the exclusive list of the federal government. The functions included prisons, registration of business names, registration of tourist businesses, regulation of political parties, the census, and public holidays.

The Shagari Years (1979-1983)

The governmental system that functioned during the years of the presidency of Alhaji Shehu Shagari was a muddled combination of the features of three different regime types: parliamentary, military, and presidential. Although the senior politicians (especially the leaders of the main political parties) combined familiarity with the parliamentary system with exposure to military rule, the younger politicians had been exposed only to military rule, and both groups were unfamiliar with a presidential system. A good illustration of the result of this confusing reality was the importance attached to the role of political parties in governance at all levels--a carry-over from the influence of the British parliamentary system, in which parties play a central role. In these circumstances, the fifty-one-month civilian rule interlude was dominated by inter- and intraparty political struggles, and little attention was paid to promoting economic and social progress. A product of the intensity of partisan politics was the emergence of federal "liaison officers," political appointees of the federal government who were posted to each state of the federation. This policy was also an illustration of continued centralization and federal dominance.

Each liaison officer was to serve as the political representative of the federal government, and each was expected to help promote smooth intergovernmental relations. Predictably, the state governments that were controlled by parties different from the ruling party at the center objected to these liaison officers, some of whom comported themselves as "alternative governors." Some opposition governors even regarded them as agents provocateurs. The controversy they generated increased the intensity of partisan politics and poisoned intergovernmental relations, the very opposite of the ostensible reason for their appointment. In the majority of cases, all the liaison officers could do was to serve as conduits for the distribution of patronage, euphemistically couched as enforcement of the "federal character" provision in the 1979 Constitution. Without question, the appointment of federal liaison officers was a carry-over from military centralism with an overlay of partisan politics.

Federal dominance was also ensured through maintenance of the revenue-allocation system inherited from the military and used up to 1981, when a new system was adopted. However, only a few changes were made in the new system. The federal government continued to keep most of the national revenues, and its share in spending remained almost as high as under the military. The only notable change was that a few states (e.g., Lagos State) were able to increase the internally generated revenue that they spent on their own development priorities.

Development Performance. The Fourth National Development Plan (1981-1985), produced under the Shagari administration, was long on vision and strategy but short on implementation. Poor performance was due to the same combination of diversion of attention to partisan politics and weak implementation capacity that caused the failure of the preceding Third National Development Plan. The implementation of some development initiatives in the areas of infrastructure, education, agriculture, and housing was vitiated by the primacy accorded to partisan political calculations and rent seeking. For example, the decision to provide affordable housing in different parts of the country was largely a failure because the implementation was totally controlled from the center, with attention focused on the contracting aspects (and the accompanying kickbacks, that is, bribes collected by public officials from contractors). There was little or no consultation with the state governments. Furthermore, no attention was paid to matching the design of houses with widely divergent local climates and cultures. Many of the houses were never completed, and a good proportion of those that were completed remained uninhabited in some parts of the federation for many years. Another example is agriculture, where the emphasis was also on contracting for the importation of both agricultural inputs (notably fertilizers) and food (notably rice). Again, the attention was on contracts and kickbacks. Overall, the administration left the economy in a shambles, and there was a sharp decline in the quality of life of citizens in many parts of the country.

The Obasanjo Years (1999 to Date)

The federal dominance enshrined in the 1979 Constitution is maintained in the 1999 Constitution, under which civilian rule has been operating since May 1999. The intense partisan politics that characterized the Shagari years have reemerged in the operation of the federal system under President Olusegun Obasanjo since 1999. However, unlike the strong attachment to the centrality of political parties between 1979 and 1983, partisan politics has revolved almost as much around ethnic nationalities and Muslim-Christian rivalry as around political parties. For example, the unending complaints since 1999 about "marginalization" in the distribution of political and top bureaucratic appointments, social services, economic amenities, and infrastructure facilities have been championed in many cases by ethnic leaders and religious groups. As was the case under the Shagari administration, there has been an attachment to federal dominance, with policing and local governance emerging as two major conflict areas in federal-state relations. Two other issues that deserve attention are the controversy over Sharia (secularism versus state religion) and resource control (extent of control that a constituent unit of the federation should have over the resources in its territorial area). A review of these three issues is followed by a brief assessment of development performance to date.

Federal Dominance. Because of the strong evidence of the incapacity of the Nigerian Police, formerly called the Nigeria Police Force, to assure public safety and prevent crime throughout the federation, there has been a strong demand for the establishment of state police forces. The Obasanjo administration has opposed this demand. The federal government's main argument is that state governments could use state police forces to harass political opponents and terrorize citizens for partisan political reasons, as witnessed in parts of the country during the first phase of the federal system, when regional governments had their own police forces. However, this argument falls flat in the face of the Nigerian Police being used by the ruling party in the federal government for partisan political purposes. More important, given the level of violence, criminal activity, and general insecurity in different parts of a fairly large federation with about 130 million people, continued reliance on a single police force is untenable. State governments need to have their own police forces, and they, in turn, would need to involve their respective communities in policing. Institutional arrangements for effective policing must involve the federal, state, and local governments, as well as local communities. This cannot be achieved by a single centralized police force with its strategic, policy, and operational base in Abuja (the political capital), which is between 300 and 1,000 kilometers (by road) from such large metropolises as Lagos, Ibadan, Port Harcourt, and Kant.

One incident that illustrates the federal government's interest in being a key player in local governance was its decision in 2004 to withhold payments of statutory allocations from the Federation Account to local governments in states where new local governments have been created. The federal government asserts that the states have violated the 1999 Constitution, which provides a list of 774 local government areas (LGAs) that are entitled to receive such allocations. Given a situation in which the federal government itself does not rigorously comply with several provisions of the Constitution, it appears disingenuous for it to act in this manner. However, federal dominance has triumphed as the few states concerned (with the exception of Lagos State) have abolished the new local governments they had created.

A related issue was the determination of the federal government to bring the Joint State Local Government Accounts Committee (responsible for sharing revenues among local governments in each state) under the oversight of the accountant general of the federation. Notwithstanding the protests of state governments, the legislature and the executive agreed on the Monitoring of Revenue Allocation to Local Government Act 2005. This act, which came into force in April 2005, prohibits state governments from borrowing any funds or revenue allocated to local government councils from the Federation Account. It provides for the establishment of a joint local government account allocation committee in each state and in the Federal Capital Territory. Each committee is to ensure that all allocations from the Federation Account are paid into the Joint Accounts and distributed among local governments as prescribed by the Constitution. Monthly returns are to be rendered to the Federation Account Allocation Committee. In case of default by a state government, the same amount is to be a first charge on the state's next allocation from the Federation Account and credited to the affected local governments.

Sharia. In January 2000, Zamfara State in the northwestern zone of the country extended Sharia to cover both civil and criminal matters, in contrast to the established practice that had allowed customary or Sharia courts to deal only with civil matters. Within a year or so, twelve other states followed the Zamfara example, all of them located in the northwestern, northeastern, and north-central zones. As an assertion of the autonomy of a constituent state in a federal system in the legal and religious spheres, this development would be consistent with the concept of choice that was mentioned for praise during the "golden age" of Nigerian federalism. However, this assertion of autonomy amounts to the adoption of Islam as a state religion, contrary to the provision in the 1999 Constitution (Section 10). An assertion of autonomy that is a violation of a provision of the Constitution is inconsistent with maintaining Nigeria as a law-based state. It has also had the negative effect of accentuating religious conflict and violence, resulting in the flight of a significant number of Christian technicians and professionals from some of the Sharia states. A notable example is Kano State, which has witnessed the closure of about half of its manufacturing and industrial companies since 2000. However, the federal government asserts that the challenge that Sharia states pose to Nigeria as a law-based state is only in appearance because the federal courts of appeal and the Supreme Court can overturn judgments passed by Sharia courts and the Sharia courts of appeal. To date, two judgments by Sharia courts that have been condemned as inhuman both within and outside the country have been reversed by the Sharia court of appeal in the states concerned. For now, the debate on secularism versus state religion remains subdued, but the newly empowered Sharia courts pose serious threats to the judicial and legal order in the country. This issue needs to be addressed in the review of the 1999 Constitution.

Resource Control. This is a code used by some constituent states and some opinion leaders to demand the restoration of the primacy of the principle of derivation in revenue sharing among the federal, state, and local governments. According to some resource-control advocates, it also seeks to vest the exploitation of mineral resources in capable indigenous companies with a view to assuring transfer of technology, development of local skills, promotion of local entrepreneurship, and acceleration of the pace of development. Although review of the revenue-allocation system has been a subject of controversy for several decades, the controversy had never been as contentious as it has become since 1999. Not even a unanimous judgment of the Supreme Court (delivered in 2002) could put the controversy to rest. The Court asserted that the boundaries of the country's six oil-producing littoral states do not extend to the exclusive economic zone or continental shelf of Nigeria. In other words, it affirmed an onshore/offshore dichotomy. This would mean that the 13 percent of oil revenues paid into the Federation Account that the 1999 Constitution requires to be allocated to oil-producing states would exclude offshore production. In 2004, a political "solution" set aside the Supreme Court's decision, and derivation was to cover both onshore and offshore oil production. A bill incorporating this solution was passed into law, namely, the Allocation of Revenue (Abolition of Dichotomy in the Application of Principles of Derivation) Act 2004. Although the oil-producing states were generally satisfied with this solution, all the nineteen northern states and two non-oil-producing states in the southwest have resolved to challenge the solution in the Supreme Court.

In May 2005, the revenue-allocation formula determined by the president in 2002 through an executive order was still in use because the National Assembly was yet to enact a new formula. The current formula has maintained existing practice (dating back to the military era) of allocating the lion's share of the Federation Account to the federal government, and with the same consequence, namely, maintenance of federal dominance. The manifestations of continued federal dominance include use of its abundant resources to take over functions that are assigned to state and local governments in the Constitution (notably, primary education, primary health, and aspects of agriculture) and inadequate allocations to state and local governments to carry out their constitutionally assigned functions. Predictably, the subnational governments are dissatisfied with this unending centralism, and this dissatisfaction contributes significantly to the tensions in intergovernmental relations in the country.

Development Performance. At the beginning of his second term, President Obasanjo introduced the National Economic Empowerment Development Strategy (NEEDS), prepared by an economic team he had assembled. The purpose of the strategy is to achieve significant improvement in the standard of living of all citizens in the country. The main thrusts of the strategy are toward macroeconomic stability, deregulation and liberalization of the economy, privatization, transparency and accountability, anticorruption efforts, and improving the performance of public sector institutions. NEEDS has been hailed as a solid and credible development strategy by key stakeholders within the country and by the country's key development partners. It has been marketed to the National Assembly and brought to the attention of states through the National Economic Council. For NEEDS to produce results that would make a dent in the problem of poverty through better economic performance as well as targeted delivery of some goods and services, the prevailing confusion on the allocation of functions and resource control would need to be sorted out very soon. The critical determining factor of the success of the strategy will be implementation capacity. Although some of the economic policy reform changes envisaged in NEEDS are being implemented already, successful implementation of development activities depends on how quickly the strengthening of public sector institutions can be carried out. Sustainability of the economic policy reform measures and improved service delivery depend, to a great extent, on satisfactory resolution of the centrifugal forces encapsulated in the controversies over marginalization (alias "federal character"), policing, local governance, and resource control. This important point is examined in some detail below.

The Way Forward: Devolve or Die

To keep Nigeria one, federalism is a necessity not a choice. The challenge is to accommodate the ethnic, linguistic, religious, cultural, regional, and geographical divisions within a federation that is, at the same time, democratic and capable of advancing socioeconomic progress. In this circumstance, continued maintenance of the centralism and uniformity of the military era is antithetical to the goal of keeping Nigeria one; devolution is the only viable way forward. It is worth recalling that each of the constituent regions of the federation at its birth in 1954 had threatened to secede at one time or the other: the North in 1950 (before the federation was formally established) and in 1966 following the declaration of Nigeria as a unitary state; the West in 1953 (again, before the formal establishment of the federation) and a virtual "secession threat" in 1998-1999; and the East in 1966, resulting in a thirty-month civil war. A putative independent "Delta Peoples Republic" was declared in 1966, but the military promptly arrested its leaders and the so-called republic died. In 1990, an abortive coup d'etat led by a military officer from one of the north-central zones announced the "suspension" of the Hausa-Fulani and Muslim states of the northeastern and northwestern zones from the federation.

The obvious starting point in discussing Nigeria's way forward is to define devolution. Instead of providing a dictionary definition or a selection of definitions from the literature on politics and public administration, some examples of what devolution means in practice in selected federal, quasi-federal, and unitary states are provided. The following conclusion from a recent systematic review of the constitutions of both old and new federations is also relevant: "Generally, the more homogeneity within a society, the greater the powers that have been allocated to the federal government, and the more diversity, the greater the powers that have been assigned to the constituent units of government." From the lessons from operating the Nigerian federal system to date as well as the lessons from both the examples of devolution and the international good practices cited, one can argue that the following two critical issues need to feature prominently in the design of a new devolved federal system for Nigeria: (1) political restructuring and autonomy for nationalities and (2) reallocation of functions and resources.

Political Restructuring and Autonomy

There is a broad agreement among the three arms of government (executive, legislative, and judicial) as well as among opinion leaders within the society on the need for a review of the 1999 Constitution because it contains many loopholes, inconsistencies, and illogicalities. A significant number of opinion leaders from different parts of the country would like change to go beyond constitutional review to involve a comprehensive restructuring of the polity. The different viewpoints have been documented in various newspapers, magazines, and books. For example, the ambivalence of the Supreme Court, which sometimes supports expansion of federal power and sometimes supports its diminution, is due partly to the inconsistencies in the Constitution. The purpose of political restructuring would be to produce a new constitution that not only would remove these deficiencies but would specifically establish Nigeria as a devolved federation.

The overall objective of political restructuring should be to establish autonomous (self-governing) nationalities or groups of nationalities within a federal union with a small coordinating national government. Two examples of issues that would need greater clarity than exists in the 1999 Constitution are institutional arrangements for local serf-governance and how best to accommodate the enforcement of "national minimum standards" in certain policy areas. Because full clarity cannot be spelled out in a constitution, a negotiated memorandum of understanding could be adopted as a companion document to the Constitution. In the memorandum, operational guidelines relating to certain concepts and issues would be spelled out in detail. Examples are the concepts of federal character and local self-governance and such issues as mechanisms for conducting relations between the federal, state, and local governments; enforcing national minimum standards for specific public services; and ensuring checks and balances.

Of course, those who fear that fundamental political restructuring (devolution) could lead to the balkanization or disintegration of the country could point to some international experiences, such as the unending referendums on "sovereignty" in Quebec, Canada, and talk of a "free state associated with Spain" (and represented in the European Union) by some separatists and regionalists in Spain. But it can also be argued that each of these countries has remained one because it has implemented significant devolutions of powers in response to demands by its disaffected constituent parts. Nigeria's postindependence experience to date constitutes a strong case for what one might call the inevitability of devolution. It is important to stress that subnational governments that would enjoy greater degrees of devolved powers would need to match their autonomy with consistent practice of good governance, notably respect for the rule of law and human rights, citizen participation, and governmental transparency and accountability. Otherwise, new groups within the different subnational governments would cry out against new forms of marginalization.

Reallocation of Functions and Resources

A major aspect of political restructuring and autonomy relates to the allocation of functions and resources in the new federal system. Drawing on functional allocation under the 1954 Constitution and international good practices, the responsibilities of the federal government should be limited to currency and foreign exchange, external security and aspects of internal security, external affairs, foreign trade, railways, interstate transportation, and aspects of regulatory administration. State and local governments should have responsibility for all other functions. In turn, the revenue-allocation formula applied to the Federation Account should reflect this assignment of functions. In particular, the revenue-allocation system should accord to derivation the same 50 percent share as was the case in the 1954 Constitution, including a recent suggestion on vesting aspects of the exploitation of mineral resources in capable indigenous companies. This approach to the allocation of functions and resources would result in decentralized economic policy and management.

Next Step: Convocation of a Sovereign National Conference

Although a Joint Committee of the National Assembly on Review of the 1999 Constitution is at work, it does not enjoy the public trust required to tackle the two key issues highlighted above. The kind of political restructuring and autonomy that are required for a new devolved federal system would include a significant reduction in the powers of the National Assembly. Therefore, it would be asking too much to expect the assembly to preside over the diminution of its own powers. Furthermore, the record of the assembly to date does not inspire confidence that it would act decisively on the reassignment of functions and resources and provide a road map for achieving decentralized economic policy and management. Therefore, the only viable alternative is convocation of a sovereign national conference (SNC). Even an older federation, Canada, organized three national conferences between 1987 and 1999 to review the state of the union. Extensive suggestions on the modalities and expected outputs and outcomes of this conference have been provided in many of the published materials on political restructuring and autonomy. Perhaps the one big problem that remains to be tackled satisfactorily is how best to reconcile an SNC with the legitimacy of the incumbent federal powers (the executive and the legislative). One possible solution would be to hold a referendum on the new constitution to be produced by the SNC just before the presidential and legislative elections of 2007. One final point on the desirability of an SNC is its potential usefulness as a trust-building mechanism.

Instead of a genuine SNC, President Obasanjo, in response to persistent pressure for a national conference to discuss the problems of the federation, constituted a presidential committee to advise him on an agenda for political reform. The committee, which was established in December 2004, completed its work within a few weeks, and in February 2005 the president inaugurated the 400-person National Political Reform Conference (NPRC). The NPRC was given a broad mandate covering issues ranging from constitutionalism to the economy and including fiscal federalism and revenue allocation, political parties, electoral systems, and social justice. In his opening address at the conference, the president asserted that the following nine areas of governance in Nigeria were "settled" and NPRC members were asked only to "strengthen, update, and refine" them. The areas are the oneness of Nigeria, federalism, a federal system of government, presidentialism, multireligiosity, federal character, popular participation, the fundamental objectives and directive principles of state policy, and the separation of powers. The committee is expected to complete its work by mid-June 2005.

A significant number of opinion leaders, some ethnic nationalities, and many civil-society groups that distrusted the genuineness of the president's "conversion" to the idea of a national conference promptly announced that they would organize a separate conference, baptized the People's National Conference (PNC). The organizers of the PNC, called the Pro-National Conference (PRONACO) group, questioned the idea of "settled areas" in the federal system, pointing out the widespread contestations about each of them, except the "oneness of Nigeria." They also highlighted two important contrasts between the NPRC and the PNC: (1) the selection of participants to the NPRC by the president and state governors in contrast to the proposed election or selection of participants to the PNC by the constituencies they would represent (for example, ethnic nationalities, civil-society groups, and professional associations) and (2) the uncertainties about what the National Assembly would do with the recommendations of the NPRC in contrast to the proposed public adoption of the recommendations of the PNC, possibly through a nationwide polling survey. PRONACO's preferred option of subjecting its recommendations to a referendum would not happen unless it managed to reach a rapprochement with both the incumbent executive and the National Assembly. The PNC is scheduled to begin during the second half of 2005 and to be concluded before the end of the year.

It is a good development that the future of the country will be debated in these two conferences, well ahead of legislative and presidential elections that are due during the first half of 2007. It is reasonable to expect that the various issues subsumed under the rubric "national question" (that is, the problems of the federation) since the early 1990s will be addressed in the two conferences. However, the holding of two conferences means that the possible advantage of a national conference as a trust-building mechanism has been lost. And only time will tell whether or not the new constitution that would be produced for use from 2007 onwards would contain provisions that would help assure a well-performing federal democracy.

Concluding Observation

While reemphasizing the credit the military deserves for keeping Nigeria one through the thirty-month civil war of 1967-1970, it is important to stress that the enduring unity of the Nigerian federation cannot be assured through military-style centralism and uniformity. Persistent fears about the fragility of the federation after almost three decades of strict application of that approach, and about ten years of imitations of the same approach, constitute a strong justification for adopting and implementing a different approach. The desirable approach is a devolved federal system with the characteristics spelled out above. Only devolution can unleash the forces for consolidating democracy and achieving accelerated socioeconomic progress in Nigeria. The alternative to devolution will likely be the death of the federation.

References

Adamolekun, Ladipo, *Politics and Administration in Nigeria* (London: Hutchinson and Ibadan: Spectrum Books, 1986), chaps. 3-4.

Afigbo, Adiele, "Background to Nigerian Federalism: Federal Features in the Colonial State," *Publius: The Journal of Federalism*, 21 (Fall 1991): 13-29.

Akande, Jadesola, "The Legal Order and the Administration of Federal and State Courts," *Publius: The Journal of Federalism*, 21 (Fall 1991): 61-73.

Akindele, S., O. Olaopa, and A. Obiyan, "Fiscal Federalism and Local Government Finance in Nigeria: An Examination of Revenue Rights and Fiscal Jurisdiction," *International Review of Administrative Sciences* 68 (Fall 2002): 557-577.

Amuwo, Kunle, Suberu, Rotimi, Agbaje, Adigun, and Herault, George, eds. *Federalism and Political Restructuring in Nigeria* (Ibadan: Spectrum Books, 1998), pp. 99-210.

Atta, Victor (governor of oil-producing Akwa Ibom State), "Resource Control: A Misunderstood Phenomenon," *The News* (Lagos), 26 January 2004, p. 49.

Elaigwu, J. Isawa and Galadima, Habu, "The Shadow of Sharia over Nigerian Federalism," *Publius: The Journal of Federalism* 33 (Summer 2003): 123-144.

Falae, Olu, *The Way Forward for Nigeria: The Economy and Polity* (Akure: Flocel Publishers, 2004).

Maier, Karl, *This House Has Fallen: Midnight in Nigeria* (New York: Public Affairs, 2003). He presents Nigeria as a failing state.

Phillips, Adedotun, "Managing Fiscal Federalism: Revenue Allocation Issues," *Publius: The Journal of Federalism*, 21 (Fall 1991): 103-111.

Soyinka, Wole "Centralism and Alienation," *International Social Science Journal* 167 (March 2001).

Tamuno, Tekena, "Separatist Agitations in Nigeria Since 1914," *Journal of Modern African Studies* 8 (Fall 1970): 563-583.

Telford, Hamish, "The Federal Spending Power in Canada: Nation-Building or Nation-Destroying?" *Publius: The Jourual of Federalism* 33 (Winter 2003): 23-44.

The Punch (Lagos), 4 October 2004; see also the editorial "State of Insecurity," The Punch (Lagos), 23 March 2004.

The Punch (Lagos) "Nigeria May Become a Failed State--Report,", 27 May 2005.

Watts, Ronald L., "The Distribution of Powers, Responsibilities and Resources in Federations," Handbook of Federal Countries, ed. Ann Griffiths (Montreal: Forum of Federations, 2002), pp. 448-471.

World Bank, "Nigeria: State Finances Study," Report No. 25710-UNI, April 2003.

Index

1979 world development report 284
1992 Copenhagen World Summit for Social Development 290
1993 Vienna Conference on Human Rights 290
1995 Copenhagen World Summit for Social Development Declaration and Programme of Action 279
1999 Lome Agreement 268

Afghanistan 32, 37
African Development Bank (AfDB) 90, 91, 97, 103
African development report 6, 140
African Growth and Opportunity Act (AGOA) 92, 100, 107
African Peer Review Mechanism (APRM) 13, 77, 78, 79, 83, 137, 138
African socialism 184
African union 13, 23, 60, 86, 90, 91, 137, 139, 151, 152, 165, 170, 289, 291
Afro-centric 184, 201, 202
Algeria 1, 3, 6, 12, 78, 133, 230, 231, 232, 250
antiretroviral drugs 263
Apprenticeship 319
Armed conflict 4, 35, 121, 224
Authoritarian 3, 24, 29, 32, 49, 54, 63, 64, 65, 67, 68, 73, 76, 77, 78, 79, 80, 83, 258, 260, 261, 264, 269
Autocratic 36, 53, 54, 56, 61, 65, 238, 251
Autonomy 5, 23, 167, 173, 190, 260, 270, 276, 328, 330, 331, 332

Bakili Muluzi 66
Barons 66, 74, 118, 119, 135, 191
Basic needs 6, 184, 280, 283
Beneficiaries 32, 78, 127, 280, 285, 290
Benin 19, 28, 31, 78, 147, 150-161, 234, 235, 258
Botswana 3, 6, 19, 20, 28, 31, 61, 64, 76, 230, 231, 232, 250, 299, 315

brain drain 98, 102, 209, 210, 222, 296, 297, 302
Bretton woods 124, 125, 128, 131, 132, 133, 135, 215
Bureaucracies, also bureaucratic 27, 69, 70, 75, 77, 78, 124, 158, 175, 182, 184, 286, 326
Burundi ix, 4, 20, 21, 23, 24, 31, 102, 234, 235

Capacity building 60, 61, 103, 132, 149, 177, 283
Capitalist 37, 44, 50, 61, 78, 87, 88, 89, 92, 117, 180, 182, 194, 206, 291
Casamance Democratic Forces Movement (MFDC) 24
Centre-periphery 180, 195
Chad 2, 4, 20, 23, 25, 29, 31, 72, 302
Charles De Gaulle 35
Checks and balances 23, 331, 332
Civil liberties 5
Civil service 5, 11, 51, 61, 158, 275, 284, 322, 324
Civil war 28, 71, 72, 80, 145, 209, 210, 211, 218, 219, 222, 268, 322, 324, 330
Class 29, 40, 43, 47, 48, 52, 53, 70, 73, 77, 78, 80, 93, 187, 256, 259, 260, 269, 279, 321
Clientelism 69, 81, 83
Cold war 18, 33, 120, 128, 143, 179, 182
Colonial regime 51, 53, 54, 57, 72, 73, 80
COMESA 92, 93, 94, 100, 103, 155, 233
Comprehensive development frameworks (CDF) 132
Comprehensive peace agreement 1
Conflict management xi, 15, 22, 23, 25, 26, 32, 34, 122, 145, 173
Congress of Berlin 3
Constitutionalism 332
Conventions 147, 148, 155, 170, 279, 289

Corruption 5, 8, 13, 18, 28, 29, 63, 67, 69, 71, 72, 74, 75, 82, 83, 148, 182, 190, 195, 203, 258, 259, 314, 325
Cotonou Agreement 98, 99
Cox 295, 315
Cultures 3, 39, 73, 190, 192, 199, 200, 286, 326

Darfur peace agreement 1
Debt relief 270, 286
Debt servicing 10, 12, 13
Decolonisation 196, 198, 204, 207
Democracy 19, 25, 28, 30, 35, 44, 49, 50, 61, 65, 66, 68, 73, 79, 108, 110, 137, 138, 146, 148, 184, 185, 191, 259, 263, 264, 265, 273, 274
Democratic Republic of Congo 3, 5, 47
Dependency – 37, 180, 181, 186, 188, 189, 190, 193, 195, 196, 198, 200, 205, 297
Djibouti x, 3
Dominican Republic 69, 82

East African Community 96, 99
Economic Commision for Africa (ECA) 86, 87, 90, 91, 95, 123, 124, 125, 131, 133, 155, 175, 290
Economic Community of West African States (ECOWAS) 23, 103, 143 178, 233, 302
Elites 1, 6, 17, 18, 19, 20, 21, 29, 36, 60, 71, 74, 75, 181, 182, 186, 188, 268, 286
Enterprises 70, 87, 90, 91, 97, 98, 102, 117, 144, 182, 297, 308
Entrepreneurship 104, 297, 328
Eritrea 1, 21, 23, 25, 29, 72, 76, 93
Ethiopia 3, 4, 20, 23, 25, 28, 72, 76, 78, 87, 93, 94, 230, 231, 232, 234, 235, 250
Ethnicity 38, 39, 40, 41, 42, 53, 55, 56, 203, 204, 256, 283
European union 59, 92, 96, 136, 331
Exchange rates 86, 97, 102, 299, 300, 305, 307, 314
Exploitation 37, 143, 200, 202, 203, 328, 331

faith based organisation (FBOs) 256, 257, 258, 264, 265, 266, 268, 269, 270, 276

Fanon 14, 187, 192, 196, 199, 200, 206
Feudalism 87
Fiscal 18, 21, 23, 26, 60, 86, 90, 95, 97, 102, 183, 236, 238, 239, 240, 241, 244, 246, 247, 248, 249, 250, 313, 314
Fluctuations 211, 212, 216, 222, 228, 235, 239, 300
Foreign aid 22, 31, 75, 111, 280, 285, 296
Foreign direct investment 88, 110, 137, 212, 296, 298, 308, 310, 314
Frederick Chiluba 65, 83
Free trade area 95, 144
French revolution 19

G8 107, 111, 134, 136, 195
Gambia 3, 147, 150-160, 162, 230, 231, 232, 234, 235, 250
Gender 279- 294
George W Bush 299
Ghana x, 4, 19, 22, 23, 25, 28, 31, 78, 85, 150, 153, 156, 180, 230, 231, 232, 250, 258, 274, 302
Good governance 35, 37, 58, 63, 75, 78, 1020, 138, 146, 148, 195, 219, 331
Guinea Bissau 4, 22, 23, 147, 150, 153, 230, 231, 232
Gunder frank 181

Hastings Kamuzu Banda 66
HIV/AIDS x, 11, 13, 115, 263, 269, 270, 272, 273, 287, 288
human capital 97, 98, 210, 218, 221, 280, 281, 296
Human development 6, 15, 35, 61, 111, 119, 120, 121, 123, 127, 220, 221, 295
Human insecurity 58
Human rights ix, 24, 26, 43, 46, 66, 70, 76, 77, 256, 263, 269, 270, 272, 273, 279, 281, 286, 287, 289, 290, 291, 297, 331
Hutu 3, 20, 24, 30, 269

Ideology 2, 37, 44, 49, 54, 61, 116, 118, 199, 255, 261, 282
Immanuel Wallerstein 1, 38
Imperialism 75, 180, 181, 197, 200, 201
Import Substituting Industrialisation (ISI) 100
Income gap 295

Indigenous 14, 50, 53, 80, 183, 188, 190, 191, 264, 308, 328, 331
Indirect rule 40, 52, 53, 54, 72, 180, 181, 197, 320
Industrialisation 85, 88, 87, 91, 93, 97, 100, 102, 130, 194
Inflation 10, 97, 236, 237, 239, 240, 241, 242, 243, 244, 246, 247, 248, 249, 251, 258, 300, 301, 302, 307
Infrastructures 86, 88, 96, 98, 102, 110, 127, 130, 133, 137, 143, 164, 174, 188
Insecurity 1, 2, 26, 58, 80, 117, 327
Interest groups 81, 175, 256, 274
Inter-governmental organisations (IGOs) 145, 170
International community 14, 18, 90, 91, 107, 121, 122, 123, 125, 186, 195, 196, 205, 273
International Financial Institutions (IFIs) 27, 32, 49, 56, 59
International Monetary Fund (IMF) 8, 9, 12, 15, 24, 37, 54, 131, 136, 233, 250, 252, 297, 298
Iraq 37, 69, 275
Ivory Coast 2, 4, 21, 22, 23, 25, 28, 30, 72, 80, 250, 302

Kenneth Kaunda 65
Kenya 4, 13, 19, 23, 28, 31, 52, 78, 92, 93, 96, 99, 100, 230, 231, 232, 233, 250, 258, 259, 264
Kwame Nkrumah 6, 85, 180, 189, 194, 199

Lagos Declaration 14
Lagos Plan Action (LPA) 107, 108, 109, 111, 115, 117, 119, 130, 131, 133, 138, 184
Laisser-faire 191
Latin America 9, 56, 73, 124, 181, 214, 223, 225
Least Developed Countries (LDCs) 91, 99, 110, 136, 213, 229
Leninist 72, 180
Leviathan 2
Liberal democracy 35, 37, 44, 49, 50, 61, 77, 137, 184
Liberia 2, 3, 4, 19, 20, 21, 23, 29, 31, 72, 73, 79, 129, 145, 146, 150, 156, 286
Libya 6, 69

Lome I Convention 98

Macro-economic policy x, 8, 9, 128, 296, 312
Malaria 75, 257, 258, 269, 288
Malawi Congress Party 66
Marginalisation 11, 86, 100, 109, 111, 125
Marxist 38, 47, 72
Mauritius 6, 64, 78, 92, 100, 101, 103, 230, 231, 232, 250
Mexico Plan for Action 280
Millennium Development Goals 60, 91, 287, 291
Movement for Multiparty Democracy (MDD) 65
Mozambican National Movement (RENAMO) 24
Multi-party 4, 191

National Resistance Movement (NRM) 64
National Union for the Total Independence of Angola (UNITA) 24
Nation-state 15, 20, 22, 35, 38, 46, 49, 51, 55, 59
Nelson Mandela 273
Neo-colonial 36, 48, 49, 61, 115, 180, 185, 187, 188, 189, 190, 196, 197, 199, 203
Neo-liberal 45, 118, 126, 127, 135, 138, 139
Neo-patrimonialism 68, 69, 78, 79
Nepotism 56, 70, 74
New global age 117, 118, 141
New Partnership for African Development, NEPAD 13, 33, 60, 77, 79, 86, 91, 102, 107, 108, 109, 111, 117, 119, 121, 125, 129, 134, 135, 136
Nigeria 4, 5, 7, 12, 19, 22, 23, 26, 27, 85, 86, 129, 133, 137, 150, 151, 156, 302, 303, 304, 306, 307, 310, 311, 312, 323, 328, 332, 333

OECD 6, 7, 117, 118, 135, 141
Oil crisis 8
Organisation of African Unity (OAU) 17, 25, 86, 87, 122, 129, 133, 184, 186
Organisation of the Petroleum Exporting Countries (OPEC) 7

Patronage 66, 128, 192, 261, 267, 268, 279, 326
Patron-client 69, 180, 195
Peace Keeping Operations (PKOs) 23
Pluralism 27, 63, 76, 80
Policymaking 122, 125, 174
political economy 49, 86, 209, 222
Post-fordist 46
Poverty reduction strategy papers (PRSP) 132
Privatisation 10, 108, 135, 182, 191
Protocol to the African charter 289

Regional cooperation x, 96, 130, 143, 148, 174, 175, 184
restrictive trade policies 225
Revolutionaries 47, 77
Revolutionary United Front (RUF) 29, 269
Robert Mugabe 20, 68, 73, 76, 261
Rule of law 43, 69, 331
Rwanda 2, 3, 4, 13, 20, 23, 29, 30, 31, 72, 76, 78, 102, 230, 231, 232, 250, 286

Senegal 4, 19, 20, 22, 27, 28, 30, 31, 45, 61, 64, 67, 150, 151, 152, 153, 154, 155, 156, 158, 159, 162, 188, 230, 231, 232, 234, 267, 2698, 297, 319
Sierra Leone 2, 5, 19, 21, 23, 26, 29, 31, 32, 78, 145, 150, 159, 230, 231, 232, 250, 268, 269
Small and medium enterprises (SMEs) 90, 91, 94, 104
social capital 258, 259, 265, 270, 276
Social contract 2, 18, 23, 267
Social Darwinism 191, 199
Somalia 1, 2, 4, 20, 21, 23, 31, 32, 47, 80, 93
South Africa 4, 6, 19, 20, 22, 23, 25, 28, 31, 49, 51, 61, 78, 86, 89, 93, 95, 100, 103, 112, 132, 133, 137, 230, 231, 232, 250, 258, 260, 263, 270, 271, 272, 273, 304
South Africa's Treatment Action Campaign (TAC) 264, 270, 271, 272, 273, 274, 276, 277
Sovereign 2, 17, 18, 20, 32, 285, 332
Soviet Union 24, 69, 179

Structural Adjustment Programmes (SAPs) 8, 9, 10, 11, 12, 90, 100, 122, 125, 130, 131, 132, 133, 139
Sub-Saharan Africa 8, 12, 14, 35, 41, 47, 48, 49, 51, 55, 61, 95, 114, 115, 141, 209, 212, 226, 233, 234, 235, 244, 245, 298, 304
Sudan 1, 3, 4, 21, 23, 25, 30, 72, 78, 80, 93, 235, 296
Sudan Peoples Liberation Movement (SPLM) 24
Sustainable development 86, 91, 135, 140, 203, 205, 281, 285
Swaziland 6, 19, 20, 92, 93, 230, 231, 232, 236, 250
Syria 69

Tanzania 12, 13, 19, 21, 28, 31, 50, 76, 78, 96, 99, 100, 185, 233, 234, 291
Technological transfer 188
think tanks 139, 256, 257, 274, 275, 276, 277
Third wave 18, 63, 68
Third world 73, 74, 80, 111, 117, 188, 189
Thomas Hobbes 2
Totalitarian state 24
Trade Related Intellectual Property Rights (TRIPS) 271
Trajectories 30, 31, 32, 52, 107, 109, 111, 113, 115, 117, 119, 121, 123, 125, 127, 129, 131, 133, 135, 137, 139, 141
Transnational companies 104, 117
Tunisia 69, 230, 231, 232, 250
Tutsi 21, 24, 30, 269

UN Convention on the Elimination of all forms of discrimination against women (CEDAW) 291, 292
Underdevelopment 14, 46, 55, 57, 74, 91, 127, 181, 185, 186, 187, 188, 189, 193, 195, 196, 198, 200, 201, 205, 206
United Kingdom Department for International Development (DFID) 253, 263, 316
United National Independence Party (UNIP) 65

United Nations 5, 6, 59, 90, 118, 122, 124, 133, 136, 182, 184, 186, 261, 273, 296
United Nations development programme (UNDP) 6, 7, 13, 15, 111, 122, 155, 177, 178, 296
US Agency for International Development (USAID) 138, 141, 263, 316

Washington consensus 111, 115, 118, 133, 139, 182
Watchdog institutions 5
Welfare state 108
Westernization 189, 267

Women 2000: Gender, Equality, Development and Peace in the 21st Century 287
Women and Development (WAD) 282, 284, 293
Women in development (WID) 280, 281, 282, 283, 293
World Trade Organisation (WTO) 87, 99, 100, 104, 110, 135, 154, 225, 233, 271
Yoweri Museveni 64, 76

Zambia 12, 13, 19, 28, 31, 40, 42, 51, 52, 53, 54, 56, 57, 58, 65, 66, 78, 100, 185, 230, 231, 232, 234, 235, 250,

For Product Safety Concerns and Information please contact our EU representative GPSR@taylorandfrancis.com
Taylor & Francis Verlag GmbH, Kaufingerstraße 24, 80331 München, Germany

www.ingramcontent.com/pod-product-compliance
Lightning Source LLC
Chambersburg PA
CBHW071234290426
44108CB00013B/1406